MECHANISMS IN TRANSMISSION OF SIGNALS FOR CONSCIOUS BEHAVIOUR

MECHANISMS IN TRANSMISSION OF SIGNALS FOR CONSCIOUS BEHAVIOUR

Edited by

T. DESIRAJU

Indian Council of Medical Research Laboratory
Department of Physiology
All-India Institute of Medical Sciences
New Delhi 110016

and

Department of Neurophysiology
National Institute of Mental Health and Neurosciences
Bangalore 560027, India

ELSEVIER SCIENTIFIC PUBLISHING COMPANY
AMSTERDAM / OXFORD / NEW YORK   1976

ELSEVIER SCIENTIFIC PUBLISHING COMPANY
335 Jan van Galenstraat
P.O. Box 211, Amsterdam, The Netherlands

AMERICAN ELSEVIER PUBLISHING COMPANY, INC.
52 Vanderbilt Avenue
New York, New York 10017

Library of Congress Cataloging in Publication Data
Main entry under title:

Mechanisms in transmission of signals for conscious
  behaviour.

    Proceedings of a symposium held in India.
    Includes index.
    1. Neural transmission--Congresses. 2. Con-
sciousness--Congresses. I. Desiraju, T. [DNLM:
1. Neurophysiology--Congresses. 2. Consciousness
--Congress. 3. Behavior--Congresses. WL102 M486]
QP363.M44   612'.82   75-37986
ISBN 0-444-41397-9

QP
363
.M44
1976

Printed in The Netherlands

LIST OF CONTRIBUTORS

D. ALBE-FESSARD
Université de Paris, Physiologie des Centres Nerveux, Faculté des Sciences, 4 avenue Gordon-Bennett, 75-Paris-16ᵉ, France

E.A. ASRATYAN
Institute of Higher Nervous Activity and Neurophysiology, Butlerova 5a, Moscow 117485, U.S.S.R.

N.P. BECHTEREVA
Institute of Experimental Medicine, 69/71 Kirovsky Pr., Leningrad 197022, U.S.S.R.

M.V.L. BENNETT
Department of Neuroscience, Division of Cellular Neurobiology, Rose Fitzgerald Kennedy Center for Research in Mental Retardation and Human Development, Albert Einstein College of Medicine, 1410 Pelham Parkway South, Bronx, N.Y. 10461, U.S.A.

J.-M. BESSON
Unversité de Paris, Laboratoire de Physiologie des Centres Nerveux, 4 avenue Gordon-Bennett, 75016-Paris, France

M.H. CHASE
Departments of Physiology and Anatomy and the Brain Information Service, The Center for Health Sciences, University of California, Los Angeles, Calif. 90024, U.S.A.

T. DESIRAJU
Department of Neurophysiology, National Institute of Mental Health and Neuro Sciences, Bangalore 560 027, India

J. FEGER
Physiologie des Centres Nerveux, Facultés des Sciences, 4 avenue Gordon-Bennett, Paris, France

S. GILMAN
Department of Neurology, College of Physicians and Surgeons, Columbia University, New York 10032, U.S.A.

G. GUILBAUD
Laboratiore de Physiologie des Centres Nerveux, Facultés des Sciences, 4 avenue Gordon-Bennett, Paris, France

S. HIGHSTEIN

Division of Cellular Neurobiology, Department of Neuroscience, Rose Fitzgerald Kennedy Center for Research in Mental Retardation and Human Development, Albert Einstein College of Medicine, 1410 Pelham Parkway South, Bronx, N.Y. 10461, U.S.A.

G. HORN

Department of Anatomy, The Medical School, University of Bristol, Bristol BS8 1TD, Great Britain

M. ITO

Department of Physiology, Faculty of Medicine, University of Tokyo, Bunkyo-ku, Hongo, Tokyo, Japan

K. KUBOTA

Department of Neurophysiology, Primate Research Institute, Kyoto University, Inuyuma City, Aichi 484, Japan

P.G. MODEL

Department of Neuroscience, Albert Einstein College of Medicine, 1410 Pelham Parkway South, Bronx, N.Y. 10461, U.S.A.

C. OHYE

Université de Paris VI, Physiologie des Centres Nerveux, Faculté des Sciences, 4 avenue Gordon-Bennett, 75-Paris-16ᵉ, France

Y. OOMURA

Department of Physiology, Faculty of Medicine, Kyushu University, Fukuoka City, 812 Japan

C.G. PHILLIPS

Department of Physiology, University of Oxford, Oxford OX1 3PT, Great Britain

K.H. PRIBRAM

Department of Psychology, Stanford University, Stanford, Calif. 94305, U.S.A.

D.P. PURPURA

Department of Neuroscience, Rose Fitzgerald Kennedy Center for Research in Mental Retardation and Human Development, Albert Einstein College of Medicine, 1410 Pelham Parkway South, Bronx, N.Y. 10461, U.S.A.

M. STERIADE

Laboratory of Neurophysiology, Department of Physiology, Faculty of Medicine, Laval University, Quebec-10ᵉ, Canada

M. TAKIGAWA

Department of Physiology, Faculty of Medicine, Kyushu University, Fakuoka City, 812 Japan

INTRODUCTION

The quest for the understanding of consciousness has been with man for many millennia. By scrutinizing experiences resulting out of looking within, the ancient seers realised that consciousness of the "self" is the most important for any being, and that by understanding this one would attain the loftiest plane. Such conclusions and theorisations reached more than twenty-five centuries ago have been reported extensively in the Upanishads *. It is appropriate to briefly recall these here, to give a few comparative glimpses of the profound and logical approach of that ancient age to the most sophisticated audience of this symposium and readers of this proceedings on the subject of consciousness.

The Brihadaranyakopanishad expounded on the elemental biological property of the preservation of self, as well as on the central principle of conscious human behaviour in a higher plane as:

"Verily, it is not for the sake of the husband that a husband is dear, but for the sake of the self is a husband dear."

"Verily, it is not for the sake of the wife that a wife is dear, but for the sake of the self is a wife dear."

"Verily, it is not for the sake of the gods that gods are dear, but for the sake of the self are gods dear."

"Verily, O Maitreyi, it is the self that should be seen, heard of, reflected on and meditated upon."

"Verily, when the self is seen, heard of, reflected on and understood all is known."

The Kenopanishad characterised consciousness as:

"That which is not thought by the mind, but that by which, they say, the mind is made to think."

"That which is not expressed through speech, but that by which speech is expressed."

"That which is not seen by the eye, but that by which the eyes are made to see."

The Mandukyopanishad explains that man passes through four states of consciousness:

"The first is *Vaisvanara*, whose sphere is the waking state, who cognizes external objects."

"The second is *Taijasa*, whose sphere is the dream state, who cognizes internal objects."

---

* Hume, R.E. (1931) Upanishads (Translation from the Sanskrit). Oxford University Press.

Muller, F.M. (1879) The Upanishads (Translations of The Sacred Books of the East). Clarendon Press, Oxford.

Sarma, D.S. (1964) The Upanishads (An Anthology). Bharatiya Vidya Bhavan, Bombay.

"The third is *Prajna,* whose sphere is the sleep of deep sleep, where one does not desire any desire and does not see any dream whatsoever, who has become unified, who is verily a mass of cognition, who is full of bliss and who enjoys bliss and whose opening is thought."

"The fourth is *Atman* or *Turiya,* that which does not cognize either internal objects or external objects, which is not a mass of cognition, which is neither cognitive nor non-cognitive . . . that which cannot be seen, which cannot be described, which cannot be grasped, which has no distinctive marks, which cannot be thought of, which cannot be designated, . . . that of which the essence is the knowledge of the oneness of the self, that in which the world ceases to exist . . . the peaceful, the benign, the non-dual . . . such, they think is that."

The first three states cited above correspond to stages in our present classification of behaviour, but the fourth state, being an unbounded abstraction of some psychic state of mind, can not be commented upon under the present state of knowledge on the brain. It is only in recent decades that the scientific community has acquired courage enough to accept the reality of mind, however indefinable and mystic the mind be, and to find the neurological basis of it. It will remain a standing problem of major researches for a very long time to come.

We recognise that brain tissue is the sole organic abode of consciousness. The unparallelled versatility of the operations of the brain arises out of highly regulated interactions in the precise and plastic communication systems within it. The almost infinite number of gross and subtle psychological potentialities for human conscious behaviour may ultimately be based on some unique physicochemical organisations of the matter in the brain substance. We hope that one day the configurations of the organisations of matter underlying even such mental states as enlightenment will become part of our knowledge on consciousness. At the moment even to frame questions or conceive speculations on such issues may appear to be an exercise in mysticism or metaphysics. However, several fundamental foundations of nature's most complex living edifice — the brain — seem to have been touched upon already, so that we are beginning to feel the augur of unravelling, at least in an elementary way, the basic plans of construction and operation of brain. The data reviewed in the papers reported in this volume testify to this amply.

In recent years, brain research has advanced very rapidly in multidisciplinary directions, with progressive changes in trends and emphasis. In neurophysiology, techniques using behaving experimental subjects are yielding neurological correlates of some facets of conscious behaviour. Relating this type of data with the data on modes of communication and the properties of transmission of codes in the brain, revealed through other sophisticated experimental methods, have improved the possibilities and scope of understanding of the mechanisms of conscious behaviour. Parallel advances are also taking place in the approaches of research in neuropsychology and other allied behavioural disciplines. The growth of brain research in specialisations and the information explosion on diverse aspects have created a necessity for frequent meetings of the specialists, to promote exchange of ideas and findings, scrutiny and debate, review and synthesis, dissemination of existing knowledge highlighting fresh trends, and to trigger the formulation of questions in the minds of investigators for future pursuits. The wide-angle coverage in this somewhat multidisciplinary Satellite symposium of the XXVIth International Congress of Physiological Sciences, is impelled by that necessity.

In the symposium on which this book is based, elucidations of the mechanisms of the functional organisation of the brain were presented by eminent investigators actively engaged in deciphering some of the principles of brain organisation and programming . The presentations in the symposium were scheduled under sessions of: (i) general principles of neural communication; (ii) neural organisation for survival; (iii) programming of motor apparatus, and (iv) brain mechanisms underlying plasticity of behaviour. This categorization is not made in this publication as the papers are pluriscopic and plenteous in implications and can illuminate more than one theme. Further the contributions of the volume are not chosen to be all-inclusive on the wide title theme of the symposium, but to be restricted to certain selected facets at the forefront.

The symposium was the first of its kind held in this subcontinent in the field of brain research. The commendable support and understanding displayed by the contributors to the symposium should first be acknowledged with sincerest appreciation. Historically this may go a long way in this part of the world to stimulating further growth and development of neurological science.

Dr. C. Gopalan, Director-General of the Indian Council of Medical Research, New Delhi gave encouraging financial support and permission to undertake the task.

Dr. V. Ramalingaswami, Director of the All-India Institute of Medical Sciences, New Delhi granted facilities for conducting the symposium. He and Dr. B.K. Anand, President of the XXVIth International Physiological Congress courteously joined me in welcoming and greeting the participants personally at the beginning of the symposium.

The hospitality extended to the participants by the firms: Therapeutic Pharmaceuticals (Bombay), T.E. Patterson (India) Private Ltd. (New Delhi), Sarabhai Chemicals (Squibb) Private Ltd. (New Delhi), May and Baker Ltd. (New Delhi), and Cadila Laboratories (Ahmedabad), is appreciated.

Arrangements were helped by Drs. N. Kochu Pillai, V. Mohan Kumar, S. Kesar, N. Bhattacharya, Prem Kumar and Harleen.

T. Desiraju
New Delhi

CONTENTS

CEREBELLAR LEARNING CONTROL OF VESTIBULO-OCULAR MECHANISMS

MASAO ITO

Department of Physiology, Faculty of Medicine, University of Tokyo (Japan)

GENERAL VIEW OF CEREBELLAR FUNCTIONS

Since the earlier ablation experiments indicated that the cerebellum is involved in motor functions (Rolando, 1809) and plays an important role in coordination of movements (Flourens, 1824 and 1842), numerous observations have been made on the nature of the motor disturbances which follow lesions of the cerebellum. A variety of symptoms may be seen, depending on what part of the cerebellum is involved, but there are certain outstanding aspects characteristic to cerebellar lesions (Dow and Moruzzi, 1958). For example, the symptom called 'dysmetria' is a clear indication that the cerebellum normally contributes to motor control by providing measures of the animal's body relative to environmental objects. The cerebellum estimates positions of fingers, arms, legs, face and other parts of the body in space from time to time and thereby enables various willed and unwilled movements to be performed successfully. Other symptoms, such as 'ataxia', 'intention tremor' and 'Stewart-Holmes phenomenon', in some way give similar indications. The disturbance in saccadic eye movement (Kornhuber, 1971) may also be understandable as a sort of dysmetria, as the saccade is the quick eye movement to catch up to a fast moving visual target. Here the cerebellum appears to be responsible for the process by which the animal derives an accurate prediction of the future position of the target.

Another outstanding feature of cerebellar action is the ability to produce a plastic modification of motor functions. Flourens (1824 and 1842) produced disturbances in body equilibrium by removing the superior half of the cerebellum in a young cock. Fifteen days later, however, the equilibrium was totally re-established. On the other hand, he noted that if he removed the entire cerebellum, no recovery was seen even four months after the operation. Luciani (1891) further showed that if additional cerebellar lesions are made in an animal already compensated, then the resulting deficits exceed in intensity those which would have occurred as a result of the second lesion alone. This suggests that the cerebellum itself is directly involved in the process of compensation, an action of cerebellar tissues well known to neurosurgeons and neurologists. It has also been shown that postrotatory nystagmus undergoes a marked decline when angular acceleration was repeatedly applied (Hood and Pfaltz, 1954), and that this habituation was no longer effected after cerebellectomy (Halstead et al., 1937; Giorgio and Pestellini, 1948).

These signs from cerebellar lesions suggest that the cerebellum contributes to various motor functions by providing measures of the body in space and time, and that this cerebellar function involves something like a learning process.

FUNCTION DIVISIONS OF THE CEREBELLUM

In discussing cerebellar function, it is important to realize that its role in actual motor control varies from region to region. From the phylogenetical and anatomical viewpoints, the cerebellum can be divided into four major portions (Herrick, 1924; Jansen and Brodal, 1954; Brookhart, 1960; Evarts and Thach, 1969). First, the vestibulocerebellum is the phylogenetically oldest part of the cerebellum (archicerebellum) and its evolutional development is closely connected with the vestibular organ. It receives vestibular afferents and projects to vestibular nuclei. Second, the vermis, which is also an old part of the cerebellum (paleocerebellum), receives spinal afferents and projects mainly to the medial cerebellar (fastigial) nucleus. The fastigial nucleus in turn projects to the medulla and innervates vestibulospinal and recticulospinal tract neurons. The vermis also projects directly to certain vestibulospinal tract neurons in Deiters' nucleus. Thus, the vermis is closely bound to the spinal cord. Third, the paravermis, often called the intermediate part, receives not only spinal afferents, but also afferents from the cerebral cortex (cf. Allen et al., 1974), while it projects to the interpositus nucleus. The interpositus nucleus innervates rubrospinal tract neurons and, further, thalamocortical relay cells. Hence the paravermis is linked with both the spinal cord and the cerebral cortex. Fourth, the cerebellar hemisphere, the phylogenetically newest part (neocerebellum), receives afferents from the cerebral cortex and innervates the lateral cerebellar (dentate) nucleus. The lateral cerebellar nucleus projects to the cerebral cortex via thalamocortical relay cells. These connections form the so-called cerebrocerebellar communication loop.

Different functional roles can be assigned to the above-described anatomical divisions of the cerebellum (Chambers and Sprague, 1955a and b). The vermis regulates the tone, posture, locomotion and equilibrium of the entire body. The paravermis controls the spatially organized and skilled movements, and the tone and posture associated with these movements, of the ipsilateral limbs. The hemisphere is involved in the skilled and spatially organized movements of the ipsilateral limbs, but without any apparent regulation of their posture and tone. The vestibulocerebellum serves in regulating vestibular systems and contributes to body equilibrium and eye movements (Fernandez and Fredrickson, 1963). Because of these varieties involved, any study of cerebellar functions needs to specify clearly both the cerebellar area concerned and the relevant motor function.

NEURONAL CIRCUITRY IN THE CEREBELLUM

In the past decade, the construction of neuronal circuitry in the cerebellum, as well as in related brain tissues, has been studied extensively (cf. Eccles et al., 1967; Eccles, 1973). The cerebellar cortex can be viewed as a nerve net (Fig. 1A) composed of five types of neurons. Of these, four: the Purkinje, Golgi, basket and superficial stellate cells, have inhibitory actions, while only one, the granule cells, is specialized for excitation. Two distinctly different types of afferents, mossy and climbing fibers, enter the cerebellar cortex, while Purkinje cell axons are the sole efferent to send out cortical signals. At the level of the subcortical nuclei (cerebellar and vestibular nuclei), collaterals of cerebellar afferent fibers supply excitatory signals to counteract inhibitory signals from Purkinje cells (Fig. 1B).

On the basis of these analytical data of cerebellar structures, efforts have been devoted to building a nerve net model which may represent essential features of cerebellar functions. Marr (1969) conceived his theory of cerebellar cortex which ascribes a pattern-recognizing and learning capability to the cortical nerve net. Albus (1971) later formulated a similar idea, closely in connection with Rosenblatt's (1962) theory of the *simple per-*

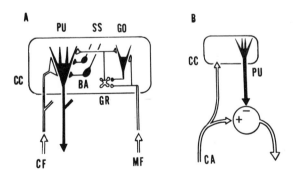

Fig. 1. Neuronal connections in the cerebellum. A: intracortical connections. Abbreviations: CF, climbing fiber; PU, Purkinje cell; SS, superficial stellate cell; BA, basket cell; GO, Golgi cell; GR, granule cell; MF, mossy fiber and CC, cerebellar cortex. B: relationship between the cerebellar cortex and a subcortical nucleus. + and − indicate excitatory and inhibitory synaptic action, respectively. CA, cerebellar afferent. In this, as well as in succeeding figures, inhibitory neurons are filled in black, while excitatory neurons are indicated by hollow structures.

ceptron. The *simple perceptron* is formed of three layers of threshold elements, i.e., receptor cells in the first, association cells in the second, and effector cells in the third layer. Signals are received by the first layer and from there are transferred to the second layer through connections with fixed efficacies. In the further transmission from the second to the third layer, the weight of connections is modifiable and this modifiability is controlled by an outside teacher. When the machine responds correctly to a given stimulus, the teacher enhances the weight of connections at all those modifiable junctions which are transmitting signals at that moment of operation. If the response is wrong, the weight will be reduced instead of being increased. As this procedure is repeated, the machine acquires the ability to always respond correctly to the same stimulus. The *simple perceptron* is now regarded as a basic model of man-made learning machines (Minsky and Papert, 1969).

Fig. 2 illustrates the cerebellar circuitry in the form of the *simple perceptron.* Cells of origin of mossy fibers, granule cells and Purkinje cells are arranged in three layers, as in the *simple perceptron.* It is assumed that the synaptic connections from granule cells to Purkinje cells are modifiable, and that this modifiability is under the control of climbing fiber impulses from the inferior olive. The inferior olive is placed in the role of the outside teacher who evaluates the performance of the cerebellum and thereby modifies internal parameters of the cerebellar cortex, to lead to a better performance. Marr (1969) assumes that when a climbing fiber impulse coincides at a Purkinje cell with an impulse from a granule cell, the efficacy of the synapse that is transmitting the granule cell impulse becomes more potent. Albus (1971) postulates that such collisions of two types of im-

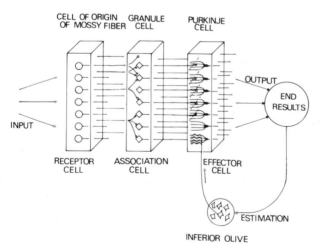

Fig. 2. Perceptron model of the cerebellum.

pulses are followed by depression of the granule cell-to-Purkinje cell synapse involved. These two assumptions have the same theoretical implication.

The model of Fig. 2, the *perceptron model of the cerebellum* as it may be called, visualizes in a very attractive way the cerebellar cortex as a sort of learning machine. Unfortunately, there has been no experimental evidence supporting the two basic assumptions introduced in the model: the modifiability of the granule cell-to-Purkinje cell synapses and the heterosynaptic interference between these and the climbing fiber synapses. Only on morphological grounds has it been shown that degeneration of climbing fibers leads to a certain structural modification — loss of dendritic spines — at the synaptic contact of granule cells and Purkinje cells (Hámori, 1973).

THE CEREBELLO-VESTIBULO-OCULAR SYSTEM

In order to examine the model of the cerebellum on physiological and functional grounds it is important to choose a system in which the meanings of input-output signals and of its overall performance can be defined and evaluated explicitly. In this sense attention has been drawn to the cerebellar flocculus which belongs to the vestibulocerebellum and which is combined with the vestibulo-ocular reflex arc in a relatively simple fashion (Ito, 1970, 1972a, b and 1974).

Fig. 3 illustrates the neuronal diagram of the cerebello-vestibulo-ocular system as worked out by histological and electrophysiological studies. The flocculus receives primary afferent signals from the vestibular organ as a mossy fiber input (Brodal and Høivik 1964; Precht and Llinás 1969; Llinás et al., 1971; Wilson et al., 1972) and, as output, sends Purkinje cell impulses which inhibit certain second-order vestibular neurons (Angaut and Brodal, 1967; Fukuda et al., 1972; Baker et al., 1972; Ito et al., 1973c; Highstein, 1973b). These second-order neurons are driven by excitatory impulses from the vestibular organ, and in turn excite or inhibit oculomotor neurons to produce ocular movement (Baker et al., 1969; Highstein et al., 1971; Precht and Baker, 1972). Fig. 3 also shows that visual signals are conveyed through the accessory optic tract and the central tegmental tract to the inferior olive, to eventually reach the flocculus via the climbing fibers (Maekawa and Simpson, 1973). Receptive areas have been defined in the visual field from which not only excitation, but also inhibition, is elicited through climbing fibers onto Purkinje cells in the flocculus (Maekawa and Natsui, 1973; Maekawa and Kimura, 1974). The basic structure of the vestibulo-ocular reflex arc thus appears simple in the sense that the arc contains only three neurons in series, as shown in Fig. 3. However, at another level, it is complex because of its multiplicity of parallel arrangements.

Labyrinthine signals arise from five different end-organs, i.e., three semicircular canals, utricle and saccule. The second-order neurons are distributed in four different structures, i.e., superior and medial vestibular nuclei,

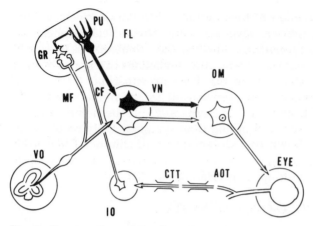

Fig. 3. Construction of the flocculo-vestibulo-ocular system. Abbreviations: OM, oculo-motor neuron; IO, inferior olive; CTT, central tegmental tract; AOT, accessory optic tract; VO, vestibular organ; FL, flocculus and VN, second-order vestibular neurons. (Modified from Ito, 1972a.)

group y of Brodal and Pompeiano (1957) and the lateral cerebellar nucleus (Highstein et al., 1971; Highstein, 1973a). The final output is distributed among 12 subnuclei (six on each side) of oculomotor neurons located in the IIIrd, IVth and VIth nuclei. Hence, the validity of Fig. 3 had to be tested separately in each component pathway of the vestibulo-ocular reflex arc

TABLE I

Principal pathways for vestibulo-ocular reflexes and their inhibition by the cerebellar flocculus

Abbreviations: AC, HC and PC, anterior, horizontal and posterior canals; YG, y group of vestibular nuclear complex; MV, medial and SV, superior vestibular nuclei.i-, ipsilateral; c-, contralateral; SR, superior rectus; IO, inferior oblique; MR, medial rectus; LR, lateral rectus; SO, superior oblique; IR, inferior rectus; + ,present; —, absent. (From Ito et al., 1973c.)

VESTIBULO–OCULAR PATHWAYS				INHIBITION FROM	
REFLEX ACTION	NO.	RECEPTOR CANAL	RELAY NUCLEUS	EFFECTOR MUSCLE	FLOCCULUS	OX,AOT
EXCITA-TORY	E_1	AC	YG	i–SR	+	—
	E_2			c–IO	+	—
	E_3	HC	MV	i–MR	+	+
	E_4			c–LR	—	—
	E_5	PC	MV	i–SO	—	—
	E_6			c–IR	—	—
INHIBI-TORY	I_1	AC	SV	i–SO	+	—
	I_2			c–IR	+	—
	I_3	HC	MV	i–LR	+	+
	I_4		SV	c–MR	—	—
	I_5	PC	SV	i–IO	—	—
	I_6			c–SR	—	—

arising from one end-organ and ending in an eye muscle. With the technique of selectively stimulating each semicircular canal (Cohen et al., 1964), 12 principal pathways for vestibulo-ocular reflexes were identified in rabbits in terms of the receptor canal, reflex action, relay nucleus and target muscle, as listed in Table I (Ito et al., 1973a, b and c). The inhibitory action of flocculus Purkinje cells is exerted upon six of these 12 pathways. Climbing fiber impulses evoked by stimulation of the optic tract caused Purkinje cell inhibition in only two of the six pathways. Both of these pathways originated at the horizontal canal; one excites the medial rectus and the other inhibits the lateral rectus motoneurons for the ipsilateral eye. Therefore, the neuronal diagram of Fig. 3 applies to the reflex arc from the horizontal canal to the ipsilateral eye of rabbits.

THE ROLE OF THE FLOCCULUS IN EYE MOVEMENT

The vestibulo-ocular reflex produces eye movements compensatory for head rotation so as to keep retinal images steady. The horizontal semicircular canal is activated by horizontal head rotation to the ipsilateral side. The resulting vestibular signals are forwarded to excite the medial rectus and to inhibit the lateral rectus motoneurons of the ipsilateral eye. This causes movement of the ipsilateral eye in the nasal direction and prevents slipping of the retinal image in that eye.

The end effect of the vestibulo-ocular reflex, i.e., the constancy of retinal images, can be monitored by vision. However, there is no straightforward connection of feedback, such as provided by muscle spindle afferents in the spinal myotatic reflex, to return visual signals to the vestibular organ. Therefore, superficially, the vestibulo-ocular reflex arc is essentially an open loop control system. In engineering systems, an open loop control system may be simpler in design and easier to construct than a closed loop control system because the feedback loop is not required. On the other hand, however, the performance of such a system is very susceptible to external disturbances as well as changes in internal parameters. Any misperformance once introduced would remain unless it is corrected by some device which replaces the feedback loop. For such a device a computer may be used in engineering control systems. It seems to be legitimate to assume that the flocculus plays a role similar to such a computer (Ito, 1970, 1972a, b and 1974). Generalization of this view to the whole cerebellar system has been attempted previously (Ito, 1970 and 1974).

More substantially, the cerebellar flocculus would have the following functions. First, the flocculus forms a sidepath to the vestibulo-ocular reflex pathway and contributes to the dynamic characteristics of vestibulo-ocular reflexes. Ablation of the flocculus causes no vestibular signs, such as disturbance of the body equilibrium and positional nystagmus (Fernandez and Fredrickson, 1963), but it alters the gain of the tonic vestibulo-ocular reflex (Manni, 1950) as well as that of the accelerating one (Carpenter, 1972; Robinson, 1975). Second, the flocculus may serve for a temporary adjustment of the vestibulo-ocular reflex by utilizing visual information. This adjustment would have the effect of improving the stability of retinal images of the visual field during head movement. Takemori and Cohen (1974a and b) demonstrated in monkey that the horizontal vestibulo-ocular reflex provoked by labyrinthectomy, caloric stimulation or administration of alcohol, was depressed by vision, and that this visual effect was lost when the cerebellar flocculus had been extirpated. Third, the flocculus may be capable of learning so as to acquire the performance of a vestibulo-ocular reflex repeatedly adjusted by vision. Gonshor and Melvill-Jones (1973) found that in human subjects the horizontal vestibulo-ocular reflex was gradually depressed, or even reversed in polarity, if the visual input was kept reversed in the horizontal plane by means of prism glasses. Robinson (1975) demonstrated that the plasticity similarly producible in cat's vestibulo-ocular reflex was indeed lost after cerebellectomy including the flocculus. Miles and Fuller (1974) recently revealed that the vestibulo-ocular responses of the rhesus monkey exhibits adaptive plasticity when the visual field was enlarged or reduced by means of telescopic glasses.

Demonstration of the floccular function in rabbits

In the experiments of Ito et al. (1974a and b), the horizontal canal was stimulated by sinusoidal rotation of an alert rabbit on a motor-driven turntable with frequencies of 0.05—0.25 Hz. The eye movements evoked by rotation in darkness gives the net effect of the vestibulo-ocular reflex. The retina was stimulated by a vertically oriented slit light, which was either fixed in front of an eye or rotated concentrically with the turntable. The fixed slit light represents the normal situation where visual environments stay stationary. When the slit light rotates by an angular amplitude twice as large as that for the rotation of the turntable, this results in a reversal of the direction of movement of the retinal image and simulates the vision reversal obtained by the use of prism glasses.

Sinusoidal horizontal rotation of the rabbit produced not only a smooth periodic eye movement closely following the head rotation, but also a quick eye movement which abruptly set back the shifted eye position. However, with relatively small angular amplitudes, around 10° (peak-to-peak), for the head rotation, occurrence of the quick eye movement was infrequent, and the movement of the eye could be followed continuously by observing under a binocular microscope a scratch mark on the cornea. Fig. 4 plots the extreme nasal and temporal positions of the cornea mark registered during continuous smooth periodic eye movement. The angle of horizontal rotation of the eye ball was calculated from the shift of the cornea mark by assuming the radius of the eye ball as 8.9 mm.

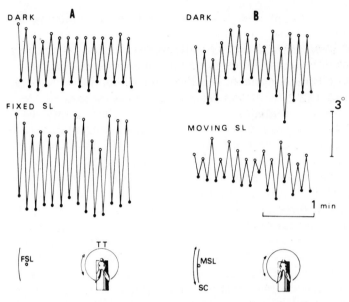

Fig. 4. Horizontal eye movement induced by sinusoidal head rotation and its modification during presentation of slit lights in the visual field: A and B were obtained in two rabbits. Open circles indicate the most nasal, and closed circles the most temporal, positions of the cornea mark on the left eye during each cycle of 10° head rotation. Plottings on the top indicate the eye movement in darkness and provide the control for the immediately succeeding measurement with slit light (SL) to the left eye, as plotted below. Diagrams at the bottom indicate dorsal views of the turntable (TT) mounting the rabbit, rotating screen (SC), fixed slit light (FSL) and 20° inphase moving slit light (MSL). (From Ito et al., 1974a.)

In darkness, where there was no light except for the faint illumination on the cornea mark, the angular amplitude of the eye rotation during 10° head rotation was usually 3—5°. The vestibulo-ocular reflex in rabbits has, therefore, a considerably lower gain as compared with that in cats and human subjects (Gonshor and Melvill-jones, 1973; Robinson, 1975). When a stationary slit light was visible to an eye, the horizontal movement of that eye, during head rotation, was significantly enhanced as illustrated in Fig. 4A. The angular amplitude of eye rotation with the fixed slit light was increased by 20—110% in comparison with that in darkness. On the other hand, the slit light moving with the turntable reduced the eye movement by 20—50%, as shown in Fig. 4B.

The enhancement of the horizontal vestibulo-ocular reflex, as seen in Fig. 4A, should have the effect of reducing the slip of the retinal image of the slit light. Likewise, the reduction of the horizontal vestibulo-ocular reflex, as in Fig. 4B, should be favorable for seeing the moving slit light, as the light moves in the opposite direction to reflex eye movement. Hence, vision modifies the eye movement always in the direction of stabilizing the retinal images during head rotation.

Visual stimulation with the slit light produced not only a temporary adjustment of the vestibulo-ocular reflex but also a progressive modification when the visual stimulation continued. In Fig. 5A, when the rabbit was rotated continuously for 12 h with the fixed slit light presented, the eye movement was gradually augmented as measured either in temporary darkness or with the slit light illuminated. At 12 h after starting the rotation, the eye movement, particularly that with the slit light presented, attained much improved compensation of the head rotation. Likewise, continuous rotation with the moving slit light caused gradual reduction of the eye movement, as shown in Fig. 6A. At 12 h there was only very small rotation of the eye. These effects were in the direction of improving the constancy of retinal images of the slit light, either stationary or moving.

The above-mentioned immediate, as well as progressive, effects of visual stimulation on the horizontal vestibulo-ocular reflex were totally absent when the flocculus had been extirpated on the side of the stimulated eye. Inversely, in those rabbits whose cerebral visual cortex or the cerebellar visual area (lobules VI and VII) had been destroyed chronically, the effects were the same or even more prominent as compared with those in normal rabbits (Figs. 5B and C; 6B and C). Evidently, the flocculus plays an essential role in the vision-guided modification of the horizontal vestibulo-ocular

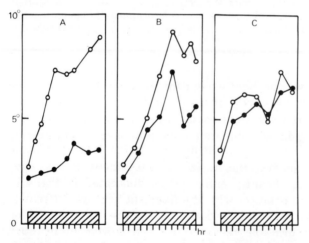

Fig. 5. Changes of rabbit's horizontal vestibulo-ocular reflex during sustained head rotation with the fixed slit light presented. A: normal rabbit. B: from a rabbit with the cerebellar posterior vermis removed chronically. C: another rabbit with the right cerebral occipital lobe removed chronically. Ordinates, mean angular amplitudes of the horizontal eye movement during 10° head rotation. Abscissae, time. ○, eye movements measured with the fixed slit light shown: ●, that measured in temporary darkness. (A from Ito et al., 1974b; B and C, unpublished data by the same authors.)

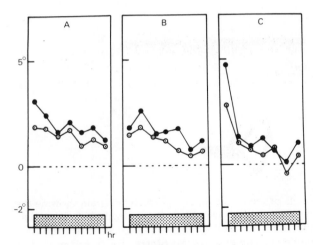

Fig. 6. Changes of rabbit's horizontal vestibulo-ocular reflex during sustained head rotation with the inphase moving slit light. Similar series to Fig. 5 but with the slit light moving with the turntable by 20°. ☉, eye movement measured with the moving slit light illuminated. (A from Ito et al.. 1974b; B and C, unpublished data by the same authors.)

reflex, as expected from the neuronal construction of the cerebello-vestibulo-ocular system.

'Simple' spike activity in flocculus Purkinje cells

As described above, the basic neuronal diagram of the cerebello-vestibulo-ocular system is now available and the functional role of the flocculus is defined in connection with the vestibulo-ocular reflex. It is of great interest to know about the neuronal events that occur in the flocculus and to see how the *perceptron* model applies to them.

With a microelectrode in extracellular position, two kinds of spikes can be recorded from Purkinje cells, i.e., *simple* and *complex* spikes (Thach, 1968; see Fig. 7). *Complex* spikes represent the activity induced via synapses from climbing fibers, while *simple* spikes reflect activities at other synapses. Lisberger and Fuchs (1974) demonstrated in the alert monkey that *simple* spike responses of flocculus Purkinje cells to horizontal rotation were modified very effectively during visual fixation. The observed effect accounts for the suppression of the horizontal vestibulo-ocular reflex that occurs when the animal gazed at the lamp on the turntable. In the experiments by Ghelarducci et al. (1975), Purkinje cell spikes were recorded from the alert rabbit rotated on a turntable and subjected to visual stimulation with the slit light as described in the foregoing section (Fig. 7).

Simple spikes were discharged from flocculus Purkinje cells in alert rabbits at 10—60/sec in the absence of both vestibular and visual stimuli.

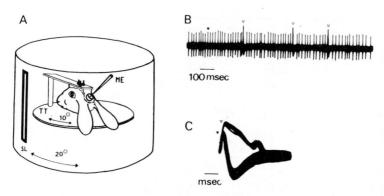

Fig. 7. Recording from Purkinje cells of alert rabbits. A: schematic diagram showing the experimental arrangement. Abbreviations: TT, turntable; SL, slit light; ME, Microelectrode. The body and limbs of the rabbit are omitted for simplicity. B: spikes recorded from a Purkinje cell of the flocculus. ∇, *complex* spikes; others, *simple* spikes. C: fast sweep recording. Sweeps were triggered by *complex* (∇) and *simple* (▼) spikes. (From Ghelarducci et al., 1975.)

This activity was modulated when the animal was rotated in darkness. As seen in Fig. 8B and C, the spike density per unit time (bin width, 0.42 sec) was calculated during 10—100 successive rotations by 10° at 0.15 Hz. The spike density was altered sinusoidally at the frequency of the head rotation. The amplitude and phase of the modulation were determined on a best-fit sine curve extracted by a Fourier analysis. The amplitude is expressed relative to the mean spike density calculated within the period of rotation. The phase angle was determined relative to the head velocity curve (Fig. 8A). The polar diagram of Fig. 8D illustrates distribution of the amplitude and phase angle of *simple* spike modulation in 113 Purkinje cells tested with rotation in darkness. In view of the irregularity of the spike density histogram causing a deviation from the best-fit sine curve, only modulation amplitudes greater than 5% were regarded as significant. The largest amplitude obtained was 83%. The phase angle of modulation varied from cell to cell, but there were two major populations of about equal sizes, one with the phase angle around 0° (±45°, *inphase* type) and the other near 180° (±45°, *outphase* type). A minority of cells had phase angles around 90° and 270° (*intermediate* type).

In the absence of vestibular stimulation, the slit light moving sinusoidally around the stationary rabbit produced little modulation of *simple* spike discharges. However, visual stimulation was very effective in modifying the amplitude and phase angle of *simple* spike modulation provoked by simultaneous head rotation. With the fixed slit light presented, it frequently happened that an outphase response was augmented, as shown in Fig. 9A and B, an inphase response was depressed, or an inphase response was converted to another response type. Even though the effect was opposite

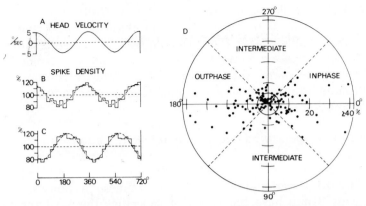

Fig. 8. Modulation of 'simple' spikes of flocculus Purkinje cells during head rotation in darkness. A: sine curve representing the head velocity (ordinate) during two successive periods of rotation. Positive values of the velocity are for the ipsilateral head rotation and negative ones for the contralateral head rotation. B and C: spike density histograms obtained for two Purkinje cells during 30 and 40 rotations, respectively. Ordinates, number of *simple* spikes recorded per bin, relative to the mean spike number calculated over one period of rotation. The histogram obtained for one period is duplicated to cover two periods of rotation in order to facilitate visual estimation of the modulation. Broken lines show the best fitting sine curves. These sine curves are given in the form $r \cos(\frac{1}{8}\pi n - \Phi)$, where r is the amplitude of modulation on the ordinates, n, bin number on the abscissae, and Φ, the phase angle. D: polar diagram plotting values of r and Φ for *simple* spike activity of 113 Purkinje cells. Interrupted lines passing the center of the diagram with 45° inclination separate the plotted points into *inphase*, *intermediate* and *outphase* types. The circle at the center encloses those points representing insignificant modulation by less than 5%. (From Ghelarducci et al., 1975.)

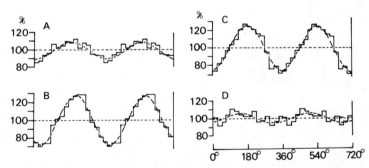

Fig. 9. Visual stimulus modification of vestibular effects on simple spike discharges. A: spike density histogram obtained by 16 rotations in darkness. B: same as in A but by 16 rotations with the fixed slit light presented. C and D: in another Purkinje cell. C: 20 rotations in darkness. D: 20 rotations with the moving slit light. (From Ghelarducci et al., 1975.)

14

in a minority of examined cells, or neutral in another minority, the fixed slit light caused a shift of the dominance to the outphase response type. Conversely, the slit light moving with the turntable by 20° caused a shift of the dominance to the inphase response type; in the majority of examined cells, the observed changes were augmentation of an inphase response, reduction of an outphase response, as shown in Fig. 9C and D, or conversion from an outphase to another response.

Implication of the simple spike modulation and its modification by visual stimuli

As pointed out by Lisberger and Fuchs (1974), inphase responses of flocculus Purkinje cells would have the effect of cancelling the excitatory action of primary vestibular signals upon second-order vestibular neurons (Fig. 10), since the primary vestibular afferents discharge impulses in phase with head velocity (Fernandez and Goldberg, 1971). Hence, the dominance of the *inphase* response during presentation of the moving slit light satisfactorily accounts for the depression of the horizontal vestibulo-ocular reflex (Fig. 4B). By contrast, *outphase* responses of the flocculus Purkinje cells would facilitate the excitatory action of primary vestibular afferents, for the Purkinje cell inhibition wanes and waxes in the opposite direction to the excitation (Fig. 10). Hence, the dominance of the *outphase* responses of flocculus Purkinje cells produced by the fixed slit light is in accordance with the enhancement of the horizontal vestibulo-ocular reflex induced by

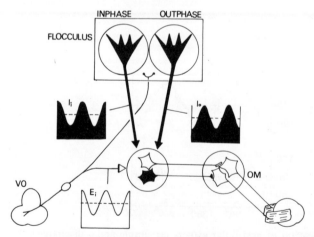

Fig. 10. Modification of the vestibulo-ocular reflex by inphase and outphase responses of flocculus Purkinje cells. E_i, spike density histogram for the primary vestibular afferent impulses; I_i and I_o, those for Purkinje cell discharges. Note that when superposed at second-order vestibular neurons (VN), I_i cancels E_i, while I_o facilatates E_i.

the fixed slit light (Fig. 4A). The postulated mechanisms of visual influences on the vestibulo-ocular reflex are illustrated schematically in Fig. 11.

The above-described observations point to two kinds of neuronal mechanisms which have not been illustrated in the neuronal diagram of Fig. 3. First, how are the two major response types of Purkinje cells, *inphase* and *outphase*, generated? One may speculate that the *inphase* response is driven by primary afferent impulses arising from the vestibular organ ipsilateral to the flocculus concerned and the *outphase* response by those from the contralateral vestibular organ. The contralateral vestibular impulses may be passed to the flocculus through a relay at the descending vestibular nucleus (Brodal and Torvik, 1957). However, in a preliminary experiment on decerebrate rabbits (Ghelarducci, Ito and Yagi, unpublished), destruction of a labyrinth, either ipsilateral or contralateral, resulted in immediate disappearance of both *inphase* and *outphase* responses. Hence, it appears that both *inphase* and *outphase* responses are generated through integration of both ipsilateral and contralateral impulses. As to the possible mechanisms of this integration, it is pointed out that the intracortical inhibitory neurons would invert response patterns of vestibular impulses. For example, when the ipsilateral vestibular impulses evoke *inphase* discharges in Golgi, basket and superficial stellate cells, these in turn cause an *inphase* inhibition of granule and Purkinje cells. This *inphase* inhibition would be equivalent to an *outphase* excitation exerted upon Purkinje cells by the contralateral vestibular impulses. Hence, it is possible that *outphase* responses of flocculus Purkinje cells are supported by both the converted ipsilateral, and the straightforward contralateral, vestibular actions. Similarly, *inphase* responses of Purkinje cells may depend on both the ipsilateral and the converted contralateral, vestibular actions. The observation in decerebrate rabbits (see

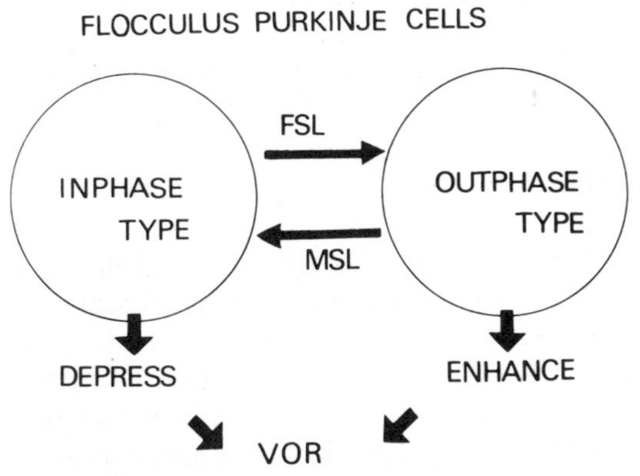

FLOCCULUS PURKINJE CELLS

Fig. 11. Neuronal process that accounts for the visual stimulus modification of the vestibulo-ocular reflex. FLS, fixed slit light; MSL; moving slit light; VOR, vestibulo-ocular reflex.

above) may then be explained by assuming that the cooperation between the ipsilateral and contralateral vestibular impulses in the cortex of the flocculus occurs in a non-linear fashion; Purkinje cells would be effectively influenced only when the vestibular actions from both sides are summated, the action from only one side being subthreshold.

Second, how does vision affect the *simple* spike activity? A possibility is that there exists a mossy fiber pathway which conveys visual signals to the flocculus and which has not yet been identified. Another possibility, however, remains, namely that impulses of the climbing fiber pathway influence Purkinje cells not only directly, but also indirectly via intracortical neurons. It has been shown that collaterals of climbing fibers make synaptic contact with basket and Golgi cells (Eccles et al., 1967), and even with granule cells (Palay and Chan-Palay, 1974). It is not possible to distinguish these two possible pathways at the present stage of this investigation. Since visual signals have little effect on *simple* spike activity in the absence of vestibular stimuli, it is likely that visual signals primarily impinge onto Golgi cells, which in turn influence granule cells by inhibition; effective modification of transmission of vestibular signals via a mossy fiber-granule cell pathway may thereby be expected in spite of the absence of a direct influence of visual signals on the Purkinje cells. One may further infer that if the stationary slit light presented to the rotating rabbit raises excitation of Golgi cells with an *inphase* pattern, this will cause an *inphase* inhibition of granule cells which would cooperate with the *outphase* excitation from the contralateral vestibular organ; augmentation of *outphase* responses in Purkinje cells would thus be expected. Likewise, if the slit light moving with the turntable provokes an *outphase* activity in Golgi cells, this would facilitate the *inphase* excitation of granule cells driven by the ipsilateral vestibular organ; intensification of *inphase* responses in Purkinje cells would thereby be expected. These are nothing more than vague possibilities, but they may point to the way along which the neuronal mechanisms of *simple* spike modulation and its modification by visual stimuli will be explored in future experiments.

'Complex' spike activity in flocculus Purkinje cells

'Complex' spikes were discharged in the flocculus of alert rabbits at a relatively low rate of 1—2 impulses/sec. During vestibular and visual stimulation, significant modulation of *complex* spike discharges of 10—60% in amplitude was frequently induced. In contrast to *simple* spikes, *complex* spikes were affected by visual stimuli in the absence of vestibular stimuli; this is to be expected from the previous study by Maekawa and Simpson (1973). Rather surprising was the fact that in many Purkinje cells the *complex* spike activity was affected by vestibular stimuli, in the absence of visual stimuli. This is in accord with the previous report of Ferin et al. (1971)

that caloric and galvanic stimulation of the labyrinth causes modulation of not only *simple* but also *complex* spikes in the cerebellum.

Just as for *simple* spikes, visual stimulation was very effective in modifying the modulation of *complex* spikes provoked by vestibular stimulation. Response patterns of *complex* spikes, as determined by a Fourier analysis, varied from cell to cell, but there was a certain tendency that the *inphase* pattern prevails under the fixed slit light and the *outphase* pattern under the moving slit light. This contrasts to the effects on *simple* spikes which exhibited dominance of *outphase* responses under the fixed slit light and that of *inphase* responses under the moving slit light. Further, when both *simple* and *complex* spikes were tested under the same series of alternated rotation in darkness and rotation with the slit light, the opposite effects for *simple* and *complex* spikes were consistently observed in 13 of the 15 Purkinje cells examined.

Implication of complex spike modification and its modulation by visual stimuli

The fact that *complex* spikes were modulated by vestibular stimuli, even in the absence of visual stimuli, indicates that vestibular signals impinge onto the visual pathway somewhere in its course through the midbrain to the inferior olive. No connection has been known to exist between the vestibular system and the inferior olive, but this does not exclude the possibility that the inferior olive receives vestibular information via some polysynaptic route. Another possible site for interference of the visual pathway by vestibular signals is the midbrain, because second-order vestibular impulses reach the midbrain structures such as the IIIrd nucleus and interstitial nucleus of Cajal, and because the visual pathway to the inferior olive is also relayed in the midbrain, possibly at Darkschewitsch's nucleus (Walberg, 1974). However, there is no direct evidence supporting either of these possibilities.

As mentioned above (Figs. 10 and 11), the activity of *simple* spikes, behaving oppositely to *complex* spikes, satisfactorily explains the effect of visual stimulation on the vestibulo-ocular reflex. Further, *complex* spikes discharge at a considerably lower rate than *simple* spikes (1 : 10—50); even though one *complex* spike may be equivalent to several *simple* spikes as a propagating signal, *simple* spikes would predominate over *complex* spikes in their effects upon the second-order vestibular neurons. Hence, it is unlikely that the *complex* spikes are responsible for the immediate visual stimulus modification of the vestibulo-ocular reflex.

Even if *complex* spikes have nothing to do with the immediate modification of the vestibulo-ocular reflex by visual stimuli, the possibility remains that *complex* spikes contribute to the progressive modification of the reflex. One may imagine that *complex* spikes serve for a process intrinsic to the cerebellar cortex, such as controlling the plastic modifiability of synaptic transmission from granule cells onto Purkinje cells, as postulated in the *perceptron* model of the cerebellum (Fig. 2). Conclusion on this point should await an experiment where Purkinje cell discharges will be tested during sustained application of combined vestibular and visual stimulation which causes plastic modification of the rabbit's vestibulo-ocular reflex (Figs. 5 and 6).

COMMENTS

Several lines of approach in the study of cerebellar function have now converged at the cerebello-vestibulo-ocular system. The basic neuronal diagram is given and experimental conditions to drive the system with natural stimuli are established. Neuronal events actually occurring in the flocculus are now being studied in close connection with the overall performance of the system. The performance of this system accords with the general view that the cerebellar cortex provides measures of the animal's body (the eye in this case) in space and time, and that it involves a learning process.

However, there is still a certain gap between our knowledge and the reality. Observations of neuronal events in alert animals during natural stimulation have revealed several important points which are not explicable on the basis of the neuronal diagram of Fig. 3. This may not be surprising because the initial diagram is based upon electrophysiological analysis in anesthetized rabbits using electric pulses as stimuli. The diagram of Fig. 3 should, therefore, be considered as a skeleton of the cerebello-vestibulo-ocular system which must be elaborated by further investigations.

At the present stage of investigation, application of the *perceptron* model to the flocculus appears to be more remote than it was thought before for the following two reasons. First, the initial scheme of a clearcut dichotomy between vestibular signals as a mossy fiber input and visual signals as a climbing fiber input is no longer valid, for both signals influence both *complex* and *simple* spikes. Second, visual correction of vestibulo-ocular misperformance is exerted from time to time through *simple* spikes but not through *complex* spikes. This finding does not allow placing the inferior olive in the role of the outside teacher who must correct misperformance of the *simple perceptron*. The possibility, remains, however, that the inferior olive contributes to the postulated learning through a progressive modification of the system's performance.

In order to fill these gaps, further, continued exploration is needed. Yet emphasis may be placed on the hope that elaboration of our knowledge on the cerebello-vestibulo-ocular system will lead to an answer to the question: 'what sort of information processing is operating in the cerebellum?'

REFERENCES

Albus, J.S. (1971) A theory of cerebellar function. Math. Biosci., 10, 25—61.
Allen, G.I., Azzena, G.B. and Ohno, T. (1974) Somatotopically organized inputs from fore- and hindlimb areas of sensorimotor cortex to cerebellar Purkyne cells. Exp. Brain Res., 20, 255—272.
Angaut, P. and Brodal, A. (1967) The projection of the vestibulo-cerebellum onto the vestibular nuclei in the cat. Arch. ital. Biol., 105, 441—479.
Baker, R.G., Mano, N. and Shimazu, H. (1969) Postsynaptic potentials in abducens motoneurons induced by vestibular stimulation. Brain Res., 15, 577—580.
Baker, R.G., Precht, W. and Llinás, R. (1972) Cerebellar modulatory action on the vestibulo-trochlear pathway in the cat. Exp. Brain Res., 15, 364—385.
Brodal, A. and Høivik, B. (1964) Site and mode of termination of primary vestibulo-cerebellar fibers in the cat. Arch. ital. Biol., 102, 1—21.
Brodal, A. and Pompeiano, O. (1957) The vestibular nuclei in the cat. J. Anat. (Lond.), 91, (1957) 438—454.
Brodal, A. und Torvik, A. (1957) Über den Ursprung der sekundären vestibulocerebellaren Fasern bei der katge. Eine Experimentelle anatomische Studie. Arch. Psychiat. Z. ges. Neurol., 195, 550—567.
Brookhart, J.M. (1960) The cerebellum. In Handbook of Physiology, Sect. I, Neurophysiology, II. Amer. Physiol. Soc., Washington D.C., pp. 1245—1280.
Carpenter, R.H.S. (1972) Cerebellectomy and the transfer function of the vestibulo-ocular reflex in the decerebrate cat. Proc. roy. Soc. B, 181, 353—374.
Chambers, W.W. and Sprague, J.M. (1955a) Functional localization in the cerebellum. I. Organization in longitudinal corticonuclear zones and their contribution to the control of posture, both extrapyramidal and pyramidal, J. comp. Neurol., 103, 105—129.
Chambers, W.W. and Sprague, J.M. (1955b) Functional localization in the cerebellum. II. Somatotopic organization in cortex and nuclei. Arch. Neurol. Psychiat. (Chic.), 74, 653—680.
Cohen, B., Suzuki, J. and Bender, M.B. (1964) Eye movement from semicircular canal nerve stimulation in the cat. Ann. Otol. (St. Louis), 73, 153—170.
Dow, R.S. and Moruzzi, G. (1958) The Physiology and Pathlogy of the Cerebellum, Univ. Minnesota Press, Minneapolis, Minn.
Eccles, J.C. (1973) Review lecture. The cerebellum as a computer: patterns in space and time. J. Physiol. (Lond.), 229, 1—32.
Eccles, J.C., Ito, M. and Szentágothai, J. (1967) The Cerebellum as a Neuronal Machine. Springer, New York.
Evart, E.V. and Thach, W.T. (1969) Motor mechanisms of the CNS: cerebrocerebellar interrelations. Ann. Rev. Physiol., 32, 451—498.
Ferin, M., Grigorian, R.A. and Strata, P. (1971) Mossy and climbing fibre activation in the cat cerebellum by stimulation of the labyrinth. Exp. Brain Res., 12, 1—17.
Fernandez, C. and Fredrickson, J.M. (1963) Experimental cerebellar lesions and their effect on vestibular function. Acta oto-laryng. (Stockh.), Suppl. 192, 52—62.
Fernandez, C. and Goldberg, J.M. (1971) Physiology of peripheral neurons innervating semicircular canals of the squirrel monkey. II. Response to sinusoidal stimulation and dynamics of peripheral vestibular system. J. Neurophysiol., 34, 661—675.
Flourens, P. (1824 and 1842) quoted in Dow and Moruzzi (1958).
Fukuda, J., Highstein, S.M. and Ito, M. (1972) Cerebellar inhibitory control of the vestibulo-ocular reflex investigated in rabbit IIIrd nucleus. Exp. Brain Res., 14, 511—526.
Ghelarducci, B., Ito, M. and Yagi, N. (1975) Impulse discharges from flocculus Purkinje cells of alert rabbits during visual stimulation combined with horizontal head rotation. Brain Res., 87, 66—72. ·

Giorgio, A.M.D. e Pestellini, G. (1948) Inhibizione acquisita del riflessi vestibolari. Significato degli emisferi cerebrali e del cerevelleto. Arch. Fisiol., 48, 86—110.

Gonshor, A. and Melvill-Jones, G. (1973) Changes of human vestibulo-ocular response induced by vision — reversal during head rotation. J. Physiol. (Lond.), 234, 102—103.

Halstead, W., Yacorzynski, G. and Fearing, F. (1937) Further evidence of cerebellar influence in the habituation of after-nystagmus in pigeons. Amer. J. Physiol., 120, 350—355.

Hámori, J. (1973) Developmental morphology of dendritic postsynaptic specializations, Recent Develop. Neurobiol. Hung., 4, 9—32.

Herrick, C.J. (1924) Origin and evolution of the cerebellum. Arch. Neurol. Psychiat. (Chic.), 11, 621—625.

Highstein, S.M. (1973a) The organization of the vestibulo-oculomotor and trochlear reflex pathways in the rabbit. Exp. Brain Res., 17, 285—300.

Highstein, S.M. (1973b) Synaptic linkage in the vestibulo-ocular and cerebello-vestibular pathways to the VIth nucleus in the rabbit. Exp. Brain Res., 17, 301—314.

Highstein, S.M., Ito, M. and Tsuchiya, T. (1971) Synaptic linkage in the vestibulo-ocular reflex pathway of rabbit. Exp. Brain Res., 13, 306—326.

Hood, J.D. and Pfaltz, C.R. (1954) Observations upon the effects of repeated stimulation upon rotational and caloric nystagmus. J. Physiol. (Lond.), 124, 130—144.

Ito, M. (1970) Neurophysiological aspects of the cerebellar motor control system. Int. J. Neurol., 7, 162—176.

Ito, M. (1972a) Neural design of the cerebellar motor control system. Brain Res., 40, 81—84.

Ito, M. (1972b) Cerebellar control of the vestibular neurons. In A. Brodal and O. Pompeiano (Eds.), Basic Aspects of Central Vestibular Mechanisms, Progr. Brain Res., Vol. 37. Elsevier, Amsterdam, pp. 377—390.

Ito, M. (1974) The control mechanisms of cerebellar motor system. In F.O. Schmitt and F.G. Worden (Eds.), The Neurosciences, Third Study Program. MIT Press, Boston, Mass., pp. 293—303.

Ito, M., Nisimaru, N. and Yamamoto, M. (1973a) The neural pathways mediating reflex contraction of extraocular muscles during semicircular canal stimulation in rabbits. Brain Res., 55, 183—188.

Ito, M., Nisimaru, N. and Yamamoto, M. (1973b) The neural pathways relaying reflex inhibition from semicircular canals to extraocular muscles of rabbits. Brain Res., 55, 189—193.

Ito, M., Nisimaru, N. and Yamamoto, M. (1973c) Specific neural connections for the cerebellar control of vestibulo-ocular reflexes. Brain Res., 60, 238—243.

Ito, M., Shiida, T., Yagi, N. and Yamamoto, M. (1974a) Visual influence on rabbit horizontal vestibulo-ocular reflex presumably effected via the cerebellar flocculus. Brain Res., 65, 170—174.

Ito, M., Shiida, T., Yagi, N. and Yamamoto, M. (1974b) The cerebellar modification of rabbit's horizontal vestibulo-ocular reflex induced by sustained head rotation combined with visual stimulation. Proc. Jap. Acad., 50, 85—89.

Jansen, J. and Brodal, A. (1954) Aspects of Cerebellar Anatomy. Johan Grundt Tanum Forlag, Oslo.

Kornhuber, H.H. (1971) Motor functions of the cerebellum and basal ganglia; the cerebello-cortical saccadic (ballistic) clock, the cerebello-nuclear hold regulator, and the basal ganglia ramp (voluntary speed smooth movement) generator. Kybernetik, 8, 157—162.

Lisberger, S.G. and Fuchs, A.F. (1974) Response of flocculus Purkinje cells to adequate vestibular stimulation in the alert monkey: fixation vs. compensatory eye movements. Brain Res., 69, 347—353.

Llinás, R., Precht, W. and Clarke, M. (1971) Cerebellar Purkinje cell responses to physiological stimulation of the vestibular system in the frog. Exp. Brain Res., 13, 408—431.

Luciani, L. (1891) Il Cervelletto, Le Monnier Publ. Co., Florence.
Maekawa, K. and Kimura, M. (1974) Inhibition of climbing fiber responses of rabbit's flocculus Purkinje cells induced by light stimulation of the retina. Brain Res., 65, 347—350.
Maekawa, K. and Natsui, T. (1973) Climbing fiber activation of Purkinje cells in rabbit's flocculus during light stimulation of the retina. Brain Res., 59, 417—420.
Maekawa, K. and Simpson, J.I. (1973) Climbing fiber responses evoked in the vestibulo-cerebellum of rabbit from visual system. J. Neurophysiol., 36, 649—666.
Manni, D.E. (1950) Localizzazioni cerebellari corticali della cavia nota 29, effetti di lesioni delle 'parti vestibolari' del cervelletto. Arch. Fisiol., 50, 110—123.
Marr, D. (1969) A theory of cerebellar cortex. J. Physiol. (Lond.) 202, 437—470.
Miles, F.A. and Fuller, J.H. (1974) Adaptive plasticity in the vestibulo-ocular responses of the rhesus monkey. Brain Res., 80, 512—516.
Minsky, M. and Papert, S. (1969) Perceptrons. MIT Press, Boston, Mass.
Palay, S.L. and Chan-Palay, V. (1974) Cerebellar Cortex, Cytology and Organization. Springer, Berlin.
Precht, W. and Baker, R. (1972) Synaptic organization of the vestibulo-trochlear pathway. Exp. Brain Res., 14, 158—184.
Precht, W. and Llinás, R. (1969) Functional organization of the vestibular afferents to the cerebellar cortex of frog and cat. Exp. Brain Res., 9, 30—52.
Robinson, D.A. (1975) Oculomotor control signals. In C. Fernandez abd R.F. Naunton (Eds.), 'The Vestibular System'. Chicago, April. Academic Press, New York.
Rolando, L. (1809) quoted in Dow and Moruzzi (1958).
Rosenblatt, F. (1962) Principles of Neurodynamics: Perceptrons and the Theory of Brain Mechanisms. Spartan Books, Washington, D.C.
Takemori, S. and Cohen, B. (1974a) Visual suppression of vestibular nystagmus in rhesus monkey. Brain Res., 72, 203—212.
Takemori, S. and Cohen, B. (1974b) Loss of visual suppression of vestibular nystagmus after flocculus lesions. Brain Res., 72, 213—224.
Thach, W.T. (1968) Discharge of Purkinje and cerebellar nuclear neurons during rapidly alternating arm movements in the monkey. J. Neurophysiol., 26, 785—797.
Walberg, F. (1974) Descending connections from the mesencephalon to the inferior olive: an experimental study in the cat. Exp. Brain Res., 21, 145—156.
Wilson, V.J., Anderson, J.A. and Felix, D. (1972) Semicircular canal input to pigeon vestibulo-cerebellum. Brain Res., 45, 230—235.

DISCUSSION

PURPURA: Does visual activity get into the mossy fiber system?

ITO: There may be a special mossy fiber pathway which has not been identified so far for this. This examination so far has been done on the anesthetized animal, so there may be the possibility of this being missing. However, just visual stimulation does not modify the simple spikes at all. It modifies simple spikes only when combined with rotation, so even if there is such a mossy fiber pathway, it must be a pathway of a special kind that may be connected to intracortical inhibitory neurons, but not be directed to granule cells.

PURPURA: Let me ask that again. When you have this setup, and suppose you have injected a very small amount of barbiturate, could you show the sensitivity of the system which would interrupt the coupling between the visual stimulus and (rotatory) movement? Or does barbiturate depress the system? I mean a very small amount. I am trying to understand Maekawa's results which are mostly under barbiturates.

ITO: Well, with very very low anesthesia by barbiturates Maekawa says that there is no mossy fiber activity in most parts of the flocculus. But in a very limited area, Meiu and Rosso sometimes find field potentials which may represent mossy fiber activity after ocular stimulation or occipital stimulation. So I think this possibility still remains. But a second possibility is there; the climbing fiber is known to have axon collaterals going to the Golgi cells and basket cells, so the same input from the inferior olive can influence simple spike activity.

GILMAN: You said unilateral ablation of the flocculus removes the effect, and you think there is much crossing between vestibular nuclei. Should there be bilateral effects?

ITO: Well, this may be a special case in the rabbit. I do not know, but as I showed in the initial diagram there is no crossing over in this particular system. Crossing over is just at the higher end of the final output.

GILMAN: The inferior olive crosses in that.

ITO: That is right. But that only receives information from the eye which is on the same side of the flocculus, so there is double crossing.

HIGHSTEIN: The finding of the climbing fibers being modified by vestibular stimulation is bizarre. This is at variance with the previous idea that there is no modification of climbing fiber input into the flocculus. How do you think it is getting into the flocculus?

ITO: That idea can also be supported by the findings of Strata who made caloric stimulation and got climbing fiber discharges in nodulus. The explanation may be, as Valverde is proposing, that the visual pathway may be deranged at the Draschaevich nucleus in the brain stem and that this area is receiving, in fact, the second order vestibular projection. So a possibility is that modulation happens at the level just half-way between the retina and the inferior olive. At the very beginning of our experiments we never expected this and thus overlooked it, but later on there were so many cases where the complex spikes were modulated by rotation in darkness, that we cannot disregard it now.

PHILLIPS: Is it true that what you have described could account for the arresting or enhancing of the vestibulo-ocular reflex, but not for reversing the direction of it?

ITO: Perhaps this is just a supposition, but when the inphase type of output from the Purkinje cell exceeds the excitatory action from the vestibular organ, there may well be reversal.

2

PATTERNS OF MOTONEURON RESPONSES TO NATURAL STIMULI

SID GILMAN

Department of Neurology, College of Physicians and Surgeons, Columbia University,
New York, N.Y. 10032 (U.S.A.)

INTRODUCTION

According to current concepts of spinal motoneuron function, skeletal muscle contraction results from coactivation of alpha-motor and fusimotor neurons, the former serving to control muscle length and tension, the latter to prevent unloading of muscle spindle receptors during muscle shortening. These concepts have evolved from observations of the behavior of muscle spindle afferents during muscle contraction and of the discharge sequence of alpha-motor and fusimotor neurons during various types of movement (Granit, 1970; Matthews, 1972; Stein, 1974). It has been shown repeatedly that discharge of fusimotor efferents accompanies alpha-motoneuron activation. Correspondingly, muscle spindle afferents commonly show an increase rather than a decrease in discharge rate during muscle contraction.

There is strong evidence implicating the cerebellum in the central control of coactivation processes. Granit et al. (1955) found that ablation of the cerebellum disrupted the coactivation sequence; the discharge rate of spindle afferents decreased during muscle contraction, indicating that some impairment of fusimotor function had occurred. The mechanism of this impairment has not been worked out. Indeed, subsequent studies showed that, even in the recently decerebellate animal, fusimotor activation may still precede alpha-motor discharge (Gilman and McDonald, 1967a; Gilman, 1969a). Thus, the concept of coactivation appears to apply even to the completely decerebellate animal. The role of the cerebellum in regulating responses of fusimotor and alpha-motor neurons to natural stimuli requires further study.

The present communication contains data bearing on the problem of cerebellar involvement in coactivation processes. I have compared the responses to natural stimuli of fusimotor and alpha-motor neurons innervating the triceps surae muscles of control and decerebellate animals. The purpose of this comparison is to determine whether (a) both types of neurons respond similarly to each stimulus; (b) cerebellar ablation alters the pattern similarly for both types of neurons and (c) coactivation persists in the recently decerebellate animal.

METHODS

Procedures common to all preparations

Data were derived from five studies reported previously (Gilman and McDonald, 1967a and b; Gilman, 1969a; Gilman and Ebel, 1970; Copack et al., 1975). The studies were performed in cats weighing 1.7—4.8 kg. Ablation of the cerebellum, including nuclei, was performed by subpial aspiration using sterile surgical techniques. Sodium pentobarbital, 35—40 mg/kg, was used for anesthesia. Approximately 2 mm of the rostral portion of flocculus was preserved bilaterally to avoid injury of vestibular nuclei. At the time of unit recording, control and 1—6-day decerebellate cats were anesthetized with 30 mg/kg of pentobarbital. Some findings in anesthetized preparations were reproduced in unanesthetized decerebellate cats decerebrated acutely by spatula at precollicular levels under ether anesthesia.

A laminectomy was performed from L_4 to S_2. The branch of the left sciatic nerve innervating the hamstring muscles was sectioned. The L_3 dorsal spine and pelvis were fixed in a steel frame to which the distal portion of the left femur was attached with a metal pin. The ankle was immobilized with a clamp. Muscles of the left triceps surae were separated from the surrounding tissues; the proximal attachments, blood vessels, and nerves were preserved. Severed from its insertion, the gastrocnemius tendon was attached with a short length of light chain to a force-displacement transducer which was mounted in a rack and pinion manipulator clamped permanently to the steel frame. Skin flaps of the hindlimb and lumbar region were attached to the frame to form pools for paraffin oil equilibrated with 95% O_2-5% CO_2, and warmed to 37°C. Monitored continuously, body (rectum) and oil pool temperatures were maintained between 36 and 38°C by external heating lamps.

Recordings from fusimotor neurons

The left MG nerve was separated from the surrounding tissues and placed intact on bipolar Ag-AgCl recording electrodes. The left ventral roots (VRs) L_6 through S_2 were sectioned, sparing either S_1 or L_7, which was placed intact on bipolar Ag-AgCl stimulating electrodes with the cathode oriented distally. A black glass plate, inserted beneath the intact left MG nerve at the nerve-muscle junction, immobilized the nerve and provided a surface for dissection. Small fascicles of the nerve were sectioned at a point immediately adjacent to the muscle and separated for about 1 cm centrally. Dissected under a microscope with fine scissors and forceps, small filaments of the fascicles were laid across fine bipolar Ag-AgCl recording electrodes at periodic intervals to sample the activity. The dissection was continued until single action potentials were recorded which occurred spontaneously or could be evoked by a pinna twist (Granit et al., 1952). Selecting for these discharge characteristics may produce a sampling bias, favoring particular groups of fibers (Hunt and Paintal, 1958). The action potentials were shown to originate in fusimotor fibers by determining the conduction velocity (CV) of each, using the conduction distance and the latency of the unit response to electrical stimuli of the VRL_7 or VRS_1 at twice threshold intensity.

The conduction distance was determined at the end of the experiment by excising the nerve from the site of the stimulating cathode to the site of the proximal branch of the recording electrode. The nerve was placed on paper in a straight line without stretching and its length measured. The latency of each unit to VR stimulation was determined by computing the mean of three latency values. A unit was accepted for further evaluation only if occlusion of the electrically evoked response by spontaneously active units could be demonstrated (Hunt and Paintal, 1958). Occlusion and an all-or-nothing response to threshold electrical stimulation demonstrated that each unit was completely isolated. Units with axonal CVs at or below 50 m/sec were considered to be fusimotor efferents and above 50 m/sec, alpha-motor efferents (Hunt and Kuffler, 1951; Kuffler et al., 1951). Misclassification of fusimotor and alpha-motor efferents may result from errors in CV measurements due to branching (Eccles and Sherrington, 1930) of peripheral nerve fibers. An analysis of such errors has indicated that they are minimal in the conditions of the present experiments (Ebel and Gilman, 1969).

Records were made on moving film. Zero length for the gastrocnemius muscle was the length at which progressive muscle extension would deflect slightly the tracing of a myograph set at high sensitivity (2 g/mm). Length in mm refers to the degree of gastrocnemius muscle extension beyond that point.

Recordings from alpha-motoneurons

Four nerves in the left hindlimb were dissected free of surrounding tissues: medial gastrocnemius (MG); lateral gastrocnemius (LG); anterior tibial (AT); posterior tibial (PT). The nerves of the popliteal fossa were dissected so that the soleus nerve was included with the LG and the plantaris nerve plus the many branches to muscles of the toes with the PT. Ventral roots L_6 -S_2 were exposed. Recordings were taken from the ventral root which, upon stimulation, caused contraction of the MG or LG muscle with minimal contraction of other muscles. In most experiments, this root was S_1 . Ventral roots L_6 -S_2 were then severed at the dural exit zones. Recording from the distal end of the cut ventral root made it possible to determine whether a reproducible response with a fixed latency occurred upon stimulation of each dissected peripheral nerve. Small filaments of the ventral root were separated with fine forceps under a microscope and laid across bipolar Ag-AgCl electrodes with an interpolar distance of 2 mm until single alpha-motoneuron units could be identified by orthodromic electrical stimulation of nerves of the triceps surae. Units showing fixed latencies compatible with either monosynaptic or polysynaptic relay were studied.

The units were monitored with an oscilloscope after conventional amplification. Responses to orthodromic electrical stimulation at twice threshold strength of nerves of the triceps surae were recorded on film. Amplitudes and latencies of action potentials were subsequently measured from the film. Responses to the natural stimuli described below were recorded on film moving at 50 mm/sec. Data were tabulated and cards were keypunched for analysis by IBM 360 and 1130 digital computers.

Recordings from muscle spindle afferents

Except for the MG, nerves to the left hip, tail, and leg were sectioned. A pair of Ag-AgCl stimulating electrodes was inserted under the medial gastrocnemius nerve near its junction with muscle. Small filaments of S_1 or L_7 dorsal roots were dissected in paraffin oil with fine forceps under a microscope. The dissected filaments were laid across bipolar Ag-AgCl electrodes and action potentials were displayed on an oscilloscope after amplification. The fact that recorded action potentials were derived from afferent fibers related to spindles in the medial gastrocnemius muscle was established by noting (a) the response to electrical stimulation of the medial gastrocnemius nerve, (b) the increased discharge frequency associated with passive stretch, and (c) the pause in discharge during active muscle contraction. Dissection was carried out until single action potentials were isolated. A unit was not accepted unless occlusion of electrically evoked responses could be produced by muscle stretch. This and an all-or-nothing response to threshold electrical stimulation demonstrated each unit to be single. Conduction velocities were computed using the length of nerve measured from the cathode and the latency of unit responses to electrical stimuli of twice threshold intensity. Only data obtained from spindle afferents with velocities above 72 m/sec were used for analysis (Hunt, 1951).

Level of anesthesia

Barbiturate anesthetics may depress to various degrees the 'background' discharge of fusimotor efferent fibers (Diete-Spiff and Pascoe, 1959; Andrew, 1961; Voorhoeve and Van Kanten, 1962; Langfitt et al., 1963). In addition, these anesthetics may alter fusimotor responses to particular natural stimuli. For example, pinna stimulation enhances the discharge of lumbar extensor fusimotor neurons in unanesthetized animals, but diminishes this discharge in barbiturate anesthetized animals (Schomburg, 1968). To control these effects, the following precautions were observed. (a) A constant, light level of anesthesia was maintained during the experiment by small (0.5—1.0 mg/kg) intravenous doses of pentobarbital (animals were considered lightly anesthetized if they responded to pinna twist by head-shaking and forelimb progression movements) and (b) recordings of unit discharge were taken no sooner than 30 min following each dose of barbiturate.

Application of stimuli

Natural stimuli were applied manually according to a Latin square design for randomization of presentation. The following stimuli were used. (1) *Pinna stimulation* (Pt), the left pinna was firmly kneaded for 4 sec; (2) *neck flexion* (Nf), the neck was flexed passively 60° from the horizontal position over 0.5 sec, maintained in flexion for 4 sec, then returned to the neutral position; (3) *neck extension* (Ne), the neck was extended passively 60° from the horizontal position over 0.5 sec, maintained and returned to neutral as in Nf; (4) *toe dorsiflexion* (Td), the left hindtoes were passively dorsiflexed through 45° from the neutral position, then maintained and returned as in Nf; (5) *toe ventral-flexion* (Tv), the left hindtoes were passively plantarflexed through 45° from their neutral position, then maintained and returned as in Nf; (6) *noxious stimulation* (Nx), the pad of the right hindfoot was compressed with a bronchus clamp continuously for 4 sec; (7) *static extension of the triceps surae* (ST), the left triceps surae were extended in 4 mm increments from slack, through 0 length to 16 mm (the muscle was maintained at each length for 5 sec before recordings of unit activity were made; slack length refers to the muscle length in the absence of applied stretch; 0 length refers to the amount of muscle extension required to produce a 2 g tension as measured with a strain gauge). For all stimuli except ST, unit discharge was recorded for 2 sec prior to stimulus application, 4—5 sec during, and 2 sec after cessation of stimulus application. For passive neck and toe movements (Ne, Nf, Td, Tv), the effects of cutaneous stimulation were minimized by maintaining continuous contact with the body part manipulated prior to and during the movement.

RESULTS

Pattern of fusimotor responses to natural stimuli

The discharge rate of single fusimotor fibers in MG nerve was recorded from unoperated control (79 units) and 3—5-day decerebellate (63 units) cats under light pentobarbital anesthesia. Measurements were made of the discharge rate prior to application of phasic natural stimuli (prestimulus

28

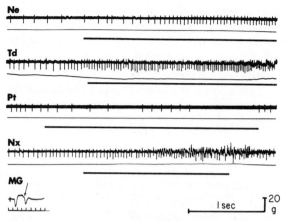

Fig. 1. Medial gastrocnemius (MG) fusimotor unit responses to natural stimuli recorded from a control animal. Upper trace: fusimotor unit discharge; middle trace: myographic response of gastrocnemius muscle; lower trace: onset of a natural stimulus. Ne, neck extension; Td, dorsiflexion of left hindtoes; Pt, pinna twist; Nx, noxious stimulation of contralateral hindtoes. Traces in lower left corner show conducted spike (arrow) from VRS_1 stimulation (CV = 37.0 m/sec) and time scale in 1.0 msec divisions. Gastrocnemius muscle extended 10 mm beyond zero length. Spikes retouched. In Td stimulus application, cutaneous contact with the left hindlimb was initiated 0.5 sec in advance of the applied proprioceptive stimulus, inducing a slight change in fusimotor discharge rate and artifactual passive displacement of the myographic trace. (Modified from Gilman and Ebel, 1970, by courtesy of the Editor of Brain Research.)

discharge rate, PDR) and of the discharge rate in response to such stimuli (reactive discharge rate, RDR). Statistical testing (Gilman and Ebel, 1970) revealed that the PDR for decerebellates (mean = 10.2 impulses/sec) was significantly ($P < 0.01$) less than for controls (mean = 23.2).

During recordings from a few units, as a result of shunting effects or fiber deterioration, data were not obtained for all applied stimuli. To avoid systematic bias in comparison of stimulation effects, these units were eliminated from the data analysis, leaving n = 69 for control and 59 for decerebellate preparations. Patterns of responses to natural stimuli were similar in control (Fig. 1) and decerebellate (Fig. 2) preparations, though differences in absolute values reflected the marked differences in PDRs (Fig. 3). For each individual stimulus, comparison of mean RDRs between preparations indicated that the responses of controls were significantly greater than those of decerebellates ($t > 2.44$, df = 126, $P < 0.01$ for each comparison). The ordering of magnitude of mean RDR with respect to the individual stimuli was compared between preparations using the Spearman rank-correlation test. The significant correlations obtained ($r_s = 0.94$, $P < 0.01$) indicated that relative stimulus-response effects for individual stimuli were similar in control and decerebellate preparations.

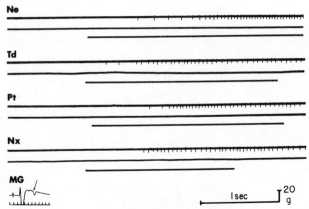

Fig. 2. Medial gastrocnemius (MG) fusimotor unit responses to natural stimuli recorded from a 4-day decerebellate cat. Upper trace: fusimotor unit discharge; middle trace: myographic response of gastrocnemius muscle; lower trace: onset of a natural stimulus. Ne, neck extension; Td, dorsiflexion of left hindtoes; Pt, pinna twist; Nx, noxious stimulation of right hindtoes. Traces in lower left corner show conducted spike (arrow) from VRS_1 stimulation (CV = 36.2 m/sec) and time scale in 1.0 msec divisions. Gastrocnemius muscle extended 10 mm beyond zero length. In Td stimulus application, cutaneous contact with the left hind limb was initiated 0.5 sec in advance of the applied proprioceptive stimulus, inducing an artifactual passive displacement of the myographic trace. (Modified from Gilman and Ebel, 1970, by courtesy of the Editor of Brain Research.)

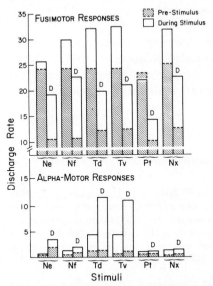

Fig. 3. Graphs of mean prestimulus discharge rates (bars with slanted lines) and reactive discharge rates (open bars) in control (unmarked) and decerebellate (D) preparations for each of the applied stimuli (Ne, neck extension; Nf, neck flexion; Td, dorsiflexion of the left hindtoes; Tv, ventral-flexion of the left hindtoes; Pt, pinna twist; Nx, noxious stimulation of the right hindfoot). Upper graph contains data from fusimotor neurons, lower from alpha-motor neurons.

TABLE I

Mean dDR (signed difference between PDR and RDR) of fusimotor neurons as a function of stimulus category and preparation. (From Gilman and Ebel, 1970; reproduced through courtesy of the Editor of Brain Research.)

Stimulus	Control	Decerebellate
Ne	1.4	8.2
Nf	5.4	12.0
Td	7.8	7.1
Tv	9.2	8.9
Pt	−0.7	4.2
Nx	6.3	9.5

In Table I, these stimulus-response relationships are expressed as a change in discharge rate (dDR) as a consequence of stimulation. The dDRs for each unit were obtained by subtracting PDR from the corresponding RDR for each stimulus. Statistical analysis, accomplished with t-tests of the dDRs to individual stimuli, indicated that the dDR in decerebellates was significantly enhanced for all stimuli except Td and Tv ($t > 2.03$, df = 126, $P < 0.05$ for each significant comparison).

Pattern of alpha-motor neuron responses to natural stimuli

The discharge rate of single alpha-motor fibers innervating triceps surae (Table II) was recorded from unoperated control (58 units) and 1—6-day decerebellate (58 units) cats under light pentobarbital anesthesia. Most units responded with fixed latency to electrical stimulation at twice thresh-

TABLE II

Distribution of peripheral nerves producing spike discharge of alpha-motoneurons ortho-dromically

Number of alpha-motoneurons responding with a fixed latency spike discharge to ortho-dromic stimulation of only a single nerve, to either one of two nerves, or to any one of three nerves of the hindlimb in control and decerebellate animals. (From Copack *et al.*, 1975.) MG, medial gastrocnemius; LG, lateral gastrocnemius; PT, posterior tibial.

Nerve stimulated	Control	Decerebellate
MG or LG alone	40	38
MG and LG	14	8
MG and PT	2	2
LG and PT	0	3
MG, LG and PT	2	7

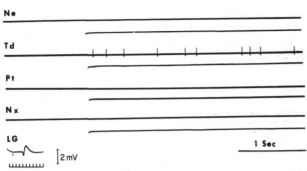

Fig. 4. Lateral gastrocnemius (LG) alpha-motoneuron unit responses to natural stimuli recorded from a control animal. Unit response to orthodromic electrical stimulation of LG nerve at 1.5 times threshold strength shown in lower left corner. Upper trace of each pair contains recording of unit responses; lower trace shows onset and duration of each stimulus. Ne, neck extension; Td, dorsiflexion of toes of the left hindfoot; Pt, pinna twist; Nx, noxious stimulation of the contralateral hindlimb. Spikes retouched. (Data taken from Copack et al., 1975.)

old strength of only the MG or LG nerve (Table II). Some responded with an identical wave-form, latency, and amplitude to stimulation of both MG and LG nerves, and the remainder to MG and PT, LG and PT, or to all of the three nerves. None of the units responded to stimulation of the anterior tibial nerve. Thus, these units represented the discharge of alpha-motoneurons that responded to orthodromic stimulation of nerves of the triceps surae and were, accordingly, presumed to innervate these muscles (Lloyd, 1943, 1946a and b; Eccles et al., 1957 and 1958; Matthews, 1966). Because the triceps surae muscles are all physiological extensors, no distinction was made between units responding to stimulation of the individual nerves for the data analyses. Measurements were made of the PDR and the RDR in response to natural stimuli. A t-test revealed that the PDR for decerebellates (mean = 0.7 impulses/sec) was not significantly different from that for controls (mean = 0.9). The responses to natural stimuli of a representative motoneuron in a control animal are shown in Fig. 4. The motoneuron responded to electrical stimulation of the LG nerve with a spike discharge at a latency of 3 msec (bottom left) but did not respond to electrical stimulation of any of the other hindlimb nerves. This unit responded to Td but not to Ne, Pt, or Nx.

Fig. 5 shows three units recorded from a ventral root filament in a 2-day decerebellate animal which responded with short latency (3—4 msec) spikes to electrical stimulation of LG nerve (Fig. 5, bottom left), but not to stimulation of the other nerves. The smallest unit discharged sporadically in the absence of applied stimulation. All three units discharged intensely to Ne; the largest unit showed a marked response to Td, but none of the units discharged in response to Pt and there was only a slight effect from Nx.

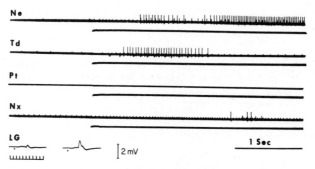

Fig. 5. Lateral gastrocnemius (LG) alpha-motoneuron unit responses to natural stimuli recorded from a 2-day decerebellate cat. Responses of three units to orthodromic electrical stimulation of the LG nerve shown in the lower left corner; single spike obtained at threshold strength, two additional spikes at 1.5 times threshold. Upper trace of each pair contains recording of unit responses; lower trace shows onset and duration of stimulus. Stimuli as in Fig. 4. Spikes retouched. (Data taken from Copack et al., 1975.)

Examination of collected data revealed that the patterns of responses to natural stimuli were different in control and decerebellate preparations, despite similarities of PDRs (Fig. 3). For each individual stimulus, statistical comparison of mean RDRs between preparations indicated that the responses of controls were not significantly different from those of decerebellates except for three stimuli, Ne, Td, and Tv ($P < 0.002$, Mann-Whitney U-test). In Table III the stimulus-response relationships are expressed as a change in discharge rate (dDR) as a consequence of stimulation. Analysis of these data revealed significant differences between preparations for Ne, Td, and Tv ($P < 0.001$ for all comparisons); there were no significant differences for the remaining stimuli ($P > 0.11$, Mann-Whitney U-test).

TABLE III

Mean dDR (difference between PDR and RDR) of alpha-motor neurons as a function of stimulus category and preparation. (From Copack et al., 1975.)

Stimulus	Control	Decerebellate
Ne	0.19	1.45
Nf	0.37	1.05
Td	3.07	10.30
Tv	3.70	9.90
Pt	0.53	0.56
Nx	1.09	0.95

Coactivation of fusimotor and alpha-motor neuron responses to natural stimuli

The data presented above indicate that the patterns of responses to natural stimuli of fusimotor neurons differ from those of alpha-motor neurons. These patterns show further differences in decerebellate cats. We studied the sequence of activation of fusimotor and alpha-motor neurons to determine whether cerebellar ablation changes this pattern. In nine recordings from control and six from decerebellate animals, the discharge of a single fusimotor and a single phasic alpha-motor unit was recorded simultaneously from the same filament of MG nerve (Gilman, 1969a). 'Phasic units' refers to units that are silent until some stimulus is applied. The activation sequence after natural stimuli was studied. In eight of the recordings in control and all six in decerebellate animals, fusimotor discharge increased before the onset of alpha-motor discharge and muscle contraction (Fig. 6). To determine whether coactivation of fusimotor and alpha-motor neurons results in muscle spindle

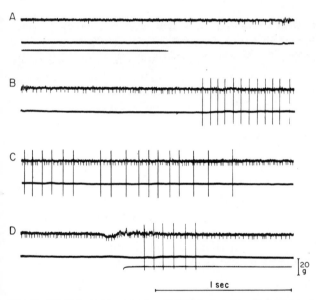

Fig. 6. Medial gastrocnemius (MG) fusimotor and alpha-motor unit responses to noxious stimulation of the contralateral hindlimb recorded from a 5-day decerebellate cat anesthetized lightly with pentobarbital. A recording from single fusimotor (small spike, conduction velocity 15.8 m/sec) and alpha (conduction velocity 88.7 m/sec) units in a filament of MG nerve (upper trace). Middle trace shows gastrocnemius muscle tension. The break in the lower trace indicates the onset of stimulation which evokes a crossed extensor reaction. Records B—D are parts of a continuous recording begun in A. An increase of fusimotor discharge (A) precedes alpha-motor firing and muscle contraction (B). A burst of alpha-motor discharge recurs when the stimulus is discontinued (D). (Reproduced from Gilman, 1969a, by courtesy of the Editor of Brain Research.)

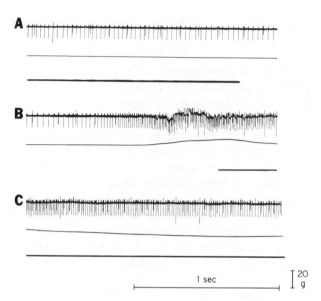

Fig. 7. Responses of two medial gastrocnemius (MG) spindle primary afferents to pinna twist recorded from an unanesthetized 3-day decerebellate cat decerebrated acutely by precollicular section. A: recordings from spindle primary afferents in a filament of S_1 dorsal root (upper trace). Middle trace shows gastrocnemius muscle tension. The break in the lower trace indicates the onset of stimulation. Records B and C are parts of a continuous recording begun in A. An increase of spindle afferent discharge precedes the onset of muscle contraction. (Previously unpublished records from Gilman and McDonald, 1967a.)

activation during muscle contraction, the responses to natural stimuli of spindle primary afferents were studied while recording muscle tension to detect the onset of muscle contraction (Gilman and McDonald, 1967a). In both pentobarbital-anesthetized and unanesthetized decerebrate cats, it was found that an increase of spindle afferent response preceded the onset of muscle contraction and that spindle activity increased during the muscle contraction, rather than pausing as would occur if the spindles were passive (Fig. 7).

DISCUSSION

Fusimotor neurons of extensor hindlimb muscles may show 'background' discharge in decerebrate (Hunt, 1951; Kobayashi et al., 1952; Voorhoeve and Van Kanten, 1962), spinal (Hunt, 1951; Hunt and Paintal, 1958), and anesthetized (Kobayashi et al., 1952; Diete-Spiff and Pascoe, 1959; Voorhoeve and Van Kanten, 1962) animals. Such background discharge varies considerably as a function of the type of preparation and depth of anesthesia. In unanesthetized, acute spinal cats, Hunt and Paintal (1958) found that less than 50% of MG fusimotor units showed background discharge. Voorhoeve and Van Kanten (1962) found that the lateral gastrocnemius fusimotor fibers showing background discharge in decerebrate cats ceased firing a few minutes following high lumbar spinalization.

The present experiments demonstrated a significant decrease of mean background discharge rate in the first week following cerebellar ablation, indicating that a tonic facilitatory influence upon spinal fusimotor neurons was lost. This cerebellar facilitation, presumably derived from the cerebellar nuclei (Henatsch et al., 1964; Manni et al., 1964), probably contributes to 'brain stem' facilitation of extensor fusimotor neurons which, in decerebrate cats, is lost following medullary section (Diete-Spiff et al., 1962) or spinalization (Diete-Spiff et al., 1962; Voorhoeve and Van Kanten, 1962; Barrios et al., 1968). The present findings confirmed previous studies showing that cerebellar ablation depresses the responses to extension of muscle spindle afferents (Granit et al., 1955; Van Der Meulen and Gilman, 1965; Gilman and McDonald, 1967a and b). The loss of cerebellar facilitation of fusimotor neurons evidently accounts for the abnormalities of spindle afferent stretch response previously observed in decerebellates: (a) decreased frequency response to static (Gilman and McDonald, 1967a) and dynamic (Gilman, 1969b) muscle extension; (b) increased stretch threshold (i.e. the amount of muscle extension required to initiate afferent discharge (Gilman and McDonald, 1967a)) and (c) enhanced effects of adaptation of responses to static muscle extension (Gilman, 1969b).

In control preparations, the fusimotor responses to each individual stimulus showed a strong linear relationship between the PDR and RDR variables, suggesting considerable dependence of RDR upon PDR levels. A linear model of the PDR-RDR relationship in controls provided excellent predictive value for the new RDR levels in decerebellates, based upon PDR shifts attributable to cerebellectomy (Gilman and Ebel, 1970). The model had accurate predictive value under essentially all stimulus conditions, indicating that ablation of the cerebellum does not alter the pattern of fusimotor response to individual stimuli. Thus, the changes of fusimotor neuron discharge in response to applied external stimuli are not mediated by cerebellar circuits. In addition, the quantitative differences in response to individual stimuli between control and decerebellate preparations can be explained by differences in prestimulus discharge rates. Consequently, the major effect of cerebellar ablation on MG fusimotor neurons appears to be a lowering of prestimulus ('background') discharge rates.

In contrast to the behavior of fusimotor neurons, alpha-motoneurons innervating hindlimb extensor muscles of the recently decerebellate cat showed no change of PDR. RDR values were greater in decerebellate than control animals only in response to specific natural stimuli: extension of the neck and movement of toes in the ipsilateral hindfoot. Other natural stimuli evoked RDR values no greater than in control animals. Manipulation of the neck activated vestibular as well as cervical joint proprioceptive receptors, and both probably contributed to the enhanced responses, since the receptors commonly act in unison (Gernandt and Gilman, 1959). Manipulation of toes of the hindfoot activated cutaneous, muscle proprioceptive, and joint proprioceptive receptors, but probably only joint receptors evoked the heightened responses since separate stimulation of muscle proprioceptive and cutaneous afferents produced responses no greater than in control animals (Copack et al., 1975).

Purkinje cells of the cerebellum maintain potent inhibitory control over brain stem vestibular neurons (Ito and Yoshida, 1966). Removal of this control by cerebellar ablation in the cat enhances vestibular activity leading to alpha rigidity of the limbs (Pollock and Davis, 1927; Batini et al., 1956a, b and 1957). Indeed, the limb rigidity of the decerebellate cat has been termed 'labyrinthine extensor rigidity' (Dow and Moruzzi, 1958; Denny-Brown, 1966). The vestibulospinal and reticulospinal pathways are doubtless involved in the heightened alpha-motoneuron responses to neck movement (Nyberg-Hansen, 1960 and 1970). Vestibular nuclei, particularly the lateral nuclei, receive afferents from the labyrinths (Precht et al., 1967; Ito et al., 1969), spinal cord (Pompeiano and Brodal, 1957; Brodal et al., 1962) and cerebellum (Dow, 1936; Brodal and Høivik, 1964). The vestibular nuclei make numerous connections with reticular neurons (Lorente de Nó, 1933; Gernandt and Gilman, 1959; Ladpli and Brodal, 1968) and thus the latter may be influenced by both natural (Duensing and Schaefer, 1960) and artificial (Gernandt and Gilman, 1959) stimulation of the vestibular apparatus. Electrical stimulation of vestibular nerve fibers evokes responses thought to be mediated by vestibulospinal and reticulospinal pathways to cervical and lumbosacral alpha-motoneurons; these responses are enhanced by cerebellar ablation (Gernandt and Gilman, 1959). Electrical stimulation within parts of the brain stem reticular formation induces extensor rigidity in limbs of the deafferented decerebrate cat through direct activation of alpha-motoneurons, probably via reticulospinal fibers (Sprague and Chambers, 1953). The finding that cerebellectomy affected the background and reactive discharge rates of fusimotor neurons differently from alpha-motor neurons indicates that the cerebellum influences these neurons, at least in part, through separate descending pathways. Nevertheless, coactivation persists in the decerebellate animal, suggesting that this process is not affected directly by the cerebellum.

Barbiturate anesthesia influenced the present experiments. The level of anesthesia was sufficient to depress the intensity of limb rigidity on clinical examination in the decerebellate cats. Correspondingly, prestimulus firing rates for motoneurons were low. However, anesthesia was not sufficiently deep to prevent opisthotonos, including extension of the forelimbs and, to a lesser extent, the hindlimbs, upon passive extension of the neck. Motoneuron responses to neck extension were correspondingly enhanced.

Data from control animals revealed the potency of various natural stimuli in altering spike discharge rates of hindlimb extensor motoneurons. Local segmental stimuli induced a change of rate in a larger percentage of neurons than stimuli acting from more remote sites; passive manipulation of ipsilateral hindtoes and extension of triceps surae (data not included; cf. Copack et al. (1975)) altered the rate of the highest percentage of neurons and evoked the highest discharge frequencies. In contrast, passive manipulation of the neck, pinna stimulation, and noxious stimulation of the contralateral hindfoot were relatively ineffective stimuli. The responses in decerebellate animals were not simply an exaggeration of a pre-existing pattern. If this were the case, local segmental stimuli would have been enhanced uniformly in the decerebellate animals. However, the responses to a local segmental stimulus (muscle proprioceptive stimulation) were unchanged but responses to another local segmental stimulus (joint proprioceptive stimulation) and a long spinal reflex (vestibular-cervical stimulation) were exaggerated, suggesting that the 'release' phenomena underlying limb rigidity in the decerebellate feline represent highly specific, stimulus-related effects.

It is concluded that cerebellar ablation decreases the baseline discharge rate of extensor fusimotor efferents, but does not diminish the frequency change induced by natural segmental and suprasegmental stimuli. There is no change in the activation sequence of fusimotor and phasic alpha-motor fibers. The disorder of 'alpha-gamma linkage' from cerebellar lesions may be viewed as a depression of tonic fusimotor activity and an increase of tonic alpha-motor activity, without alteration of the phasic fusimotor-phasic alpha-motor excitation pattern (coactivation) induced by natural external stimuli.

SUMMARY

The responses of single fusimotor and alpha-motor neurons innervating the triceps surae to various natural stimuli were recorded in lightly anesthetized control and recently decerebellate cats. Fusimotor activity was recorded from dissected medial gastrocnemius nerve filaments, and alpha-motor activity from ventral root filaments. Measurements were made of the discharge rate prior to application of stimuli (prestimulus discharge rate, PDR) and of the responses to such stimuli (reactive discharge rate, RDR). For fusimotor neurons, the mean PDR and the mean RDR for each stimulus were significantly less in decerebellates than in controls. However, the mean difference between PDR and RDR for each stimulus in decerebellates was equal to or greater than that in control preparations. The RDR pattern in controls was approximately parallel to that in decerebellates. Furthermore, a strong linear correlation between RDR and PDR was observed for each of the individual stimuli. Thus, each RDR level was a function of both the type of applied stimulus and the PDR associated with that stimulus. For alpha-motor neurons, the mean PDR of controls was not significantly different from that for decerebellates. The mean RDR was significantly greater in decerebellates than controls for only three stimuli: neck extension, ipsilateral hindfoot dorsiflexion, and ipsilateral hindfoot ventral-flexion; for other stimuli there was no difference between preparations. The pattern of motoneuron discharge in response to natural stimuli, characterized by coactivation of fusimotor and alpha-motor neurons, was preserved after cerebellectomy. It is concluded that the effect of complete cerebellectomy on motoneuron discharge is a decrease of the 'background' discharge of fusimotor neurons and an enhancement of the responses of alpha-motor neurons to vestibular and joint proprioceptive stimuli with preservation of the coactivation process.

Acknowledgements

Supported in part by USPHS Grants NS10612, NS 2356 and NS 2682.

REFERENCES

Andrew, B.L. (1961) The effect of certain anaesthetics on the activity of small motor fibres serving the hind limb of the rat. J. Physiol. (Lond.), 155, 59—71.
Barrios, P., Haase, J., Nassr-Esfahani, H., Noth, J. und Ropte, H. (1968) Statische und dynamische Aktivitätsänderungen primärer Spindelafferenzen aus den Fussextensoren und prätibialen Flexoren der anaesthesierten und deafferentierten Katze nach intercolliculärer Dezerebrierung, tiefer Spinalisierung und Deafferentierung. Pflügers Arch. ges. Physiol., 299, 128—148.
Batini, C., Moruzzi, G. e Pompeiano, O. (1956a) Componenti labirintiche ed estralabirintiche nelle manifestazioni spastiche del gatto decerebrato e decerebellato. R.C. Accad. Lincei., 21, 328—332.
Batini, C., Moruzzi, G. e Pompeiano, O. (1956b) Origine e meccanismi di compensazione dei fenomeni dinamici di Luciani. R.C. Accad. Lincei., 21, 474—479.
Batini, C., Moruzzi, G. and Pompeiano, O. (1957) Cerebellar release phenomena. Arch. ital. Biol., 95, 71—95.
Brodal, A. and Høivik, B. (1964) Site and mode of termination of primary vestibulocerebellar fibres in the cat. An experimental study with silver impregnation methods. Arch. ital. Biol., 102, 1—21.
Brodal, A., Pompeiano, O. and Walberg, F. (1962) The Vestibular Nuclei and Their Connections, Anatomy and Functional Correlations. Oliver and Boyd, Edinburgh, pp. 1—193.
Copack, P.B., Lieberman, J.S. and Gilman, S. (1975) Alpha motoneuron responses to natural stimuli in decerebellate cats. Brain Res., 95, 75—87.
Denny-Brown, D. (1966) The Cerebral Control of Movement. Liverpool University Press, Liverpool.
Diete-Spiff, K. and Pascoe, J.E. (1959) The spindle motor nerves to the gastrocnemius muscle of the rabbit. J. Physiol. (Lond.), 149, 120—134.
Diete-Spiff, K., Dodsworth, H. and Pascoe, J.E. (1962) An analysis of the effect of ether and ethyl chloride on the discharge frequency of gastrocnemius fusimotor neurones

in the rabbit. In D. Barker (Ed.), Symposium on Muscle Receptors. Hong Kong Univ. Press, Hong Kong, pp. 43—47.

Dow, R.S. (1936) Fiber connections of posterior parts of cerebellum in rat and cat. J. comp. Neurol., 63, 527—548.

Dow, R.S. and Moruzzi, G. (1958) The Physiology and Pathology of the Cerebellum. Univ. of Minnesota Press, Minneapolis, Minn.

Duensing, F. und Schaefer, K.P. (1960) Die Aktivetät einzelner Neurone der Formatio reticularis des nicht gefesselten Kaninchens bei Kopfwendungen und vestibulären Reizen. Arch. Psychiat. Nervenkr., 201, 97—122.

Ebel, H.C. and Gilman, S. (1969) Estimation of errors in conduction velocity measurements due to branching of peripheral nerve fibers. Brain Res., 16, 273—276.

Eccles, J.C. and Sherrington, C.S. (1930) Numbers and contraction-values of individual motor-units examined in some muscles of the limb. Proc. roy. Soc. B, 106, 326—357.

Eccles, J.C., Eccles, R.M. and Lundberg, A. (1957) The convergence of monosynaptic excitatory afferents on to many different species of alpha motoneurons. J. Physiol. (Lond.), 137, 22—50.

Eccles, J.C., Eccles, R.M. and Lundberg, A. (1958) The action potentials of the alpha motoneurons supplying fast and slow muscles. J. Physiol. (Lond.), 142, 275—291.

Gernandt, B.E. and Gilman, S. (1959) Descending vestibular activity and its modulation by proprioceptive, cerebellar, and reticular influences. Exp. Neurol., 1, 274—304.

Gilman, S. (1969a) Fusimotor fiber responses in the decerebellate cat. Brain Res., 14, 218—221.

Gilman, S. (1969b) The mechanism of cerebellar hypotonia: an experimental study in the monkey. Brain, 92, 621—638.

Gilman, S. and Ebel, H.C. (1970) Fusimotor neuron responses to natural stimuli as a function of prestimulus fusimotor activity in decerebellate cats. Brain Res., 21, 367—384.

Gilman, S. and McDonald, W.I. (1967a) Cerebellar facilitation of muscle spindle activity. J. Neurophysiol., 30, 1494—1512.

Gilman, S. and McDonald, W.I. (1967b) Relation of afferent fiber conduction velocity to reactivity of muscle spindle receptors after cerebellectomy. J. Neurophysiol., 30, 1513—1522.

Granit, R. (1970) The Basis of Motor Control. Academic Press, London.

Granit, R., Job, C. and Kaada, B. (1952) Activation of muscle spindles in pinna reflex. Acta physiol. scand., 27, 161—168.

Granit, R., Holmgren, B. and Merton, P.A. (1955) The two routes for excitation of muscle and their subservience to the cerebellum. J. Physiol. (Lond.), 130, 213—224.

Henatsch, H.D., Manni, E., Wilson, J.H. and Dow, R.S. (1964) Linked and independent responses of tonic alpha and gamma hind-limb motoneurons to deep cerebellar stimulation. J. Neurophysiol., 27, 172—192.

Hunt, C.C. (1951) The reflex activity of mammalian small-nerve fibres. J. Physiol. (Lond.), 115, 456—469.

Hunt, C.C. and Kuffler, S.W. (1951) Further study of efferent small-nerve fibres to mammalian muscle spindles. Multiple spindle innervations and activity during contraction. J. Physiol. (Lond.), 113, 283—297.

Hunt, C.C. and Paintal, A.S. (1958) Spinal reflex regulation of fusimotor neurones. J. Physiol. (Lond.), 143, 195—212.

Ito, M. and Yoshida, M. (1966) The origin of cerebellar-induced inhibition of Deiters neurones. I. Monosynaptic initiation of the inhibitory postsynaptic potentials. Exp. Brain Res., 2, 330—349.

Ito, M., Hongo, T. and Okada, Y. (1969) Vestibular-evoked postsynaptic potentials in Deiters neurones. Exp. Brain Res., 7, 214—230.

Kobayashi, Y., Oshima, K. and Tasaki, I. (1952) Analysis of afferent and efferent systems in the muscle nerve of the toad and cat. J. Physiol. (Lond.), 117, 152—171.

Kuffler, S.W., Hunt, C.C. and Quilliam, J.P. (1951) Function of medullated small-nerve fibres in mammalian ventral roots: efferent muscle spindle innervation. J. Neurophysiol., 14, 29—54.

Ladpli, R. and Brodal, A. (1968) Experimental studies of commissural and reticular formation projections from the vestibular nuclei in the cat. Brain Res., 8, 65—96.

Langfitt, T.W., Kamei, K., Koff, G.Y. and Peacock, S.M. (1963) Gamma neuron control by thalamus and globus pallidus. Arch. Neurol. (Chic.), 9, 593—606.

Lloyd, D.P.C. (1943) Neuron patterns controlling transmission of ipsilateral hind limb reflexes in cat. J. Neurophysiol., 6, 293—315.

Lloyd, D.P.C. (1946a) Facilitation and inhibition of spinal motoneurons. J. Neurophysiol., 9, 421—438.

Lloyd, D.P.C. (1946b) Integrative pattern of excitation and inhibition in 2-neuron reflex arcs. J. Neurophysiol., 9, 439—444.

Lorente de Nó, R. (1933) Vestibulo-ocular reflex arc. Arch. Neurol. Psychiat. (Chic.), 30, 245—291.

Manni, E. Henatsch, H.D., Henatsch, E.M. and Dow, R.S. (1964) Localization of facilitatory and inhibitory sites in and around the cerebellar nuclei affecting limb posture, alpha and gamma motoneurons. J. Neurophysiol., 27, 210—228.

Matthews, P.B.C. (1966) The reflex excitation of the soleus muscle of the decerebrate cat caused by vibration applied to its tendon, J. Physiol. (Lond.), 184, 450—472.

Matthews, P.B.C. (1972) Mammalian Muscle Receptors and their Central Actions. Williams and Wilkins, Baltimore, Md.

Nyberg-Hansen, R. (1960) Functional organization of descending supraspinal fibre systems to the spinal cord. Anatomical observations and physiological correlations. Ergebn. Anat. Entwickl.-Gesch., 39, 3—48.

Nyberg-Hansen, R. (1970) Anatomical aspects on the functional organization of the vestibulospinal projection, with special reference to the sites of termination. In Fourth Symposium on the Role of the Vestibular Organs in Space Exploration. NASA, SP-187, 167—181.

Pollock, L.J. and Davis, L. (1927) The influence of the cerebellum upon the reflex activities of the decerebrate animal. Brain, 50, 277—312.

Pompeiano, O. and Brodal, A. (1957) Spinal-vestibular fibers in the cat; an experimental study. J. comp. Neurol., 108, 353—381.

Precht, W., Grippo, J. and Wagner, A. (1967) Contribution of different types of central vestibular neurons to the vestibulospinal system. Brain Res., 4, 119—123.

Schomburg, E.D. (1968) Fusimotorische Forderung und Hemmung bei Pinna-Reizung in Abhängigkeit vom zentralnervösen Zustand. Pflügers Arch. ges. Physiol., 304, 164—182.

Sprague, J.M. and Chambers, W.W. (1953) Regulation of posture in intact and decerebrate cat. I. Cerebellum, reticular formation, vestibular nuclei. J. Neurophysiol., 16, 451—463.

Stein, R.B. (1974) Peripheral control of movement. Physiol. Rev., 54, 215—243.

Van Der Meulen, J.P. and Gilman, S. (1965) Recovery of muscle spindle activity in cats after cerebellar ablation. J. Neurophysiol., 28, 943—957.

Voorhoeve, P.E. and Van Kanten, R.W. (1962) Reflex behaviour of fusimotor neurons of the cat upon electrical stimulation of various afferent fibers. Acta physiol. pharmacol. néerl., 10, 391—407.

DISCUSSION

PURPURA: Do you see any differences if you make more regional ablations? For example, if you just take off the anterior lobe (or maybe nuclei) versus the entire cerebellectomy or pedunculotomy. If you do the entire cerebellectomy or pedunculotomy can you see the same?

GILMAN: Yes, is the question whether there is any difference if one does regional cerebellar ablations or selective lesions in nuclei?

PURPURA: Along functional lines.

GILMAN: The answer is that I have not done that. The Granit group did so by making ablations in the anterior lobe, and their results were highly variable. One animal showed the effect and another animal did not. They also used the Pollack-Davis method which ablates the anterior lobe specifically, and they found that there was again tremendous variability. I don't think anybody has gone through the requisite task, which is a rather tedious one, of ablating specific portions of the cerebellum to look at differences in spindle responses. I am trying to follow it now. I have made lesions of the superior cerebellar peduncle and looked at spindle responses in these animals, comparing these data with data obtained from animals with complete cerebellectomy. The degree of impairment of spindle responses is less in animals with the superior cerebellar peduncular lesion. As a matter of fact, they fall just about half-way between control and completely cerebellectomized animals' data. I think this means that this tonic facilitation is probably coming out of the nuclei, or coming out of the nuclei proceeding up to the ventrolateral nucleus to the precentral cortex and then proceeding downwards through various pathways. There is some second source of facilitation to the spindle apparatus and this probably comes through the fastigial nucleus. I have now looked at the effects of selective ablations there, but one finds similar behavioral patterns as Pompeiano has shown.

KUBOTA: You said you have seen after ablation that your results are different from Granit's. How do you explain the differences?

GILMAN: I think the difference is probably due to the fact that we have carried out very complete cerebellar ablations, waiting several days, and then recording from the animals. This provides a period of time for reorganization, to recover from the effects of the ablation procedure. This is one aspect. The second aspect is that Granit, Holmgren and Merton emphasized the break in the alpha-gamma linkage, and yet in their recordings it is clear that the linkage is not broken. As I showed you in the slides there is still considerable fusimotor activation, as shown by the fact that there is no spindle unloading in most recordings in their own paper. So, I think the differences are due to slight differences in technique and perhaps differences in emphasis.

ALBE-FESSARD: I would like you to explain your technique or method of ablation. How you are totally ablating the cerebellum?

GILMAN: The difficulty was the preparation of the animals because of the wound after cerebellectomy. We carry out the cerebellar ablation through a posterior fossa exposure, ablate by means of suction, stop the bleeding, close the wound completely (including skin), allow the animals to recover for a period of time of up to weeks (in the case of cat experiments) and then carry out the various sections and relate anesthesia for recording purposes. At the end of our recording session we kill the animal, remove the nervous system and examine the brain stem for evidence of damage to vestibular and reticular nuclei and discard all data from animals which have any evidence of damage in the brain stem. We also looked at the completeness of the cerebellum ablation. In fact it is quite difficult to remove the flocculi in animals without damaging the vestibular nuclei, and so usually there are 2 mm or so pieces of flocculus still intact in cat and also in monkey. This period of time allows the animal to recover to a substantial standard of fluid balance and electrolyte balance, so that the animal can withstand many hours of recording. However, some of the experiments were carried out in decerebrate cats. Again, these experiments were done in animals which had cerebellar ablations several days in advance of the recording procedures, for the same reasons. It worried me a bit to carry out an acute ablation at the time of recording because of the chance of infarction of areas that one would have no information about or have no histological evidence of. Also, it is a nice technique to apply a piece of ice to a part of the nervous system and see a change in physiological behavior, vis-à-vis the problem of ice water dripping on the brain stem.

PHILLIPS: Are you thinking of doing any intracellular recording from animals in these experiments? There may be a general factor of the sort of reticular depolarization of the motor neurons so that they are impelled nearer or farther away from their firing level, and in that case descending pathways could still exert an equal amount of excitatory or inhibitory action and would have their response completely unbalanced. That may be part of what we mean by alpha-gamma coactivation, and may not be so much a difference in the descending control signals, as a general change in the reactivity of the gamma motor neuron, so that it is tripped in one way or the other. . . . I do not know whether this makes satisfactory sense.

GILMAN: No, on the contrary, it is a very big point. Yes, I want to do that very much. We have restricted ourselves to recording unit activity coming down the ventral root, which ignores the terribly important synaptic activity at the level of the spinal cord, not to mention elsewhere. But the purpose of recording unit activity and not the synaptic activity in these experiments was to look at the behavior with respect to the natural stimulus. We want to see what was going on outside of the muscle. Now, when I emphasize the specificity of the stimuli, that emphasis has to do with an action potential proceeding down the nerve, and not with what might happen at the synapse. It certainly is possible that at the synapse itself there is a general enhancement of activity which is non-specific, i.e., it is possible that the noxious stimulus would produce an equal number of EPSPs and IPSPs in the motor neurons, to vestibular stimulation. I cannot rule out that possibility, and in fact if we examine the cerebellar cat it does appear to develop opisthotonic postures to a variety of stimuli. However, I think that we chose this method of recording as a first approach in order to see whether there would be specificity in terms of spinal pathways, and in fact I was very pleased.

PHILLIPS: Yes, I think everybody is pleased. It is a question of whether some further analysis is needed for comparison.

GILMAN: Yes, I think it certainly would be worthwhile to do that and also to look at the pathways involved, and to examine this curious effect that local segmental stimuli are terribly important for the motor neuron responses. There has been an interesting study carried out in Germany in which vestibular nuclear responses to various stimuli were examined, and it was found that the vestibular nuclei respond very specifically to neck proprioceptive input and not to muscle proprioceptive input. It is possible that many of the reactions we see here are due to an input to vestibular nuclei and were not immediately generated.

PHILLIPS: There is a powerful monosynaptic connection from vestibular nuclei to extensor motor neurons.

GILMAN: Yes.

3

STUDY IN AWAKE MONKEYS OF CONNECTIONS BETWEEN THE CORPUS STRIATUM AND PALLIDUM WITH THE SUBSTANTIA NIGRA AND SUBTHALAMUS

CHIHIRO OHYE*, JEAN FEGER** and DENISE ALBE-FESSARD

Université Pierre et Marie Curie, Laboratoire de Physiologie des Centres Nerveux, 75016 Paris (France)

INTRODUCTION

For a better understanding of neural mechanisms of 'conscious behavior', an experiment on awake monkeys might be one of the most attractive. Recently, in this laboratory, a new technique has been developed which facilitates the stereotaxic approach to the subcortical deep structures in animal without anesthesia (Gallouin and Albe-Fessard, 1973).

With this technique, the present investigation was undertaken to elucidate the function of the striatonigral connection in awake monkeys. In fact, it seemed to be somewhat puzzling that the striatonigral system, which makes a closed circuit with reciprocal nigrostriatal dopaminergic system (essentially inhibitory; see Hornykiewicz, 1966) has also been considered to be inhibitory (Yoshida et al., 1972).

And so, it was considered interesting to study electrophysiologically the possibility of striatonigral excitatory connections, several evidences of which will be presented here. During this work, an interesting connection between the striatum and the subthalamic nucleus was also found.

METHODS

Five monkeys (*Macaca cynomolgus*) weighing 2.5—3.0 kg were used in this study. Under ketamine analgesia, the head of the animal was fixed on an ordinary stereotaxic apparatus with the aid of a special contention device previously attached to the skull; the rest of the body was supported

---

* Fellowship INSERM. On leave of absence from Dept. of Neurosurgery, Gunma University, Maebashi, Japan.
** Université R. Descartes, U.E.R. de Psychologie, Paris, France.

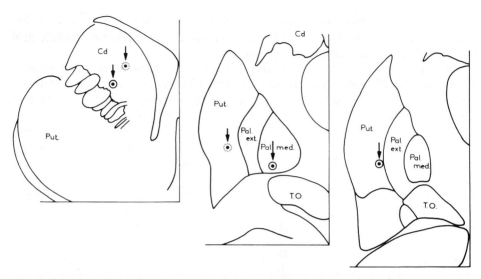

Fig. 1. Schematic drawing of transverse sections through the corpus striatum and lenticular nucleus to show the sites of stimulation reconstructed from the histological sections. Point with solid circle indicates the site of stimulation lying about 2 mm in front of the point with dotted circle. Drawings are made from laboratory atlas (see footnote p. 47) corresponding to A23 (left), A18 (middle) and A17 (right), respectively. Cd, caudate nucleus; Pal. ext., external segment of pallidum; Pal. med., medial segment of pallidum; Put, putamen; T.O., tractus opticus.

in a hammock. Thus, the animal was kept awake throughout the experiment without pain and fear. The details of this technique have already been presented (Féger et al., 1975).

Bipolar concentric stimulating electrodes (diameter 0.7 mm; tip distance 0.5 mm) were implanted prior to the first recording experiment in the head of the caudate ($\times$ 2), the putamen ($\times$ 2) and the internal segment of the globus pallidus ($\times$ 1) (Fig. 1).

The electrodes were placed on one side and then another set of electrodes was implanted on the other side after a series of recording experiments, except for one case in which bilateral implantation was performed at one time. Electrical stimulation was given with the following parameters: 1—4 shocks (200—300 c/sec), 0.5 msec and 150—250 μA. Before this first experiment, the animal was carefully examined to check if the stimuli gave rise to any muscular contraction or behavioral reaction, but this was never the case.

Extracellular unitary recording was made by a glass micropipette (filled with 1 M KCl and pontamine blue) (tip diameter, about 5 μm; electrical resistance, 10 MΩ).

In order to arrive at deep seated structures, such as the substantia nigra

(SN), with the minimal error, the stereotaxic coordinates* (Olszewski, 1952) were adjusted, referring to the third ventricle by previous radiological study (Percheron and Lacourly, 1973).

Through a small burr hole in the skull, a guide tube (external diameter, 1 mm; length, 50 mm) was introduced vertically down to the cortical surface and cemented temporarily. A bipolar concentric electrode was then lowered through this guide tube. The neural activity was recorded to delineate various subcortical structures (cell layers or fibers). The upper border of the thalamus was characterized by a sudden increase of neural noise contrasting to that of the surrounding structures (Albe-Fessard et al., 1963; Fukamachi et al., 1973). At the entrance of the thalamus thus determined, the bipolar concentric electrode, which also served to make a guide hole, was replaced by a micropipette. Unitary recording started from this level of the thalamic entrance to the deep structures, exploratory distance being 12,000—15,000 μm.

Together with the conventional recording system, a dot display on a memory scope was used on-line to facilitate the analysis of poststimulus sequences.

Systematic vertical trajectories toward SN were carried out from A12 to A16 rostrocaudally and from L1.5 to L7 mediolaterally. Generally, one or two complete tracks were enough in each experimental session to be tolerated by the animal in such condition.

Considering the survival time (about one month from the first preparation), the end point of each tract was marked, if necessary, by injecting pontamine blue iontophoretically in several later experiments of each case (see Fig. 8).

At the end of the series of experiments, the animal was perfused with 10% formalin under deep Nembutal anesthesia. The points of stimulation and sites of recording in each trajectory were reconstructed on the histological sections.

RESULTS

Striatonigral connections

Among a total of 40 trajectories, 26 were histologically verified to have passed through a part of the substantia nigra (SN). During the experiment, this area was recognized by spontaneous activity which contrasted with the

---

* In this study, we used Olszewski's (1952) atlas mainly to refer to the details of the structures. However, from the practical point of view, we used our 'laboratory atlas' of *Macaca cynomolgus* more. Therefore, the coordinates given in this text are represented according to the latter. There are certainly some differences between them, for example, the commissure anterior and posterior in Olszewski's atlas are 17.1 and 2.7, respectively, but 22 and 10 in our laboratory atlas.

rather silent fibrous structures dorsal to SN. However, because of pulsations probably due to the nearby passing basilar artery, stable recording of SN neurons was not always easy. Unstable neurons were thus discarded and the responses of only 57 neurons in SN were retained.

All 57 neurons showed spontaneous activity in a rather regular continuous fashion, the frequency being stable between 10 and 100, depending on the cell. Burst activity was never encountered in the normal awake condition.

These 57 neurons responded to stimulation of either the caudate (Cd), the putamen, or both.

(a) Response to caudate stimulation

Electrical stimulation of the head of Cd nucleus exerted two different types of effects on the background spontaneous activity of 40 SN neurons. In 22 neurons, the effect was a pure inhibition (Fig. 2, left). In 18 neurons, an excitation was followed by an inhibition and, in some cases, followed further by a rebound of excitation. In the former 22 neurons, the spontaneous discharge was abruptly interrupted at about 20—50 msec after Cd stimulation and reappeared suddenly, also with its original firing rate. The firing rate could play a role in this regard: the more active was the spontaneous discharge, the shorter was the duration of inhibition, in general. Thus, duration of the inhibitory effect varied from 30 to 200 msec (mean 80 msec), but it was constant for a given neuron. Frequently a negative slow wave of the same duration as the inhibitory phase was recorded concomitantly (Fig. 2, left, juxtacellular recordings).

In the latter 18 cells, the initial excitation of one or two spikes with a fluctuating latency of 10—20 msec was followed by an inhibitory phase of longer duration (50—500 msec, mean 200 msec).

These two types of response were often obtained one with the other in one penetration of the SN, apparently without topographic distribution.

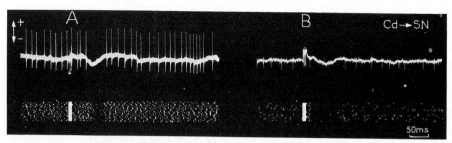

Fig. 2. Two different types of responses of SN neurons to Cd stimulation. Pure inhibitory (A) and excitatory-inhibitory sequences (B). In each pair of illustrations, the upper trace is an example of ordinary oscillographic recording and in the lower each spike is represented as a dot (to be read from the bottom upward). Note that on the left the spontaneous activity is very strong.

(b) Responses to putamen stimulation

Twenty-three SN neurons responded to electrical stimulation of the putamen. As in the case of Cd stimulation, two different types of response were observed: pure inhibitory and excitatory-inhibitory effects, but with some quantitative differences in latency and duration of excitation or inhibition (Fig. 3). A pure inhibitory effect was found in 10 SN neurons. The latency was comparable to that observed with Cd stimulation, but the duration was somewhat longer (50—250 msec, mean 140 msec). Thirteen neurons responded to putamen stimulation with excitatory-inhibitory sequences. The initial excitation started between 15 and 50 msec, depending on the recorded neuron, and the subsequent inhibitory phase also varied, from 25 to 200 msec (mean 130 msec). Postinhibitory rebound was also observed in several cases.

The two stimulating electrodes placed in one nucleus were not in general both effective in producing a response in the same cell. This fact suggests point-to-point projections between striate nuclei and SN. However no systematic organization was found, possibly because of the small number of cells studied.

(c) Convergent responses to caudate and putamen

In 23 neurons tested with stimulations, only six responded to both Cd and putamen stimulation. In four neurons the type of response was the same (pure inhibitory, two; excitatory-inhibitory, two) and in two other neurons the type of response was different.

It might be noteworthy that the latency of initial excitation was not necessarily shorter after putamen stimulation than Cd stimulation on consideration of the geometrical situations between them. These results are

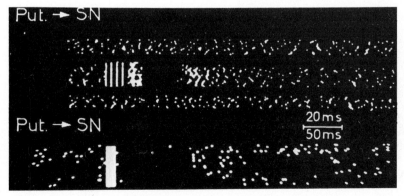

Fig. 3. Two different types of responses of SN neurons to putamen stimulation. The excitatory-inhibitory sequences with rebound excitation (upper) and the pure inhibitory response (lower) are demonstrated by dot-displays.

on the same line as the anatomical knowledge that Cd-nigral fibers were
not relayed in the putamen (Nauta and Mehler, 1969).

(d) Responses to globus pallidus stimulation

Although stimulation of the globus pallidus (GP) was not always tried in
this study, among 20 SN neurons tested only one neuron was inhibited by
GP stimulation with a postexcitatory effect.

(e) Orthodromic origin of the excitatory responses

The nigral excitatory responses to striatal stimulation generally required
repetitive trains of stimuli (3—4 shocks at 200—300 c/sec) in order to appear.
The number of spikes of the responses was not always equal to the number
of shocks. This was in favor of an orthodromic origin of the spikes, but the
other tests of orthodromicity were difficult to apply in this case. However,

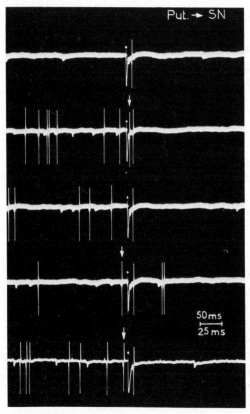

Fig. 4. The spontaneous and putamen-induced spike activities of a SN neuron showing
the absence of collision between them. Arrows indicate critical spontaneous activities
which may block the evoked response.

in several cases, only a single shock was enough to produce excitatory as well as inhibitory responses. In such cases, special care was taken to find whether the collision between spontaneous and electrically elicited spikes occurred in due sequences. As shown in Fig. 4, the early excitatory response to striatal stimulation (putamen, in this case) persisted even if a preceding spontaneous spike fell within the interval in which they might cause the collision, if any. The apparent absence of collision suggested that the early excitatory response was orthodromic in nature. As a matter of fact, the spike response due to nigrostriatal antidromic excitation has not been found, so far.

Striatosubthalamic connections

In a very limited area between the thalamus and SN, a particular group of neurons was found which received a strong excitatory input from the striatum and a pure inhibitory influence from GP. A total of 28 cells were studied at this level. Seventeen responded to Cd stimulation, 17 to putamen and seven of these cells showed convergent responses to Cd and putamen. Further, six cells which were excited by one of these stimulations and one independent cell, were also inhibited by pallidal stimulation.

Examples of excitatory responses are shown in Fig. 5. Electrical stimulation of Cd (or putamen) induced short latency repetitive spikes followed by an arrest of spontaneous discharge for about 100 msec. The detail of the Cd-induced response is demonstrated in Fig. 5B. The initial excitatory effect was so strong that a single shock applied to Cd nucleus was enough to induce repetitive spike discharges placed on the rising phase of the positive slow wave to which succeeded a large negative slow potential corresponding to the inhibitory phase. The latency for initial excitation was about 10—20 msec in most of the cases, and the repetitive discharge of several spikes continued to about 50 msec. Moreover, the initial excitation followed repetitive stimulation, as high as 30/sec, with a fluctuation of the latency of the first spike as demonstrated in Fig. 6. Duration of the subsequent inhibitory phase varied from 40 msec up to 300 msec depending on the particular case (mean 110 msec). In every respect, no difference was found between Cd-induced and putamen-induced responses, even if some preferential dominancy was seen in the case of convergent response as in Fig. 7, in which responses to putamen stimulation were more marked than those to Cd stimulation.

In the case of inhibition from pallidal origin, arrest of spontaneous discharge started in half of the cases almost just after the stimulus artifact, or with a little delay, as shown in Fig. 7, and in the other half of the cases with a latency of about 50 msec. The mean duration of GP-induced inhibition was 90 msec.

The localization of this thin layer of neurons was first assumed to be in the zona incerta, or the superior part of the subthalamic nucleus. Further

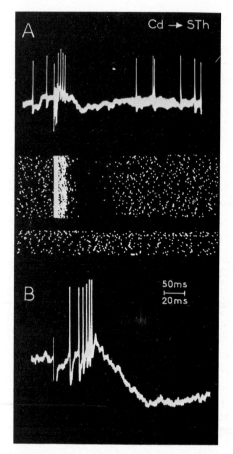

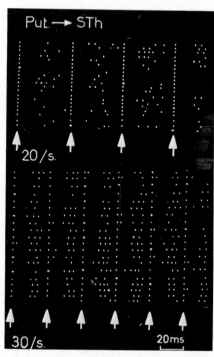

Fig. 5. A: Excitatory-inhibitory response of a neuron of the subthalamic nucleus to Cd stimulation. Each spike, A upper, is represented in A lower, as a dot (to be read from the bottom upward). B: the initial excitation induced by a single shock to Cd nucleus is shown with the faster sweep in B. A and B are from different neurons.

Fig. 6. Responses of a subthalamic neuron by repetitive (20/sec and 30/sec) stimulation of putamen nucleus. Dots in a line with an arrow show the stimulus artifacts. The other dots represent spike responses.

verification through coloration of cells (Fig. 8) assigns this response to corpus Luysii. These cells are present in clusters between A13 and A16 anteroposteriorly, L3 and L5 mediolaterally and, dorsoventrally, they covered only less than 1 mm in depth. This small area corresponded to the dorsal part of the subthalamic nucleus. But the precise localization must be confirmed by further accumulation of recordings from the same type of neurons.

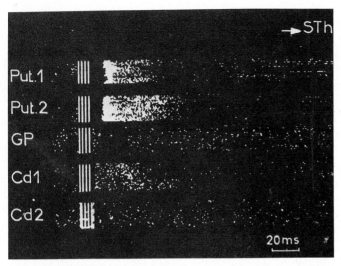

Fig. 7. Convergent responses of a neuron of the subthalamic nucleus to caudate (Cd), internal segment of globus pallidus (GP) and putamen (Put.) stimulations. 1 and 2 denote anterior and posterior parts of each nucleus respectively.

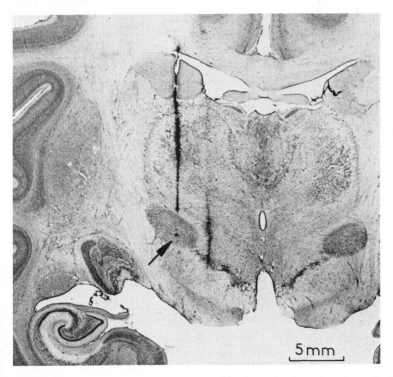

Fig. 8. Photomicrograph of transverse thionin-stained section through the left half of the diencephalon showing the tracking of micropipette and its end point (arrow) of recording in the subthalamic nucleus. At this point, the striatum-induced field potential diminished markedly, while four characteristic neurons were found just dorsal to it (200—400 μm apart).

DISCUSSION

Excitatory pathway from the striatum

The present investigation demonstrated that the electrical stimulation of the striatum exerted an excitatory effect on SN neurons, as well as on a special group of subthalamic neurons in awake monkeys.

In both cases, the latency of the initial excitation was about 10—20 msec, with considerable fluctuations. The fluctuation of the latency as well as the lack of collision with spontaneous activity seems to demonstrate the orthodromic origin of this excitatory response. Thanks to the advantage of the anatomical situation that the internal capsule is far from the head of Cd nucleus at least, it is presumed that the initial excitation might be attributed to be orthodromic activation of the striatum and putamen, suggesting fine myelinated descending fibers as an anatomical substrate (Verhaart, 1950).

Although the striatonigral excitatory connection has been reported on the basis of intracellular recording in the 'encéphale isolé' cat experiment (Frigyesi and Purpura, 1967), the majority of authors claimed it to be a capsular or antidromic excitation, because it was absent in the anesthetized conditions (Goswell and Sedgwick, 1971). However, a recent study on the striatopallidal pathway has also revealed EPSP-IPSP sequences in the GP neurons (Levine et al., 1974). This result is in favor of the present assumption that striatal efferents to SN contain excitatory pathways as well as inhibitory.

Striatonigral inhibitory connection

Since the work of Yoshida et al. (1972), the GABA mediated striatonigral inhibitory connection has been well known. As already discussed in a previous paper (Féger and Ohye, 1975), as far as pure inhibition found in awake monkeys is concerned, it is comparable to their finding in anesthetized cat. However, as, apparently, two different types of inhibition: pure inhibition and inhibition after initial excitation, were found in this study, the origin of respective inhibitory effects should be clarified.

Striatosubthalamic projection

The close excitatory connection between the striatum and the restricted zone in the subthalamic area is a striking finding, never being observed in the cat (Frigyesi and Rabin, 1971; Tsubokawa and Sutin, 1972) nor in the monkey. A cluster of cells responded to the striatal stimulation in quite a similar manner, with a short latency repetitive firing followed by an inhibition of long duration. The shortest latency for excitation was about 5 msec, and the initiation of a slow positive wave accompanying the repetitive firing spikes also started around 5 msec; the initial excitation followed well the high frequency repetitive stimulation. All these findings suggested an oligosynaptic connection between the structures, if not a monosynaptic one. In fact, as such a direct pathway has not yet been described anatomically (Nauta and Mehler, 1969), the most plausible alternative might be the striato-pallido-subthalamic system, relaying at the level of the external pallidal segment which almost exclusively projects to the subthalamic nucleus (Carpenter et al., 1968).

This point will be solved by recordings of the activities of pallidal neurons in response to the same striatal stimulation, which are now going on.

Finally, it might be relevant to recall that this location in the subthalamic area is very close to the target of choice for the control of abnormal movements, such as parkinsonian tremor in one part (Fukamachi et al., 1973; Velasco et al., 1972) and the production of experimental dyskinesia in the other (Carpenter et al., 1950). As the neurophysiological basis for these operations is still lacking, the present series of investigations might contribute to some extent in the future.

SUMMARY

An electrophysiological study has been made on the striatonigral and striatosubthalamic connections in five waking monkeys. With the aid of a special contention device on the skull, the extracellular unitary activities were recorded stereotaxically from the neurons of the subthalamic area and substantia nigra.

Electrical stimulation of the caudate nucleus and putamen induced a pure inhibitory response in half of the neurons in the substantia nigra and a short latency excitation followed by inhibition in the other half of the neurons Pallidal stimulation produced an inhibition in only one neuron.

The same striatal stimulation elicited marked short latency excitation followed by inhibition in neurons of the dorsal subthalamic nucleus. About a quarter of the same neurons was inhibited by pallidal stimulation.

A possible descending excitatory pathway from the caudate nucleus and putamen was emphasized.

REFERENCES

Albe-Fessard, D., Arfel, G. et Guiot, G. (1963) Activités électriques caractéristiques de quelques structures cérébrales chez l'homme. Ann. Chir., 17, 1185—1214.
Carpenter, M.B., Whittler, J.R. and Mettler, F.A. (1950) Analysis of choreoid hyperkinesia in the rhesus monkey. Surgical and pharmacological analysis of hyperkinesia resulting from lesions of the subthalamic nucleus of Luys. J. comp. Neurol., 92, 293—331.

Carpenter, M.B., Fraser, R.A.R. and Shriver, J.E. (1968) The organization of pallido-subthalamic fibers in the monkey. Brain Res., 11, 522—559.

Féger, J. and Ohye, C. (1975) The unitary activity of the substantia nigra following stimulation of the striatum in the awake monkey. Brain Res., 89, 155—159.

Féger, J., Ohye, C., Gallouin, F. and Albe-Fessard, D. (1975) A stereotaxic technique for stimulation and recording in non-anesthetized monkeys: application to the determination of connections between caudate and substantia nigra. Advanc. Neurol., 10, 33—45.

Frigyesi, T.L. and Purpura, D.P. (1967) Electrophysiological analysis of reciprocal caudate-nigral relations. Brain Res., 6, 440—456.

Frigyesi, T.L. and Rabin, A. (1971) Basal ganglia-diencephalon synaptic relations in the cat. III. An intracellular study of ansa lenticularis, lenticular fasciculus and pallido-subthalamic projection activities. Brain Res., 35, 67—87.

Fukamachi, A., Ohye, C. and Narabayashi, H. (1973) Delineation of the thalamic nuclei with a microelectrode in stereotaxic surgery for parkinsonism and central palsy. J. Neurosurg., 39, 214—225.

Gallouin, F. et Albe-Fessard, D. (1973) Stéréotaxie chez le macaque éveillé: étude des cortex somatiques, moteurs et moteur supplémentaire. J. Physiol. (Paris), 67, 274A—275A.

Goswell, M.J. and Sedgwick, E.M. (1971) Inhibition in the substantia nigra following stimulation of the caudate nucleus. J. Physiol. (Lond.), 218, 84P—85P.

Hornykiewicz, O. (1966) Dopamine (3-hydroxytyramine) and brain function. Pharmacol. Rev., 18, 925—964.

Levine, M.S., Hull, C.D. and Buchwald, N.A. (1974) Pallidal and entopeduncular intracellular responses to striatal, cortical, thalamic and sensory inputs. Exp. Neurol., 44, 448—460.

Nauta, W.J.H. and Mehler, W.R. (1969) Fiber connections of the basal ganglia. In G. Crane and R. Gardner (Eds.), Psychotropic Drugs and Dysfunctions of the Basal Ganglia, Public Health Service Publ. No. 1938. U.S. Government Printing Office, Washington, D.C., pp. 68—74.

Olszewski, J. (1952) The Thalamus of the Macaca mulatta. An Atlas for use with the Stereotaxic Instrument. Karger, Basel.

Percheron, G. et Lacourly, N. (1973) L'imprécision de la stéréotaxie thalamique utilisant les coordonnées crâniennes de Horsley-Clarke chez le macaque. Exp. Brain Res., 18, 355—373.

Tsubokawa, T. and Sutin, J. (1972) Pallidal and tegmental inhibition of oscillatory slow waves and unit activity in the subthalamic nucleus. Brain Res., 41, 101—118.

Velasco, F.C., Molina-Negro, P., Bertrand, C. and Hardy, J. (1972) Further definition of the subthalamic target for arrest of tremor. J. Neurosurg., 36, 184—191.

Verhaart, W.J.C. (1950) Fiber analysis of the basal ganglia. J. comp. Neurol., 93, 425—440.

Yoshida, M., Robin, A. and Anderson, M. (1972) Monosynaptic inhibition of pallidal neurons by axon collaterals of caudate nigral fibers. Exp. Brain Res., 15, 333—347.

DISCUSSION

PURPURA: I want you to speculate. This is a very informal meeting and I would like you to draw a diagram of how you think the zone incerta cells * are activated. What is

---

* Editor's note: the authors have later revised their inference of recording location from zona incerta to subthalamus, see bottom of pp. 51 and 52.

going from the caudate putamen and how do you conceive of the synaptic pathways that are concerned?

ALBE-FESSARD: I think that is a direct pathway. I think Mehler and Nauta have described some fibers coming out at this level but going out to the Forel's field. The zona incerta is a part of the Forel's field and so I think it is a direct pathway.

PURPURA: Not to nigra?

ALBE-FESSARD: Not to nigra.

PURPURA: Not by nigrothalamic connections?

ALBE-FESSARD: No, I don't think so. If you look to Mehler's picture . . .

PURPURA: I think, Madame Fessard, that in the more recent work of Carpenter in the Journal of Comparative Neurology, where he has done nigral lesions both in the reticularis and compacta areas, he has plotted a projection from the nigra to the VAM, VAL area, but there is a definite loop that enters towards the centrum median region with some possible fibers left as dots, as they are entering the zona incerta, so that the excitatory loop could involve caudate to nigra and the excitation from nigra to zona incerta.

ALBE-FESSARD: No, because the delay is impossible.

PURPURA: I have noticed that it is 20 msec.

ALBE-FESSARD: Yes, but for the nigra the stimulation is not so. It is quite the same latency in nigra and zona incerta. Mehler and Nauta showed Forel's field, but it is very difficult to know what difference there is in anatomy between Forel's field and the zona incerta. It is difficult to know. But what is the zona incerta is a place where neurosurgeons have found the best place to make the smaller lesion, with cooling for example. I have seen myself that with cooling in this place you have an immediate arrest of the tremor, and it is a place where the smaller lesion is very efficacious.

STERIADE: What kind of neurons are there in the zona incerta? Small size neurons?

ALBE-FESSARD: Large size neurons. You have very big neurons.

PURPURA: They are some of the biggest cells in the brain.

STERIADE: Discharging in bursts?

ALBE-FESSARD: No.

STERIADE: Discharging in bursts.

ALBE-FESSARD: Yes, to the stimulation, but they are not normally (spontaneously) discharging in bursts. But, in the patient with tremor, they are discharging in bursts and their bursts are very different from the bursts in the thalamus. They are special bursts. The possibility is that these cells are freed from something from the caudate or the pallidum, but I am not sure. There is no anesthesia and no other problem in these animals.

GILMAN: May I ask your neurosurgical results? You were saying that this applies to Parkinson's disease. To any other neuromuscular disease, or just Parkinson's disease?

ALBE-FESSARD: Just for Parkinson's disease. I know that people are making lesions at this region in the zona incerta for tremor. There is a group of Germans; the Japanese and some French are operating at this level too.

GILMAN: So the comments pertain to tremor of Parkinson's disease and not to rigidity.

ALBE-FESSARD: It is working well on rigidity too.

GILMAN: That is a little bit at variance with the neuropathology which has been worked up by several people, including Marian-Smith, who say that if you look at the brains of people who had these results, the lesion can be anywhere from the ventrolateral nucleus across the capsule to the pallidum. It is not quite restricted.

ALBE-FESSARD: No, that is old work. The pallidum is not now destroyed by anybody.

PURPURA: Let me ask you the last question, because you have carefully avoided something. You looked at sixty cells and stimulated the striatum. What about the antidromic response?

ALBE-FESSARD: There was none. There was no antidromic response.

PURPURA: Did you see any?

ALBE-FESSARD: No.

PURPURA: Then, that would suggest that you have activated the nigrostriatal pathway.

ALBE-FESSARD: No, we have not activated the nigrostriatal pathway. We have looked at all these cells which are not antidromically activated.

PURPURA: I know that. But you see the point I am trying to make is: are you capable of distinguishing the nigrostriatal from the striatonigral? What you are saying is that it is much easier to find the striatonigral system. Why cannot you activate antidromically the fibers of this pathway which is more prominent than the others?

ALBE-FESSARD: Possibly they are not the same cells and we are making the choice of the big cells, it is always the same thing. We use glass micropipettes in our laboratory because I think that with the other microelectrodes you make a choice of the bigger cells. But, even with micropipettes, you make a choice of the bigger cells and it is difficult to detect antidromically activated cells because they are possibly smaller.

PURPURA: I don't think it is the microelectrodes.

ALBE-FESSARD: I think it is.

PURPURA: No, the problem is something else. Namely, the cells that contain the dopamine are among the largest cells in the nigra. If you are selecting the large cells, you should be selecting the antidromically activated cells. I don't think that is the answer, but I think it is the nature of the pathway in the caudate and the putamen that turns out the fibers which permits electrical stimulation to be avoided if you will, because of their threshold or other characteristics. Something that you cannot stimulate that easily. How big are the cells that you are recording from?

ALBE-FESSARD: We have searched for antidromic responses. Not systematically, but we have searched.

PURPURA: Are the terminals so diffuse that it is hard to stimulate them?

ALBE-FESSARD: Yes. We are not at a good place for that, possibly because they are diffuse at the caudate.

PHILLIPS: Is it true that the anatomists first had difficulty in identifying this, until the fluorescence technique?

PURPURA: When we looked at this carefully in electrophysiology, we really, I must say, hedged on this in our first paper because we were still not certain that we were looking at a nigrostriatal thing. The only things that convinced us are some of the antidromic latencies.

ALBE-FESSARD: We are working on the same thing.

PURPURA: I want to see recording of an antidromic response from caudate stimulation of a fairly identifiable cell in pars compacta.

PHILLIPS: There must be some explanation why the anatomists cannot find it.

PURPURA: Because fluorescence fibers may turn out to be non-suppressive. It is simply a chemical reaction, something about the catecholaminergic systems are not good for silver suppression. And, the Nauta method may not be suitable. However good the horseradish peroxidase method turns out to be, that may not be good either.

ALBE-FESSARD: Has somebody tried horseradish peroxidase here?

PURPURA: One cannot identify the horseradish peroxidase thing that will identify the bouton. Nauta Jr., has tried caudate injection and then, of course, the pars compacta cells light up. They are silver suppressants.

PHILLIPS: They are funny neurons, not the funny microelectrodes.

PURPURA: But, after all, they were finally shown to be big cells.

4

PREFRONTAL PROGRAMMING OF LEVER PRESSING REACTIONS IN THE MONKEY

KISOU KUBOTA

Primate Research Institute, Kyoto University, Inuyama City, Aichi 484 (Japan)

INTRODUCTION

Traditionally, functions of the prefrontal cortex have been studied primarily by ablation methods (Rosvold and Schwarcbart, 1964; Teuber, 1972). While prefrontal monkeys in the outside field show deficits of a wide range of behaviors, such as social, sexual and maternal behaviors (Franzen and Myers, 1973), those in individual cages show few deficits. It has only been shown that the bilateral lesions of a circumscribed area in the dorsolateral prefrontal cortex produced a permanent deficit of the delayed response type behavior, such as delayed response and delayed alternation, and of conditional positional response (Jacobsen, 1935; Mishkin and Pribram, 1956; Butters and Pandya, 1969; Goldman and Rosvold, 1970).

Stimulation of this area during performance of the task disturbed the correct choice of the reward and apparently did not interfere with the voluntary movement (Stamm, 1969). At least, no one described the disturbance of the voluntary movement after the prefrontal lesion. From stimulation studies this cortex was regarded as a silent area because no visible movement was evoked (Brutkowski, 1965). According to conditioning studies in the macaque with cortical stimulation, various loci within the cortex, including the prefrontal cortex, are capable of becoming a site for conditioning stimuli for lever pressing if appropriate parameters are chosen (Doty, 1965). If the neural activity within the prefrontal cortex is related to an expressed behavior of the animal, that activity should be transmitted in some way to the motor system. It follows that the single unit activity of the prefrontal cortex should show, more or less, a correlation to the voluntary movement. To discover such a unit activity, a first attempt has been made to elucidate the programming in the prefrontal cortex. The terminology of programming is used in the broadest sense. Prefrontal unit activity temporally related to the voluntary movement was first described by Kubota and Niki in 1971. A unit activity was correlated to lever pressing. It is confirmed that unit activity did not show correlations with horizontal eye movements. I should like to start my presentation by introducing this finding.

E UNIT ACTIVITY IN DELAYED ALTERNATION AND SIMPLE ALTERNATION

Units were recorded from the middle one-third portion of the periprincipal area while the monkey was performing the delayed alternation task.

Fig. 1 shows a drawing of a panel and a monkey seated in a monkey chair. On the panel were placed two levers 15 cm apart. A vinyl tube, through which the artificial juice reward was delivered, was guided to the mouth. In the task the monkey was allowed to press the lever alternately. Between the panel and the monkey's face was placed a vertical sliding screen made of aluminum plate. This plate was lowered during the delay period and raised after the delay until the lever was pressed. The chair was constructed from a metal frame and acrylate plate. In the center of this plate two rectangular holes (6—8 × 4—6 cm) were made so that the monkey's hand could reach either of two levers when the screen was raised. The monkey used only one of his hands and the other hand was restrained. Position of the used hand during delay period was not determined, so the monkey placed his hand on positions where he liked. In this task situation two kinds of unit activity were recorded. One kind was activated prior to and during the lever press, and the other was depressed at this time. The former was designated as E unit, and the latter as D unit.

Fig. 2 illustrates the response pattern of a single E unit. Spike discharges were plotted as dots alternately for right or left lever presses. After the screen was raised, indicated by SC and vertical lines, units were activated for several hundred milliseconds until reward delivery, as indicated by upward directed arrows. Inverted triangles indicate the EMG onsets of the triceps brachii muscle, which are approximately 100—300 msec later than the first spike activity. This muscle activity was recorded as an index of the onset of the lever pressing behavior. The time values from the initiation of spike activity to EMG onset were about 100—300 msec (176 msec for the left and 305 msec for the right lever; 13 units). If the lever was pressed without up and down shifts of the screen (simple alternation), this unit was also activated, as seen in the brackets at the bottom. Similarly to the pattern in the delayed alternation task, discharges appeared before the triceps EMG. Time difference between first spike discharge and EMG was more than that of the motor cortex pyramidal tract neurons for the wrist movement (Evarts, 1966). In general, compared to the discharge during delayed alternation, units tended to discharge closer to the EMG onset. Some units failed to discharge during simple lever pressings. Since the position of the hand was

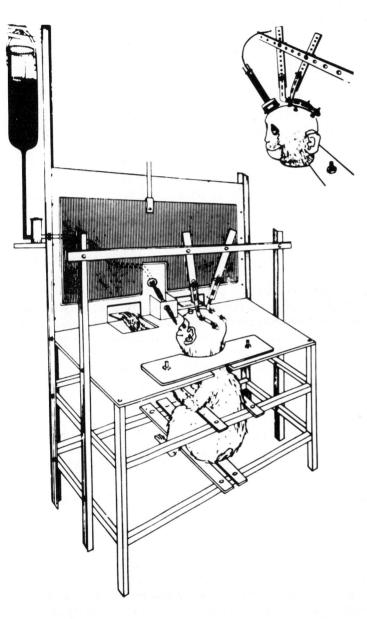

Fig. 1. A monkey seated in the primate chair used for a delayed alternation task. Levers can be reached through rectangular holes in the horizontal Plexiglas plate. Juice reward was delivered through a solenoid valve from the reservoir to the left. Access to levers was prevented during the delay periods by lowering the opaque screen shown as a vertically lined panel. Detail of the head restraint and micromanipulator attachment is shown at upper right. (From Kubota and Niki, 1971.)

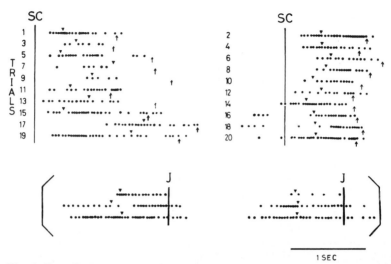

Fig. 2. Dot displays of a unit activity activated synchronously with the lever press during delayed alternation performance (above) and simple alternation performance (below) (E unit activity). Above: delayed alternation trials were performed in the sequence indicated by the numbers to the left of each display (odd numbers, right-lever press; even numbers, left-lever press). These records were related to screen raising (SC) for timing signalling an end of the delay period. The small inverted triangles indicate onset of the triceps EMG activity; arrows indicate onset of juice reward. Below: sample records from the same unit during simple alternation performance related to onset of juice reward (J) for timing. Left-lever presses to the right; right-lever presses to the left. Onset of EMG activity indicated by small inverted triangles. Time bar, 1 sec. (From Kubota and Niki, 1971.)

not predetermined, further studies on the temporal characteristics were required.

Thus, it was shown that the E units become active several hundred milliseconds before the muscle contracted, and remained active until the juice was delivered. This result guided us to continue work to further understand their nature.

UNIT ACTIVITY IN VISUAL LAMP SIGNAL-LEVER PRESS REACTION

As the unit activity related to lever pressing was found in the prefrontal cortex, one of my colleagues, Dr. M. Sakai analyzed the prefrontal units in the visually guided lever pressing reaction. In front of the monkey there was a panel in which a pair of lamps was fitted above the levers (similar to Fig. 3). Between the monkey and panel was placed another lever which the monkey used to rest his right hand during the waiting period. This key was designated as the holding key. Monkeys were asked, releasing his hand from the holding key, to press the lever just below the lighted lamp. Lamp signal

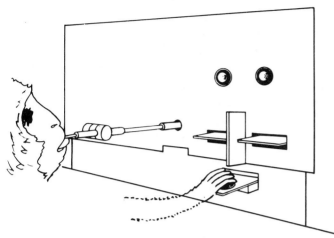

Fig. 3. A panel used for delayed response-type tasks with visual cues. A monkey, facing the panel in front and depressing the holding key with his right hand. On the panel are two levers at the level of the mouth and two lamps at or slightly above the level of the eyes. The holding key at the level of the monkey's shoulder extends 12 cm from the panel toward the monkey. Levers were 6.5 cm below the lamps. A small Plexiglas plate was placed between levers to avoid simultaneous depression of two levers by a single hand. Distance between holding key and the lever was about 14 cm. (From Kubota et al., 1974.)

was the cue for the lever depression which was rewarded by artificial juice. Half of the sampled units (80 units) were facilitated and the other half was depressed during reaction period. Fig. 4 illustrates responses of a prefrontal unit which was activated immediately after the lamp signal onset and represented 31% of the sampled units (V type unit). In Fig. 4a the light was presented, as indicated by the bar above the trace, the monkey released the hold key, as indicated by a triangle below the trace, and touched the lever, as indicated by a line below the trace. Activation, starting after 140 msec, continued for over 1 sec. After being rewarded, the monkey returned his hand to an initial hold key position, as indicated by an inverted triangle. The activity was the highest around the time of the hold key release. In Fig. 4b the same signal is presented, but the hand movement was restrained. The unit was activated with a similar latency but the evoked number of spikes was far less. If the monkey was allowed to press the lever without light signal, as illustrated in Fig. 4c, activation was not seen. Thus, in this unit an increase is striking when light and lever presses are present in combination. And there is no increase when light or lever pressing is separately present. The highest activity is coupled to that voluntary movement to be rewarded.

Another type of unit activity with facilitation during lever press (M type) was observed in 11% of the sampled units. This type of unit was

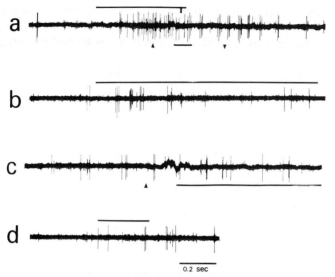

Fig. 4. A unit activated during visually guided lever press reaction. a: activity in a light-lever press trial. b: activity during presentation of the light signal without lever pressing. The used hand was restrained by a tied rope. c: activity during lever pressing without light signal. d: activity to the lamp signal uncoupled to the reward. Horizontal bars above trace indicate the period of light signal. A short vertical bar indicates the delivery of the reward. The shorter line below the trace indicates the timing of the lever press. A triangle to the left of the lever press below the trace indicates the timing of the hold key release. The second, inverted, triangle to the right of the lever press indicates the timing of the hold key press. (From Sakai, 1974.)

activated during lever press whenever the monkey pressed the lever, irrespective of the presence of the light stimulus. Its onset was later than the timing of hold key release and was earlier than the timing of lever press.

The former type of prefrontal units cannot be categorized as a sensory neuron nor as a motor neuron. It may be said that this unit is an internuncial with a dual property: sensory and motor, and it is not a simple algebraic sum of these two properties. Later studies of prefrontal units with respect to movement should be directed to determine more precise correlations to determine whether an increase is related to a shift of hand from the hold key or to the lever pressing movement itself. It is possible that other factors such as attention to the goal may be related.

VISUOKINETIC UNIT IN 'VISUAL' DELAYED RESPONSE

Responses of prefrontal units to the visual lever press reaction were further analyzed during a delayed response-type task with visual cues (Kubota, 1974; Kubota et al., 1974). In these tasks the primary concern was to find a prefrontal unit activity with higher activity in the delay period, and possibly related to a spatial short-term memory. In a recent paper (Kubota et al., 1974) I emphasized the importance of the unit which I designated as visuo-

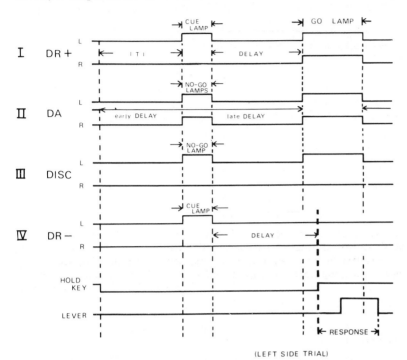

(LEFT SIDE TRIAL)

Fig. 5. Schematic illustrations of the temporal sequence of four different kinds of tasks in delayed response studies. Sequence of one trial started as soon as the monkey depressed the hold key (for details of experimental situation, refer to Fig. 3). I: delayed response with go signal (DR+). Left (L) or right (R) cue lamp was presented for 1 sec according to a Gellerman's series. After 3 sec delay both left and right lamps were presented as 'go' signal. As soon as the monkey, after releasing the hold key, depressed the lever located just below the lit lamp as visual cue, two lamps were turned off and reward juice was delivered to the mouth. Before visual cue, there was an intertrial interval time (ITI) of several seconds which started after depressing the hold key. II: delayed alternation with visual cues (DA). 'Go' lamp signals were rewarded if one of two (left and right) levers were pressed alternately. Delay was started as soon as two lamps were turned off after the reward and ended when 'go' signal was presented. In the middle of the delay time, two lamp signals were presented for 1 sec, as 'no-go' signal. If the monkey depressed the lever to the 'no-go' lamps, the sequence was reset. III: discrimination task (DISC). At the response phase left or right lamp was presented as 'go' signal and if the monkey depressed the lever located just below the lamp, he was rewarded and the lamp was turned off. At the phase when the cue or no-go lamps were presented, the same lamp was presented for 1 sec, but the monkey should hold the holding key ('no-go' lamp). If he released, the sequence was reset. Left or right lamp signal was given according to a Gellerman's series. IV: delayed response without go signal. Left or right cues were presented as in task I. After 1 sec delay the monkey had to press the lever coupled to the lamp lit in the cue phase. Therefore, there was no clear separation between delay and response periods.

kinetic. Similar to the V-type unit of Sakai, this unit showed a sensory-motor dual property. Results to be described will only be concerned with the activity in association with lever pressing in these tasks. Their possible relationship to memory functions will not be referred to in this paper. Two lamps, two levers and a holding key were arranged on the panel as illustrated in Fig. 3. The temporal sequence of tasks performed with this panel are illustrated in Fig. 5.

In the first task (a delayed response with go signal) the sequence was the intertrial interval (3 sec), cue (1 sec), delay (3 sec) and response period (timing from the signal onset to hold key release). During the response period two lamps were lit simultaneously, and the monkey released his hand from the holding key and pressed the lever just below the lamp which was lit during the preceding cue period. The second task was a visual delayed alternation of which the sequence is illustrated in Fig. 5_{II}. The first task was slightly modified: instead of one lamp in the cue period, two lamps were lit and monkeys were not allowed to press the lever. During the response period two lamps were signaled as in a delayed response task. In the third task, instead of two lamps in the response period, one lamp was lit which was lit in the preceding cue period. This task may be called a two-choice visual discrimination task. The final and fourth task was called the delayed response without go signal, monkeys were asked to press the lever after a certain period of delay time (usually 1 sec). Therefore, as the go signal was not given, the monkey must learn to wait, for at least 1 sec, and press the lever below the lamp lit in the cue period. In any of these tasks the majority of prefrontal units were activated by no-go visual cue or signal and during the response period with or without go signal. Fig. 6 illustrates the response of a unit in the delayed response with go signal. There was no activity in the intertrial interval time. When the initial cue was turned on, as shown by a line above the traces, a burst of 2—4 spikes appeared, with a latency of about 100 msec. After this, the unit ceased firing during the earlier part of the delay period. Then it resumed discharging and continued to fire with irregular intervals, at a rate of 4—9/sec during the later part of the delay period. On presenting the response cue, as shown by two lines above the traces, the monkey released the holding key in 200—400 msec. Then, he moved his hand toward a correct lever and pressed it; consequently both lamps were turned off and reward juice was delivered. During this sequence of behavior, a burst of spike discharges was evoked at the response cue and its latency was slightly shorter than that at the initial cue. Fig. 7 illustrates responses during delayed response (DR, above) and delayed alternation (DA, below). Each includes left (L) cue and right (R) cue trials. In these, discharges were facilitated by the visual cue and response cue in delayed response and also by no-go signal and go signal in delayed alternation. In these cases more discharges were evoked when the lever was pressed in the response period. Fig. 8 illustrates responses of a single unit during

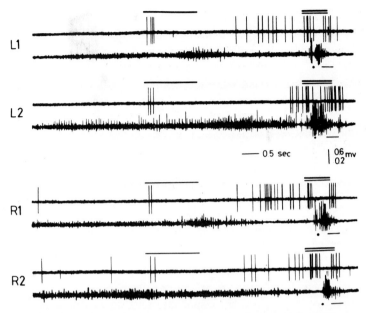

Fig. 6. A visuokinetic unit and delayed response. Temporal sequence of the discharges of the unit in two series of delayed response trials (left-side lever press (L1 and L2) and right-side lever press (R1 and R2)). Upper trace: unit activity. Lower trace: EMG of the right triceps brachii. Horizontal lines above traces in the center indicate cue light presentation. Left cue lamp is shown by the thicker line and right cue lamp by the thinner line. The response cue is indicated by the two parallel lines. Dots and lines below the traces at the right indicate timing of hold key release and of lever depression by the right hand. Traces started as soon as the monkey depressed the hold key. (From Kubota et al., 1974.)

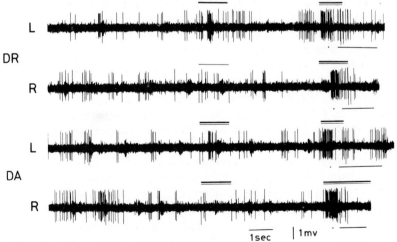

Fig. 7. Activity of a visuokinetic unit during delayed response performances (DR, above) and delayed alternation performances (DA, below). In each case left and right correct lever presses are shown.

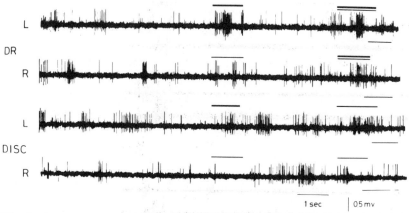

Fig. 8. Activity of a visuokinetic unit during delayed response performances (DR, above) and discrimination performances (DISC, below).

a delayed response with go signal and a no-go—go discrimination task. It is also seen that discharges are evoked by visual cue and go response phase. Magnitudes of the change were compared between delayed response and other tasks in many units, and results are shown by graphs in Fig. 9. In Fig. 9_I the average values between delayed response (DR, solid histograms) and delayed alternation (DA, broken lined histograms) were compared. These values are calculated from 15 paired units. At any phase no significant differences were found between these tasks. The rate at the intertrial interval was 6.0 for left and 6.1 spikes/sec for right, and that at early delay was of a similar order, being 6.7 for left and 5.6 spikes/sec for right. During cues, the rate increased to 10.5 (left) or 9.5 spikes/sec (right). During no-go signals the rate was 10.4 (left) or 11.4 spikes/sec (right). During delays of both tasks the rate was about 1.2—1.6 times the control rate. In the go period the rate became 2.7—3.1 times the control rate in the intertrial interval, and 1.5—1.8 times the rates at cue or no-go lamps. When lever press was accompanied, the rate increased to about three times the control of 50% increase from the rate during lamp signal without lever press. Fig. 9_{II} compares the average rates in DR with those in discrimination (DISC) tests. Values were calculated from average values of eight paired units. In the intertrial interval phase the average was about 7 spikes/sec (6.5—8.9 spikes/sec); during cue the rate was higher (12—17 spikes/sec) and in the succeeding delay it returned to a value slightly above the control rate (7.0—8.5 spikes/sec). During the go phase the rate became 2.5—3.0 times that of the control. In discrimination the rate was higher than the corresponding values in any phases of delayed response of which the cause was not found. The increase in go phase was about 1.5 times that of the no-go phase. From these values between these tasks, i.e. between delayed response

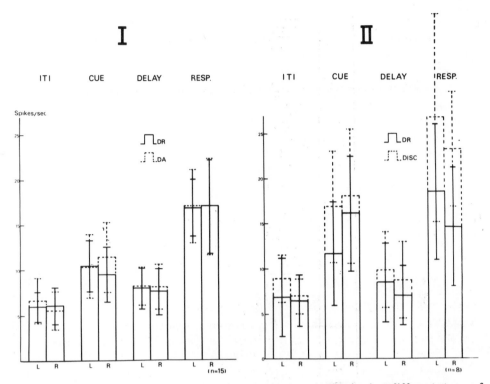

Fig. 9. Graphic comparisons of averaged discharge rates (spikes/sec) at different stages of the task between DR and DA (I) and between DR and DISC (II). I: in 15 paired visuo-kinetic units in which ten DR correct trials were alternately tested, values are averaged over four different phases separately for left and right trials and plotted vertically. Vertical lines at the bar top indicate averages of S.D.s. Bars with solid lines represent DR task and those with dotted lines DA task. II: in eight paired visuokinetic units similarly tested as in I, values are averaged at four different phases of the task, separately for left (L) and right (R). Bars with solid lines are from DR task and those with dotted lines from discrimination task.

and delayed alternation, and between delayed response and discrimination task, there were no obvious differences. On the average, on the no-go cue the rate increased to 1.5 times control and during the go phase it increased to 3.0 times control in these three tasks. These show more activity when the voluntary movement is accompanied.

The dot displays of Fig. 10 illustrate an example of a unit during delayed response without go signal. After the cue signal the monkey had to wait for 1 sec and then the monkey released his hand from the holding key. Remarkable discharges appeared before the hold key release, as indicated by a dot below spike train dots. More than 10 spikes appeared in most trials for over 500 msec. There was no difference of the rates between left and right

72

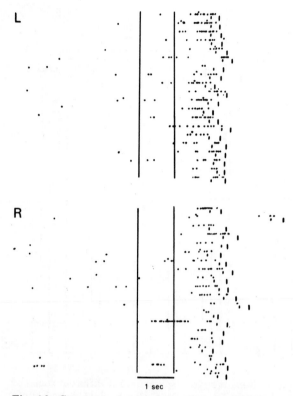

Fig. 10. Computer dot displays of a visuokinetic unit during delayed responses without go signal. Left (L) and right (R) cue trials are shown separately (20 trials each). Shorter vertical line below a train of dots for spike activity indicates a timing of the hold key release. Longer vertical line at the right end of each train of dots indicate a timing of lever press. Occasional dot above a trains of dots indicates that spike activity occurred twice in a 20-msec bin. (From Kojima and Kubota, 1974.)

trials. Since there is a slight activation by the left cue and this unit is activated during the delay period and prior phase to the hold key release, these results demonstrate that the activation is observed without the go signal, coupled to the lever press. As for the increase, it was difficult to separate increases during delay, from increases in the go phase (cf. Kubota et al., 1974). These appeared in a mixed fashion. Out of 182 visually activated prefrontal units tested in task IV, 70% of units showed a significant increase immediately before the hold key release (Kojima and Kubota, 1974). How an increase associated with the voluntary movement to the goal is transferred to the motor system is not known. Out of more than 200 units studied in the delayed response with go signal, about 70% of them showed activations by visual cue and during or prior to lever press. Hence I gave a designation of a visuokinetic unit (Kubota et al., 1974).

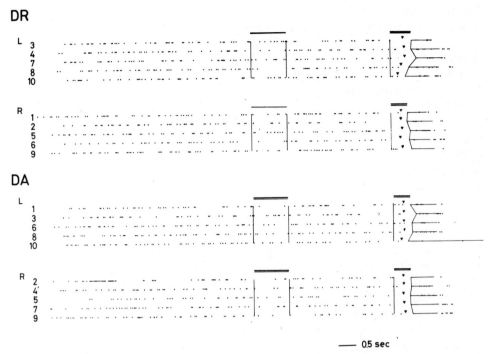

Fig. 11. Dot displays of a depression type of unit activity in delayed response (DR) and delayed alternation (DA). For designations refer to Fig. 5.

Of them, 9% were depressed by a visual cue and/or during response. One example of the depression type of unit is illustrated in Fig. 11. This unit showed an irregular spontaneous activity in intertrial intervals at 7—8 spikes/sec, and was moderately depressed by either of the cues, reducing its rate to half of the control rate (4.0—5.4 spikes/sec), and in the succeeding delay phase it resumed its previously steady activity. During the go period the activity was depressed as soon as the go signals were presented. At the phase between lamp onset and hold key release, the reduced rate was 3.3—5.4 spikes/sec and at the phase between hold key release and the lever touching, the depression was complete. Therefore, it may be said that this unit was slightly suppressed by the lamp signal, be it cue or go signal, and was more suppressed during lever press. The rate in early delay of delayed alternation was not different from that in the intertrial interval (8.3 spikes/sec). The rate was reduced by no-go signals into half of the initial rate. After that, in the late phase of the delay, the lowered rate continued (left, 6.7 and right, 4.8 spikes/sec). In the late phase of delay the depression was more in the right than in the left. With go signals the activity was further depressed. At phase from lamp onset to hold key release in the right side

74

the rate was reduced to 0.8 spikes/sec, while in the left the reduction was not as much (6.3 spikes/sec). At a time between the hold key release and the lever touching, the depression was also complete, as in the delayed response depression. If sequences of no-go signal and succeeding delay phase were omitted, the temporal changes of this unit's activity were not different from the activity known as D unit in delayed alternation (Kubota and Niki, 1971). From these correspondences, although there is a slight depression by cue signal, it is concluded that the D unit in delayed alternation, and depression unit in delayed response, belong to the same category of the unit activity recorded in different task situations. The onset of the depression was usually more than 120 msec and was later than the onset latency of the visuokinetic unit (80 msec).

Of the units 15% were not influenced by visual cue and were only activated during lever depression. Their onset was always after the hold key release. One example of the discharges of this kind of unit is shown in Fig. 12. Discharges are seen synchronous to the EMG of the triceps brachii. Short latency visual on-off units and units activated by juice reward were also found, and the number was very small. The functional significance of these units is not well understood.

As for the efferent connections of the periprincipal area, the only area known anatomically to receive the projection is the rostral portion of the caudate head (Johnson et al., 1968). It was expected that studies of single unit activity might give some insight on possible efferent neurons of the prefrontal cortex in the task of delayed alternation which I mentioned at the beginning of this chapter. Single units were also recorded from the head of the caudate nucleus. Corresponding to an area which receives projections from the principal area, discharge patterns similar to the cortical E unit were observed. Their temporal relationships with the task behavior were not different from those of the prefrontal E units. Differently from the prefrontal cortex, depression type units were not found in the caudate

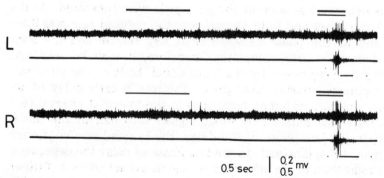

Fig. 12. Discharges of a unit activated during lever press in delayed response performances.

head. Discharges of a caudate E unit are illustrated in Fig. 13 in which responses during delayed alternation and simple alternation are shown. Timing is adjusted to the juice reward time, as shown by vertical lines labeled J. Small vertical lines in each trial indicate timing of the screen release. Inverted triangles indicate onset of the EMG of the triceps brachii. From these observations of the E-type pattern in the prefrontal and caudate, it was inferred that E units may be the efferent neurons and information of the cortical E units may be transmitted not only to the caudate head but also to unknown structures. It is totally unknown if the category of unknown structures includes a structure for the sensory system.

The next question is: which of the neurons are possible efferent neurons from the prefrontal cortex in the delayed response? Those neurons may be included within the category of the visuokinetic unit. Fig. 14 illustrates a unit which has little spontaneous activity in the intertrial interval and delay periods of both delayed response and delayed alternations. This unit was little activated by visual cues. In both delayed response and delayed alternation the unit was slightly activated during cue, no-go lamp, and was not activated during delay and early and late delays. But the unit was activated before the right side lever press of the response phase and no significant activation was seen in the left side press. During delayed alternation delays, both early and late, no rate strikingly higher than in the control

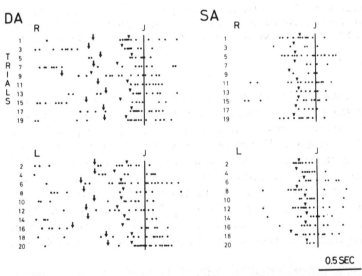

Fig. 13. Dot displays of caudate nucleus unit during delayed alternation performance (DA) and simple alternation performance (SA). Right (R) and left (L) lever pressing took place in the order indicated by the numbers on the left. All records are related to juice delivery (J labeled vertical line) for timing. Arrows indicate the time of screen raising and small inverted triangles indicate onset of triceps EMG activity. (From Niki et al., 1972.)

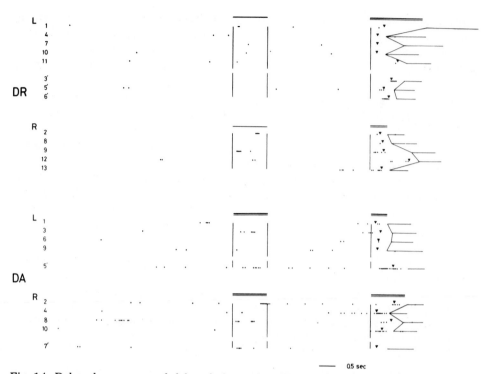

Fig. 14. Delayed response and delayed alternation (DA) performances and a visuokinetic activity with little spontaneous activity in the intertrial interval phase. Note that an increase is observed in right-side lever press but not in left-side press. Designations are same as in Fig. 5.

was seen. In a previous study on delayed alternation (Kubota and Niki, 1971), E units had little spontaneous activity in the delay. The unit illustrated in Fig. 14 had features described as E unit in an earlier paper. Among units designated as visuokinetic, 8% had no spontaneous activity in the intertrial interval and delay period and were little activated by cue. It is suggested that these would be efferent neurons of the prefrontal cortex. Histology data do not support this but are not contradictory. While cortical E units are distributed evenly, with no preferred cortical layers (Kubota and Niki, 1971), visuokinetic units with activation during delay are distributed in all layers while those without activation are distributed only deeply (Kubota et al., 1974).

From these data it is inferred that the role of the prefrontal units, particularly visuokinetic, in the visually guided lever pressing behavior, is to respond to the visual stimulus in a given visual space and obtaining yet unidentified information of its location and induce a movement to the events or objects which, by learning, are known to be coupled to that stimulus. It is unlikely that efferent neurons are connected to neurons which have a fixed strong coupling to the muscles, like the precentral pyramidal neurons.

SUMMARY

Single unit activity was recorded from the dorsolateral prefrontal cortex of the monkey while the conscious monkey was performing various kinds of tasks, such as the visual lever press reaction, visual delayed responses, visual and non-visual delayed alternations and visual discrimination. A minority of units were activated only by visual cue or during response, but the majority of units were activated not only by visual cue, but also during the response period and were regarded to be of primary importance in the execution of the above-mentioned tasks.

REFERENCES

Brutkowski, S. (1965) Functions of prefrontal cortex in animals. Physiol. Rev., 45, 721—746.
Butters, N. and Pandya, D. (1969) Retention of delayed-alternation: effect of selective lesions of sulcus principalis. Science, 165, 1271—1273.
Doty, R.W. (1965) Conditioned reflexes elicited by electrical stimulation of the brain in macaques. J. Neurophysiol., 28, 623—640.
Evarts, E.V. (1966) Pyramidal tract activity associated with a conditioned hand movement in the monkey. J. Neurophysiol., 29, 1011—1027.
Franzen, E.A. and Myers, R.E. (1973) Neural control of social behavior: prefrontal and anterior temporal cortex. Neuropsychologia, 11, 141—157.
Goldman, P.S. and Rosvold, H.E. (1970) Localization of function within the dorsolateral prefrontal cortex of the rhesus monkey. Exp. Neurol., 27, 291—304.
Jacobsen, C.F. (1935) Functions of the frontal association area in primates. Arch. Neurol. Psychiat. (Chic.), 33, 558—569.
Johnson, F.N., Rosvold, H.E. and Mishkin, M. (1968) Projections from behaviorally-defined sectors of the prefrontal cortex to basal ganglia, septum, and diencephalon of the monkey. Exp. Neurol., 21, 20—34.
Kojima, S. and Kubota, K. (1974) Prefrontal neuron activity and a delayed response without go signals. In Abstracts 38th Annual Meeting Japan Psychological Soc., Hiroshima, Oct. 9—11, pp. 368—369.
Kubota, K. (1974) A neurophysiological approach to study the functions of the prefrontal cortex. Seitai no Kagaku., 25, 12—24. (In Japanese)
Kubota, K. and Niki, H. (1971) Prefrontal cortical unit activity and delayed alternation performance in monkeys. J. Neurophysiol., 34, 337—347.
Kubota, K., Iwamoto, T. and Suzuki, H. (1974) Visuo-kinetic activities of primate prefrontal neurons during delayed response performance. J. Neurophysiol., 37, 1197—1212.
Mishkin, M. and Pribram, K. (1956) Analysis of the effects of frontal lesions in the monkey: 2. Variations of delayed response. J. comp. physiol. Psychol., 49, 36—40.
Niki, H., Sakai, M. and Kubota, K. (1972) Delayed alternation performance and unit activity of the caudate head and medial orbitofrontal gyrus in the monkey. Brain Res., 38, 343—353.

Rosvold, H.E. and Schwarcbart, M.K. (1964) Neural structures involved in delayed-response performance. In J.M. Warren and K. Akert (Eds), The Frontal Granular Cortex and Behavior. McGraw-Hill, New York, pp. 1—15.

Sakai, M. (1974) Prefrontal unit activity during visually guided lever pressing reaction in the monkey. Brain Res., 81, 297—309.

Stamm, J.S. (1969) Electrical stimulation of monkeys' prefrontal cortex during delayed-response performance. J. comp. physiol. Psychol., 67, 535—546.

Teuber, H.-L. (1972) Unity and diversity of frontal lobe functions. Acta neurobiol. exp., 32, 615—656.

DISCUSSION

ALBE-FESSARD: Is the response influenced by cue of the presentation?

KUBOTA: I am sorry I could not follow the later part of your question.

PHILLIPS: The question is whether it is something which an animal does straightaway, or whether it is going to be after a prolonged experience or training. Am I right?

ALBE-FESSARD: Yes.

KUBOTA: The question is whether the prefrontal units are activated in a naive state or after experience or with a different response after learning?

ALBE-FESSARD: To the cue?

KUBOTA: I do not know yet. Fuster studied single units of almost the same area, and in what he called dry runs there are units which responded to the cue stimulus, but in his case a parallel stimulus is coming in because he shows the big box's screen as going up and down and he showed that this can have an effect.

PHILLIPS: So there are several things going on, the effects of which are different.

KUBOTA: Anyway, the point I would like to state is that the unit activated by the visual stimulus is related to the movement in some way.

GILMAN: Is there any tight relationship between the nature of the stimulus and the response of the unit? For example, if you use the auditory cue do you still get the same relationship?

KUBOTA: We have not studied this yet, but we expect so. These units in the prefrontal cortex are very polymodal. So they will be responding proportionally to the auditory stimuli, and also they will be related to the movement. But we do not know the answer yet.

PHILLIPS: It has not been tested, but according to Jones and Powell, there is a strong input from the visual cortex to this part of the frontal cortex.

KUBOTA: We do not know whether it is from the visual cortex or somewhere from the visual system.

PHILLIPS: But there is this anatomical link from the visual cortex?

KUBOTA: Yes.

GILMAN: The next question is whether a lesion of the corpus callosum or the striate cortex will interrupt this data.

KUBOTA: We don't know.

ASRATYAN: The kind of changes you interpreted, you consider as an integration of only visual input. How do you interpret the mechanism of this good mode of action?

KUBOTA: This is a hard question to answer. Somewhere the unit activity will influence the neurons within the motor system. The mode we don't know. Also, as Teuber has suggested, very often what he calls the corollary discharge is sent from the prefrontal cortex to the sensory systems. It is also possible that it will be transferred to the movements although we do not know; that kind of refined experiment should be done in the future.

BUCHWALD: One of the other paths can be the caudate, and it is good to study the caudate units. The caudate projections evoke excitatory-inhibitory effects in the thalamus.

PHILLIPS: What is the technical difficulty in recording from caudate neurons?

KUBOTA: I don't know. What I am thinking is that they are not related to this kind of task.

PURPURA: I want to introduce some questions of controversy that relate to caudate neurons and pallidal neurons. What is happening to the pallidum and how indeed is activity from the neostriatum affecting the pallidum? Several years ago we showed that there were two kinds of things happening during caudate stimulation. (1) In the entopeduncular nucleus, which is a homologue of the medial pallidum in the cat, you can see early excitation followed by considerable inhibition. (2) Then came the studies with the caudate, which was only inhibitory to the outflow cells of the pallidum, something I could never understand because how in the world then could the caudate affect any output to the thalamus, if its major outflow system was going to be inhibitory? It now turns out that some other people are seeing again that there are indeed the early excitatory effects, and I suspect that your data (Buchwald's) can only be explained by the fact that there have got to be a number of projections from the caudate that are going to be excitatory to the thalamus. The inhibition is afterwards and it is not a problem.

BUCHWALD: Yes.

PHILLIPS: I am also enquiring whether you have shown the caudate cells as afferent or efferent to the prefrontal cortex. In the picture you have shown there was an arrow going from the caudate to the prefrontal cortex, thus maybe you said afferent.

KUBOTA: There are anatomical papers to show connections from the prefrontal cortex to the caudate. Since the prefrontal cortex and some of the caudate units show similar patterns, some of the units similar to the caudate may be the afferents to the caudate.

PHILLIPS: Yes, I mean that Kemp and Powell's work showed several reciprocal connections between caudate and cortex, and the arrow that you showed was going up from caudate to the cortex.

PURPURA: You mean reciprocal connection from caudate to the cortex? There has never really been shown any such connection directly.

PHILLIPS: Yes, yes. It goes always from cortex to caudate, to thalamus and back to cortex. That is the same.

PHILLIPS: Let me see that slide once again? Now this is an arrow going from the caudate to the prefrontal cortex. Isn' t it?

PURPURA: I don't think that really means that.

PHILLIPS: Does it? Could you tell us what it means?

PURPURA: It is not a neuron ascending, that is a neuron that is descending.

PHILLIPS: I see. I am sorry. I thought it was an arrow. I am very sorry it is my misunderstanding.

GILMAN: What is the timing of the onset of discharge in dorsolateral cortex relative to that of the caudate?

KUBOTA: It is hard to determine. One cannot say.

DESIRAJU: The figure you show is made by Dr. Mishkin to emphasize two corticofugal subsystems of the prefrontal cortex: the dorsolateral prefrontal cortex connected to the dorsal part of the head of the caudate, and the orbital surface of the frontal cortex connected to the ventral part of the caudate and from there they are relayed further right up to thalamus. That was the concept proposed by Mishkin and Rosvold and other workers on the basis of certain behavioral and anatomical observations.

5

PHYSIOLOGICAL MECHANISMS OF GOAL-DIRECTED MOVEMENTS

E.A. ASRATYAN

Academy of Sciences of the U.S.S.R., Moscow (U.S.S.R.)

It was in the middle of the last century, at the laboratory headed by Sechenov, when the first ambitious experiments of introducing electrodes into the deep formations of the dog's brain and their stimulation were made, with a view to checking the correctness of the principle fact of the central inhibition established by the scientist on frogs not long before.

Many decades after this pioneer event, namely, in the 1930s, Hess (1949) and Ranson (1937) considerably modified the techniques of such experiments, and by their systematic research made a big step forward along the yet unexplored paths of knowledge of the functions of deep formations of the brain.

Further scientific and technological progress in physiology and contiguous branches of science widely opened the gates for many concerned researchers to the remarkable and puzzling world of nervous formations of the brain.

Thus, with the combined efforts of a large number of neurophysiologists and experimental psychologists of many countries, and within a relatively short period of time, there were accumulated ample facts on the functions of the deep formations. This experimental material is big in its scale and, although not free of contradictions, is basically reliable, original in essence and, on the whole, exceptionally valuable from the point of view of science. It will not be an overstatement to regard this material as the most significant achievement in experimental research of the functions of the brain during the recent decades.

More complicated is the interpretation and theoretical analysis and synthesis of this wealth of multiform and valuable experimental material relating, in its most part, to the problem of the drive-motivation.

For obvious reasons the differences in the views of investigators on this or other important matters of the problem are more considerable than those in the corresponding experimental material. Since I have no time to discuss here all the existing concepts of the problem I will only state that most of them are characterized by a global psychological approach to the interpretation of complicated acts of behavior, called motivated, that they do not give proper consideration to the physiological mechanisms of the phenomena in question, that they disregard the reflex theory of the activity of the nervous system and that they do not properly use the achievements of neurophysiology. The prevailing points of view in all these concepts of the priority of the subcortex in these acts of behavior over the cortex of the brain, of the priority of inborn forms of brain activity over its attained forms, of the priority of endogenous over exogenous factors, correlate with the commonly known Freudian concepts and are in full contradiction, or to say the least of it, are not in harmony with Pavlov's (1973) teachings of the higher nervous activity.

But among the investigators of the problem there are also those (Coons, 1963; Valenstein, 1970; Miller, 1968; Bindra, 1969; Grossman, 1968), who, supported by the reliable facts obtained by them, keep to the point of view that environmental factors and conditioned reflexes are of great importance in motivated behavior.

However, the views of representatives of this progressive, but not fully consistent, scientific trend contain only separate elements of Pavlov's teaching.

It is essential that this great materialistic teaching should be more thoroughly and consistently utilized for a more satisfactory investigation of complicated questions of the drive-motivation problem, for a purely scientific interpretation of the principle facts relating to it, as well as for improving the prospects of further experimental and theoretical research of this vital scientific problem as a whole.

I will now present, in short, a few results of our investigations in this field. To make easy both my task and the task of the readers I will allow myself first to recall some principles and ideas of the founder of the teaching and of the concept which we were guided by and proceeded from in our research.

Pavlov (1973) defined the higher nervous activity as brain activity which provides for complex relations of the whole organism with its environment, for its dynamic and perfect adaptation to external life conditions. He believed that this activity is of a reflex nature and consists of several instances or stages which are in close relationship and interaction: (a) most complex special inborn reflexes (alimentary, defensive, sexual, etc.), performed mainly by subcortical nervous formations; (b) conditioned reflexes, performed in higher animals by the brain cortex and (c) second signaling system inherent in human brain cortex.

It should be noted that according to Pavlov (1973) each of the inborn reflexes is accomplished not by a single level of the central nervous system, but by its many levels, including the brain cortex. He considered a reflex or neural center as a system or constellation of neural structures which are located in different parts of the central nervous system and closely interconnecting, both structurally and functionally, forming an integral framework responsible for the performance and regulation of a particular function of the organism. Based on this Pavlovian concept and on the theoretical propositions of Sherrington (1906) and Magnus (1924) relating to different subordinated levels in the neural integration of organism functions, which are consistent with those of Pavlov (1973), as well as on the results of our special study on the consequences of decortication for the various simple and composite unconditioned reflexes, we proposed, many years ago, a new formulation of the functional architecture of the unconditioned reflex arc which we consider to be a further development and a precise definition of the above-mentioned Pavlovian concept. Without going into detail, our concept is essentially as follows.

The central part of the unconditioned reflex arc is not unilinear, traversing a particular region of the central nervous system, but is multistaged and multibranched, with each branch traversing one of the essential levels of the system (I—V in Fig. 1). As suggested by the reliable evidence reported by a number of investigators and that obtained in our laboratory, each of these branches is specific and imparts a certain functional feature to the respective unconditioned reflex, raising it to a certain level of perfection. There is every reason to assume that the specific significance of each of these branches is different for different unconditioned reflexes and varies with the kind, type, degree of complexity and other characteristics of the reflexes concerned. Although every reflex (alimentary, protective, orienting, sexual, cardiovascular, respiratory, etc.) is represented at all the main levels

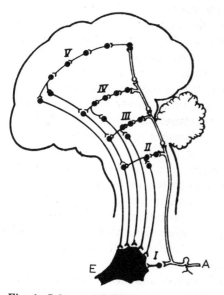

Fig. 1. Scheme illustrating the multistage arc of an unconditioned reflex. I—V: branches of the central part of the reflex arc at different levels of central nervous system. A, afferent neuron; E, efferent neuron.

of the central nervous system, the main branch of the arc of each of these reflexes may pass via different levels of the system. For example, while the main branches of the arcs of the cardiovascular and respiratory reflexes pass via the bulbar level (II), the main branches of the arcs of the alimentary, protective and sexual reflexes pass at the hypothalamic level (III). The highest branch of the arc serves, in the form of a cortical representation of a given unconditioned reflex (V), as the basis for the formation of respective conditioned reflexes. Local and general alternations in the functional state of the central nervous system under the effect of various specific and non-specific endogenous and exogenous factors bring about wide variations in the degree of involvement of each of the branches in the performance of the particular unconditioned reflex. In this context, inborn motivational behavioral acts may be considered as the manifestations of a composite, specific and vitally important unconditioned reflex, the main branch of whose arc is represented in the hypothalamic region. The formation of respective conditioned reflexes on the basis of the cortical branch of this arc makes motivational behavior more perfect, and of full value from a biological point of view.

We think that the above point of view could serve as a reliable physiological basis for explanation in a more satisfactory way of some obscure problems of motivational behavior; in particular, the well known phenomenon of participation of many subcortical formations in its performance. As pointed out in the early work by Hess (1949) and Ranson (1937) and confirmed later by many other researchers, each kind of motivational behavior, such as alimentary, drinking, sexual, etc., can be elicited by electrical stimulation not only of hypothalamic regions but also of structures of the amygdaloid complex, of the hippocampus and even of the gyrus cinguli and of the orbital region of the cortex. Individual elements of the respective complex behavioral acts can also be evoked through the stimulation of bulbar and other neural structures of the stem. A striking demonstration of the existence of multiple, differently localized neural structures has been provided by Anand (1971) and his associates with special reference to alimentary motivation. The intimate relationship existing among the structures of the reticular formation, hypothalamus and differents part of the limbic system which are concerned with particular kinds of motivational behavior, has been pointed out by adherents of quite different lines and trends of research into the problem under consideration. The interpretations of the observed phenomena, however, are usually limited to either the mere statement of the fact itself or are based on an assumption of non-reflex forms of nervous activity and thus confuse rather than clarify the whole problem.

It is generally recognized that one of the most characteristic and essential features of motivational behavior is the selection and performance of goal-directional or purposeful actions by animals in the form of certain combinations, or sets, of specialized motor acts. But there is as yet no meaningful answer to questions on the mechanism of those purposeful actions, or how the motivational excitation that has arisen by way of a particular mechanism, under the effect of certain factors and in particular structures, selects and performs adequate movements and leads the animal to move in the required direction. It has been suggested, however, that purposeful movements in motovational behavior are determined by existing goals, that they are performed under the directing action of an image or the effect of environmental factors, etc. Yet, strictly speaking, neither of these suggestions can be considered as a sufficiently specific and precise answer to the question under discussion.

It appears to us that the most satisfactory, and most discussed, answer to this question can be given at present in the light of the concepts of bilateral conditioned connections as understood by Pavlov (1973) and experimentally confirmed by some of his followers: Kupalov (1949), Asratyan (1955), Fedorov (1955), Skipin (1947), Dostalek (1964), Schastny (1972). We have been highly interested in the problem of the bilateral conditioned connections for many years and the results of these investigations are known from our previous publications (Asratyan, 1955, 1965 and 1968). There is no need to dwell on them here. It seems appropriate, however, to mention certain points emerging from these studies and of special interest for the subject under discussion.

In order to reveal and study two-way conditioned connections in a clear form for elaboration of reflexes, we, as a rule, combine two such stimuli each of which, taken separately, evokes easily observable and graphically registrable reactions; for instance food and electrocutaneous stimulation, a puff of air into the eye and the flexion of a leg, food and lifting of a leg etc. After several combinations each of the stimuli acquires the property of evoking in a conditioned way the reflex of its partner (Figs. 2, 3, 4). We regard this as a manifestation of elaboration of bilateral or two-way conditioned connections: direct or forward connection — from the cortical point of the first of the stimuli to the cortical point of the second stimulus — and backward connection — from second point to the first point.

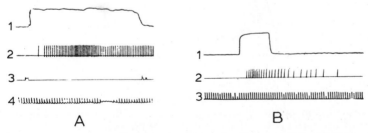

A   B

Fig. 2. The two-way primary motor-alimentary conditioned reflex. A: presentation of food (3) evokes salivation (2) and a conditioned flexion reflex (1). B: flexion of the paw (1) evokes conditioned reflex salivation (2). In this and subsequent figures the bottom line shows time in seconds.

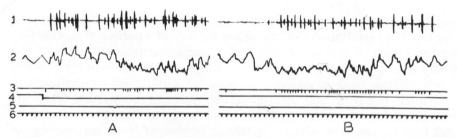

Fig. 3. Two-way primary alimentary eyelid reflex. A: air-puff (4) to the eye elicits the eyelid reflex (1) and conditioned reflex salivation (3). B· presentation of food (5) elicits salivation (3) and conditioned eyelid reflex (1).

It is possible to elaborate secondary conditioned reflexes on the basis of such kinds of primary conditioned reflexes (Figs. 5 and 6). In these cases, both forward and backward conditioned connections may be activated by the secondary stimuli in an indirect way (see Fig. 10).

The research of our colleagues proves that backward conditioned connections also occur when chained conditioned reflexes are acquired. In a series of experiments dogs were given successively the following stimuli: a tone, a passive lifting of the paw and air puff into the eye, with 10 sec intervals between them. It has been shown that after establishing a stable chain alimentary conditioned reflex, isolated application of the second or third stimulus produces not only the inherent unconditioned reflex and alimentary conditioned reflex, but also the conditioned reflex to the previous stimulus

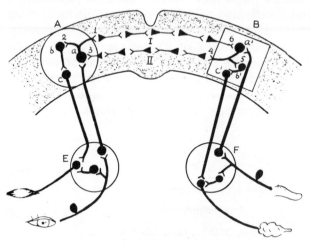

Fig. 4. Schematic representation of the conditioned reflex arc with a two-way connection. A, cortical point of the eyelid reflex; B, cortical point of the food reflex; I, forward conditioned connection; II, backward conditioned connection; E, subcortical center of the eyelid reflex; F, subcortical center of the food reflex. Neurons and synaptic contacts in cortical points are marked by figures and letters.

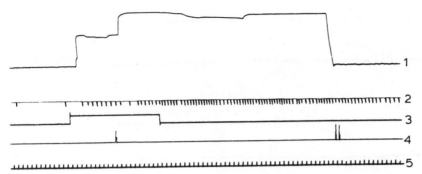

Fig. 5. Secondary alimentary instrumental conditioned reflex. Acoustic conditioned stimulus (3) elicits conditioned reflex salivation (2) and conditioned motor reflex (1) before presentation of food (4).

in the chain. For instance the air-puff evokes the blinking unconditioned reflex and alimentary conditioned reflex along with the lifting of the paw (Fig. 7).

The establishing of the classical conditioned reflex by way of associating the so-called indifferent stimulus — a sound, light, etc. — with biologically essential stimulus (food, pain) provides an obvious manifestation of backward conditioned connections. To demonstrate this it is necessary to have an objective graphic registration of the innate or orienting reflex to the respective indifferent stimulus. After consolidation of the conditioned reflex, for instance an alimentary conditioned reflex to switching on and off the light, the animal turns its head towards the source of light not only at the

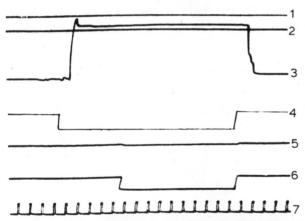

Fig. 6. Secondary electrodefensive instrumental reflex. 1 and 2, lines delimiting the safety zone; 3, motor reflex, avoiding electrostimulation; 4, acoustic conditioned stimulus; 5, electrical shock received by animal; 6, electrical current present in chain; 7, time in seconds.

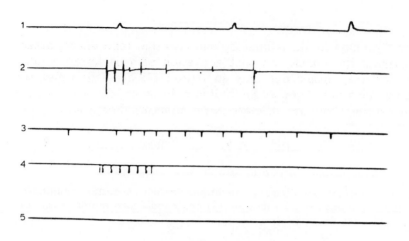

Fig. 7. Two-way conditioned connections in chain alimentary conditioned reflex. 1, flexion of paw; 2, eyelid reflex; 3, salivation; 4, air-puff into eye; 5, presentation of food; 6, time in seconds.

beginning of the light action (that is before the food was given) but also at its switching off (Rudenko, 1974; Fig. 8).

We were able to investigate the forming of backward conditioned connections by means of an objective graphic registration of orienting reflexes to two heterogenous indifferent stimuli (sound and light) which were systematically associated (Davidova, 1974), a phenomenon widely discussed by both physiologists and psychologists since Ebbinghaus (1885).

Our results, obtained mainly with the help of traditional conditioned methods, have been confirmed lately by our colleagues and also by other

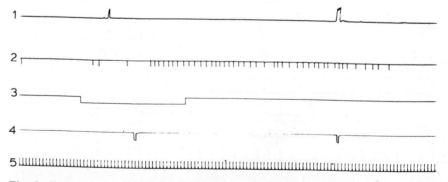

Fig. 8. Two-way conditioned connections between conditional and reinforcing stimuli. 1, orienting reflex toward the conditioned stimulus; 2, salivation; 3, presentation of conditioned stimulus; 4, presentation of food; 5, time in seconds.

investigators with the help of up-to-date electrophysiological methods.

The evidence obtained in our laboratory and also that reported by other researchers warrants the conclusion that activation of a backward conditioned connection may result not only in reproduction of the reflex to the preceding stimulus but also may be limited only to an increase of excitability of the central structures of this latter stimulus. For instance, we believe that this mechanism plays an important role in increasing the excitability of the cortical points of the stimuli.

In our data on the physiology of backward conditioned connections, as well as in results of Pankratov's (1955) and Schastny's (1972) experiments, it is noteworthy that well-formed backward conditioned connections are characterized by considerable specificity. Thus, for example, if flexion of a forepaw provided the dog with food and that of the other forepaw provided it with water then, after the respective instrumental conditioned reflexes had been elaborated, each kind of motivational excitation entailed flexion of the adequate paw (Popova, 1972; Fig. 9). If flexion of a paw provided the dog with food from the left food bowl, while flexion of the other paw also provided it with food but from the right food bowl, then, after the elaboration of appropriate instrumental reflexes, food, presented from each of the food bowls entailed an easy flexion of the adequate paw (Kolotygina, 1974).

It is the last point in our studies on the physiology of the two-way conditioned connection, which is of special interest from the point of view of the question mentioned above. While a bilateral conditioned connection is a part of every type of conditioned reflex, our results indicate that this capacity is particularly well defined in instrumental conditioned reflexes. It is noteworthy that Pavlov (1973) advanced his idea on bilateral conditioned con-

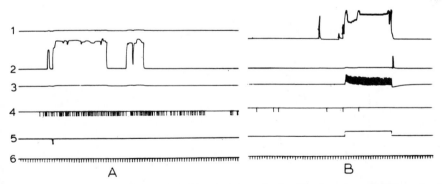

Fig. 9. Specificity of the backward connections in food and water conditioned reflexes. Flexion of right forepaw in food motivation (A) and flexion of the left paw in water motivation (B). 1, mechanogram of the left limb; 2, that of the right limb; 3, swallowing movements during drinking (in B); 4, salivation; 5, food (in A) or water presentation (in B); 6, time in seconds.

nections on the basis of analysis of experimental facts relating precisely to that kind of conditioned reflexes.

Careful and comprehensive analysis carried out by this author with many coworkers, of the primary and secondary alimentary and electro-defensive instrumental conditioned reflexes in dogs, have led us to conclude that the cortical point of the secondary signal is connected with each reflex in a dual manner: directly to each of them and indirectly, i.e. via each of them to the other, and that the mediated pathway from the point of the signal stimulus via the point of the biologically important unconditioned reflex to the point of instrumental movement is formed earlier, is more stable, and plays a more important role than direct pathway from the point of the signal stimulus to that of instrumental movement (Fig. 10).

In the case of increased excitability of the alimentary center (Ap) selected local movement of a given leg (L) may be evoked in several ways: by activation of primary backward connections (b) between alimentary and motor cortical points; by activation of the indirect pathway (c + b) from distant or secondary conditioned stimuli (Ds) to the motor cortical point (Mp), and by activation of the direct connection between the same points (d).

The instrumental conditioned reflex is regarded by many researchers, and not without reason, as a model of motivational behavior. However, these researchers do not yet have any distinct notion on the concrete physiological mechanisms of the instrumental movement itself, and their point of view was of no help in understanding the physiological mechanisms of complex purposive movements in motivational behavior.

Since, according to the Pavlovian idea, which backgrounds our above-mentioned studies, an instrumental movement is viewed as one resulting

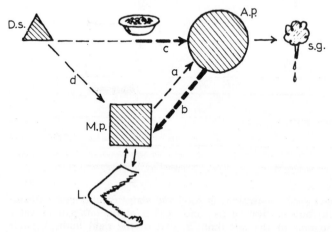

Fig. 10. Schematic representation of the secondary instrumental alimentary conditioned reflex arc. (Explanation in text.)

mainly from excitation of the backward conditioned connection, i.e. of a connection from the cortical point of a vitally important unconditioned stimulus to the cortical point of the respective motor organ, there is a real possibility for a more complete and effective utilization of this model in attempting to answer the above question, namely that of selection and performance of aquired or purposeful movements in motivational behavior.

We note here several facts relating to complex behavior acts in higher animals, obtained by our collaborators and by other researchers in experiments on freely moving animals. It seems that these data may be more satisfactorily understood if we take into consideration the important role of backward conditioned connections in the voluntary movements.

In these experiments performed in our laboratory several food boxes were put on the floor of a large room. Stimuli of different kinds were placed on different sides of the room. In unrestrained dogs various complex alimentary conditioned reflexes were elaborated and studied.

The following result established in these experiments is of particular interest. In response to a conditioned stimulus the dog pressed a certain pedal which was located a short distance away from a definite food box. When the food was presented in the window of the food box the dog approached and ate it. Pressing on the pedal without a previous special stimulus was not reinforced and so became extinguished. Under such conditions, in the intervals between applications of the special conditioned stimuli, the experimental animal stood most of the time near the pedal (Struchkov, 1975). This expectant pose near the pedal and similar phenomena noted by other researchers can be regarded as evidence of activation of the backward conditioned connection from the food center to the cortical structures of pedal place and motor acts, involved in the complex acquired reaction.

In Kupalov's (1949) laboratory many years ago an original method of investigation of a complex form of conditioned reflex ('situational conditioned reflex') was devised. Two to three tables with food boxes on each of them were placed at different points in a large room. The floor of this room was divided into squares by means of well discernible lines. All the squares were numbered. A small carpet was put for the dog in one of these squares. The animal moved freely. By means of elaboration of an alimentary motor conditioned reflex to a sound which accompanied the presentation of food in the food box and by means of gradual complication of the conditioned reflex system (elaboration of conditioned reflexes to a certain place in the room, to different special stimuli etc.), the formation of an integrated structure of behavioral acts is achieved. The animal stands on a certain square of the floor, then, in response to a given stimulus, it runs to the proper table, jumps on it, eats the food and goes back to the carpet.

We shall discuss here only those data obtained by Kupalov (1949) which we regard as manifestations of the forming and the functioning of backward conditioned connections. First, it should be mentioned that in the intervals between stimuli the dog places itself electively on a certain square on the floor, from here it starts when the signal is given and here it returns after eating the food. The second interesting fact is that often the animal eats the food, goes to the signal stimulus, stays near it for a long time and then goes back to the proper square. We think that both these facts may be explained as a display of processes of forming and activating backward conditioned connections from the cortical representation of the food center to the cortical representations of signal stimuli (among them the initial square on the floor) and of those motor acts which lead the animal to these places.

Now I shall acquaint you with a few facts from the large experimental material referring to simple and complex behavioral acts of anthropoids, obtained in the cooperative work of many experimental psychologists (Kohler, 1929; Yerkes, 1943; Ladigina-Kotz, 1959; Wolfe, 1936; Cowles, 1937) and physiologists of the brain (Pavlov, 1973; Denisov, 1958; Vatsuro, 1948; Schastny, 1972).

It is not our task to discuss here the great divergence of opinions and contradictions existing in the tendencies, modes and theoretical views of these scientists regarding the topic in general. In particular, they concern the facts which will be mentioned below as being of special interest for the discussed question. It is essential, however, to point to the notable similarities of experimental methods used by these scientists of different trends, and to the remarkable similarity of the facts obtained by them.

In these researches it has been clearly established, among other things, that anthropoids are able to perform multiform manipulations of accessible objects in the process of active communication with the environment. After a phase of random search utilization of these objects the animal forms, by trial and error, resultant modes of action and new habits useful for satisfaction of their urgent needs. These include the building of pyramids from boxes of various sizes in order to get food which is hung high above them; the extinguishing of fire with water when the food is enclosed by fire and the selection and utilization of the key adequate for a lock when the food is enclosed inside a locked box.

Being fully in accordance with Pavlov's (1973) point of view that this cognition of cause and consequence relations between objects and phenomena, that this 'object thinking' is acquired by anthropoids by way of developing new association or reflexes, and proceeding again from Pavlov's (1973) ideas we believe at the same time that the development of two-way conditional connections between the alimentary center and the cortical structures of effector organs involved in the activity play an important role. If initial random movements in case of their definite composition are followed by chance food reinforcement and this is repeated several times, then it would be correct to consider this as a manifestation of formation of a direct, or forward, connection. Also, it would be correct to consider the performance of an elaborated complex of movements in the case of increased excitability or excitation of the alimentary center as mainly being a result of activation of the formed backward conditioned connection between the same cortical points.

Although the behavioral acts described above, as well as similar behavioral acts, have a rather complex functional architecture and are a product of integration of a number of elementary elaborated reflexes, it has been established experimentally that subsequent integration of these acts leads to formation of more complex undivided behavioral acts of anthropoids. Pavlov (1973) and his followers showed that by a successive accumulation of simple behavioral acts a complex chain of behavior could be achieved. For instance, a chimpanzee opens the door of a cabin with a key, enters the cabin, extingushes alcohol burning on the window, climbs through the window into the chamber where fruits are hung beyond its reach, and constructs from boxes laying on the floor a pyramid on to which it climbs and reaches the food.

Later, Wolfe (1936), Cowles (1937) and Schastny (1971) similarly obtained in anthropoids even more complex integrated behavioral acts.

One can regard these facts as new evidence substantiating the correctness of Sechenov's (1935) and Pavlov's (1973) concepts considering complex behavioral acts as complicated chains of simpler motor acts, as an integration of a multitude of elementary movements, as a complex association composed of simpler associations. Then it would be quite logical to assume that the set of purposeful movements in motivational behavior is determined mainly by the activation of the system of backward connections from the exited cortical points of the vitally important complex unconditioned reflex (in other words drive or motivational center) to the cortical point of the motor organs taking part in an integrated chain of conditioned reflexes of the second, third, and higher orders. Exogenous stimuli of different modalities coinciding with the above movements and becoming conditioned signals, may orient the animal to the probable location of the object looked for, via the direct conditioned connections to the cortical points of these movements as well as activate the central nervous structures of the vitally important complex unconditioned reflexes.

Such an explanation is equally applicable to those cases where a central motivational state is created by congenital neurohumoral shifts in the organism as well as to those where this state arises or increases under the action of environmental factors including conditioned stimuli. This is more clearly illustrated by the scheme in Fig. 11.

Suppose that in the presence of increased excitability of the neural substratum of some vitally important complex unconditioned reflex (AC in Fig. 11), or, in other words, in the presence of a particular drive, the movements performed by the animal in the form of a chain of a certain

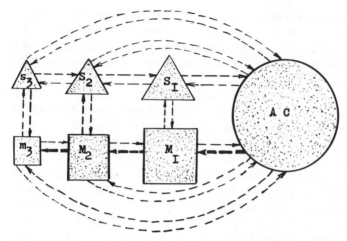

Fig. 11. Schematic representation of the formation and performance of alimentary motivational behavioral acts. (Explanation in text.)

composition (M_1, M_2, M_3) accompanied by the action of various stimuli (S_1, S_2, S_3) would be accidentally completed by the finding of an adequate biologically significant object, then, if such a process occurs several times in its main features, it will be correct to believe that motor acts of a given composition and sequence in conjunction with external stimuli of different modalities would become a complicated conditional stimulus of a complex of a chain or another type. When a conditioned reflex elaborated to such a multicomponent stimulus with multichain conditioned connections becomes sufficiently stable and specialized owing to repetition of the situation, and when the excitability of neural structures of this vitally important unconditioned reflex (or motivation) becomes enchanced under the effect of certain endogenous and exogenous factors, then it would acquire the ability to reproduce the appropriate chain of movements already as selected, or purposeful movements, via the backward conditioned connections. Here, accompanying conditioned stimuli also may play a more important role than in the case of unitary instrumental conditioned reflexes by way of activation of the direct connections to the appropriate motor points (S_3-M_3, S_2-M_2, S_1-M_1). This is especially important if we take into account the fact that central motivational structures along with activation of the complex of backward conditioned connections to the cortical points of motor organs simultaneously may also increase the excitability of central structures of these conditioned stimuli via the mediation of backward conditioned connections to them (AC-S_1, AC-S_2, AC-S_1).

We are well aware, of course, that this assumption is quite hypothetical, being made on the basis of reliable experimental data obtained in our laboratory and by other investigators into the physiology of unitary or particular instrumental conditioned reflexes and non-complex behavioral responses (i.e., is essentially an extrapolation of these facts to the integrated complex of diverse conditioned motor reflexes in the form of complex integral behavioral reactions). Thus, there is need of more solid and adequate factual substantiation, and also of further special experimental studies.

Nevertheless, it appears that even in its present form this theoretical proposition is of certain interest and is worthy of attention. First, it uncompromisingly transfers the important problem of higher nervous activity to a solid physiological footing and throws it into the orbit of the powerful conditioned reflex theory. Second, at the present stage of investigation of this problem this proposition contains a direct answer to an important question, namely, the question of physiological mechanisms of so-called purposeful motivational behavioral responses, and this makes it different from all other general and indirect answers. Third, it seems to us that from the above angle, and in the light of the conditioned reflex theory in general, one may, strictly physiologically and without any eclectism, provide quite a satisfactory explanation to at least the main and more reliable known facts related to motivational behavior.

REFERENCES

Anand, B.K. (1971) Regulation of food and water intake. In Proc. Int. Union Physiol. Sci., Vol. 8, pp. 11—12.
Asratyan, E.A. (1955) Conditioned reflex and contemporary neurophysiology. Zh. vyssh. nerv. Deyat. Pavlova, 5, 480—491. (In Russian.)
Asratyan, E.A. (1965) Compensatory Adaptations, Reflex Activity and the Brain. Pergamon Press, Oxford, 194 pp.
Asratyan, E.A. (1968) Some peculiarities of formation, function and inhibition of conditioned reflex with two-way connections. In E.A. Asratyan (Ed.), Brain Reflexes, Progr. Brain Res., Vol. 22. Elsevier, Amsterdam, pp. 8—20.
Bindra, D. (1969) The interrelated mechanisms of reinforcement and motivation, and the nature of their influence on response. In Nebraska Symposium on Motivation, Vol. 17, pp. 1—33.
Coons, E.E. (1963) Motivational Correlates of Eating Elicited by Electrical Stimulation in the Hypothalamic Feeding Area. Doctoral thesis, Yale University, New Haven, Conn.
Cowles, I.T. (1937) Food-tokens as incentives for learning by chimpanzees. Comp. Psychol. Monogr., 14, 96.
Davidova, E. (1974) Forward and backward connections in association of indifferent stimuli. In Proc. XXIVth USSR Conference on Higher Nervous Activity, Moscow, p. 257. (In Russian.)
Denisov, P.K. (1958) The analytic and synthetic function of ape's brain. Zh. Vyssh. nerv. Deyat. Pavlova, 8, 845—854. (In Russian.)
Dostalek, C. (1964) Rückläufige Bedingte Verbindungen. Verlag der Tschechoslovakischen Akademie der Wissenschaften, Praha.
Ebbinghaus, H. (1885) Untersuchungen zur experimentallen Psychologie, Duncker und Humboldt, Leipzig.
Federov, V.K. (1955) Physiological Pecularities of Dog's Motor Analyzer. Izdat. Meditsina Nauka, Leningrad. (In Russian.)

Grossman, S.P. (1968) Drive centres and drive state. Neurosci. Res. Progr. Bull., 6, 50—57.

Hess, W.R. (1949) Das Zwischenhirn: Syndrome, Localization, Functionen. Schwabe, Basel.

Kohler, W. (1929) Gestalt Psychology. Lawright, New York.

Kolotygina, R.F. (1974) Change of signal significance of 'overcovered' stimuli. In Proc. XXIVth USSR Conference on Higher Nervous Activity. Moscow, p. 259. (In Russian.)

Kupalov, P.S. (1949) On the mechanisms of the process of conditioned excitation, Physiol. Zh. SSSR, 35, 582—591.

Ladigina-Kotz, N.N. (1959) Constructive Activity and Using Tools in Apes (Chimpanzee). Izdatelstvo Acad. Nauka, Moscow. (In Russian.)

Magnus, R. (1924) Körperstellung. Springer, Berlin, 740 pp.

Miller, N.E. (1962) The relationship between drive and learning. Neurosci. Res. Progr. Bull., 6, 58—62.

Pankratov, M.A. (1955) Functional method study of localizations in cerebral cortex. Uchenie zapiski Gos. Ped. Inst. Gertsena, 108, 27—43. (In Russian.)

Pavlov, I.P. (1973) Twenty Years of Experience in Study of Higher Nervous Activity. Nauka, Moscow. (In Russian.)

Popova, E.I. (1972) Effect of use on the elective appearance of an instrumental reaction in dogs. Acta neurobiol., 34, 93.

Ranson, S.W. (1937) Some functions of the hypothalamus. Harvey Lect., Ser. 36, 92—121.

Rudenko, L.P. (1974) Functional Organisation of Simple and Complex Forms of Conditioned Reflex Activity. Nauka, Moscow. (In Russian.)

Schastny, A.I. (1972) Complex Forms of Anthropoid's Behaviour. Nauka, Leningrad. (In Russian.)

Sechenov, I.M. (1935) Selected Works. Medgiz, Moscow. (In Russian. English and German summary.)

Sherrington, C.S. (1906) The Integrative Action of the Neurons System. Scribner's and Sons, New York.

Skipin, G.V. (1947) On the Formation of Conditioned Alimentary Reflexes. Izdatelstvo Sovetskaja Nauka, Moscow. (In Russian.)

Struchkov, M.I. (1975) Systematicity of conditioned reflex activity in unrestricted animals. In press.

Valenstein, E.S. (1970) Stability and plasticity of motivation systems. In G.C. Quarton, T. Melnechuck and F.O. Schmitt (Eds.), The Neurosciences. Rockefeller Univ. Press, New York, pp. 207—217.

Vatsuro, E.G. (1948) Study of Higher Nervous Activity of the Anthropoids. Izdat. Acad. Sci. USSR, Moscow. (In Russian.)

Wolfe, I. (1936) Effectiveness of token rewards for chimpanzees. Comp. Psychol. Monogr., 12, 72.

Yerkes, R.M. (1943) Chimpanzees, a Laboratory Colony. Yale University Press, New Haven, Conn.

DISCUSSION

GILMAN: May I ask about your concept of the anatomical localization of the thing you called the alimentary center and put into anatomical schemes?

ASRATYAN: What is said by Pavlov concerning the anatomical structures of unconditioned reflexes seems to have some factual proof in that among all other competitive and vitally important reflexes, the alimentary reflex is also accomplished by structures which are located at different levels. For example, some of the structures are located in the bulbar medulla. Salivation could be elicited with the structural apparatus located in this level, and then we have some more complications in the hypothalamus not only for salivation but also for motive factor activity of the salivary and digestive system. Further, in the accomplishment of a behavioral act connected with the digestive activity the hippocampoamygdaloid and many different structures of the limbic system also take part. We know that the neocortex also has some function although we have only established this indirectly in the elaboration of conditioned reflexes, but we now know that, for example, it is possible to evoke activity of a salivary gland, stomach activity and so on. So my scheme is only a scheme of my own, but facts and ideas are connected with the names of Pavlov, Adrian, Magnus and others. It seems to me that similarly to other complicated functions, alimentary function is also regulated by different levels of the central nervous system. I consider these levels as different arcs of one and the same very complicated reflex. This is my simple essay, and it is simplified or else it cannot be called a scheme. Scheme is a little simplified to underline the main idea. My own ideas belong to the classics of neurophysiology. I also have some facts, as follows. On many dogs, I decorticated the brain and before and after decortication, I studied the unconditioned reflexes and inborn reflexes, among them the salivary activity, somesthetic activity, motor activity and others. These are normal in normal dogs, and afterwards I decorticated one hemisphere as in Goltz's experiments. If you decorticate one hemisphere and have their salivary glands, you can quite easily note that there is a great difference in salivation between one side and other side. I cannot say why, but in this case the salivary reflex of not the contra- but the ipsilateral side is very weakened some 2-3 times to the same food; 2-3 times less salivary dose is extracted out than the control. If you deal with a single organ, like the stomach in this case, some dysfunction is seen but by and by it is compensated. After a second decortication of the other half of the brain you can have a great change. In the same way, we were able to obtain data concerning the motor activity, concerning the respiratory system, and so on. These facts advance the correctness of the idea that the cortex is a special organ for conditioned reflexes as well as for accomplishment of unconditioned reflexes, with equal facility. This idea was expressed earlier, but our experiments directly confirm the correctness of this idea. So my scheme has not only the ideas of Pavlov, Sherrington and Magnus but also my own data.

GILMAN: I just want to raise the issue of what a center is . It is an idea passed through generations of medical students that there can be centers in the brain, as you said today that have to do with eating, and I was pleased to have you say that there are multiple anatomical sites or levels related to the conditions of eating. The word center probably should be dropped.

PHILLIPS: Yes. I reject this (center concept) completely.

GILMAN: It keeps creeping back.

ASRATYAN: Excuse me, I could not get the essence of your sentence.

GILMAN: I am sorry it is a small point, it is the use of the word center to describe a pathological activity.

ASRATYAN: You see not only this term, but many other terms are used to express the different types of activities. It seems to me that when Pavlov said 'centers', it may not be so correct as a technical point, because we now understand the word center as located

6

A MODEL OF CENTRAL NEURAL PROCESSES CONTROLLING MOTOR BEHAVIOR DURING ACTIVE SLEEP AND WAKEFULNESS

MICHAEL H. CHASE

Departments of Physiology and Anatomy and the Brain Research Institute, University of California, Los Angeles, Calif. (U.S.A.)

INTRODUCTION

Behaviorally, the distinction between active sleep and wakefulness is obvious, even though the activity of many physiological systems is similar during these states. And so one may ask: what are the key central neural mechanisms which allow for the presence of such dissimilar behaviors as active sleep and wakefulness during qualitatively comparable patterns of neuronal and hormonal discharge? The answer can best be sought by first defining the fundamental processes which differentiate the behavior of active sleep from that of wakefulness. Essentially, behavior is a reflection of the activity of the somatic motor system. Indeed, behavior can be defined and described as the contraction and relaxation of the somatic musculature (with minor contributions by the autonomic and endocrine systems).

The excitation of a central neural area that is responsible for maintaining motor control during a particular behavioral state would be expected to yield patterns of somatic muscular activity which normally accompany that state, as contrasted with other patterns, atypical of the state, which occur for brief periods in response to specific stimuli. Thus, if one can demonstrate that excitation of a neural area promotes the *same* pattern of motor activity as that which occurs throughout a given state (under homeostatic conditions), it may be the key area responsible for maintaining not only the distinctive behavioral characteristic of that state, somatic activity, but possibly the state as well. A neural area which induces a contrasting pattern of motor activity is likely to be related to special intrastate imperatives and not *primarily* to the maintenance of the state as a behavior. For the present, our interest lies in determining the central neural areas and mechanisms which maintain the basic motor patterns underlying the behavioral states of active sleep and wakefulness*.

---

* Since this paper presents a model depicting the control of somatic motor activity during active sleep and wakefulness, data relating to quiet sleep will not be specifically discussed, although it is included in the accompanying figures.

In the adult cat two areas of the central nervous system, the reticular core of the brain stem and the cerebral cortex, are of essential importance in sensory, motor and integrated activities, and play a major role in almost all aspects of behavior. These areas also exert a pattern of inhibition and excitation upon somatic reflex activity during active sleep and wakefulness (Chase and Babb, 1973; Chase and McGinty, 1970a and b). Since the somatic reflex is a fundamental component of behavior, as well as a sensitive indicator of state-dependent central neural activity, an examination of the fashion in which cerebral areas control reflex discharge should point the direction for a clearer understanding of the factors responsible for the states themselves.

Our studies of motor control have concentrated thus far upon the influence exerted by the orbital cortex and the pontomesencephalic reticular formation upon the brain stem, jaw-closing and monosynaptic masseteric reflex. We have determined the spontaneous state-dependent fluctuations in the amplitude of the masseteric reflex and the relative sensitivity and direction of response of the reflex to cortical and reticular stimulation during active sleep and wakefulness.

PONTOMESENCEPHALIC RETICULAR STIMULATION

In order to test the reticular influences on masseteric reflex activity, a series of studies were undertaken in the chronic freely-moving cat. In these investigations, permanently implanted electrodes were utilized to induce and record the masseteric reflex (Fig. 1), to stimulate the reticular formation and to monitor the EEG, EOG and EMG (Chase, 1974; Chase and Babb, 1973). In order to determine the concordance between induced patterns of reflex activity and those occurring under spontaneous conditions, it was first necessary to specify the fashion in which reflex activity normally changes as a function of the behavioral states of active sleep and wakefulness. Simply put, we found that the masseteric reflex is largest during wakefulness and smallest during active sleep (Fig. 2) (Chase et al., 1968). Against this background data, the variations in activity induced by reticular stimulation were examined. The critical reticular zone that we have been working with lies in the vicinity of A 1, L 2, H −2, i.e., in the heart of the reticular formation near the pontomesencephalic junction. For the present, the site of effective reticular stimulation must be left imprecisely defined; we are currently carrying out an exhaustive localization study.

Conditioning-test paradigm

In our initial experiments, the masseteric reflex was induced continuously at rates of 0.5—2/sec while the animals were within a behavioral chamber. The effect of reticular stimulation was examined with a conditioning-test paradigm which consisted of reticular stimulation (1—4 pulses;

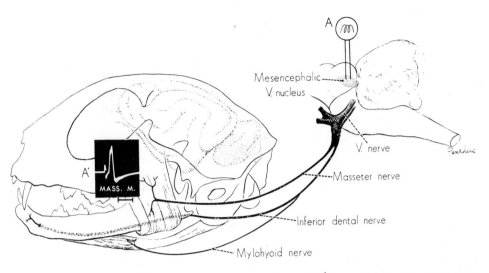

Fig. 1. Reflex activity within the masseter musculature (A') was obtained by electrical stimulation of the ipsilateral mesencephalic nucleus of the Vth nerve (A). The bipolar recording electrodes within the masseter musculature are not shown. Calibration line: 10 msec; 200 μV (under oscilloscopic figure).

interpulse interval 2.5 msec) followed by the induction of the masseteric reflex at conditioning latencies of 10—30 msec. The reflex was evoked two to four times as a control, then two to four times preceded by reticular stimulation. This alternating pattern was maintained continuously throughout consecutive sleep/waking cycles.

Oscilloscopic recordings of the masseteric reflex alone (control) and preceded by reticular stimulation are shown for all three states in Fig. 3. Stimulation of the reticular tegmentum resulted in *facilitation* of the masseteric reflex during wakefulness (and quiet sleep) and *inhibition* during active sleep. There was no evidence of any reticular evoked activity in the masseter muscle recording, i.e., the waveforms of the facilitated and inhibited reflexes were similar to their controls and no additional activity of a direct or reflexive nature was observed.

The direction of masseteric reflex response to reticular stimulation was consistent throughout the ocular and somatic movements of wakefulness (Fig. 4_{I}), spindle activity of quiet sleep (Fig. 4_{II}) and rapid eye movements of active sleep (Fig. 4_{III}). Although there were spontaneous fluctuations in reflex amplitude, which were mirrored by variability in the response to reticular stimulation, there were no qualitative changes coincident with intrastate variations in activity.

A statistical evaluation of the masseteric reflex response to reticular stimulation is presented in Fig. 5. Facilitation and inhibition, which are shown graphically in the upper part of this figure, were greater than 50% of

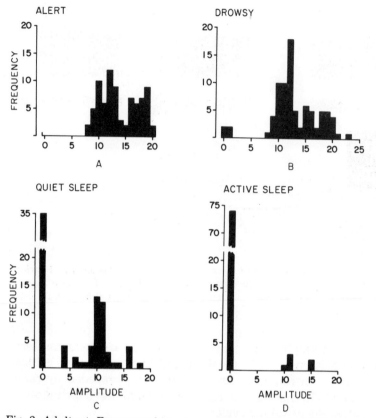

Fig. 2. Adult cat. Frequency histograms of the amplitudes of 80 consecutive masseteric reflex responses. These potentials were obtained during the alert, drowsy, quiet sleep, and active sleep states. The amplitudes of the reflex responses are plotted on an arbitrary scale as a function of the frequency of their occurrence. High amplitude potentials are reduced and then almost totally abolished as the animal progresses from wakefulness, through drowsiness and quiet sleep, into active sleep. (From Chase et al., 1968.)

the control in almost all trials for all states of sleep and wakefulness. Similar results were found for all animals.

High frequency paradigm

The response of the masseteric reflex to continuous, high frequency reticular stimulation was analyzed in order to obtain an objective index of the reflex response to sustained reticular activation and to correlate these data with the results of short pulse train stimulation. For this series of experiments, the masseteric reflex was induced continuously at a rate of 1.5/sec. The reticular formation was stimulated at random intervals (none of which was less than 3 min) for periods of 4 sec at a frequency of

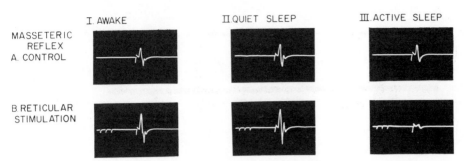

Fig. 3. Oscilloscopic recordings of the masseteric reflex response to reticular stimulation. There is a spontaneous decrease in masseteric reflex amplitude as the animal passes from wakefulness to quiet sleep. The level of reflex induction was therefore increased in this and the following figure during the sleep states in order to obtain control reflexes of equivalent magnitude. Of particular interest is the lack of any reticular evoked activity other than that affecting the amplitude of the masseteric reflex. Mesencephalic Vth nucleus. I: 4 V, 0.9 msec; II and III: 6 V, 0.9 msec. Reticular tegmentum: 5 V, 0.5 msec, 3 pulses. Calibration: 10 msec; 500 μV. (From Chase and Babb, 1973.)

100 c/sec. The average amplitude of the six reflex responses which immediately preceded reticular stimulation served as the control for the reflexes which were induced during the reticular stimulus. The following diagram illustrates the temporal relationships of this paradigm.

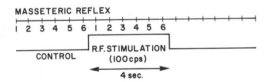

During *wakefulness*, the level of reticular stimulation was kept below that necessary to induce a behavioral or electroencephalographic reaction. The level was sufficient, however, to yield masseteric reflex facilitation (Figs. 6 and 7). In general, the degree of facilitation was more pronounced as the interval between periods of reticular stimulation was lengthened beyond the minimum 3-min intertrial interval.

Throughout *active sleep* marked reflex suppression was present during reticular stimulation (Figs. 6 and 7), both during quiescent periods as well as during episodes of rapid eye movements or muscular twitches. No obvious behavioral, ocular, myographic or electroencephalographic reactions were observed when reticular stimulation was applied during this state.

To summarize, in all animals, during every experimental period, a consistent and unvarying pattern of response was observed in conjunction with

104

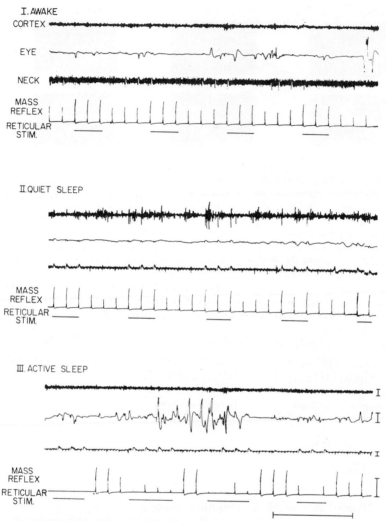

Fig. 4. Polygraphic recordings of the amplitude of the masseteric reflex and the activity of the sensorimotor cortex, eyes and neck musculature. The reflex was recorded, on-line, by employing a window circuit to isolate the reflex and a peak-amplitude pulse-lengthening circuit to deflect the polygraphic pen commensurate with the reflex amplitude. Note the consistency of the reticular effects between states and within states, especially during periods of phasic activity such as ocular movements and spindle bursts. Mesencephalic Vth nucleus. I: 5 V, 0.5 msec; II: 6 V, 0.5 msec; III: 7 V, 0.5 msec. Reticular tegmentum: 5 V, 0.9 msec, 3 pulses. Calibration: cortex, eye, neck, 50 μV; reflex, 500 μV; time, 5 sec. (From Chase and Babb, 1973.)

pulse train or high frequency reticular stimulation. When the animal was awake, reticular stimulation was accompanied by reflex facilitation. As soon

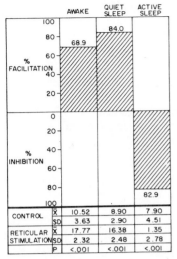

		AWAKE	QUIET SLEEP	ACTIVE SLEEP
CONTROL	X̄	10.52	8.90	7.90
	SD	3.63	2.90	4.51
RETICULAR STIMULATION	X̄	17.77	16.38	1.35
	SD	2.32	2.48	2.78
	P	<.001	<.001	<.001

Fig. 5. Graphic representation of reflex facilitation and inhibition induced by reticular stimulation: statistical evaluation of data (t-test). Each data point is based on an amplitude comparison of 40 control reflexes with 40 reticular-modified reflexes. Amplitude measurements were calculated on an arbitrary but relative scale. All parameters of reflex and reticular stimulation were held constant. Note the normal decrease in spontaneous amplitude (awake > quiet sleep > active sleep) reported previously. Mesencephalic Vth nucleus: 6 V, 0.5 msec. Reticular tegmentum: 4 V, 0.75 msec, 3 pulses. (From Chase and Babb, 1973.)

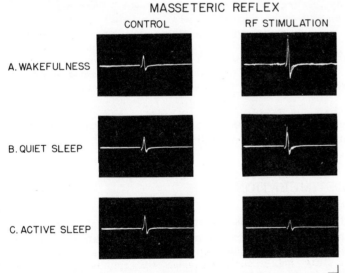

MASSETERIC REFLEX

Fig. 6. Oscilloscopic recordings of the masseteric reflex (three superimposed traces per photograph). The level of reflex induction was increased from wakefulness to quiet sleep to active sleep in order to maintain equivalent control amplitudes (A, 3 V, 0.5 msec; B, 4 V, 0.5 msec; C, 5.5 V, 0.5 msec). The level of reticular stimulation was held constant throughout all states (4 V, 0.75 msec, 100 c/sec). Note that no masseteric muscular response occurred in conjunction with reticular stimulation. Reflex facilitation was induced by reticular excitation during wakefulness (A) and quiet sleep (B), while inhibition resulted during active sleep (C). Calibration: 5 msec; 300 μV. (From Chase et al., in press.)

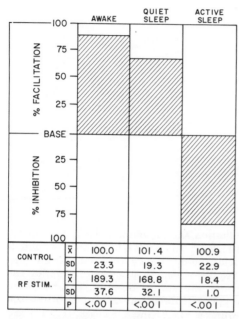

		AWAKE	QUIET SLEEP	ACTIVE SLEEP
CONTROL	x̄	100.0	101.4	100.9
	SD	23.3	19.3	22.9
RF STIM.	x̄	189.3	168.8	18.4
	SD	37.6	32.1	1.0
	P	<.001	<.001	<.001

Fig. 7. Graphic and statistical description of the masseteric reflex response to reticular stimulation. For this study the frequency of reflex induction was 1.5/sec and the level for the awake, quiet sleep and active sleep states were, respectively, 3 V, 0.5 msec; 3.5 V, 0.5 msec; and 4.2 V, 0.5 msec. Reticular stimulation (4 V, 0.5 msec, 100 c/sec for 4 sec) was held constant. The per cent variation in reflex amplitude induced by reticular stimulation (plotted on an arbitrary but relative scale) was obtained from data collected from 100 separate trials during each state (each trial consisted of a comparison of six control reflexes compared with six reflexes modified by reticular stimulation). (From Chase et al., in press.)

as the animal entered the active sleep state, using identical parameters of reticular stimulation, the reflex was dramatically suppressed.

ORBITAL CORTICAL STIMULATION

A comparable set of experiments was performed in order to determine the cortical influence upon masseteric reflex excitability and the variations in the degree of this influence as a function of state (Chase and McGinty, 1970a and b).

Chronic, freely moving cats were prepared with an array of electrodes for inducing and recording the masseteric reflex and for monitoring the EEG, EOG and EMG. Cortical stimulating electrodes were constructed of two intertwined lengths of 0.01 mm insulated stainless steel wire. At the end which was placed on the cortex, the tips were separated and the insulation was removed from one surface of each tip for a distance of 1 mm.

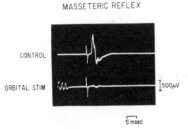

Fig. 8. This figure demonstrates the basic effect of orbitally induced inhibition of the masseteric reflex. The conditioning-test latency was approximately 15 msec. (Mesencephalic Vth nucleus: 5 V, 0.8 msec; orbital stim.: 8 V, 0 msec, 3 pulses, 500 pulses/sec.)

Electrodes of this type were implanted, bilaterally, in the subarachnoid space with the uninsulated surface resting on the orbital gyrus (Chase and McGinty, 1970a).

The reflex response was examined at varying latencies following short pulse train stimulation of the orbital gyrus. Inhibition occurred when the cortical conditioning-test response interval was approximately 15 msec (Fig. 8). Since inhibition appeared as the initial and prominent response, it, rather than facilitation which occurred at longer latencies, was considered as the principal orbitofugal pattern of effect.

In order to test the functional capacity of the orbital cortex to inhibit the masseteric reflex during active sleep and wakefulness, a second series of 'orbital' cats was prepared. The effectiveness of orbital cortical inhibition of the masseteric reflex was examined according to the following paradigms.

Fixed parameters of cortical and reflex excitation. As previously noted, the amplitude of the masseteric reflex, when liminally induced, decreases as the animal passes from wakefulness into active sleep (Fig. 2). In order to minimize this spontaneous decrease in amplitude, a suprathreshold level of reflex excitation was used. Orbital stimulation preceded every fourth reflex elicitation; the intervening reflex responses served as controls.

During the alert state the reflex was almost completely suppressed following orbital stimulation (Fig. 9A). The degree of suppression was reduced during quiet sleep and was least during active sleep (Fig. 9B and C). In Fig. 9C, the degree of orbital inhibition became greater when the animal aroused in spite of the increase in the amplitude of the baseline reflex.

Fig. 10 presents data obtained with a computer of average transients (Mnemotron). During the alert state the reflex response was maximally depressed, but was relatively unaffected by cortical stimulation when the animal passed into active sleep. Thus, the response, which was easily suppressed during the alert state, was relatively unaffected during active sleep (Figs. 9 and 10).

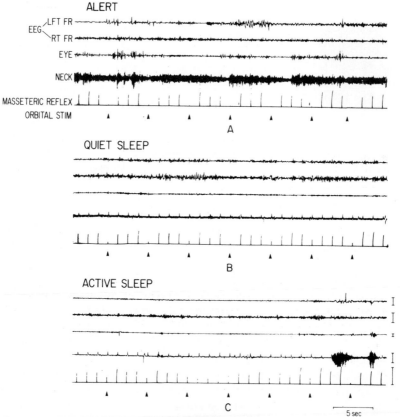

Fig. 9. By recording the masseteric reflex on a polygraph, along with the EEG, neck activity and eye movements, variations in the effectiveness of cortically induced inhibition of this reflex during sleep and waking states were examined. The masseteric reflex was evoked at a rate of 1/sec; orbital stimulation (indicated by arrowheads: ▲) preceded every fourth reflex by 15 msec. When the animal was in the alert state the degree of inhibition was greatest; it decreased during quiet sleep and was least during active sleep. Orbital stim.: 8 V, 1 msec, 4 pulses (500 pulses/sec); mesencephalic Vth nucleus stim.: 5 V, 1 msec. Calibration: masseteric reflex 500 μV; EEG, eye, neck 50 μV. (From Chase and McGinty, 1970b.)

Fixed parameter of reflex excitation: variable amplitude of orbital stimulation. A second mode of analysis utilized the stimulation paradigm depicted in the lower right-hand portion of Fig. 11. Two pulses were delivered to the orbital cortex and were followed, after a constant interval, by a pulse to the mesencephalic Vth nucleus. As before, orbital stimulation preceded every fourth reflex elicitation. The effectiveness of reflex suppression by different orbital voltages was examined during the alert, quiet sleep, and active sleep states (Fig. 11). The per cent decrease in the reflex response

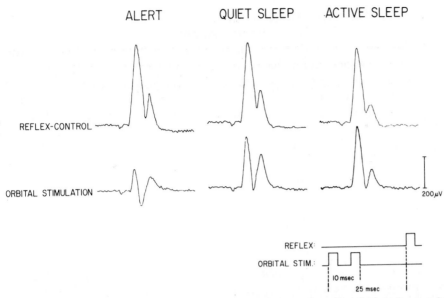

Fig. 10. Orbital cortically induced changes in the masseteric reflex during sleep and wakefulness. Each tracing is the average of 15 responses. The control reflex was maximally induced, therefore little change in amplitude was noted during the different states. Inhibition by orbital stimulation again was most evident during the alert state and least during active sleep. Orbital stim.: 9 V, 0.75 msec; mesencephalic Vth nucleus stim.: 6 V, 0.8 msec. (From Chase and McGinty, 1970b.)

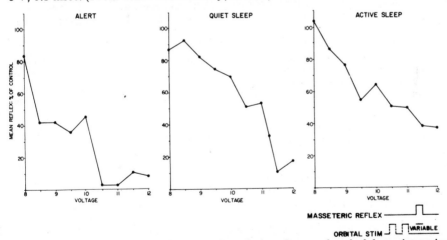

Fig. 11. Inhibition of the masseteric reflex during sleep and wakefulness in conjunction with different levels of orbital cortical stimulation. Each point indicates the per cent change in the amplitude of 10 reflex responses when preceded by orbital stimulation. At every level of orbital stimulation the masseteric reflex was more easily inhibited (15 msec latency) during the alert state than during the sleep states. Orbital cortex: 0.75 msec, 2 pulses (440 pulses/sec); mesencephalic Vth nucleus stim.: 6 V, 1 msec. (From Chase and McGinty, 1970b.)

following orbital stimulation was plotted as a function of the mean amplitude of the preceding three control reflex responses.

During low voltage orbital stimulation the reflex was suppressed only during wakefulness and quiet sleep. At higher voltages the reflex was almost completely abolished during the alert state, and slightly depressed during quiet and active sleep. Even at the highest levels of stimulation the reflex was only moderately suppressed during active sleep. Thus, at all levels of orbital stimulation which we examined, the reflex was suppressed to a greater degree during the alert state compared with active sleep.

A MODEL OF MOTOR CONTROL

In order to fit the preceding observations into an integrated scheme, a hypothetical model of motor control was developed. It essentially accounts for the two principal observations of decreasing cortical control during active sleep and reticular reflex response-reversal during wakefulness compared with active sleep. The basic underlying assumptions are summarized below. Supportive data and arguments follow.

WAKEFULNESS

(1) During wakefulness the pontomesencephalic reticular formation activates the cerebral cortex (resulting in EEG desynchronization).

(2) The pontomesencephalic reticular formation also induces masseteric reflex *facilitation*.

(3) Diffuse corticofugal inhibition of an excitatory link from the facilitatory to the inhibitory area of the reticular formation and orbitocortical activation of the medullary inhibitory area is *effective*.

(4) Pontomesencephalic activation of the medullary inhibitory formation *is* blocked by corticofugal inhibition. *These factors result in spontaneous and pontomesencephalic reticular-induced EEG desynchronization and masseteric reflex FACILITATION.*

ACTIVE SLEEP

(1) During active sleep the pontomesencephalic reticular formation activates the cerebral cortex (resulting in EEG desynchronization).

(2) The pontomesencephalic reticular formation also induces masseteric reflex *inhibition*.

(3) Diffuse corticofugal inhibition of an excitatory link from the facilitatory to the inhibitory area of the reticular formation and orbitocortical activation of the medullary inhibitory area is *ineffective*.

(4) Pontomesencephalic activation of the medullary inhibitory formation *is not* blocked by corticofugal inhibition. *These factors result in spontaneous and pontomesencephalic reticular-induced EEG desynchronization and masseteric reflex INHIBITION.*

(1) The pontomesencephalic reticular formation activates the cerebral cortex resulting in EEG desynchronization during wakefulness and active sleep

There are certainly few manipulations of the CNS that have proven as reliable and repeatable as cortical desynchronization resulting from stimulation of the pontomesencephalic reticular formation. Finely graded electrical stimulation of the reticular formation leads, with almost perfect regularity, to correlated degrees of induced low voltage fast activity over the cortical mantle (Bremer, 1961; Dell, 1963; Moruzzi and Magoun, 1949). The induction or maintenance of a desynchronized pattern during wakefulness, in conjunction with excitation of the 'reticular activating system', was also observed in our experiments. Since the EEG appears maximally desynchronized during active sleep, no specific effect of reticular stimulation was noted nor did stimulation disrupt the state itself. Therefore, excitation by the reticular formation either maintains the desynchronization of cortical activity which occurs during wakefulness and active sleep, or, at the very least, is compatible with the spontaneous EEG pattern which accompanies these states.

(2) The pontomesencephalic reticular formation induces masseteric reflex facilitation during wakefulness and inhibition during active sleep

As detailed in previous sections of this chapter, reticular stimulation modified the masseteric reflex in the same direction as those variations in amplitude which occur spontaneously during wakefulness (increase in amplitude) and active sleep (decrease in amplitude). Specifically, when reticular formation stimulation preceded the induction of the masseteric reflex (conditioning-test paradigm), or was concurrent with it (continuous high frequency paradigm), the reflex was facilitated during wakefulness and inhibited during active sleep.

In an elegant series of acute experiments on immobilized cats, Bonvallet, Dell and Hugelin also determined that stimulation of the pontomesencephalic reticular formation led to facilitation of the masseteric reflex (Dell, 1963; Dell et al., 1961; Hugelin, 1961; Hugelin and Bonvallet, 1957). In addition, Sauerland et al. (1967) also found that excitation of the pontomesencephalon resulted in masseteric reflex facilitation in the immobilized cat. In this study, the participation of lower brain stem structures was not involved, the response being of short latency. Since the studies of both groups were carried out in the immobilized preparation (Flaxedil and/or urethane), the state of the animal was unknown, but was presumably awake.

It is clear from the studies cited above, as well as our own, that reticular stimulation facilitates the masseteric reflex in the waking cat and that reticular induced reflex response-reversal (inhibition) occurs during active sleep. The following section presents a possible mechanism for this unique pattern of response-reversal.

(3) During wakefulness diffuse corticofugal inhibition of an excitatory link from the facilitatory to the inhibitory area of the reticular formation is effective and orbitocortical activation of the medullary inhibitory area is effective. Both processes are ineffective during active sleep

The data indicating that there are both specific (orbital) and diffuse cortical effects exerted upon the brain stem reticular formation and that these influences are maximal during wakefulness and depressed during active sleep begins with a description of the presumptive projection systems. The existence of a pathway mediating orbitofugal inhibition of the masseteric reflex has been demonstrated electrophysiologically by Clemente et al. (1966) and by Sauerland et al. (1967), and anatomically by Mizuno et al. (1969).

In 1966, Clemente et al. found that short pulse train electrical stimulation of the orbital gyrus in flaxedilized cats resulted in profound inhibition of the masseteric reflex. Following this observation, Sauerland et al. (1967) reported that:

> "The anterior portion of the orbital gyrus, previously implicated in the inhibition of monosynaptic and polysynaptic reflexes at all levels of the neuroaxis, was shown to project directly to the ventromedial bulbar reticular formation (chiefly to the nucleus reticularis gigantocellularis) and to the pontine tegmentum (mainly to the nucleus reticularis pontis oralis)."

As a result of single pulse excitation of the anterior portion of the orbital gyrus, short latency (0.4—0.5 msec) direct responses were obtained in the ipsilateral and contralateral pontine and medullary reticular regions. The fact that the ventromedial bulbar reticular formation participates in the mechanisms of orbital-induced inhibition of the monosynaptic masseteric reflex was demonstrated by transection experiments (Sauerland et al., 1967).

In studies designed to explore the anatomical basis for orbital inhibition of the masseteric reflex, Mizuno et al. (1969), working with Sauerland and Clemente, reported that:

> "The main orbitobulbar projections to the reticular formation in our animals were found in the caudal part of the oral pontine nucleus, the rostral part of the caudal pontine nucleus and in the rostroventromedial part of the gigantocellular nucleus. Thus, an anatomical substrate exists for the cortically induced influences on reflexes described electrophysiologically by our group."

They concluded, on the basis of preterminal degeneration following cortical lesions, that the inhibitory effects on the masseteric reflex induced by orbital stimulation could be mediated by cortico-reticulo-Vth motor pathways.

The studies in freely moving cats which support these electrophysiological and anatomical investigations are provided mainly by our work described in previous sections. Essentially, we found that with respect to the control of motor processes, orbital cortical influences were maximally effective during wakefulness and minimally effective during active sleep. Of course, the depression of orbital effects may reflect changes in the excitability of one or more sites along the pathway from cortex to motoneuron, including the orbital cortex, a subcortical relay, or the lower motoneuron itself.

As early as 1894, Tarchanoff observed that limb movements evoked by motor cortical stimulation were reduced during sleep. Hodes and Suzuki (1965) applied high frequency electrical stimulation to the 'frontal cortex' of cats and determined the threshold voltage for inducing head and forelimb movements. The threshold was lowest in the waking animal and highest during quiet sleep, with an intermediate value for active sleep. In contrast, our results indicate that the orbital cortical threshold was highest during active sleep. Iwama and Kawamoto (1966) also stimulated the frontal (motor) cortex of cats and recorded the activity of flexor hindlimb muscles following short pulse train stimulation. They found a gradual decrease in the somatic excitatory response as the animal passed from the alert state through quiet sleep into active sleep. Similarly, Baldissera et al. (1966) reported that motor cortical stimulation produced the greatest amplitude of electromyographic response during the alert state, whereas during active sleep it was almost absent. Thus, while we observed a depression in a somatic excitatory response during active sleep, as did Iwama and Kawamoto (1966) and Baldissera et al. (1966), Hodes and Suzuki (1965) found an enhancement.

The existence of diffuse cortical projections to brain stem reticular nuclei has been well established by Kuypers (1964), Grofova (1965) and Rossi and Brodal (1956), among others. However, there is no information, to the best of my knowledge, that directly substantiates the state-dependency of cortical inhibition of pontomesencephalic activation of the medullary reticular formation. However, the cortical-reticular and reticular-reticular interactions previously described, and those outlined below, lend indirect support to the existence of a functional linkage of this nature.

(4) Pontomesencephalic activation of the medullary inhibitory formation is blocked by corticofugal inhibition during wakefulness but is not blocked during active sleep

This aspect of the model is based upon the supposition that pontomesencephalic reticular activity excites the medullary reticular formation which in turn inhibits the masseteric reflex, and that the tonic excitation of the medullary inhibitory formation is blocked by corticofugal activity only during wakefulness, not during active sleep.

In a summary of reticular homeostasis and cortical reactivity, Paul Dell (1963) stated:

> "Close functional interrelationship between these bulbar inhibitory mechanisms and the activating system have been demonstrated. This suggests that each mesencephalic reticular activation brings into play a bulbar inhibitory mechanism. If one accepts some of the suggestions made here, then sleep would be only an extreme state resulting from an accumulation of bulbar inhibitory effects."

The data referred to by Dell is supported by an extensive series of related experiments (Dell, 1963). However, there is little other information which either supports or negates the proposed reticular-reticular interaction. Only indirectly, by examining some of the classically defined physiological control systems of the brain stem, can some supportive data be marshalled.

For example, the brain stem respiratory mechanisms of the medulla, pons and mesencephalon are interrelated by inhibitory and excitatory connections. Other vegetative functions similarly reflect inhibitory and excitatory loops within parenchyma of the brain stem (Chase and Clemente, 1968). Thus, while the potential for pontomesencephalic control of the medullary inhibitory area exists insofar as other functions appear to reflect similar processes (Scheibel and Scheibel, 1964), with the exception of Dell's studies, credible proof for the specific interplay proposed here is lacking at the present time.

OVERVIEW

We began our studies of the central neural systems which control motor behavior with an investigation of the spontaneous state-dependent variations in masseteric reflex amplitude, and found that the reflex was largest (facilitated?) during wakefulness and smallest (inhibited?) during active sleep. We then determined that orbital cortical stimulation inhibited the masseteric reflex during all states, and that the effect was strongest during wakefulness and minimal during active sleep. On the other hand, excitation of the pontomesencephalic reticular formation facilitated the reflex during wakefulness and inhibited it during active sleep. These data indicate that during wakefulness *and* during active sleep the reticular formation exerts a pattern — facilitation and inhibition, respectively — which occurs normally during these states, whereas the cerebral cortex exerts only one pattern — inhibition — which is opposite from that which occurs during wakefulness. This cortical effect is practically absent during active sleep when a spontaneously maintained pattern of inhibition occurs. We therefore conclude that cerebral cortical-initiated inhibition represents a departure either in direction (during wakefulness) or degree (during active sleep) from the normal state-dependent level of motor activity and that reticular stimulation induces activity which mimics the patterns which normally occur during wakefulness and active sleep.

There are a number of plausible models that could account for the 'reticular reflex response-reversal', other than that outlined in the preceding section. It may be that reticular stimulation excites a single neuronal group (or fiber tract) which exerts one function during wakefulness (and quiet sleep) and another during active sleep. Neurons that have the potential for producing both excitation and inhibition have been described in the invertebrate (Gardner and Kandell, 1972; Grillner, 1970); no concrete evidence of their existence in higher animals is available.

It is also possible that reticular stimulation may be simultaneously exciting not one fiber tract or nuclear group, but two. Both the locus coeruleus (purported to sustain the motor inhibition of active sleep) and the reticular activating system (purported to maintain wakefulness) are located in the area of reticular stimulation (Jouvet, 1972; Menini, 1972). However, such separate systems would be expected to have different excitatory thresholds, so that it should be possible at low levels of stimulation to excite only that system whose threshold is lowest, resulting in only one pattern of response irrespective of the state of the animal (Chase et al., 1967). This was not the case, for the same pattern of state-dependent response-reversal, i.e., facilitation/inhibition, was observed at both high and low levels of reticular stimulation.

On the other hand, reticular stimulation may not have a direct effect on the masseteric reflex, but may be indirectly inducing activity simultaneously in separate neuronal pools which then, *individually*, have the potential for producing reflex facilitation and inhibition. The activity of these distant neuronal pools would have to be strongly state-dependent, so that effective reflex modulation would take place only during periods of high excitability which would occur as a function of a given state. Whatever the actual processes may be, since the masseteric reflex is monosynaptic, they must eventually act presynaptically upon the mesencephalic Vth nerve terminals or postsynaptically upon the trigeminal motoneurons.

The model developed in this chapter is similar to the hypothesis presented in the preceding paragraph. It accounts for the fact that reticular modulation of the masseteric reflex is powerful during both wakefulness and active sleep and that the pattern of reflex modulation is comparable to that which occurs spontaneously during these states, i.e., facilitation during wakefulness and inhibition during active sleep.

The capability of a single reticular locus to express a dual function is explained by the shutting down of a path from (1) the pontomesencephalic reticular formation (2) to the medullary inhibitory formation (3) to the masseteric reflex during wakefulness, and the opening of this path during active sleep. The tonically active excitatory link to the medulla is blocked by corticofugal activity during wakefulness. Due to a reduction in corticofugal activity during active sleep this link becomes functional and the medullary region tonically inhibits the masseteric reflex. Direct phasic facilitation of the masseteric reflex, during arousal, occurs as a result of pontomesencephalic activation. According to this scheme, the baseline reflex level is that which occurs during wakefulness, with phasic increases during arousal or wakefulness and tonic inhibition during active sleep being due to pontomesencephalic discharge.

The model depends upon a reduction in corticofugal activity during active sleep, for the link between the facilitatory and inhibitory areas of the reticular formation is thought to be under cortical control. Since corticofugal projection systems are believed to be 'turned off' in active sleep, during this state, insofar as motor control is concerned, the adult cat is thought to be comparable to a newborn kitten prior to cortical development. One tantalizing bit of supporting evidence is that the masseteric reflex is smallest in the young kitten during wakefulness and largest during active sleep — the exact opposite pattern from that which occurs in the adult (Fig. 12; Chase, 1971 and 1972). In the kitten, during wakefulness, cortical inhibition of the proposed ponto-mesencephalic link to the inhibitory medullary reticular formation would be non-existent. Activity of the 'reticular activating system' would then result in reflex suppression via pontomesencephalic excitation of the medullary inhibitory formation. The paradoxical increase in amplitude of the masseteric reflex during active sleep in kittens would then be viewed as a release from suppression during wakefulness (although it is not clear how a steady state value is achieved during active sleep). As the kitten matures, the diffuse cortex projection system would begin blockade of the reticular-reticular link during wakefulness (allowing, of course, the expression of phasic pontomesencephalic activation of the masseteric reflex). The blockade would be released during active sleep, resulting in reflex inhibition.

The model and the data serving as its foundation suggest that it is the pontomesencephalic reticular formation that controls the basic states of motor activity during wakefulness and active sleep, and not the cerebral cortex. Since motor activity appears to be 'a' or 'the' key physiological process which provides the foundation for the expression of either active sleep or wakefulness, the pontomesencephalic reticular formation may also play a crucial role in the initiation or maintenance of these states.

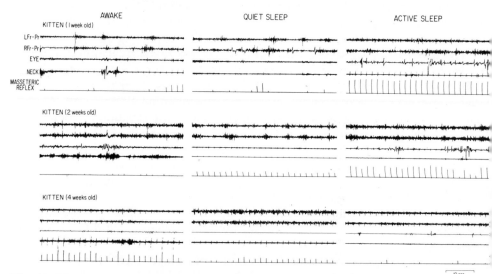

Fig. 12. Masseteric reflex modulation in the one-, two- and four-week-old kitten. This reflex was of greatest amplitude during active sleep in the one- and two-week-old kittens. By four weeks of age the mean amplitude of the reflex was largest during the awake state and smallest during active sleep. Note the lack of a clearly differentiable state-dependent EEG pattern in the one-week-old kitten. Stimulation parameters: masseteric reflex, 3 V, 0.5 msec, 0.5/sec. Calibration: EEG, EOG, EMG, 50 μV; reflex, 500 μV. The following abbreviations for the cortical recording sites were employed: LFr-Pr, left frontal to left parietal; RFr-Pr, right frontal to right parietal. (From Chase, 1971.)

The model as constructed is most likely sound, but its strength may be deceptive, for as noted some essential aspects have been deliberately left ill-defined or unaccounted for when neither the literature not our data bear directly upon them. As with any model, its chief value lies in guiding or generating concepts and providing research strategies to determine their validity. It is to be predicted that the model proposed in this chapter will shortly be replaced by another as new data is added to the store. However, the accumulated data which serves as its foundation will remain, and we will continue to approximate more and more closely an accurate picture of central neural functioning in the control of motor processes during sleep and wakefulness.

Acknowledgements

This research was supported by NIH Grants NS-09999 and MH-10083. Bibliographic assistance was provided by the Brain Information Service (NINDS Contract N01-NS-3-2306).

REFERENCES

Baldissera, F., Ettore, G., Infuso, L., Mancia, M. et Pagni, C.A. (1966) Etude comparative des réponses évoquées par stimulation des voies corticospinales pendant le sommeil et la veille, chez l'homme et chez l'animal. Rev. Neurol., 115, 82—84.

Bremer, F. (1961) Neurophysiological mechanisms in cerebral arousal. In G.E.W. Wolstenholme and M. O'Connor (Eds.), The Nature of Sleep. Little Brown and Company, Boston, Mass., pp. 30—56.

Chase, M.H. (1971) Brain stem somatic reflex activity in neonatal kittens during sleep and wakefulness. Physiol. Behav., 7, 165—172.

Chase, M.H. (1972) Patterns of reflex excitability during the ontogenesis of sleep and wakefulness. In C.D. Clemente, D.P. Purpura and F.E. Meyer (Eds.), Maturation of Brain Mechanisms Related to Sleep Behavior. Academic Press, New York, pp. 253—285.

Chase, M.H. (1974) Somatic reflex activity during sleep and wakefulness. In O. Petre-Quadens and J. Schlag (Eds.), Basic Sleep Mechanisms. Academic Press, New York, pp. 249—267.

Chase, M.H. and Babb, M. (1973) Masseteric reflex response to reticular stimulation reverses during active sleep compared with wakefulness or quiet sleep. Brain Res., 59, 421—426.

Chase, M.H. and Clemente, C.D. (1968) Central neural components of the autonomic nervous system. Anesthesiology, 29, 625—633.

Chase, M.H. and McGinty, D.J. (1970a) Modulation of spontaneous and reflex activity of the jaw musculature by orbital cortical stimulation in the freely-moving cat. Brain Res., 19, 117—126.

Chase, M.H. and McGinty, D.J. (1970b) Somatomotor inhibition and excitation by forebrain stimulation during sleep and wakefulness: orbital cortex. Brain Res., 19, 127—136.

Chase, M.H., Nakamura, Y., Clemente, C.D. and Sterman, M.B. (1967) Afferent vagal stimulation: neurographic correlates of induced EEG synchronization and desynchronization. Brain Res., 5, 236—249.

Chase, M.H., McGinty, D.J. and Sterman, M.B. (1968) Cyclic variations in the amplitude of a brain stem reflex during sleep and wakefulness. Experientia (Basel), 24, 47—48.

Chase, M.H., Monoson, R., Watanabe, K. and Babb, M.I. (1975) Somatic reflex response-reversal of reticular origin. In Press.

Clemente, C.D., Chase, M.H., Knauss, T.A., Sauerland, E.K. and Sterman, M.B. (1966) Inhibition of a monosynaptic reflex by electrical stimulation of the basal forebrain or the orbital gyrus in the cat. Experientia (Basel), 22, 844—848.

Dell, P. (1963) Reticular homeostasis and critical reactivity. In G. Moruzzi, A. Fessard and H.H. Jasper (Eds.), Brain Mechanisms, Progr. Brain Res., Vol. 1. Elsevier, Amsterdam, pp. 82—103.

Dell, P., Bonvallet, M. and Hugelin, A. (1961) Mechanisms of reticular deactivation. In G.E.W. Wolstenholme and M. O'Connor (Eds.), The Nature of Sleep. Little Brown and Company, Boston, Mass., pp. 86—107.

Gardner, D. and Kandell, E.R. (1972) Diphasic postsynaptic potential: a chemical synapse capable of mediating conjoint excitation and inhibition. Science, 176, 675—678.

Grillner, S. (1970) Is the tonic stretch reflex dependent upon group II excitation? Acta physiol. scand., 78, 431—432.

Grofova, I. (1965) Frontal cortical projections to the midbrain tegmentum in the cat. Folia morph. (Warszawa), 13, 305—315.

Hodes, R. and Suzuki, J.K. (1965) Comparative thresholds of cortex, vestibular system and reticular formation in wakefulness, sleep and rapid eye movement periods. Electroenceph. clin. Neurophysiol., 18, 239—248.

Hugelin, A. (1961) Intégrations motrices et vigilance chez l'encéphale isolé. II: Controle réticulaire des voies finales communes d'ouverture et de fermeture de la gueule. Arch. ital. Biol., 99, 244—269.

Hugelin, A. et Bonvallet, M. (1957) Tonus cortical et controle de la facilitation motrice d'origine réticulaire. J. Physiol. (Paris), 49, 1171—1200.

Iwama, K. and Kawamoto, T. (1966) Responsiveness of cat motor cortex to electrical stimulation in wakefulness. In T. Tokizane and J.P. Schadé (Eds.), Correlative Neurosciences, Part B: Clinical Studies, Progr. Brain Res., Vol. 21B. Elsevier, Amsterdam, pp. 54—63.

Jouvet, M. (1972) The role of monoamines and acetylcholine-containing neurons in the regulation of the sleep-waking cycle. Ergebn. Physiol., 64, 166—307.

Kuypers, H.G.J.M. (1964) An anatomical analysis of cortico-bulbar connexions to the pons and lower brain stem in the cat. J. Anat. (Lond.), 92, 198—218.

Menini, C. (1972) La formation reticulaire. Rev. méd. Toulouse, 8, 545—567.

Mizuno, N., Sauerland, E.K. and Clemente, C.D. (1969) Projections from the orbital gyrus in the cat. I: To brain stem structures. J. comp. Neurol., 133, 463—476.

Moruzzi, G. and Magoun, H.W. (1949) Brain stem reticular formation and activation of the EEG. Electroenceph. clin. Neurophysiol., 1, 455—473.

Rossi, G.F. and Brodal, A. (1956) Corticofugal fibers to the brain-stem reticular formation. An experimental study in the cat. J. Anat. (Lond.), 90, 42—62.

Sauerland, E.K., Nakamura, Y. and Clemente, C.D. (1967) The role of the lower brain stem in cortically induced inhibition of somatic reflexes in the cat. Brain Res., 6, 164—180.

Scheibel, M. and Scheibel, A. (1964) Some structural and functional substrates of development in young cats. In W.A. Himwich and H.E. Himwich (Eds.), The Developing Brain, Progr. Brain Res., Vol. 9. Elsevier, Amsterdam, pp. 6—25.

Tarchanoff, J. (1894) Quelques observations sur le sommeil normal. Arch. ital. Biol., 21, 318—321.

DISCUSSION

HIGHSTEIN: Do you have any data on units?

CHASE: This is the next step in our experiment on the present problem of corticofugal control of motor activity. We are going to go into both intracellular and unit studies to try to determine what the mechanisms are in this model system.

ASRATYAN: You especially chose the point of cortex which is paleocortical. Did you stimulate one point of the cortex, or did you change the points of the cortex?

CHASE: Changed points.

ASRATYAN: From each point the same results were obtained?

CHASE: Yes.

BENNETT: Are there any changes in the input-output relations that might indicate coupling of sensory afferents?

CHASE: I am hesitant to answer that. I do not know.

BESSON: Are there any results on the spinal cord?

CHASE: The change in the response pattern in the spinal cord is the question now.

BESSON: Are there any presynaptic inhibitory influences? There is a big influence of dorsal column input.

CHASE: What I am saying is that it is during wakefulness that the orbital stimulation will induce that pattern of activity. But the control of the motor process is shifted then to the reticular formation. During the active sleep state, and goal-directed activity you would expect to see the presynaptic inhibition of cortical origin. Certainly, inhibition of motor processes can arise by excitation of almost every area of the central nervous system. What I am getting at here is what area mimics the same pattern of motor variation that one normally sees. It seems that the reticular formation facilitates motor activity during wakefulness and also inhibits during active sleep, which is the same process that occurs spontaneously. So I think that the fact that autostimulation will lead to presynaptic inhibition, and that increased presynaptic inhibition during active sleep is not related directly to the point that I am trying to make.

HIGHSTEIN: Is it possible to include the digastric reflex in your model?

CHASE: I do not have any trouble in including that in the model, but the digastric reflex is unique in my knowledge in the entire body in that it is suppressed during wakefulness, increased in amplitude during quiet sleep and decreased during active sleep, probably due to the fact that there are no muscle spindles of the fusimotor system. So I do not have any trouble in putting it into the model, but it will be a very confusing explanation if you try to include that also. I think a better question is what happens to the spinal cord reflexes, and the critical question here is, am I really dealing with the local phenomena of the area, or is this also true of the spinal cord. And we are now looking at the spinal cord reflexes to see if this is a general principle of action that is true at every level of the neuraxis.

PURPURA: And it is going to be more complex because that presynaptic influence is going to be very powerful.

CHASE: But you have that to the masseter reflex too.

PURPURA: But to what extent, how powerfully is it related to the cortex?

CHASE: Nobody has looked at the presynaptic inhibition during active sleep of the masseteric reflex, but the degree of inhibition of the masseter reflex during active sleep appears equal to that of the cord. The increased inhibition during rapid eye movements and twitches, which is when the presynaptic inhibition during active sleep occurs, is also present for the masseteric reflex, so that you have masseteric reflex during active sleep which is reduced during rapid eye movements; there is a further reduction, which is a period of time during cord reflex activity when the presynaptic process is coming.

OOMURA: You have mentioned the lateral hypothalamic effect. Did you ever try to stimulate the lateral hypothalamus during this change of reflexes?

CHASE: No, we did not. We did some experiments on feeding behavior and were looking at the masseteric reflex and effects of hypothalamic ablations, but not stimulations.

ASRATYAN: Sleep is a general state which would call upon the neocortex and paleocortex. Did you try to prevent change of the neocortical activity by cooling, and look at the result?

CHASE: I think one can do that, at least theoretically, by looking at the kittens. I think a kitten is cortically decorticated, and in kitten we also see a reversal of the facilitation of reflexes during active sleep and that is why we were getting at the cord. It would be interesting to stimulate the reticular formation in the young kitten and see what happens, because I think that the young kitten in which the cortex is not functionally active might be equivalent to the experiment that you are suggesting to study. Of course, it could also be studied in the adult.

BUCHWALD: What areas are involved in facilitation and inhibition of spinal reflexes?

CHASE: Iwamura published an article last month in Archives Italiennes de Biologie in which they transected the brain stem at various levels in progression. I think it was the anterior hypothalamus which was producing facilitation during active sleep and then a period after when they made a transection of the anterior mesencephalon produced inhibition and facilitation and inhibition, a very complicated story.

BUCHWALD: Did they remove frontal cortex?

CHASE: Yes, they removed the entire anterior part of the brain, basal forebrain first, then the hypothalamus, then midbrain and found different variations in the expansiveness of these reflexes during sleep and wakefulness. But a progressive inhibition-facilitation, inhibition-facilitation occurred down the neuraxis following complete transections.

BUCHWALD: The area in front of transection is retained?

CHASE: No. They removed the entire area in front of the transections.

ALBE-FESSARD: Do you know the work of Bonvallet and Dell on the inhibition of amygdala on the masseter reflex and the lesions of the spinal pathway of the reflex between the oralis and dorsalis? Surprisingly enough, are you at the same level of your recordings and lesion?

CHASE: I have not recorded here. I was just quoting McGinty and Sterman's work.

ALBE-FESSARD: But I am thinking of your lesions.

CHASE: No. We have done stimulation studies, but it is not surprising again. What I am saying is that the amygdala will certainly influence the masseteric reflex, or, the hypothalamus or the orbital cortex, almost every area will influence motor behavior. Which is the area that influences it during sleep and wakefulness and then during which stage and in which behaviors is the control of the reflex for motor processes not changed, is my problem.

ALBE-FESSARD: Certainly the amygdala has something to do with motor reflex.

CHASE: Yes, and I expect, for example, that stimulation of the amygdala during feeding behavior will be more effective than during sleep.

PURPURA: No.

CHASE: For the modification of the masseteric reflex.

ALBE-FESSARD: That is for the next symposium.

7

REPETITIVE STIMULATION, FATIGUE AND RECOVERY OF THE MAUTHNER FIBER—GIANT FIBER SYNAPSE OF HATCHETFISH

S.M. HIGHSTEIN, P.G. MODEL and M.V.L. BENNETT

Department of Neuroscience, Albert Einstein College of Medicine, Bronx, N.Y. (U.S.A.)

INTRODUCTION

The vesicle hypothesis states that at chemical synapses, synaptic transmitter is packaged in and released from synaptic vesicles in the presynaptic terminals. The contents of a vesicle comprise a quantum of transmitter that is released from the presynaptic terminal and diffuses across the synaptic cleft to produce a quantal change in the postsynaptic conductance. The resulting potential change is called a miniature postsynaptic potential (mPSP). mPSPs generally occur spontaneously and randomly at a low rate. Further, depolarization of the presynaptic terminals increases the rate of release of quanta. An action potential causes the synchronous release of many quanta of transmitter, and a large postsynaptic potential (PSP) results. It has been shown at many synapses that this depolarization-secretion coupling requires calcium and is antagonized by magnesium. In magnesium-poisoned terminals, where the number of quanta per impulse is decreased, statistical investigation has demonstrated that the number of quanta in the PSP is a Poisson distributed variable. The implications of these results were important in demonstrating that the PSP is composed of quanta that are the same as the spontaneous mPSPs.

Evidence concerning the vesicle hypothesis can be obtained by a combined morphological and physiological approach. For example, if stimulation causes a parallel decrease in the number of synaptic vesicles and of transmitter measured physiologically, the vesicle hypothesis is supported. We have obtained evidence of this kind at the synapse between Mauthner and giant fibers in the hatchetfish. Our data indicate that the total vesicular store of transmitter is quite rapidly depleted by Mauthner fiber stimulation and that later stimuli release the contents of partially full vesicles. These vesicles probably arise through a mechanism of membrane reuse which involves recycling of membrane through the external surface and internalization by coated vesicles.

The hatchetfish synapse is unique among chemically transmitting synapses

124

in vertebrates in that both pre- and postsynaptic elements can be simultaneously penetrated with microelectrodes close to the synaptic region (Auerbach and Bennett, 1969a). Studies of the ultrastructure (Model et al., 1975) and physiology (Auerbach and Bennett, 1969a; Highstein and Bennett, 1975) of this synapse demonstrate that the Mauthner fiber is presynaptic and the giant fiber is postsynaptic. In location the Mauthner cell and axon resemble the homologous structures in other species. There are 2—7 giant fi-

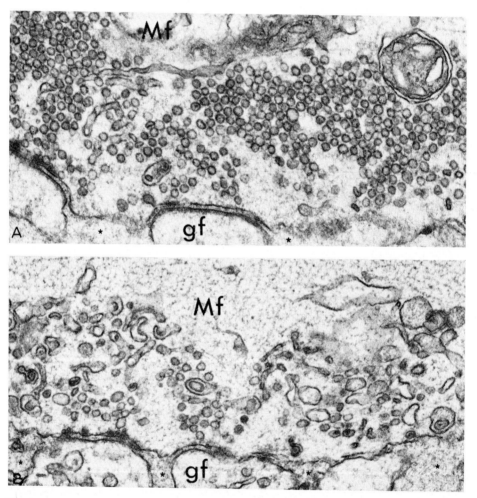

Fig. 1. A: electron micrograph of a portion of control unstimulated Mauthner fiber (Mf)-giant fiber (gf) synapse. Synaptic vesicles are numerous and clustered near the presynaptic membrane. * is extracellular space. × 57,000. B: electron micrograph of a portion of a Mauthner fiber (Mf)-giant fiber (gf) synapse which had been stimulated at 10/sec for 10 min. Synaptic vesicles are greatly reduced in number and there is an accumulation of irregular membranous compartments. * is extracellular space. × 57,000.

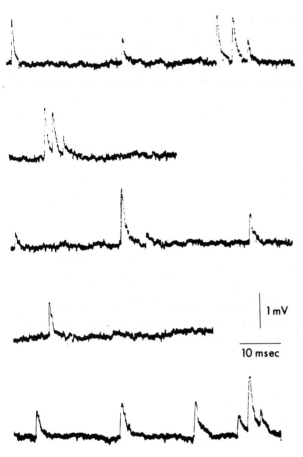

Fig. 3. Miniature excitatory postsynaptic potentials recorded from a giant fiber. All traces are intracellular records of miniature postsynaptic potentials recorded in a giant fiber.

made to disappear into the noise level (Fig. 4). The surprising finding is that even when PSP amplitude is of the same order of magnitude or smaller than a single miniature, there are no complete failures of PSPs. Fig. 4 illustrates such a result. As the frequency of stimulation is increased from 1/sec to 143/sec the PSP gradually decreases in amplitude. The PSP at 33/sec stimulation and above is relatively constant in shape and significantly longer lasting than the miniatures riding upon it. Although its amplitude is comparable to that of the mPSPs, there are no failures. If the miniatures (quanta) comprising the PSP were the same size as the spontaneous miniatures, there should be no (non-zero) PSPs smaller than a miniature, and failures should be common for amplitudes where mean number of miniatures contributing

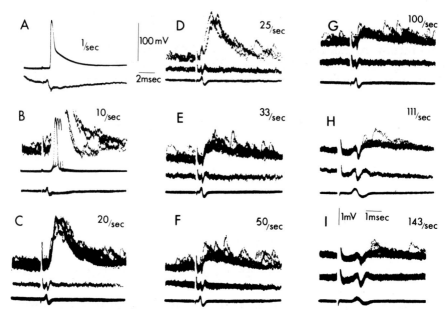

Fig. 4. Effect of increasing frequency of Mauthner fiber stimulation upon the amplitude of postsynaptic potentials recorded in a giant fiber. A: control record, upper trace DC recording of giant fiber action potential; lower trace external recording from the medulla. B: upper traces high gain, middle traces low gain records of giant fiber PSP and action potential, lower traces in this and all subsequent records are the same as lower traces in A. C—I: upper traces as in B, middle traces, just extracellular field potentials, lower traces as in A. Frequency of stimulation and calibrations as indicated.

to the PSP is small. Three hypotheses to explain the PSP amplitudes actually observed can be considered.

(1) Quantum number is high but quantum size has become much smaller, that is, the amount of transmitter per vesicle is greatly reduced. The resulting decrease of quantal size while number remains high could account for the small size of the PSP and lack of failures. This is the hypothesis we favor.

(2) The postsynaptic membrane has become desensitized, so that normal sized quanta of transmitter produce a smaller postsynaptic quantal effect. The time course of the amplitude changes of the PSP, as well as the persistence of relatively large spontaneous miniatures during high frequency stimulation, appear to contradict this hypothesis. (Also, see below.)

(3) Quantum size is unchanged and a small number are released with a high probability. This hypothesis can be rejected since PSPs of smoothly graded amplitudes smaller than normal miniatures are easily obtained (Fig. 4E—I).

EFFECTS OF TETANIC STIMULATION UPON MINIATURES

The frequency of miniatures increases markedly just after the onset of a tetanus (Fig. 5B and C, top row, and Fig. 7A), and then decreases again to a value near or below the resting level (Fig. 5B and C, bottom row). In occasional experiments miniature frequency becomes very small. The mean amplitudes of the mPSPs decrease somewhat but even when their frequency is markedly reduced they are not greatly reduced in size. In the experiment of Fig. 6, during the tetanus, there was a roughly 50% decline in mPSP amplitude from a mean 0.73 ± 0.25 to a mean of 0.38 ± 0.14 mV. However, the mPSPs could never be reduced in amplitude by more than this amount. The observed reduction in mPSP amplitude is certainly not adequate to explain the reduction in PSP amplitude given the high quantum number implied by the observed absence of failures (five or more). Within a few seconds after the tetanus the mean mPSP size increased slightly to 0.51 ± 0.17 mV, but time for complete recovery to control amplitude was not measured. There is no increase in the number of small mPSPs during recovery from a tetanus.

The miniatures that persist when the PSPs have become very small may have several origins. An important property is that tight coupling between depolarization and secretion of mPSPs is not present, since mPSPs are not preferentially released during the PSP but instead occur more or less at

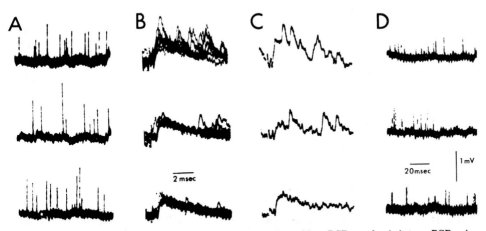

Fig. 5. Effect of prolonged tetanic stimulation on giant fiber PSPs and miniature PSPs. A: spontaneous miniature PSPs. B: PSP evoked by continuous Mauthner fiber stimulation at 20/sec. Top traces were recorded at beginning of tetanus, middle traces after one minute and bottom traces after several minutes. Note progressive decrease in number of miniature PSPs from top to bottom (5—10 superimposed traces). C: same as B top to bottom except records are single traces. D: miniature PSPs immediately after cessation of tetanic stimulation.

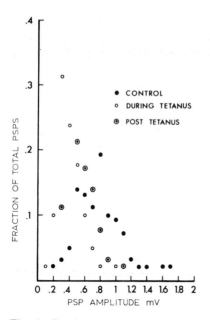

Fig. 6. Graph of the amplitude distribution of the miniature PSPs before, during and after a tetanus. The ordinate is the fraction of the total number of miniature PSPs and the abscissa is the PSP amplitude in mV. Data are from the same experiment illustrated in Fig. 5.

random during the tetanic stimulation cycle. This difference suggests a different mechanism of release and presumably different release sites that are relatively voltage insensitive. In support of this explanation electron microscopy reveals occasional clusters of vesicles close to the surface membrane in otherwise depleted synapses (Model et al., 1975). These regions might be slowly releasing vesicles relatively unaffected by the impulse activity. In this case the persistence of miniatures would be irrelevant to the question of desensitization. If, however, the persistent mPSPs are generated at the same sites as the evoked PSPs, their persistence at near normal size excludes desensitization as a mechanism of the PSP reduction. Desensitization predicts a gradual but pronounced decrease in the size of the mPSPs as PSP amplitude becomes greatly reduced. Where mPSPs are greatly reduced in frequency by tetanic stimulation, one expects that the mPSPs are arising close to the evoked PSPs. Whether the sites are close enough together to involve the same postsynaptic receptors is uncertain. Relative independence of evoked PSPs and mPSPs is also observed at the neuromuscular junction. There are several treatments that have a differential effect upon the quantal content of the PSP and the mPSP frequency. For example, hyperosmolarity has little effect on the quantal content of the PSP while the mPSP frequency increases markedly (Furshpan, 1956). Furthermore, the increase in miniature frequency that occurs with tetanic stimulation persists in high magnesium-low calcium solutions that completely block the PSP (Hurlbut et al., 1971).

RECOVERY OF PSPs FROM TETANIC STIMULATION

If a tetanus is terminated PSP amplitude recovers rapidly. Generally after a tetanus a 1 sec rest allows recovery of the PSP to where it initiates an impulse. To explore the recovery process, trains of stimuli were given at varying rates that were selected to allow partial recovery between trains. The PSP evoked by the first stimulus in the train was then studied for variability in amplitude, which allows one to infer quantal size. Such an experiment is illustrated in Fig. 7. When the train was repeated at 1/sec the amplitude of the first PSP in the train showed considerable variability. On the assumption that the amplitudes are distributed according to Poisson statistics we calculated quantal content and quantal size from the coefficient of

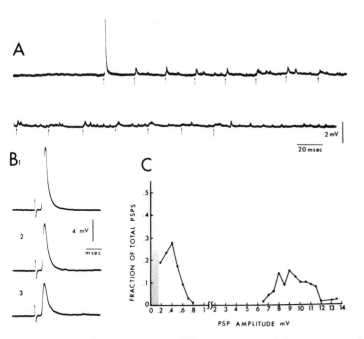

Fig. 7. Giant fiber PSPs evoked by long train stimuli. A: a sample of PSPs and miniature PSPs evoked by a train of 15 stimuli at 25 msec intervals. The train was repeated at 1/sec intervals until a 'steady state' depletion of transmitter was achieved. B: 1, 2 and 3 are the first PSP in the train viewed at a faster sweep speed. C: a normalized amplitude distribution of the miniature PSPs and the first PSP in the train repeated at 1/sec. Cross-hatching on the ordinate indicates the baseline noise in the recording system.

variation and mean amplitude. This calculated quantal amplitude agreed with the amplitude of the spontaneous mPSPs observed simultaneously. This agreement suggests that the Poisson statistics were applicable and that at this interval between stimuli the quantal size had recovered fully. As the train was repeated more frequently the spontaneous mPSP size remained unchanged but the PSP amplitude decreased. The calculated quantal content of the first PSP decreased as the intertrain interval decreased while quantal size remained unchanged at relatively long intertrain intervals. When the intertrain interval was about 400 msec calculated quantal size began to be smaller than mPSP amplitude in this case. The reduced quantal size in the PSP can be accounted for by depletion of the vesicular store of transmitter and subsequent release of the contents of incompletely filled vesicles. Thus determined in this experiment, 400 msec seems to be the minimum recovery time for the depleted preparation to release 'normal size' quanta of transmitter.

Since the PSPs can be evoked at intervals of less than 10 msec without failures, the rate limiting step in transmission appears to be the time for filling the vesicles rather than the time for their formation and movement to the release site. The 0.4 sec recovery time appears to be primarily occupied with filling of the vesicle. Since at higher frequencies of stimulation small quanta can be released, it appears that release can interrupt the filling process. If so, it follows that filling actually occurs at the release site. This idea is supported by observations that acetylcholine released by physiological stimuli is enriched in recently synthesized material (Collier, 1969; Barker et al., 1972; Birks and Fitch, 1974; Chakrin et al., 1972). We imagine that in a tetanus a vesicle is filled and immediately released. However, in the recovery period, newly filled vesicles could move to the center of the terminal for storage and subsequent release. The rapid filling inferred from the recovery may account for the failure to observe small mPSPs when PSP amplitude is reduced and during recovery. If the time to fill a vesicle is short compared to its average life before release as an mPSP, then small mPSPs will be very rare.

LONG-TERM EFFECTS OF TETANIC STIMULATION

The morphological data (Model et al., 1975) indicate that over one hour is required for full recovery of the vesicle population. Although the response to low frequency stimulation (1/sec) recovers within a second or two after a tetanus to the level required to initiate impulses, there is a much more persistent decrement to short trains of stimuli. In one experiment, a train of three stimuli at 20 msec intervals was employed. The train was repeated once per second and mean amplitudes for the second and third PSPs in the train were obtained. The first PSP was suprathreshold under these conditions. Then the train was repeated at 10/sec for 10 min in order to reduce

PSP amplitude to a low level and to deplete the synapse of vesicles (Model et al., 1975). Recovery was tested by applying the train 100 times at 1/sec after 15, 30 and 45 min. The second and third PSPs recovered to their control amplitudes in 45 min. This slow recovery correlates with the slow recovery of the vesicle population observed morphologically.

In summary, we have demonstrated a correlation between physiologically observed depression of quantum size and morphologically demonstrated depletion of synaptic vesicles. We infer that there is a mobilizable store of transmitter which is quite easily depleted by tetanic stimulation of the Mauthner fiber and that subsequent Mauthner fiber stimuli then release subnormal sized quanta. We propose that the small quanta are due to the release of the contents of partially filled vesicles. Partially filled vesicles could arise in at least two ways. For the release of transmitter the vesicles could fuse with the surface membrane in the process of exocytosis. As proposed for the neuromuscular junction, this membrane could be reclaimed in coated vesicles and reformed into smooth vesicles by passage through cisternae (Heuser and Reese, 1973). These new vesicles would at some point have their transmitter added to them. If they were released prior to complete filling, quantal size would be reduced. The morphological observations of depletion of vesicles support this explanation. Alternatively, vesicles might release their transmitter by merely transient contact with the surface membrane and maintenance of their vesicular form. If they went through subsequent release events prior to complete refilling, quantal size would be reduced. The morphological observations of depletion clearly indicate that exocytosis occurs. However, it may not occur with every release event and a combined mechanism is possible.

At the neuromuscular junction reduction in quantal size has been observed after relatively high frequency stimulation (Cooke and Quastel, 1973; Kriebel and Gross, 1974), and after prolonged stimulation that depletes the ending of transmitter (Ceccarelli et al., 1973; Elmquist and Quastel, 1965).

An uncertainty remains in the quantal hypothesis as to the number of vesicles that constitute a quantum. A single quantum could represent the release of a number of vesicles, such as all those occupying release sites in a single 'active zone' (Wernig, 1975; Zucker, 1973). Small mPSPs can be recorded at the neuromuscular junction after exhaustive stimulation and it has been suggested that the usual large mPSPs result from multiple release of the small components (Kriebel and Gross, 1974). The hatchetfish results suggest that partially filled vesicles could also underlie the small mPSPs, although in our system the rapid filling inferred from the time course of recovery allows the contents of partially filled vesicles to be released only rarely to generate spontaneous mPSPs.

The combined physiological and morphological data support the view that vesicles are lost in the release process and their membrane is recycled to form new vesicles. In addition, one can obtain a measure of the time

134

required to fill newly formed vesicles. The filling process appears accessible for study because new vesicles can be so rapidly formed that adding transmitter is the rate limiting step. The observations reported here allow a further elaboration on the hypotheses of quantal release and membrane recycling in specifying the time and site of addition of transmitter.

REFERENCES

Auerbach, A.A. (1971) Spontaneous and evoked quantal transmitter release at a vertebrate control synapse. Nature (Lond.), 234, 181—183.
Auerbach, A.A. and Bennett, M.V.L. (1969a) Chemically mediated transmission at a giant fiber synapse in the central nervous system of a vertebrate. J. gen. Physiol., 53, 183—210.
Auerbach, A.A. and Bennett, M.V.L. (1969b) A rectifying electrotonic synapse in the central nervous system of a vertebrate. J. gen. Physiol., 53, 211—237.
Barker, L.A., Dowdall, M.J. and Whittaker, V.P. (1972) Choline metabolism in the central cortex of guinea pigs. J. Biochem., 130, 1063—1080.
Birks, R.I. and Fitch, S.J.G. (1974) Storage and release of acetylcholine in a sympathetic ganglion. J. Physiol. (Lond.), 240, 125—134.
Ceccarelli, B., Hurlbut, W.P. and Mauro, A. (1973) Turnover of transmitter and synaptic vesicles at the frog neuromuscular junction. J. Cell Biol., 57, 499—524.
Chakrin, L.W., Marchbanks, R.M., Mitchell, J.F. and Whittaker, V.P. (1972) The origin of acetylcholine released from the surface of the cortex. J. Neurochem., 19, 2727—2736.
Collier, B. (1969) The preferential release of newly synthesized transmitter by a sympathetic ganglion. J. Physiol. (Lond.)., 205, 341—352.
Cooke, J.D. and Quastel, D.M.J. (1973) Transmitter release by mammalian motor nerve terminals in response to focal polarization. J. Physiol. (Lond.), 228, 377—405.
Elmqvist, D. and Quastel, D.M.J. (1965) Presynaptic action of hemicholinium at the neuromuscular junction. J. Physiol. (Lond.), 177, 463—482.
Furshpan, E.J. (1956) The effects of osmotic pressure changes on the spontaneous activity at motor nerve endings. J. Physiol. (Lond.), 134, 689—697.
Heuser, J.E. and Reese, T.S. (1973) Evidence for recycling of synaptic vesicle membrane during transmitter release at the frog neuromuscular junction. J. Cell Biol., 57, 315—344.
Highstein, S.M. and Bennett, M.V.L. (1975) Stimulation fatigue and recovery of the Mauthner fiber, giant fiber synapse of hatchetfish. Brain Res., 98, 229—242.
Hurlbut, W.P., Longenecker, H.B., Jr. and Mauro, A. (1971) Effects of calcium and magnesium on the frequency of miniature end plate potentials during prolonged tetanization. J. Physiol. (Lond.), 219, 17.
Kriebel, M.E. and Gross, C. (1974) Multimodal distribution of frog miniature endplate potentials in adult, denervated, and tadpole leg muscles. J. gen. Physiol., 64, 85—104.
Model, P.G., Spira, M.E. and Bennett, M.V.L. (1972) Synaptic inputs to the cell bodies of the giant fibers of the hatchetfish. Brain Res., 45, 288—295.
Model, P.G., Highstein, S.M. and Bennett, M.V.L. (1975) Depletion of vesicles and fatigue of transmission at a vertebrate central synapse. Brain Res., 98, 209—228.
Spira, M.E., Model, P.G. and Bennett, M.V.L. (1970) Cholinergic transmission at a vertebrate central synapse. J. Cell Biol., 47, 199a—200.
Wernig, A. (1975) Estimates of statistical release parameters from crayfish and frog neuromuscular junctions. J. Physiol. (Lond.), 244, 207—221.

Zucker, R.S. (1973) Changes in the statistics of transmitter release during facilitation. J. Physiol. (Lond.), 787—810.

DISCUSSION

GILMAN: I want to ask you about the behavior of the hatchetfish, and the cells you are involved in. During natural behavior of the hatchetfish, at what frequency will the cells fire?

HIGHSTEIN: Well, the fins can move at great frequency, but with the escape reflex it is hard to elicit more than 3 or 4 of them in a given period of time. You can elicit the reflex by banging on the tail, but we cannot tell what the mechanism is. Certainly, the natural frequency of discharge of cells is very low.

DESIRAJU: I think this is an excellent demonstration of depletion of vesicles during synaptic transmission activity. You know there is another concept. Many people have tried to see the depletion of vesicles at active synapses and they have not found it. Your data, on the contrary, is quite clear. However, I would like you to comment on what kind of transmitter these vesicles may contain. This could be one of the reasons why you found such a nice result.

HIGHSTEIN: It appears to be a cholinergic synapse, and we have not done the critical experiment which is the iontophoresing of acetylcholine and measuring the reversal potential at the postsynaptic side. The fact that it is depletable is probably related to the phasic nature of transmission. Other preparations, such as *Torpedo*, have a depletable synapse and some neuromuscular junctions are really depletable. So, I suspect that vesicle depletion is due to the nature of transmission rather than what is in the vesicles.

BENNETT: I think one other point is important for the present discussion. The synapse, once it works, may not be used again for another hour. So there is a long-term change in responsiveness which one can see with a short train of stimuli, and this has the morphological correlate in the depletion of the vesicles.

DESIRAJU: In other words, in your view this synapse has probably evolved for very slow rates of activity, and if you quickly repeat to press the tail it just cannot escape again quickly. The reason why you have found such a rapid depletion or a slow recovery is that it is only meant for occasional usage.

HIGHSTEIN: Actually I know of at least two cases of abnormally large quanta of transmitter with abnormally large synaptic vesicles which show depletion.

PURPURA: I think, on the other hand, when you look at the synapses in the central nervous system of the mammal, they have a fantastic capacity to carry information. You look at the wrong names to find an analogy. Everybody has looked at the lateral geniculate which is a nice place to look at and if you stimulate as fast in the monkey or in the cat you can well get transmission and what it finally goes down is, the vesicles are still there, the possibility of very fast recovery much more than slow recovery during the indefinite fixation.

BENNETT: You are comparing a mammal.

PURPURA: You are in the spectrum! Yes, that is in the ultraviolet range and this is in the infrared area in the spectrum of synapses.

PHILLIPS: This is such a nice big fiber that it might be interesting to find whether re-synthesis comes down from the soma or whether it is taken up as transmitter from the outside.

BENNETT: In order to have an uptake you have to have peripheral recycling of membranes. We don't really know; it is hard to evaluate, as far as the axonal flow is concerned. The vesicles are probably made from endoplasmic reticulum. Until we are able to get peroxidase data, we can not answer this question.

HIGHSTEIN: Probably the release and reclamation of the membrane would also enhance the appearance of depletion.

DESIRAJU: You can use some of the blockers of acetylcholine, for example, hemi-cholinium, if it is a cholinergic synapse. Then you can use this information for extra-polation.

HIGHSTEIN: Yes, that is in the work.

8

MODULATION OF THE TRANSMISSION OF PAINFUL MESSAGES AT THE SPINAL LEVEL

JEAN-MARIE BESSON and GISELE GUILBAUD

Université Pierre et Marie Curie (Paris VI), Laboratoire de Physiologie des Centres Nerveux, 75016 Paris (France)

INTRODUCTION

During the last several years, a great number of electrophysiological studies have considered the properties of dorsal horn interneurons of the spinal cord and their possible implication in pain mechanisms. If we consider in the cat the anatomical division of the spinal cord, as proposed by Rexed (1952) on cytoarchitectonic criteria, three layers have been considered to be the best candidates for the transmission of painful messages: laminae I, V, and VII—VIII.

In the cat, some laminae VII—VIII cells are at the origin of the spinoreticulothalamic (Levante and Albe-Fessard, 1972) or spinothalamic tract (Trevino et al., 1972); but more information is needed, especially concerning the properties of their peripheral receptive fields, the type of their afferent inputs and the control of the transmission at their level, to have a clear idea of their implication in pain processes.

Lamina I cells, first described in the cat by Christensen and Perl (1970) are of special interest since they are only activated by slowly conducting myelinated fibers (Aδ) and/or unmyelinated C fibers. Similar properties of lamina I cells have been found in the monkey by Trevino et al. (1973), Willis et al. (1974) and Price and Mayer (1974) who mentioned that these cells are activated by intense mechanical or noxious stimulation. Moreover, some lamina I cells are at the origin of spinothalamic tract neurons in the monkey (Trevino et al., 1973; Willis et al., 1974). But, if afferent inhibition has been described on lamina I cells (Christensen and Perl, 1970), no information has been obtained at the present time about the modulation of the transmission of these cells. For this reason, in this paper, devoted to the modulation of the transmission of nociceptive messages at the spinal cord level, we will only consider lamina V cells which have very particular electrophysiological properties, and which are strongly modulated by spinal and supraspinal mechanisms.

(I) CHARACTERISTICS OF LAMINA V CELLS

Since the 'gate control theory' was stated by Melzack and Wall (1965), many studies have dealt with the properties of dorsal horn interneurons.

On one hand, anatomical studies (Szentágothai, 1964; Ralston, 1965 and 1968; Scheibel and Scheibel, 1968; Rethelyi and Szentágothai, 1969) have underlined the great complexity of the synaptic organization in this area; on the other hand, electrophysiological data have been used to describe their characteristics. From the literature, it is difficult to give a general electrophysiological picture of dorsal horn interneurons admitted by all the authors. In order to give a schematic description, we have considered electrophysiological data observed by Wall and coworkers (Mendell, 1966; Wall, 1967; Pomeranz et al., 1968; Hillman and Wall, 1969) when recording the responses of dorsal horn cells to natural peripheral cutaneous stimulation. Their studies, which are based on the differentiation between laminae IV and V cells, have been confirmed by several authors. Nevertheless, we must mention that there is not always a strict correlation between anatomical locations and electrophysiological properties (especially at the boundaries between laminae IV and V and between laminae V and VI).

Lamina IV-type cells are driven by low intensity stimuli (movement of hairs, light touch) applied within a highly restricted peripheral receptive field. Descent into lamina V is accompanied by an important increase in size of the receptive field and the appearance of a threshold gradient between the field's center and periphery; low intensity stimuli are effective in the center while more intense stimuli (pinch, pressure, pin-prick) are necessary at the periphery. Fig. 1B illustrates a typical response of lamina V to the application of an intense pinch. The discharge frequency of lamina V cells is generally in direct relation to peripheral stimulus strength (Wall, 1967; Hillman and Wall, 1969; Wagman and Price, 1969). Lamina V cells are also activated by noxious heat in the cat (Price and Browe, 1973) and the monkey (Willis et al., 1974) and by intense electrical stimulation (Fig. 1A) applied into the peripheral cutaneous receptive field. Cutaneous nerve stimulation has shown that lamina V cells have convergent properties (Mendell, 1966; Wagman and Price, 1969; Price and Wagman, 1970; Gregor and Zimmermann, 1972). They are activated by large diameter fibers, but also by $A\delta$ and unmyelinated C fibers; the responses increase as a function of stimulus intensity.

The frequency and the duration of their discharge, evoked by unmyelinated fibers, are enhanced with each successive stimulus, when the stimulating rate is greater than one every 2—3 sec (Mendell, 1966; Wagman and Price, 1969; Price and Wagman, 1970). This phenomenon, termed 'wind up' by Mendell (1966) has been confirmed by intracellular recording which showed long-term postsynaptic facilitatory responses elicited by small fiber inputs (Price et al., 1971).

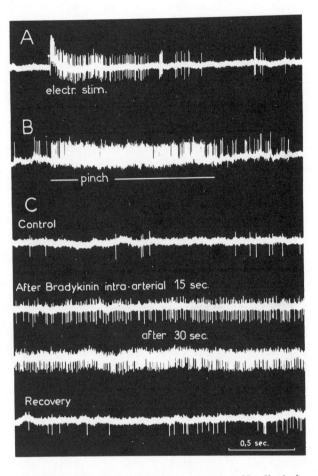

Fig. 1. Activation of three lumbar lamina V cells, induced by intense stimulation applied in the peripheral receptive field (electrical stimulation in A, strong pinch in B), or by an intra-arterial injection of bradykinin in the posterior limb (in C).

These facilitatory effects during repetitive stimulation are consistent with clinical experiments in which repetitive stimulation at 3/sec was required to produce a painful stimulus (Collins and Nulsen, 1962). They also agree with recent experiments of Price (1972) in which the characteristics of second pain obtained in human subjects are compared with the characteristics of flexion reflex elicited in spinal cats, by using percutaneous electrical shocks; second pain and flexion reflex were both increased with each successive shock, when shock frequencies exceeded 0.3/sec.

Along with the convergence of various cutaneous afferents on lamina V cells, a convergence of visceral and cutaneous inputs on lamina V cells

140

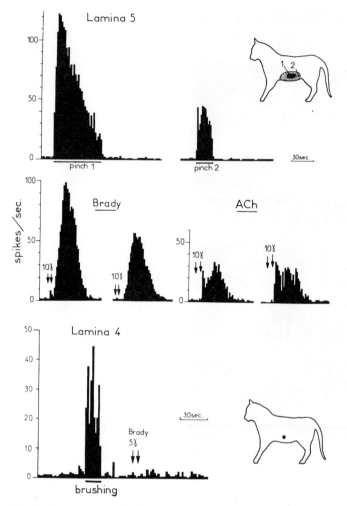

Fig. 2. Successive activations of a thoracic lamina V cell by pinches applied in the center (1) or at the edges (2) of the peripheral cutaneous field, and by bradykinin or acetylcholine injections into the superior mesenteric artery. Activation by brushing of a thoracic lamina IV cell which is not affected by the nociceptive visceral stimulation.

has also been observed at the lumbar level by stimulation of the sympathetic chain (Selzer and Spencer, 1969) and at the thoracic level by splanchnic nerve stimulation (Pomeranz et al., 1968). This important finding could explain the referral of visceral pain to the skin. Finally, in a comparative study of laminae IV and V cells (Besson et al., 1972), by using the intra-arterial injection of pain producing substance (bradykinin) into the posterior limbs, we found, at the lumbar level, that this drug preferentially modified the activity of lamina V cells (Fig. 1C). Injections of this substance and acetylcholine in the superior mesenteric artery have also strongly affected the activity of lamina V cells recorded at the thoracic level. We must emphasize the fact that these cells were also activated by stimulation of a large peripheral cutaneous field. On the contrary, always at this thoracic level, lamina IV cells, with a small receptive field, were not affected by pain-producing substances (Fig. 2) (Benelli et al., 1974).

From a psychophysiological point of view, it is interesting to note that the latency and the duration of the modifications induced by bradykinin on lamina V cells are of the same order as the latencies and the durations of

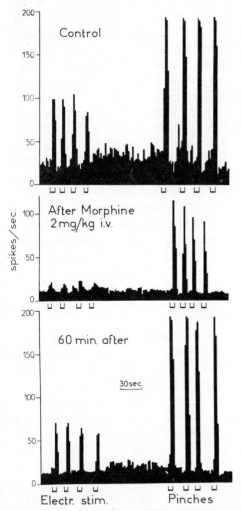

Fig. 3. Depressive action of morphine upon lamina V cell response, evoked by pinch or electrical stimulation.

painful sensations and nociceptive manifestations induced in man and animal by injection of this drug (see ref. in Lim, 1968).

From the pharmacological point of view, it must be mentioned that lamina V cell activities are extremely sensitive to anesthetics (Kitahata et al., 1971) and depressed by morphine and its derivatives (Fig. 3); these depressive effects are specific since they are immediately reversed by the injection of an opiate antagonist (Conseiller et al., 1972; Besson et al., 1973; Le Barst et al., 1974b).

Concerning the ascending projections of lamina V cells, several studies have shown that some lamina V cells are the cells of origin of the spino-cervical tract in cats (Taub and Bishop, 1965; Fetz, 1968; Hongo et al., 1968; Bryan et al., 1973) and in monkeys (Bryan et al., 1974). Dilly et al. (1968) found, in cats, that some lamina V cells of the cervical cord send their axons in the spinothalamic tract. However, they did not observe antidromic activation of these cells at the lumbar level by the same central stimulation. The same negative observations at the lumbar level have resulted from thalamic and reticular stimulations (Trevino et al., 1972; Levante and Albe-Fessard, 1972). This may be due to the existence of a polysynaptic pathway between lamina V cells and the contralateral ascending tract. Nevertheless, in the monkey, there is no doubt that some lamina V lumbar cells are at the origin of the spinothalamic tract (Levante et al., 1973; Trevino et al., 1973; Albe-Fessard et al., 1974; Willis et al., 1974).

As initially suggested by Wall, all these numerous electrophysiological data argue in favor of a role of lamina V cells in the integration of pain messages at the spinal level and in the transmission of these messages to the brain. Moreover, the activities of these cells are under the influences of controls of spinal and supraspinal origin. These controls are discussed in the following sections.

(II) SPINAL CONTROLS

(1) In 1965, Melzack and Wall proposed the 'gate control theory' as a model to relate the input-output functions of the dorsal horn to explain the phenomena of pain. In this hypothesis, the transmission on 'trigger cells' (system responsible for pain experience) would be continuously presynaptically modulated by interneurons located in the substantia gelatinosa of Rolando; the inhibitory effects exerted by these interneurons would be increased by stimulation of large afferent fibers and decreased by the activation of small fibers. As mentioned by Wall himself (1973): "the least and perhaps the best, that can be said for the 1965 paper is that it provoked discussion and experiment".

Inhibitory effects of large diameter fibers on responses of laminae V—VI cells have been demonstrated by various authors (Mendell, 1972; Wagman and Price, 1969; Price and Wagman, 1970; Gregor and Zimmermann, 1972;

Brown et al., 1973b). Due to the lack of intracellular recordings there is no direct evidence about the nature of this inhibition. But the fact that the time course of this inhibition corresponds to the time course of the negative (inhibitory) component of the dorsal root potential, or to the time course of the primary afferent depolarization, suggests that the inhibition evoked by A fibers' activity, is, in part at least, due to presynaptic mechanisms. The role of large afferent fibers in the modulation of pain has been confirmed by some clinical applications; for example, some forms of intractable pain have been suppressed by peripheral stimulation of low threshold afferents (Wall and Sweet, 1967; Meyer and Fields, 1972). Furthermore, Hillman and Wall (1969) have shown that dorsal column stimulation in spinal cats depressed the responses of lamina V cells to nociceptive stimulation. This inhibition could be explained by the fact that large diameter fibers ascending in dorsal columns send collaterals into the dorsal horn. In man, dorsal column stimulation has been successful in the treatment of severe chronic pain (Shealy et al., 1970; Friedman et al., 1974). In this case, direct spinal mechanisms may be involved, but it is also possible that this kind of stimulation activates supraspinal structures which are at the origin of descending control systems (see next section, and Brown et al., 1973c).

The hypothesis of a presynaptic facilitatory role of small fibers is still sharply discussed. This hypothesis has been advanced from an experiment showing the appearance of a positive (facilitatory) dorsal root potential or of a primary afferent hyperpolarization after selective stimulation of C fibers (Mendell and Wall, 1964). This result was confirmed by stimulation of various types of thin afferent fibers (Dawson et al., 1970; Mendell, 1970; Dubner and Sessle, 1971; Young and King, 1972; Price and Wagman, 1973). But other workers found negative dorsal root potentials only by selective C fiber stimulation (Zimmermann, 1968; Franz and Iggo, 1968; Janig and Zimmermann, 1971) and by noxious cutaneous stimuli (Vyklický et al., 1969). Nevertheless, Hodge (1972) found a presynaptic hyperpolarization of some large diameter afferent fibers by stimulation of small cutaneous and muscle fibers. This hyperpolarization is simultaneously associated with a facilitation of the responses of some spinocervical tract neurons. But this author pointed out that this hyperpolarization cannot explain the entire facilitation of afferent input.

In a detailed study of the presynaptic afferent hyperpolarization phenomenon, Mendell (1972) revealed that flexor reflex afferent stimulation mainly induced presynaptic hyperpolarization in proprioceptive afferents and primary afferent depolarization in cutaneous afferents. This finding does not support the existence of a presynaptic facilitation of the transmission of cutaneous messages by the stimulation of small cutaneous afferent fibers.

By a very sophisticated method, using single unit recording to examine the changes in polarization of afferent fibers, Whitehorn and Burgess (1973)

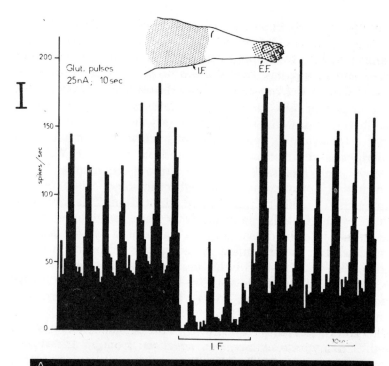

I

Glut. pulses
25 nA; 10 sec

spikes/sec

200

150

100

50

0

I.F.

E.F.

I.F.

30 sec

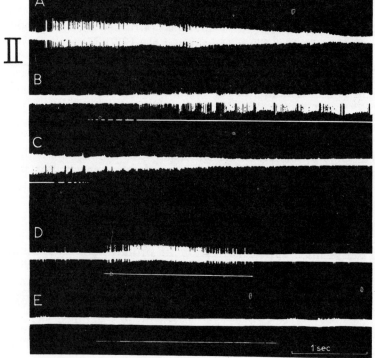

II

A

B

C

D

E

1 sec

were unable to find presynaptic hyperpolarization during nociceptive stimulations. Moreover, they mentioned that central terminals of any particular fiber type are depolarized mainly by activity arising in that same type of fiber.

From all these results, it appears that there is no clear evidence of a presynaptic facilitation due to C fibers as initially proposed in the gate control theory. In fact, Brown et al. (1973b) did not find any action of C fiber input in conditioning an A fiber discharge of the spinocervical tract.

(2) Stimulation of the largest A fibers produces an initial burst of excitation, followed by a prolonged inhibition, and we have seen that this inhibition is generally attributed to presynaptic inhibition. Nevertheless, several studies have demonstrated postsynaptic inhibitory effects. From intracellular recordings of spinocervical tract cells, Hongo et al. (1968) described a convergence of monosynaptic excitatory postsynaptic potentials and of disynaptic inhibitory postsynaptic potentials evoked from the same afferent system originating in hair receptors. IPSPs were also evoked by light natural stimulation from a relatively small receptive field which was closely related to the excitatory one, but not of the surround type. Some sequences of EPSPs followed by a long duration IPSP (50—250 msec) were also described by Price et al. (1971) when stimulating both A and C fibers. However, as mentioned by Hongo et al. (1968), it seems difficult to definitely reject the role of presynaptic inhibition in these phenomena, since Janig et al. (1968) and, more recently, Whitehorn and Burgess (1973) described a high degree of specificity of primary afferent depolarization evoked in the central terminals of cutaneous afferents.

EPSP-IPSP sequences were also obtained in spinocervical tract neurons by stimulation of the flexion reflex afferents (Hongo et al., 1968). But in this case the afferents were driven from very large receptive fields. This must be drawn in parallel with the fact that several authors have reported that lamina V cells often present an extensive inhibitory field, mainly located in the ipsi- or contralateral proximal part of the limb. By using an iontophoretic approach we demonstrated the postsynaptic nature of this inhibition (Besson et al., 1974). As shown in Fig. 4,I, chemical discharges induced by glutamate are strongly depressed by natural stimulation applied within the inhibitory recep-

Fig. 4. Postsynaptic effects on lamina V cells induced by stimulation within the inhibitory receptive field (IF) (EF, excitatory receptive field). I: activations provoked by glutamate application are strongly depressed by natural stimulation within the IF. II. A: neuronal firing of a lamina V cell induced by a continuous injection of 110 nA of glutamate with final firing blockage by excessive depolarization. B and C: glutamate injection was maintained and the firing restored (B) by stimulation of the IF (horizontal lines); renewal of firing blockage (C) when stimulation of IF is withdrawn. D and E: test of natural stimulation in the EF in the absence of glutamate injection (D) and during a sequence of excessive depolarization (E). (From Besson et al., 1974.)

tive field. Since it is generally well admitted that intense firing induced by glutamate does not result from a direct action of this substance on endings or neurons' fibers, this fact indicates that this inhibition might act postsynaptically on lamina V-type neurons. This is confirmed by another type of observation (Fig. 4,II), where we considered the effects of natural stimulation within the inhibitory field when the neuron was excessively depolarized by a continuous administration of high doses of glutamate; in this case natural stimulation within the inhibitory field restored the firing of the cell. A similar result was obtained by Zieglgänsberger and Herz (1971) on some SCT neurons. These two observations argue in favor of the postsynaptic nature of this inhibition.

All of the data presented in this section show that the transmission of cutaneous messages on dorsal horn cells, especially lamina V cells, is strongly modulated at the segmental level by presynaptic and postsynaptic controls. More precise evidence is required to clearly understand the role of each and their respective implication in the pain process itself. Nevertheless, there is no doubt about the existence of a balanced inhibition-facilitation mechanism. There can be no doubt of the inhibitory role of large fibers and the existence of a facilitatory mechanism, which might be due to prolonged excitatory postsynaptic effects of small fibers (see wind-up).

(III) DESCENDING CONTROLS ON LAMINA V CELLS

As initially demonstrated by Hagbarth and Kerr (1954) and Hagbarth and Fex (1959), the transmission of cutaneous impulses at the spinal cord level is strongly influenced by cortical and brain stem descending controls.

(1) Controls of cortical origin

Several investigations have shown that stimulation of different cortical areas induces presynaptic inhibition at the spinal cord level. In cats, these cortical regions included SI, SII, motor (precruciate) cortex (Andersen et al., 1962 and 1964; Carpenter et al., 1963) and orbital cortex (Abdelmoumène et al., 1970). These inhibitory effects were predominantly contralateral from SI, whereas the SII and orbital effects were bilateral. The stimulation of the SI (postcruciate) cortex is more effective than this of precruciate; but Andersen et al. (1964) and Morrison and Pompeiano (1965) have shown that the precruciate cortex is acting indirectly by stimulating the postcruciate. In a comparative study in the cat and the monkey, Abdelmoumène et al. (1970) found a topical organization of the descending presynaptic controls in the monkey while the organization is only of the preferential type in the cat. In the cat, these presynaptic descending effects are mainly mediated by the pyramidal tract (Andersen et al., 1964; Carpenter et al., 1963; Morrison and Pompeiano, 1965), but also by extrapyramidal pathways (Hongo and

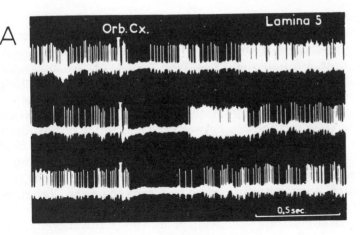

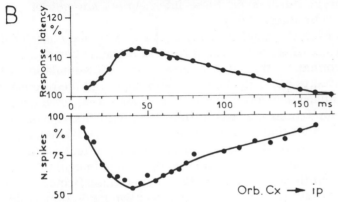

Fig. 5. A: inhibitory action by the stimulation of the orbital cortex (Orb. Cx.) upon the responses of a lamina V cell to strong pinch. B: curves illustrating the effects of conditional orbital cortex stimulation on the responses of lamina V cells to ipsilateral posterior limb stimulation; each point represents the mean value calculated for 28 cells of the same type. (From Wyon-Maillard et al., 1972.)

Jankowska, 1967). Presynaptic inhibition induced by corticospinal fibers is mediated via interneurons (D cells of Eccles et al., 1962 or interneurons described by Besson and Rivot, 1973) which could be involved in inhibitory axoaxonal synapses.

Direct evidence of descending cortical controls has been obtained by unitary recordings of dorsal horn interneurons. After the initial studies of Hagbarth and Fex (1959) and Andersen et al. (1964), detailed experiments have been performed by stimulating the pyramidal tract (Fetz, 1968) and the orbital cortex (Wyon-Maillard et al., 1972) (see Fig. 5). These two studies have shown that evoked and spontaneous activities of laminae IV and V cells were strongly inhibited by such stimulations. Stimulation of the pyramidal tract is inhibitory for 68% of lamina IV cells and for 39% of lamina V cells. This difference between the two laminae is also observed on stimulation of the orbital cortex since, in this case, 84% of lamina IV cells, but only 60% of lamina V cells are inhibited. The time course of the inhibitory effects (Fig. 5) corresponds to the time course of dorsal root potentials recorded at the lumbar level following pyramidal tract or orbital cortex stimulations. Moreover, in the study of the effects of orbital cortex we found that there is a clear relationship between the magnitude of the dorsal root potentials and the magnitude of the inhibition. These data suggest that these inhibitory effects are sustained by mechanisms of a presynaptic nature. Unfortunately, because of the small size of dorsal horn interneurons, we have little information about eventual postsynaptic mechanisms. Nevertheless, hyperpolarization of dorsal horn interneurons is only very infrequently obtained by pyramidal stimulation (Lundberg et al., 1962); this suggests that postsynaptic inhibitory influences on these interneurons are not of predominant importance (Lundberg, 1964).

Another recent study in the monkey (Coulter et al., 1974) has considered the effects of stimulation of sensorimotor cortex on the activities of spinothalamic neurons recorded at the lumbar level. Electrical stimulation of either pre- or postcentral gyrus in the hindlimb area depressed the responses of 14 of the 21 spinothalamic neurons. The affected cells were activated by light and intense stimulations applied within the peripheral cutaneous receptive field. An important finding of this study is that cortical stimulation is efficient on responses to weak stimulation and has no effect on slowly adapting responses to intense mechanical or thermal stimulation. This selectivity of effect is confirmed by the fact that the seven unaffected spinothalamic cells tended to have only high threshold receptive fields. Concerning the nature of these inhibitory effects, it is interesting to mention that the stimulation of the same hindlimb cortical area evoked dorsal root potentials at the lumbar level only (Abdelmoumène et al., 1970).

(2) Controls exerted from the brain stem

Initial studies have shown that stimulation of wide areas of the brain stem induced presynaptic inhibition of cutaneous afferent fibers, (Carpenter et al., 1962 and 1966; Taub, 1964; Chan and Barnes, 1972). Evidence for the role of the brain stem in the control of the transmission of cutaneous impulses through sensory interneurons in the dorsal horn has been provided by several studies. Taub (1964) found that electrical stimulation of the mesencephalic tegmentum and central pontobulbar core produced a constriction of the cutaneous receptive field of spinocervical tract units and also inhibited their spontaneous and evoked activities.

The influence of descending control systems originating in the brain stem have been investigated by considering the activity of a given spinal interneuron in both the decerebrate and spinal states. Temporary spinal state was obtained by a cold block of the cord.

Concerning lamina V cells, Wall (1967) observed, after reversible spinalization, an increase of their excitability in responses to peripheral stimuli and an expansion of their receptive fields. The same kind of study has been performed by Brown (1971) on spinocervical tract units. Although this author did not find size modifications of the excitatory receptive field, he reported very large increases of the spontaneous firing rate of the majority of units. He pointed out that the descending systems act particularly to inhibit responses to heavy pressure or pinch of the skin which excites receptors innervated by small fibers (Iggo, 1960; Burgess and Perl, 1967). Brown obtained similar results by considering responses to intense electrical stimulation since the descending control was more and more effective as the stimulus strength was raised. In another study, Brown et al. (1973) mentioned that stimulation of descending systems led to inhibition of C fiber evoked discharges in spinocervical tract neurons. In the same way, Zimmermann and Handwerker (1974) found that responses of dorsal horn cells to noxious heat only clearly appeared after spinal cord block. They pointed out that these descending effects especially modulated the responses to noxious heat since the discharges of neurons induced by mechanical skin stimulation were affected to a much lesser extent by the cold block. In a recent study (Le Bars et al., 1974a), we found that responses of lamina V-type cells to intraarterial injection of bradykinin were strongly inhibited by the descending system (Fig. 6). Indeed, excitatory effects of this substance were nonexistent or of minor importance in the decerebrate state while particularly intense in the temporary spinal state. These modifications are associated with a large increase of the spontaneous firing rate. Moreover, we observed that responses to light cutaneous stimulation were almost the same in both states. The pathways responsible for the tonic inhibition observed in the decerebrate cat remain to be described but they may include vestibulospinal and reticulospinal tracts (Brown et al., 1973a).

From all these data, it appears that the transmission of cutaneous messages at the spinal cord level is strongly modulated by supraspinal structures. Although more precise data are necessary, it seems that the control exerted by the somatosensory areas (SI, SII, motor cortex) acts preferentially upon responses elicited by weak stimulation (Fetz, 1968; Coulter et al., 1974). From a functional point of view, these cortical areas could be involved in a negative feedback loop, by controlling their own afferents (Towe and Zimmermann, 1962; Andersen et al., 1964). About the effects of orbital stimulation, which control not only responses to weak stimulation but also a high percentage of cells responding to intense stimulation (Wyon-Maillard et al., 1972), it must be pointed out that this area is preferentially activated by nociceptive cutaneous stimuli conveyed by the spinocervical and neospinothalamic tracts (Korn et al., 1966); moreover, it also receives

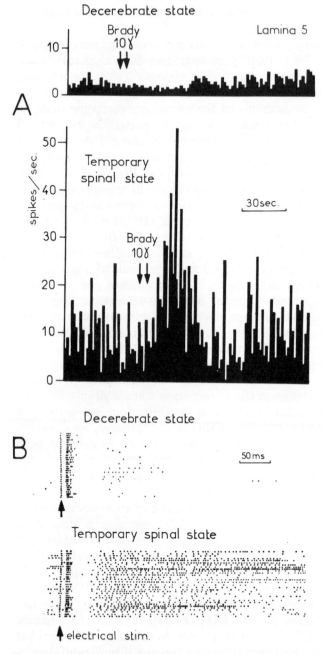

Fig. 6. A: effects on lamina V cells of intra-arterial injection of bradykinin, in decerebrate and temporary spinal state. B: responses of a lamina V cell to a strong electrical stimulation; note the weak reponse of the late component in the decerebrate state and its intense discharge during the spinal state.

vagal (Massion et al., 1966) and splanchnic afferents (Korn, 1969).

By contrast to the somatomotor cortex, we have seen that controls exerted from the brain stem seem to be particularly efficient upon responses to intense stimulation (pinch, C fiber stimulation, noxious heat and brady-kinin).

All these electrophysiological data showing the important role of the brain stem in controlling the transmission of nociceptive messages at the spinal level are reinforced by recent behavioral and pharmacological studies which emphasize the fact that there exists in the brain stem a neural system which functions in the inhibition of pain.

These studies concern the analgesia obtained by electrical stimulation of certain brain stem areas (especially the raphe nuclei) and also the modalities of morphine analgesia.

(IV) RELATIONSHIP BETWEEN ANALGESIA OBTAINED BY STIMULATION OF RAPHE NUCLEI AND MORPHINE ANALGESIA

(1) Preliminary observations from Reynolds (1969) that have shown, in the rat, that potent analgesia results from electrical stimulation in periaqueductal and periventricular structures, have been confirmed and extensively studied by Mayer et al. (1971). A recent study by Mayer and Liebeskind (1974), comparing in the rat the effects of electrical stimulation in several different brain areas, emphasizes the fact that only stimulation of the mesencephalic central gray matter and periventricular gray matter greatly reduces or totally abolishes responsiveness to all noxious stimuli employed; moreover, these authors pointed out that the magnitude of this analgesia is equal to or greater than analgesia induced by 10 mg/kg of morphine. Our recent studies in cats (Liebeskind et al., 1973; Oliveras et al., 1974a; Redjemi et al., 1974) underline the role of the raphe nuclei in this type of analgesia.

Cats were chronically implanted with concentric bipolar electrodes aimed at various sites within or adjacent to the periaqueductal gray matter. Electrical stimulation within the periaqueductal gray matter induced powerful analgesia. Analgesia was tested by applying intense pinches.

As shown in Fig. 7, points from which analgesia was obtained were located in the ventral portion of the periaqueductal gray matter in the vicinity of the dorsal raphe nucleus; moreover, the most powerful effects were found with stimulation of sites very close to this nucleus. Sites at which stimulation provoked motor or emotional reactions are broadly distributed within the periaqueductal gray matter and the adjacent reticular formation and, in these cases, it was not possible to test for analgesia since these reactions were obtained by even low levels of central stimulation.

In another experimental approach (Oliveras et al., 1974b), we tried to quantify more precisely the intensity of the noxious stimulus and the

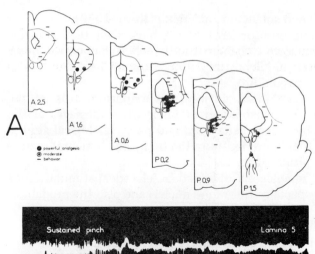

A

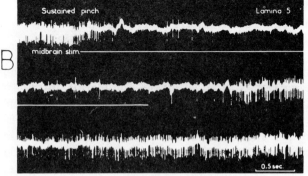

● powerful analgesia
◉ moderate
– behavior

B

Sustained pinch

Lamina 5

midbrain stim

0.5 sec.

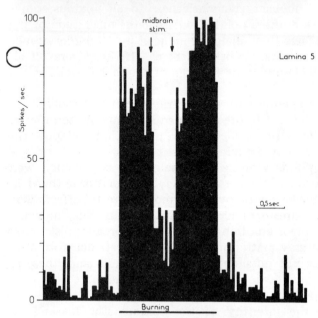

C

Spikes / sec

100

50

0

midbrain
stim.

Lamina 5

0,5 sec

Burning

magnitude of the analgesic effect by using, in the unrestrained cat, tooth pulp stimulation and by recording the jaw-opening reflex. Indeed, this procedure has several advantages since the tooth pulp is innervated solely by fibers of small diameter and its stimulation is thought to give rise to sensations of only a nociceptive nature.

A clear inhibition of the jaw-opening reflex induced by tooth pulp stimulation has been obtained by electrical stimulation at a number of sites in the midbrain of the cat. However, the nature of the inhibition varies as a function of the particular midbrain region stimulated. The maximum suppressive effects, those occurring at the shortest latencies and causing the largest increases in reflex threshold ($3-10 \times$ control threshold) have been found from stimulation of sites close to the dorsal raphe nuclei (DRN).

Thus, from all the data, it results that, in the cat the analgesic effects are only clearly observed from stimulation sites in the immediate vicinity of the DRN in the ventral portion of the periaqueductal gray matter while, by contrast, in the rat analgesic effects were obtained from a variety of sites distributed throughout the dorsal and ventral portions of the caudal periaqueductal gray matter (Mayer et al., 1971; Mayer and Liebeskind, 1974). So, there exists the possibility of an important interspecific difference between the cat and the rat. However, in the cat it is possible that aversive emotional and motor effects evoked by certain sites of stimulation prevented observation of analgesia.

Nevertheless, the role of the raphe nuclei, in general, in this type of analgesia seems to be prominent since, with similar experimental approaches, we have demonstrated (Redjemi et al., 1974) that the stimulation of other raphe nuclei (raphe magnus and raphe obscurus) also induced a potent analgesia.

To explain these analgesic effects we advanced the hypothesis that brain stimulation activates descending control systems which are involved in the modulation of the transmission of nociceptive impulses at the spinal cord level. In fact, we have seen (Section II) that several studies in acute preparations have clearly shown that the brain stem exerts powerful inhibitory controls at this level. In a second experimental approach we have studied, in acute preparations, the effects of the stimulation of the periaqueductal gray matter on the activity of dorsal horn interneurons and especially on lamina V-type cells. As shown in Fig. 7, midbrain stimulation strongly inhibited lamina V cell responses to noxious stimulation. On the contrary responses to innocuous stimuli were practically unaffected.

Fig. 7. A: schematic reconstruction of tips of all electrodes tested. (From stereotaxic atlas of Berman, 1968.) B and C: depressive effect of the midbrain stimulation upon the responses of lamina V cells to pinch (B) and burning (C). (Modified from Oliveras et al., 1974a.)

These results suggest that analgesia could, in part, be explained by descending inhibitory effects on dorsal horn interneurons. But we need additional experiments since the region from which inhibitory effects were seen on spinal cord interneurons was considerably more extensive than the region from which analgesic effects were obtained in the unrestrained cat. Inhibition of spinal interneurons by stimulation of DRN depends on the integrity of serotoninergic mechanisms. Indeed we have demonstrated (Guilbaud et al., 1973) that intravenous injection of LSD in the cat blocks the inhibition of lamina V-type cells deriving from stimulation points in the vicinity of the DRN, but not from points at a distance from this region. Although the mechanism of action of LSD is still uncertain, this finding can be understood by the known suppressive effect of this drug on the spontaneous activity of the serotonin-containing cell bodies of the DRN (Aghajanian et al., 1968).

In conclusion, serotoninergic mechanisms play an important part in the process of analgesia since, in the cat, pain suppression can be obtained by stimulation of various raphe nuclei (DRN, raphe magnus and raphe obscurus). These observations are supported by the fact that, in the rat (Akil and Mayer, 1972), injection of a serotonin synthesis inhibitor (p-chlorophenylalanine (pCPA)) strongly reduced the analgesic effect induced by stimulation of the ventral portion of the periaqueductal gray matter.

Moreover, as mentioned by several authors (Akil et al., 1972; Mayer and Liebeskind, 1974; Oliveras et al., 1974), there is a certain relationship between morphine analgesia and electrical analgesia obtained by midbrain stimulation.

(2) As in the electrical analgesia we have described, the analgesic effects of morphine seem to be in part sustained by serotoninergic mechanisms. Morphine analgesia is considerably decreased after the reduction of brain levels of serotonin by pCPA (Tenen, 1968; Lee and Fennessy, 1970; Görlitz and Frey, 1972; Vogt, 1974) and after electrolytic lesions of the DRN (Samanin et al., 1970). We have previously mentioned that, in the rat, electrical analgesia was also greatly reduced by pCPA (Akil and Mayer, 1972) and reappeared after administration of 5-hydroxytryptophan.

Moreover, direct proofs of an analogy between both types of analgesia have been advanced: in the rat, stimulation of the DRN greatly enhanced morphine analgesia (Samanin and Valzelli, 1971), in the same species administration of naloxone, a specific opiate antagonist, reduced analgesia induced by DRN stimulation (Akil et al., 1972).

In the cat we recently observed (Redjemi et al., 1974) that analgesia obtained by stimulation of raphe magnus and raphe obscurus was totally suppressed by naloxone administration.

Concerning the modalities of morphine sites of action, an hypothesis advanced by Takagi et al. (1955) and Satoh and Takagi (1971) suggested that this drug could enhance the activity of descending control systems and thereby reduce the transmission of nociceptive messages at the spinal level (see also experimental data using intracerebral injection of morphine (Herz et al., 1970; Tsou and Jang, 1964). As previously mentioned, we advanced the same hypothesis to explain electrical analgesia.

Although a direct effect of morphine and its derivatives on lamina V cells has been demonstrated in the spinal cat (Conseiller et al., 1971; Besson et al., 1973; Le Bars et al., 1974b), recent work from Vogt (1974) seems to confirm the hypothesis of Takagi and coworkers. Vogt (1974) used injection of 5,6-dihydroxytryptamine into a lateral ventricle. This drug considerably decreases the level of serotonin in the spinal cord without affecting serotonin content in the pons and medulla. After administration of this drug, the analgesic activity of low doses of morphine was considerably reduced. This experiment indicates that tryptaminergic descending impulses contribute to the analgesic effect of morphine.

In conclusion, the transmission of nociceptive messages at the spinal level is strongly modulated by spinal and descending controls. The existence of this latter type of control could explain some analgesics' effects.

REFERENCES

Abdelmoumène, M., Besson, J.M. and Aleonard, P. (1970) Cortical areas exerting presynaptic inhibitory action on the spinal cord in cat and monkey. Brain Res., 20, 327—329.

Aghajanian, G.K., Foote, W.E. and Sheard, M.H. (1968) Lysergic acid diethylamide: sensitive neuronal units in the midbrain raphe. Science, 161, 706—708.

Akil, H. and Mayer, D.J. (1972) Antagonism of stimulation-produced analgesia by p-CPA, a serotonin synthesis inhibitor. Brain Res., 44, 692—697.

Akil, H., Mayer, D.J. et Liebeskind, J.C. (1972) Comparaison chez le rat entre l'analgesie induite par stimulation de la substance grise periaqueducale et l'analgesie morphinique. C.R. Acad. Sci. (Paris), 274, 3603—3605.

Albe-Fessard, D., Levante, A. and Lamour, Y. (1974) Origin of spino-thalamic tract in monkeys. Brain Res., 65, 503—509.

Andersen, P., Eccles, J.C. and Sears, T.A. (1962) Presynaptic inhibitory action of cerebral cortex on spinal cord. Nature (Lond.), 194, 740—743.

Andersen, P., Eccles, J.C. and Sears, T.A. (1964) Cortically evoked depolarization of primary afferent fibers in the spinal cord. J. Neurophysiol., 27, 63—77.

Benelli, G.C., Besson, J.M., Guilbaud, G. et Lombard, M.C. (1974) Réponses des interneurones de la corne dorsale thoracique à des stimulations cutanées et à des stimulations viscérales nociceptives. J. Physiol. (Paris), 669, 221A.

Berman, A.L. (1968) The Brain Stem of the Cat: A Cytoarchitectonic Atlas with Stereotaxic Coordinates. Univ. of Wisconsin Press. Madison, Wisc.

Besson, J.M. and Rivot, J.P. (1973) Spinal interneurones involved in presynaptic controls of supraspinal origin. J. Physiol. (Lond.), 230, 235—254.

Besson, J.M., Conseiller, C., Hamann, K.F. and Maillard, M.C. (1972) Modifications of dorsal horn cell activities in the spinal cord after intraarterial injection of bradykinin. J. Physiol. (Lond.), 221, 189—205.

Besson, J.M., Wyon-Maillard, M.C., Benoist, J.M., Conseiller, C. and Hamann, K.F.

156

(1973) Effects of phenoperidine on lamina V cells in the cat dorsal horn. J. Pharmacol. exp. Ther., 187, 239—245.

Besson, J.M., Catchlove, R.F.H., Feltz, P. and Le Bars, D. (1974) Further evidence for postsynaptic inhibitions on lamina V dorsal interneurones. Brain Res., 66, 531—536.

Brown, A.G. (1971) Effects of descending impulses on transmission through the spino-cervical tract. J. Physiol. (Lond.), 219, 103—125.

Brown, A.G. and Martin, H.F. III (1973) Action of descending control of the spino-cervical tract by impulses ascending the dorsal column and relaying through the dorsal column nuclei. J. Physiol. (Lond.), 235, 535—550.

Brown, A.G., Hamann, W.C. and Martin, H.F. III (1973a) Descending influences on spino-cervical tract cell discharges evoked by non-myelinated cutaneous afferent nerve fibres. Brain Res., 53, 218—221.

Brown, A.G., Hamann, W.C. and Martin, H.F. III (1973b) Interactions of cutaneous mye-linated (A) and non-myelinated (C) fibres on transmission through the spinocervical tract. Brain Res., 53, 222—226.

Brown, A.G., Kirk, E.J. and Martin, H.F. (1973c) Descending and segmental inhibition of transmission through the spinocervical tract. J. Physiol. (Lond.), 230, 689—705.

Bryan, R.N., Trevino, D.L., Coulter, J.D. and Willis, W.D. (1973) Location and somato-topic organization of the cells of origin of the spinocervical tract. Exp. Brain Res., 17, 177—189.

Bryan, R.N., Coulter, J.D. and Willis, W.D. (1974) Cells of origin of the spinocervical tract in the monkey. Exp. Neurol., 42, 574—586.

Burgess, P.R. and Perl, E.R. (1967) Myelinated afferent fibres responding specifically to noxious stimulation of the skin. J. Physiol. (Lond.), 190, 541—562.

Carpenter, D., Engberg, I. and Lundberg, A. (1962) Presynaptic inhibition in the lumbar cord evoked from the brain stem. Experientia (Basel), 18, 450—451.

Carpenter, D., Lundberg, A. and Norrsell, U. (1963) Primary afferent depolarization evoked from the sensorimotor cortex. Acta physiol. scand., 59, 126—142.

Carpenter, D., Engberg, I. and Lundberg, A. (1966) Primary afferent depolarization evoked from the brain stem and the cerebellum. Arch. ital. Biol., 104, 73—85.

Chan, S.H.H. and Barnes, C.D. (1972) A presynaptic mechanism evoked from brain stem reticular formation in the lumbar cord and its temporal significance. Brain Res., 45, 101—114.

Christensen, B.N. and Perl, E.R. (1970) Spinal neurons specifically excited by noxious or thermal stimuli: marginal zone of the dorsal horn. J. Neurophysiol., 33, 293—307.

Collins, W.F. and Nulsen, F.E. (1962) Studies on sensation interpreted as pain: central nervous system pathways. Clin. Neurosurg., 8, 271—281.

Conseiller, C., Menetrey, D., Le Bars, D. et Besson, J.M. (1972) Effects de la morphine sur les activités des interneurones de la couche V de Rexed de la corne dorsale chez le chat spinal. J. Physiol. (Paris), 65, Suppl. 220—221.

Coulter, J.D., Maunz, R.A. and Willis, W.D. (1974) Effects of stimulation of sensorimotor cortex on primate spinothalamic neurons. Brain Res., 65, 351—356.

Dilly, P.N., Wall, P.D. and Webster, K.E. (1968) Cells of origin of the spinothalamic tract in the cat and rat. Exp. Neurol., 21, 550—562.

Dawson, G.D., Merrill, E.G. and Wall, P.D. (1968) Dorsal root potentials produced by stimulation of fine afferents. Science, 167, 1385—1387.

Dubner, R. and Sessle, B.J. (1971) Presynaptic excitability changes of primary afferent and corticofugal fibers projecting to trigeminal brain stem nuclei. Exp. Neurol., 30, 223—238.

Eccles, J.C., Kostyuk, P.G. and Schmidt, R.F. (1962) Central pathways responsible for depolarization of primary afferent fibres. J. Physiol. (Lond.), 161, 237—257.

Fetz, E.E. (1968) Pyramidal tract effects in the cat lumbar dorsal horn. J. Neurophysiol., 81, 69—80.

Franz, D.N. and Iggo, A. (1968) Dorsal root potentials and ventral root reflexes evoked by non-myelinated fibers. Science, 162, 1140—1142.

Friedman, H., Nashold, B.S., Jr. and Somjen, G. (1974) Physiological effects of dorsal column stimulation. In J.J. Bonica (Ed.), Int. Symp. Pain, Advances in Neurology, Vol. 4. Raven Press, New York, pp. 769—773.

Görlitz, B.D. and Frey, H.H. (1972) Central monoamines and antinociceptive drug action. Europ. J. Pharmacol., 20, 171—180.

Gregor, M. and Zimmermann, M. (1972) Characteristics of spinal neurones responding to cutaneous myelinated and unmyelinated fibres. J. Physiol. (Lond.), 221, 555—576.

Guilbaud, G., Besson, J.M., Oliveras, J.L. and Liebeskind, J. (1973) Suppression by LSD of the inhibitory effect exerted by dorsal raphe stimulation on certain spinal cord interneurons in the cat. Brain Res., 61, 417—422.

Hagbarth, K.E. and Fex, J. (1959) Centrifugal influences on single units activity in spinal sensory paths. J. Neurophysiol., 22, 321—338.

Hagbarth, K.E. and Kerr, D.I.B. (1954) Central influences on spinal afferent conduction. J. Neurophysiol., 17, 295—307.

Herz, A., Albus, K., Metys, J., Schubert, P. and Teschemacher, Hj. (1970) On the central sites for the antinociceptive action of morphine and fentanyl. Neuropharmacology, 9, 539—551.

Hillman, P. and Wall, P.D. (1969) Inhibitory and excitatory factors influencing the receptive fields of lamina V spinal cord cells. Exp. Brain Res., 9, 284—306.

Hodge, C.J., Jr. (1972) Potential changes inside central afferent terminals secondary to stimulation of large and small-diameter peripheral nerve fibers. J. Neurophysiol., 35, 30—43.

Hongo, T. and Jankowska, E. (1967) Effects from the sensorimotor cortex on the spinal cord in cats with transected pyramids. Exp. Brain Res., 3, 117—134.

Hongo, T., Jankowska, E. and Lundberg, A. (1968) Postsynaptic excitation and inhibition from primary afferents in neurones of the spinocervical tract. J. Physiol. (Lond.), 199, 569—592.

Iggo, A. (1960) Cutaneous mechanoreceptors with afferent C fibres. J. Physiol. (Lond.), 152, 337—353.

Janig, W. and Zimmermann, M. (1971) Presynaptic depolarization of myelinated fibres evoked by stimulation of cutaneous C fibres. J. Physiol. (Lond.), 214, 29—50.

Janig, W., Schmidt, R.F. and Zimmermann, M. (1968) The specific feedback pathways to the central afferent terminals of phasic and tonic mechanoreceptors. Exp. Brain Res., 6, 116—129.

Kitahata, L.M., Taub, A. and Sato, L. (1971) Lamina-specific suppression of dorsal horn unit activity by nitrous oxide and by hyperventilation. J. Pharmacol. exp. Ther., 176, 101—108.

Korn, H. (1969) Splanchnic projection to the orbital cortex of the cat. Brain Res., 16, 23—38.

Korn, H., Wendt, R. and Albe-Fessard, D. (1966) Somatic projection to the orbital cortex of the cat. Electroenceph. clin. Neurophysiol., 21, 209—226.

Le Bars, D., Besson, J.M., Guilbaud, G. et Niederlender, D. (1974a) Influences descendantes s'exerçant sur la transmission des afférences nociceptives au niveau spinal: modifications de l'activité des cellules de la courbe V de Rexed, par l'injection intra-artérielle de bradykinine chez le chat spinal et décérébré. J. Physiol. (Paris), 69, 159A.

Le Bars, D., Menetrey, D., Conseiller, C. et Besson, J.M. (1974b) Comparaison chez le chat spinal at le chat décérébré des effects de la morphine sur les activites des interneurones de type V de la corne dorsale de la moelle. C.R. Acad. Sci. (Paris), 279, 1369—1371.

158

Lee, J.R. and Fennessy, M.R. (1970) The relationship between morphine analgesia and the levels of biogenic amines in the mouse brain. Europ. J. Pharmacol., 12, 65—70.

Levante, A. et Albe-Fessard, D. (1972) Localisation dans le couches VII et VIII de Rexed des cellules d'origine d'un faisceau spino-réticulaire croisé. C.R. Acad. Sci. (Paris), 274, 3007—3010.

Levante, A., Lamour, Y. et Albe-Fessard, D. (1973) Localisation dans la couche V de Rexed de cellules d'origine d'un faisceau spino-thalamique croisé chez le Macauqe. C.R. Acad. Sci. (Paris), 276, 1589—1592.

Liebeskind, J.C., Guilbaud, G., Besson, J.M. and Oliveras, J.L. (1973) Analgesia from electrical stimulation of the periaqueductal gray matter in the cat: behavioral observations and inhibitory effects on spinal cord interneurons. Brain Res., 50, 441—446.

Lim, R.K.S. (1968) Neuropharmacology of pain and analgesia. In R.K.S. Lim, D. Armstrong and E.G. Pardo (Eds.), Pharmacology of Pain. London, pp. 169—217.

Lundberg, A. (1964) Supraspinal control of transmission in reflex paths to motoneurones and primary afferents. In J.C. Eccles and J.P. Schadé (Eds.), In Physiology of Spinal Neurons, Progress in Brain Res., Vol. 12. Elsevier, Amsterdam, pp. 197—221.

Lundberg, A., Norrsell, U. and Voorhoeve, P. (1962) Pyramidal effects on lumbodorsal interneurones activated by somatic afferents. Acta physiol. scand., 56, 220—229.

Mayer, D.J. and Liebeskind, J.C. (1974) Pain reduction by focal electrical stimulation of the brain: an anatomical and behavioral analysis. Brain Res., 68, 73—94.

Mayer, D.J., Wolfle, T.L., Akil, H., Carder, B. and Liebeskind, J.C. (1971) Analgesia from electrical stimulation in the brainstem of the rat. Science, 174, 1351—1354.

Massion, J., Korn, H. et Albe-Fessard, D. (1966) Contribution à l'analyse des afférences vagales projetant sur le cortex antérieur du chat. Acta neuroveg. (Wien), 28, 135—147.

Melzack, R. and Wall, P.D. (1965) Pain mechanisms: a new theory. Science, 150, 971—979.

Mendell, L.M. (1966) Physiological properties of unmyelinated fiber projection to the spinal cord. Exp. Neurol., 16, 316—332.

Mendell, L. (1970) Positive dorsal root potentials produced by stimulation of small diameter muscle afferents. Brain Res., 18, 375—379.

Mendell, L. (1972) Properties and distribution of peripherally evoked presynaptic hyperpolarization in cat lumbar spinal cord. J. Physiol. (Lond.), 226, 769—792.

Mendell, L.M. and Wall, P.D. (1964) Presynaptic hyperpolarization: a role for fine afferent fibres. J. Physiol. (Lond.), 172, 274—294.

Meyer, G.A. and Fields, H.L. (1972) Causalgia treated by selective large fibre stimulation of peripheral nerve. Brain, 95, 163—168.

Morrisson, A. and Pompeiano, O. (1965) Pyramidal discharge from somatosensory cortex and cortical control of primary afferents during sleep. Arch. ital. Biol., 103, 538—568.

Oliveras, J.L., Besson, J.M., Guilbaud, G. and Liebeskind, J.C. (1974a) Behavioral and electrophysiological evidence of pain inhibition from midbrain stimulation in the cat. Exp. Brain Res., 20, 32—44.

Oliveras, J.L., Woda, A., Guilbaud, G. and Besson, J.M. (1974b) Inhibition of the jaw opening reflex by electrical stimulation of the periaqueductal gray matter in the awake, unrestrained cat. Brain Res., 72, 328—331.

Pomeranz, B., Wall, P.D. and Weber, W.V. (1968) Cord cells responding to fine myelinated afferents from viscera, muscle and skin. J. Physiol. (Lond.), 199, 511—532.

Price, D.D. (1972) Characteristics of second pain and flexion reflexes indicative of prolonged central summation, Exp. Neurol., 37, 371—387.

Price, D.D. and Browe, A.C. (1973) Responses of spinal cord neurons to graded noxious and non-noxious stimuli. Brain Res., 64, 425—429.

Price, D.D. and Mayer, D.J. (1974) Physiological laminar organization of the dorsal horn of Macaca mulatta. Brain Res., 79, 321—325.

Price, D.D. and Wagman, I.H. (1970) Physiological roles of A and C fibre inputs to the spinal dorsal horn of Macaca mulatta. Exp. Neurol., 29, 383—399.

Price, D.D. and Wagman, I.H. (1973) Relationship between pre- and postsynaptic effects of Macaca mulatta. Exp. Neurol., 40, 90—103.

Price, D.D., Hull, C.D. and Buchwald, N.A. (1971) Intracellular responses of dorsal horn cells to cutaneous and sural nerve A and C fiber stimuli. Exp. Neurol., 33, 291—309.

Ralston, H.J., III, (1965) The organization of the substantia gelatinosa Rolandi in the cat lumbosacral cord. Z. Zellforsch., 67, 1—23.

Ralston, H.J. (1968) Dorsal root projections to dorsal horn neurons. J. comp. Neurol., 1321, 303—329.

Redjemi, F., Oliveras, J.L., Guilbaud, G. et Besson, J.M. (1974) Analgesie induite par la stimulation du noyau central inférieur du Raphe chez le chat. C.R. Acad. Sci. (Paris), 279, 1105—1107.

Rethelyi, M. and Szentágothai, J. (1969) The large synaptic complexes of the substantia gelatinosa. Exp. Brain. Res., 7, 258—274.

Reynolds, D.V. (1969) Surgery in the rat during electrical analgesia induced by focal brain stimulation. Science, 164, 444—445.

Rexed, B. (1952) The cytoarchitectonic organization of the spinal cord in the cat. J. comp. Neurol., 96, 415—495.

Samanin, R. and Valzelli, L. (1971) Increase of morphine-induced analgesia by stimulation of the nucleus raphe dorsalis. Europ. J. Pharmacol., 16, 298—302.

Samanin, R., Gumulka, W. and Valzelli, L. (1970) Reduced effect of morphine in midbrain raphe lesioned rats. Europ. J. Pharmacol., 10, 339—343.

Satoh, M. and Takagi, H. (1971) Enhancement by morphine of the central descending inhibitory influence on spinal sensory transmission. Europ. J. Pharmacol., 14, 60—65.

Scheibel, M.E. and Scheibel, A.B. (1968) Terminal axonal patterns in cat spinal cord. II. The dorsal horn. Brain Res., 9, 32—58.

Selzer, M. and Spencer, W.A. (1969) Convergence of visceral and cutaneous afferent pathways in the lumbar spinal cord. Brain Res., 14, 331—348.

Shealy, C.N., Mortimer, J.T. and Hagfors, N.R. (1970) Dorsal column electroanalgesia. J. Neurosurg., 32, 560—564.

Szentágothai, J. (1964) Neuronal and synaptic arrangements in the substantia gelatinosa Rolandi. J. comp. Neurol., 122, 219—239.

Takagi, H., Matsunara, M., Yanai, A. and Ogiu, K. (1955) The effect of analgesics on the spinal reflex activity of the cat. Jap. J. Pharmacol., 4, 176—187.

Taub, A. (1964) Local, segmental and supraspinal interaction with a dorsolateral spinal cutaneous afferent system. Exp. Neurol., 10, 357—374.

Taub, A. and Bishop, P.O. (1965) The spinocervical tract: dorsal column linkage, conduction velocity, primary afferent spectrum. Exp. Neurol., 13, 1—21.

Tenen, S.S. (1968) Antagonism of the analgesic effect of morphine and other drugs by p-chlorophenylalanine, a serotonin depletor. Psychopharmacologia (Berl.), 12, 278—285.

Towe, A.L. and Zimmermann, I.D. (1962) Peripherally evoked cortical reflex in the nucleus. Nature (Lond.), 194, 1250—1251.

Trevino, D.L., Maunz, R.A., Bryan, R.N. and Willis, W.D. (1972) Location of cells of origin of the spinothalamic tract in the lumbar enlargement of cat. Exp. Neurol., 34, 64—77.

Trevino, D.L., Coulter, J.D. and Willis, W.D. (1973) Location of cells of origin of spinothalamic tract in lumbar enlargement of the monkey. J. Neurophysiol., 36, 750—761.

Tsou, K. and Jang, C.S. (1964) Studies on the site of analgesic action of morphine by intracerebral microinjection. Sci. sinica, 13, 1099—1109.

Vogt, M. (1974) The effect of lowering the 5-hydroxytryptamine content of the rat spinal cord on analgesia produced by morphine. J. Physiol. (Lond.), 236, 483—498.

Vyklický, L., Rudomín, R., Zajac, F.E. and Burke, R.E. (1969) Primary afferent depolarization evoked by a painful stimulus. Science, 165, 184—186.

Wagman, I.H. and Price, D.D. (1969) Responses of dorsal horn cells of *Macaca mulatta* to cutaneous and sural nerve A and C fiber stimuli. J. Neurophysiol., 32, 803—816.

Wall, P.D. (1967) The laminar organization of dorsal horn and effects of descending impulses. J. Physiol. (Lond.), 188, 403—423.

Wall, P.D. (1973) Dorsal horn electrophysiology. In A. Iggo (Ed.), Somatosensory System, Vol. II. Springer Verlag, Berlin, pp. 253—270.

Wall, P.D. and Sweet, W.H. (1967) Temporary abolition of pain in man. Science, 155, 108—109.

Whitehorn, D. and Burgess, P.R. (1973) Changes in polarization of central branches of myelinated mechanoreceptor and nociceptor fibers during noxious and innocuous stimulation of the skin. J. Neurophysiol., 36, 226—237.

Willis, W.D., Trevino, D.L., Coulter, J.D. and Maunz, R.A. (1974) Responses of primate spinothalamic tract neurons to natural stimulation of hindlimb. J. Neurophysiol., 37, 358—372.

Wyon-Maillard, M.C., Conseiller, C. and Besson, J.M. (1972) Effects of orbital cortex stimulation on dorsal horn interneurons in the cat spinal cord. Brain Res., 46, 71—83.

Young, R.F. and King, R.B. (1972) Excitability changes in trigeminal primary afferent fibers in response to noxious and nonnoxious stimuli. J. Neurophysiol., 35, 87—95.

Zieglgänsberger, W. and Herz, A. (1971) Changes of cutaneous receptive fields of spinocervical tract neurons and other dorsal neurons by microelectrophoretically administered amino-acids. Exp. Brain Res., 13, 111—126.

Zimmermann, M. (1968) Dorsal root potentials after C-fiber stimulation. Science, 160, 896—898.

Zimmermann, M. and Handwerker, H.O. (1974) Total afferent inflow and dorsal horn activity upon radiant heat stimulation to the cat's footpad. In J.J. Bonica (Ed.), International Symposium on Pain, Advances in Neurology, Vol. 4. Raven Press, New York, pp. 29—33.

DISCUSSION

PURPURA: The inferior central nucleus has some projection downwards, at least to the magnus. I do not know whether this has been seen here in order to explain the earlier results before you slip down into the other area. The second thing is whether the descending pathway is the same pathway that is going to be operating on lamina V cells? By seeing what happens on iontophoresing serotonin onto your lamina V cells, you see whether you are getting inhibition of lamina V cells.

BESSON: By injecting serotonin?

PURPURA: Yes, by iontophoresing. The third thing I want to ask regards the question of the morphine receptors which are now being clearly shown to be very powerful in the hypothalamus and more so in the amygdala, which has the highest concentration of morphine receptors in the entire brain, i.e., Snider's work. How do you tie these things together?

BESSON: For the first question, concerning the projections of the dorsal raphe nuclei, it only has projections to the higher level, but we are not discussing that point at the moment. We still think there is a possibility of a loop to the supraspinal structures as there are interconnections between raphe nuclei, but raphe magnus and raphe obscurus have no massive projections to the spinal cord. For your second question, we have not iontophoresed serotonin. King told me that they found no particular effect, or only poor effects of serotonin on this kind of cell. I think the programme is as follows. Since, as you know, the descending mechanisms act on the interneurons, perhaps serotonin is acting at another place, and perhaps another mediator is acting here. If the descending effects are presynaptic, perhaps the descending effects are presynaptic; the mediator acting presynaptically is certainly GABA.

PURPURA: Let us get around this by injecting the serotonin precursor into the lumbar artery, to get high 5-HTP levels within the cord, and seeing whether or not this has blocked the lamina V cells. According to your theory they must be blocked, I do not care how, but only so long as you are sure that sertonin is getting into the vicinity of the interneuronal mechanism.

BESSON: Yes, that is correct. But as you know, we can study only one cell in one experiment when we do such work with morphine, 5-HTP and other substances, and the experiment is finished if you are not choosing the iontophoretic method.

PURPURA: No, it is a very simple experiment. What we want you to do is to stimulate and record from lamina V cells as you are doing and merely inject 5-HTP in 10—15 minutes. Conversion is so rapid that you will be able to see the effect, especially in spinal animal as they do not have ascending or descending reflexes.

BESSON: Yes, perhaps. About your third question on the morphine receptors: I know that there are opiate receptors in the hypothalamus and, also, Hess injected morphine into the third ventricle and found analgesia. Recently Jakke in New York injected morphine in the periaqueductal gray matter and she obtained very curious data: hyperexcitability to very weak cutaneous stimulation and a very clear analgesia to noxious stimulation. I think we also have to look to the activity of lamina V cells by injecting morphine in the raphe nuclei, and record unit activity in raphe magnus or obscurus after the morphine injection.

PRIBRAM: About the lamina V cells projections, are they always upstream?

BESSON: Some lamina V cells project in the spinocerebellar tract in the cat and in monkey. In the monkey some lamina V cells come into the spinothalamic tract, but there is a total separation between ascending projections and decending influences.

PRIBRAM: What about the orbital cortex?

BESSON: The orbital cortex has a very powerful inhibitory effect on lamina V cells. This is indicative of negative feedback.

HORN: You said that LSD depresses the activity of the dorsal raphe nucleus. Is there any hyperesthesia? What happens?

BESSON: The experiment was done on rat, not the moving rat, but the acute rat.

HORN: Are there any other reports?

BESSON: No, but it was clearly demonstrated. Aghajanian recorded raphe units and there was a strong depression of dorsal raphe nucleus, whereas the units recorded in reticular formation showed no modification one minute after LSD.

GILMAN: May I ask how the dorsal column stimulation may affect lamina V cells?

BESSON: You have two reasonable hypotheses because the fibers in the dorsal column send collaterals to lamina V cells and there are inhibitory effects in this way; it has been shown in spinal cats but not man. You can also increase the activity of descending inhibitory effects coming from the cortex, especially since there is a difference between cat and man.

GILMAN: Which descending pathway in man will be active on lamina V cells?

BESSON: I think it is the pyramidal tract and also you have the corticoreticulospinal tract. You have still the presynaptic inhibition.

PURPURA: I think one has to be very cautious about this dorsal column. The dorsal column is not just like a continuous line, there are neurons arising in the spinal cord and coarsing in the dorsal column and thus they are of intrinsic origin. It is not just a simple antidromic reflex back on to the cells of the stimulating system. One has to be very cautious about this. Also I would like you to talk about emphasising the problem of species differences in the effects and I do not think this was made quite clear, I hope that you will tell us some of these differences too.

ALBE-FESSARD: The problem is that in the cat there is no clear connection between lamina V and the thalamus. The only relation between lamina V and the thalamus is very indirect, there is only the spinocervical tract that has to play the role of the spinothalamic tract. But in man and monkey there is a clear connection between lamina V and the thalamus.

9

INPUT-OUTPUT ORGANIZATION BETWEEN THE FRONTAL CORTEX AND THE LATER L HYPOTHALAMUS

YUTAKA OOMURA and MORIKUNI TAKIGAWA*

Department of Physiology, Faculty of Medicine Kyushu University, Fukuoka 812 (Japan)

The objective of this paper is a deeper perception of the connection between motivational status, interneural activity of the cerebral frontal cortex and the lateral hypothalamus, and their association with feeding and satiation.

From observations of single unit discharges from the feeding and satiety centers of the hypothalamus of the chronic cat, their reciprocal relationships under various behavioral conditions have been clarified (Oomura et al., 1969a and b). During sleep discharges from the satiety center in the ventromedial nucleus (VMH) were high in frequency while discharges from the feeding center in the lateral hypothalamic area (LH) were low. Upon arousal when hungry, and during search and feeding activities, these discharge patterns reversed. Arousal during satiation changed the relative discharge frequency only slightly. In order to establish a correlation between motivational state and neuronal activity, a cat was trained to bar-press for food in a fixed ratio program, neuronal discharges from both the LH and the VMH were then recorded as a function of time before and after bar-press. In the 0.2 sec period immediately preceding the bar-press, discharges from the LH decreased in frequency. Prior to the 0.2 sec period of low frequency discharge, occasional periods of higher than average discharge frequency were observed. Because these frequency increases occurred randomly, and although they appeared to have some association with the position of the cat in relation to the lever, no motivational correlation could be determined with certainty (Ono et al., 1976).

To obtain closer control of test conditions, the above procedure was repeated using restrained monkeys in order to establish more satisfactory control of the position of the subject in relation to the manipulandum. Under

* Present address: Department of Neuropsychiatry, Faculty of Medicine, Kagoshima University, Kagoshima, Japan.

these conditions, spontaneous LH unit discharge frequency increased significantly during the period 0.6—1.2 sec prior to bar-press, with a correspondingly significant decrease in frequency occurring in the 0.6 sec period immediately preceding bar-press, and a second increase in frequency occurring during the 0.6 sec period immediately following bar-press. Similar variations in frequency could not be observed in other parts of the hypothalamus and thalamus (Ono et al., 1976). These observations do not disagree with any results obtained with the conditioned cat, although some of the results from the cat could not be established as statistically significant.

The temporal relationship between overt behavior and the observed pre-press frequency increase of neuronal discharge strongly indicates a motivational correlation. The origin of the frequency decrease is assumed to be in the cerebral frontal cortex. The inference is that the frontal cortex may inhibit LH activity. This conclusion is based on studies of other investigators which associate frontal cortex activity with inhibition of feeding behavior. Just before bar-press for food, accelerated neural discharges have been shown in the caudate nucleus (Buser et al., 1974), which has a direct connection with the frontal cortex (Tigner, 1974). This may imply that the inhibition is a specific phenomenon observed in the hypothalamus.

It has been reported that the frontal cortex inhibits on-going operant behavior associated with food intake (Siegel and Wang, 1974), hunger-induced behavioral arousal (Moorcroft, 1971), and bite-attack behavior provoked by LH stimulation (Siegel et al., 1974). Eating and drinking behavior has been elicited by the arrival of a spreading depression wave at the frontal cortex (Huston and Bureš, 1970). Frontal cortex lesion has resulted in increase of bar-pressing rate in a fixed ratio program for food intake (Manning, 1973), and increased running wheel activity over an extended period of time (Lynch et al., 1971). Demonstrating the importance of the anatomical connection is the fact that inhibition of this behavior via the frontal cortex could not be accomplished until three weeks of age, before which the connection had not matured. The existence of a direct anatomical connection from the frontal cortex to the LH has been established (Nauta, 1972), as has a similar connection from the LH to the frontal cortex. Further correlation is established by the diminishing or discontinuing of self stimulation to the LH following application of procaine to the frontal cortex (Rolls and Cooper, 1974). Unit activity of the frontal cortex, and no other brain location, is enhanced by stimulation of the effective site for self stimulation in the LH (Rolls and Cooper, 1973).

The above citations clearly point out both anatomical and functional connections between the frontal cortex and the LH. The following data from the present experiment should enhance comprehension of the functional relationship between the frontal cortex and LH activity. Interconnection between the frontal cortex and the LH was established by stimulating one while recording from the other. LH neurons project axons which terminate directly on, and excite frontal cortex neurons. Excitatory and inhibitory interneurons located in the ventral LH, but not in the dorsal LH, may result in a modulating effect by frontal cortex stimulation. This modulation appears as an excitation-inhibition pattern in the dorsal LH, with inhibition only occurring in the ventral LH. Despite these laminar distinctions between the dorsal and ventral halves of the LH, a specific columnar structure is also shown to exist, projecting functionally through the dorsoventral portions.

Since the medial forebrain bundle, with some synaptic terminations, passes through the dorsal portion of the LH as distinct from the ventral part, possible differences between the two halves were investigated by stimulating them separately.

METHODS

Forty Wistar BR 46 rats of both sexes (180—200 g body weight) were used. Animals were placed under urethane anesthesia (1.5 g/kg, intraperitoneally), the EEG showing slow waves with moderate amplitude. After each animal was fixed in the stereotaxic apparatus, a hole (8 × 10 mm) was drilled in the skull using a dental drill. Dura mater was cautiously removed, and the exposed cortex covered with 2% agar, 3 mm thick, to prevent drying and suppress pulsations of the brain. Body temperature was kept at $37 \pm 1°C$.

Microelectrodes. Glass microelectrodes (Pyrex tubing, 0.4 mm i.d.) filled with 4 M NaCl solution with 5—10 MΩ DC resistance were employed for recording. The electrode was advanced 3 μm per pulse with a pulse motor and moved perpendicularly in a dorsal to ventral direction.

Recording and stimulation. The coordinates of recording and stimulating sites were taken from the brain atlases of Krieg (Krieg, 1946) for the frontal cortex, i.e. area 10, frontopolaris and area 6, frontalis agranularis, and of König and Klippel (1963) for the LH (A 4.6; L 1.5; H —2.0 to —3.0). The areas 10 and 6 correspond to the orbitofrontal cortex and prefrontal extrapyramidal center in the higher mammals, respectively. The recording electrode was connected to a preamplifier. An indifferent electrode was placed at the neck muscle. Extracellular unit activity was monitored with a storage oscilloscope and recorded by a long recording camera. The time constant of the amplifier was adjusted to 0.2 sec for the evoked potential of the frontal cortex or LH and 3 msec for single unit discharges. Modulation of spontaneous unit discharges of LH neurons following frontal cortex stimulation was analyzed in the form of poststimulus histograms by using a CAT computer (computer of average transients) which averages 50 stimulus trials. In each CAT display the abscissa represents time, and the ordinate the number of spikes. The time display goes from 500 msec prior to stimulus input, the control period, to 500 msec after, for a total display time of 1 sec. The 1 sec display period is divided into 400 intervals or 'bins' of 2.5 msec each. The ordinate represents the accumulated sum of all the pulses occurring in each 2.5 msec time period of all the sweeps. Thus, each display indicates the accumulated number, out of 50 possible single unit discharges, which have occurred during any one of two hundred 2.5 msec time intervals before and after application of the stimulus, which occurs at t = 0. Stimulus artifacts are suppressed by the recording circuit.

For the stimulation loci in the frontal cortex, the pyramidal cell layer of 0.5—0.7 mm depth was chosen (Krieg, 1946). For the stimulation loci in the LH, the dorsal (H −2.0), middle (H −2.5) and ventral (H −3.0) thirds of the LH were chosen respectively. Concentric bipolar stimulating electrodes were used. The outer pole was made of 25 gauge (0.4 mm o.d.) stainless steel tubing insulated with enamel or teflon while the inner electrode, 0.1 mm diameter, was enamel-coated stainless steel wire. Insulation at the tip of the outer and inner electrodes was removed 0.2 mm from the tip. The tip separation was 0.2 mm and the DC resistance was 50—70 kΩ. Rectangular stimulating pulses of 0.05 msec duration were used, with the inner electrode negative.

Anatomical identification of recording sites. After each experiment, a concentric bipolar stimulating electrode was placed at the exact coordinates of the microelectrode recording site. Anodal current (2 mA) was applied for 10 sec between the inner and outer poles of the concentric electrode. The rat was then sacrificed and decapitated, and its brain fixed with neutral 10% formalin Ringer solution. A Nissl staining procedure was used on the 20—30 μm thick brain sections (Oomura et al., 1969a and b).

RESULTS

Evoked potentials on the frontal cortex by stimulation of the LH

Fig. 1 shows recordings from the frontal cortex, area 10, as a function of electrode depth and dorsal vs ventral stimulation of the LH.

Dorsal LH stimulation (left), recorded from the surface of the cortex (top) shows a slow negative wave with a latency of 2 msec having a peak at 5.3 msec after stimulation. The duration is about 10 msec. As the recording electrode penetrates through 0.5 mm (left, center) to 1.0 mm (left, bottom) this slow negative wave changes to a slow positive wave starting at 4.5 msec, peaking at 6 msec, and enduring 7.5 msec, preceded by a short negative wave with latency of approximately 1.5 msec, peak at 2.8 msec and duration of 2.5 msec. A small negative notch with latency of 0.7 msec can occasionally be seen just prior to the short negative wave. This may be presynaptic in nature but is not considered in detail.

Ventral LH stimulation (right), recorded from the surface of the cortex (top) shows short sharp spikes with a latency of 0.7 msec and a duration of 0.3 msec. As the recording electrode penetrates to 0.5 mm (right, center)

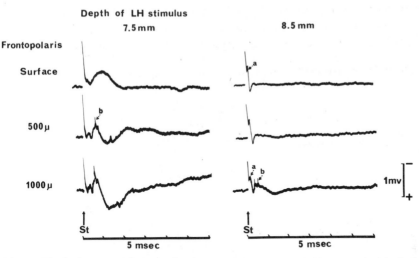

Fig. 1. Evoked potential from the frontal cortex area 10 (frontopolaris). Left: stimulation of dorsal half of LH (7.5 mm depth from the surface of the cortex). Slow negative wave changes its polarity at 0.5 mm depth from the surface. Right: stimulation of ventral half of LH (8.5 mm depth from the surface). Recording at surface (top), 0.5 mm depth (center), and 1 mm depth (bottom). a, antidromic spikes; b, driven spikes on the short negative wave.

and then to 1.0 mm depth (right, bottom) the short sharp spike remains, but it is followed by a short negative wave with a latency of approximately 1.5 msec, peak at 2.8 msec and a duration of about 3.0 msec, and a slow positive wave with its peak at about 7 msec. These short negative and slow positive waves are similar to those elicited by dorsal LH stimulation when recorded from 1 mm depth, but the latter is slightly shorter in time, somewhat less in amplitude, and is preceded by the sharp spike which is absent from the ventral LH stimulation recordings. The absence of the slow negative wave at the frontal cortex surface when stimulating the ventral LH might be explained by the absence or low density of near surface synaptic terminations of neuronal elements originating in the ventral LH.

One or more spikes appear superimposed on the short negative waves recorded from 0.5 and 1.0 mm depths of the frontal cortex for both dorsal and ventral LH stimulations. These negative waves are probably EPSPs in nature.

Fig. 2 shows recordings from 1.0 mm depth in the frontal cortex as a consequence of repetitive stimulation of the dorsal (left) and ventral (right) LH. The dorsal LH was stimulated with a single pulse (top), two pulses (center), and six pulses (bottom), all having interpulse intervals of 4.0 msec.

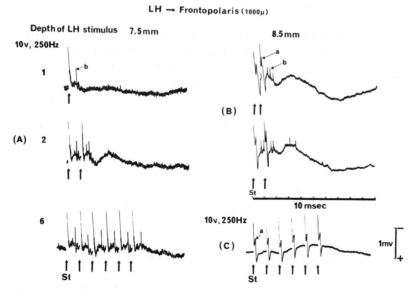

Fig. 2. Effect of repetitive stimulations on evoked potential from the frontal cortex area 10. Left (A): stimulation of dorsal half of LH. Right (B and C): stimulation of ventral half of LH. A: single stimulus (1), two stimuli (2), 6 stimuli at 4 msec intervals (6). Neither the short negative wave nor the driven spikes on it (b) disappear. B and C: two stimuli at 5 msec interval (top), at 10 msec interval (center), 6 stimuli at 4 msec interval (bottom). Antidromic spikes (a) and short negative wave with driven spikes on it (b) do not disappear until 200 Hz stimulation.

The very high sharp spikes which appear are stimulus artifacts. The short negative waves with superimposed spikes, manifest in the single stimulus trials shown in Fig. 1, still appear, but they are necessarily abbreviated in time whenever a subsequent stimulus prematurely causes termination. The right hand figures show recordings from double stimulus pulses to the ventral LH separated by 5 msec (top) and 10 msec (bottom). Again, as in the case of the dorsal LH multistimulus results, the single stimulus effect, including the initial short sharp spikes, appears in its entirety up to the time it is aborted by the next stimulus. During the experiment, the short negative wave responses remained in evidence for stimulus interpulse intervals as short as 4 msec, and disappeared when such periods diminished to approximately 3 msec. The short sharp spikes recorded as a result of ventral LH stimulation followed until periods were reduced to 1.7 msec. The ability of the neural system to follow such high frequencies is strong evidence that the connections on the frontal cortex from the dorsal and ventral LH portions are monosynaptic (Eccles, 1955; Bruckmoser and Hepp-Reymond,

1970) while the short sharp spikes observed from ventral LH stimulation are antidromic spikes.

The conduction velocity over the roughly estimated 1 cm distance from the LH to the frontal cortex is about 14 m/sec for antidromic spikes, and averages 3.6 m/sec (fastest, 6 m/sec) for short negative waves.

The slow negative waves observed at the surface of the frontal cortex by dorsal LH stimulation, appear to have a conduction velocity averaging 2.2 m/sec (fastest, 5 m/sec). These change to positive waves at depths of 0.5—1.0 mm, indicating a high density of synaptic terminations of LH neurons òn the apical dendrites of frontal cortex neurons. The weaker waves, which appear when stimulating the ventral LH, indicate that the population of LH neurons terminating synaptically on apical dendrites of frontal cortex neurons is much more concentrated in the dorsal LH layer than in the ventral LH layer. The slow positive wave of Fig. 1 is completely different from the positive wave, of inhibitory synaptic nature, recorded at the LH when the frontal cortex is stimulated (Fig. 4A), because the short negative wave is not inhibited during the slow positive wave (see Fig. 5, 1).

The short negative wave appearing in recordings made between 0.5 and 1.0 mm depth is evidence of synaptic termination of LH neurons near the cell bodies of frontal cortex neurons. Further evidence of the existence and nature of these terminations is the presence of the driven spikes which are superimposed on this wave. These terminations are probably the source of frontal cortex neuron excitation, and their existence can be detected only by reason of the close proximity of the recording electrode to the frontal cortex neurons. The small size of the wave, together with its absence at the surface, is strongly indicative of the small population of such terminations. The synaptic terminations on the apical dendrites of the frontal cortex neurons may also contribute to these excitations, though more detailed study of this is necessary.

A recent electron microscope investigation, following lesion of the LH, has detected degenerated terminal buttons on the dendritic trees of frontal cortex neurons. This finding is consistent with the above conclusions regarding the negative slow waves at the frontal cortex surface. Similar degenerated buttons were not observed, however, on the cell soma of the frontal cortex neurons (Yamamoto and Shibata, 1975). If the population is very small such terminations may not be evident, regardless of the electron microscope, but their presence, even in small numbers, can be detected electrically. From the occurrence of antidromic spikes in the ventral LH and their absence in the dorsal LH, one can deduce that frontal cortex neurons send out axons which invade the ventral LH, but not the dorsal LH.

The picture thus appears to be one in which the signals from the dorsal LH to the frontal cortex are orthodromic and operate mainly on the apical dendrites and partly on the soma, while those from the ventral LH to the frontal cortex act predominantly on the soma.

Evoked potentials in the LH by stimulation of the frontal cortex

Potentials evoked in the LH as a result of stimulation of the frontal cortex were recorded and evaluated as functions of single or multiple stimulus pulses, interpulse interval, stimulus intensity, position in the LH from dorsal to ventral extremes, and stimulating site.

Fig. 3 shows single stimulus evoked potential profiles as a function of depth of recording while stimulating area 10. Depth of recording corresponds to the positions indicated on the scale at the left. As shown, a single pulse stimulus produces a slow negative wave followed by a slow positive wave at the extreme dorsal position. As the recording site shifts towards the ventral position the negative wave gradually diminishes until it completely disappears from recordings made in the ventral third of the LH. The amplitude of the positive wave, which is present in recordings from the dorsal third, does not change substantially as depth is increased.

Area 10 was stimulated with pulses of varying intensity while recordings were made from the dorsal third of the LH as a function of such intensity. Intensity levels below 4 V were ineffective. Four volts appeared to be the threshold level, with both positive and negative waves being definitely evident at 5 V. As stimulus intensity was further increased, up to 19 V, the amplitudes of the positive and negative waves increased accordingly. When

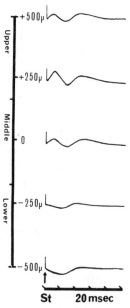

Fig. 3. Evoked potential profiles as a function of recording depth within LH. Corresponding depth shown at left. St, test stimulation.

such shocks were applied in pairs separated by 50 msec, both the negative and the positive waves produced by the second pulse were consistently 60% greater in amplitude than their counterparts produced by the first pulse.

The negative and positive waves peaked at about 7.5 msec and 17.2 msec, respectively, after stimulus time. The durations of the negative and positive waves were about 10 and 20 msec respectively. The positive wave, with a latency of about 4 msec, recorded at the ventral position was approximately 40 msec in duration.

Using a crude approximation of 1 cm as the distance from the frontal cortex to the LH, the above times were calculated to represent conduction velocities of 3.3 m/sec for the negative wave and 2.5 m/sec for the positive wave.

Increasing the number of repetitive stimulus pulses, at 10 msec intervals, evinced a further summing effect for the negative or positive waves in direct proportion to the number of pulses administered. Both the negative and positive waves produced by five pulses of 100 Hz were approximately five times the amplitude of the corresponding negative and positive waves produced by a single pulse of the same intensity and duration. Intermediate numbers of pulses produced intermediate results; i.e. the relationship was a continuous one.

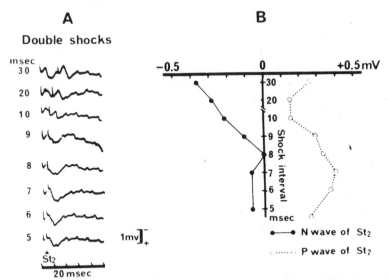

Fig. 4. A: time course of test negative waves during conditioning positive waves. Test stimulations were applied at intervals indicated in msec beside each record. The plots in B show negative and positive wave amplitude in the evoked potentials following test stimulation corresponding to shock interval times shown on the vertical line. St_2, test stimulation.

Fig. 4A shows evoked potentials recorded in the dorsal third of the LH as double shocks, with constant intensity but variable interpulse interval, are applied to the frontal cortex. Fig. 4B shows the relationship between the amplitude of evoked potentials and stimulus intervals. For a 30 msec interval the second negative and positive waves are definitely greater in amplitude than the first, indicating summation. As the interval is decreased to 20 and 10 msec the second positive wave occurs during the first negative wave, and appears to be cancelled in the recording; however, the second positive wave, which occurs after the first waves are completed, indicated summation since it had a greater amplitude than the first positive wave. For shorter intervals, 8 and 9 msec, the second test pulse is merely superimposed on the negative wave of the first pulse. For all intervals from 5 to 9 msec the second negative wave virtually disappears, indicating that it is being inhibited by the first positive wave. At the same time the positive wave, having a 1.7 times greater amplitude and about 1.5 times greater duration than it has when the intervals are longer, is an indication of its summation.

In a second example of double pulse stimulation, spike discharges were elicited on the negative waves produced by both stimulus pulses for pulse intervals from 50 msec down to less than 20 msec. With 8 and 9 msec intervals, inhibition of the second negative wave and its superimposed spike occurred, while the positive wave, in both cases, summated for these intervals. The same effect was observed on the positive wave recorded in the ventral third of the LH.

Regarding area 6 stimulation, the evoked potential throughout the entire depth of the LH is a predominantly positive wave with approximately the same latency and duration, about 4 and 40 msec respectively, as that recorded at the ventral position from area 10 stimulation. The different evoked potentials are recorded at the same position by the same recording electrode while stimulating areas 10 and 6 alternately. This is in agreement with the different modulation of single unit discharges by stimulation at the two different sites, as discussed later.

Results to this point indicate synaptic transmission. The negative and positive waves exhibit synaptic characteristics, the negative wave is excitatory and the positive wave inhibitory. The very slow conduction velocity estimated probably indicates multisynaptic transmission. Taken together, these facts present strong evidence that transmission to the LH from both area 10 and area 6 is synaptic in nature.

Pathway between the frontal cortex and LH

In order to verify the possible pathway between the frontal cortex and the LH the following experiments were conducted. The lateral preoptic region was stimulated while recording from 0.5 mm below the surface of

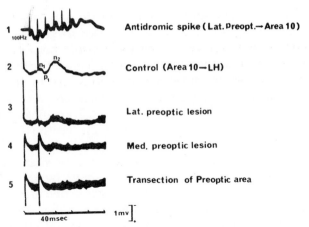

Fig. 5. An acute lesion experiment for the study of pathways from area 10 to the LH.
1: antidromic spikes produced by 100 Hz stimulation of the lateral preoptic region recorded at 0.5 mm below surface of area 10. 2: evoked potentials in the LH produced by
area 10 double shocks. 3: acute lesion of the lateral preoptic region, made by passing DC
(5 mA for 30 sec), resulted in the disappearance of the short negative (n_1) and long positive waves (p_1). 4 and 5: spreading of the lesion to the medial preoptic area and transection of preoptic area resulted in disappearance of the evoked potentials in the LH.

the frontal cortex area 10. Antidromic spikes followed by negative and
positive waves in that order were detected in area 10 as a result of stimulation by six pulses at 100 Hz (Fig. 5, 1). Evoked potentials were then recorded
in the dorsal LH from double stimulations 0.5 mm below the surface of
area 10 while leaving the original stimulating electrode in place in the
preoptic region (Fig. 5, 2). Again, negative waves (n_1) followed by positive
waves (p_1), in that order, were recorded from the LH. This indicates that
axons from the LH to the frontal cortex pass through the lateral preoptic
region. Using the original stimulating electrode a lesion in the lateral preoptic
region was created with DC current (5 mA for 30 sec). The effect of this
lesion on area 10 evoked potentials measured in the dorsal LH was then
observed. As shown in Fig. 5, 3, the negative and positive waves disappeared,
indicating that they had been passing through the lateral preoptic region.
Enlargement of the lesion to include the medial preoptic region resulted in
disappearance of the evoked potentials, including the second negative
waves from the LH. Transection of the preoptic area had no further influence, thus indicating that the electrical lesion had effectively severed the
involved axons. It can be concluded from these results that signals between
the frontal cortex and the LH are principally mediated in the medial forebrain bundle which passes through the preoptic region.

Axons in the rat medial forebrain bundle are mainly non-myelinated.
Conduction velocity measurements on nerve fibers in this region establish

the velocity at 0.6—1.0 m/sec through these fibers (Izquierdo and Merlo, 1966). The velocities of 2.5 and 3.3 m/sec that were calculated from earlier data of these experiments did not agree with the above range, indicating conduction between the frontal cortex and the LH via thin myelinated fibers.

The high conduction velocities observed from the ventral LH to the frontal cortex, indicating not only monosynaptic conduction but also a velocity as high as 14 m/sec, suggest an involvement of large myelinated axons plus the fact that they may pass directly through the ventral LH without terminations. As mentioned in the following section, the rapid suppression of LH neurons, i.e. the complete suppression immediately following frontal cortex stimulation, may not be brought about by these high velocity axons. The lower velocity of about 2.5 m/sec is what one might expect in monosynaptic transmission through a thin myelinated fiber. Discrepancies between the conduction velocities of the afferent and efferent systems will be discussed in the discussion section.

Single unit discharges in the LH by stimulation of the frontal cortex

Experiments were performed to ascertain the effects of frontal cortex stimulation on single unit discharges of LH neurons. Independent parameters were: depth of recording site in the LH, number of stimulus pulses, time interval between pulses, magnitude of stimulating pulse and stimulating site. One series of tests examined the effects of intensity variation, otherwise the stimulus amplitude was fixed at 10 V. The dependent variables consisted of: type of effect, latency of effect, duration of suppression, and presence or absence of double suppression. The observed effects fall into one of three categories: no effect (absence), driven discharge which is always followed by suppression, and suppression only (non-driven).

The effects of stimulus intensity on inhibition were measured and found to change between 6 V and 10 V. Six volts was the observed threshold, with little or no change in effect for values above 10 V up to 18 V.

In Fig. 6, consider first the inserts in the upper right portions of each of the seven histograms. These inserts are photographs of storage oscilloscope displays. The horizontal trace of each display consists of 20 superimposed 500 msec time bases. The vertical pattern includes all the single unit discharges which occurred during each of the 20 horizontal sweeps, or all of the single unit discharges which occurred during a total elapsed time of 10 sec. The upper, control, display of each insert shows spontaneous single unit discharges. In the lower test display of each insert, stimulation occurs at the beginning (left) of each of the 20 sweeps. Each of the test displays thus presents the superimposed cumulative results of the 500 msec periods following 20 stimulations of an LH neuron. At the left of each test display the stimulus artifact appears as a pulse with amplitude slightly greater than

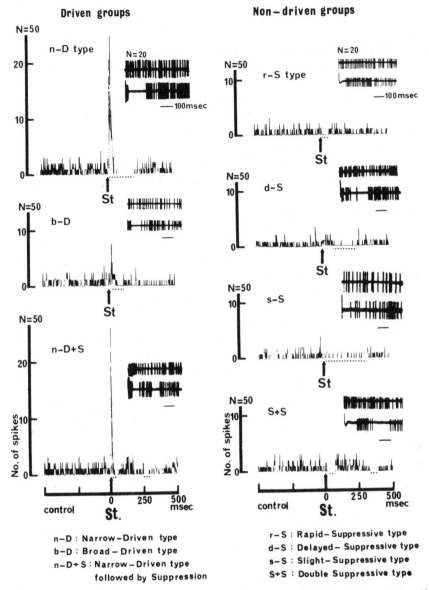

Fig. 6. Patterns of the poststimulus time histogram (PSTH). Driven types (facilitation followed by suppression) and non-driven (suppression) types were two principal patterns of PSTHs in the LH following stimulation in area 10. Three variants of PSTHs were observed in the former and four variants in the latter. The inset photographic records show 20 superimposed sweeps of spontaneous unit discharge, before (upper) and after (lower) stimulation, recorded simultaneously with the PSTHs. At the left of each lower display is a pulse with amplitude slightly greater than average, the stimulus artifact. On PSTHs ordinate is summation of unit discharges per 2.5 msec, and abscissa is time in msec. Dotted line under PSTHs is inhibitory period in msec. Sample window, 2.5 msec in computer summation. St, stimulation. Stimulus artifacts are suppressed by the recording circuit.

average. Those discharges which occur immediately after the stimulus artifact are driven discharges (except in one case, delayed-suppresive type to be discussed later). Next in time, in all cases, is a period devoid of discharges, the suppression period, and in some cases a second suppression period occurs.

The histograms in Fig. 6 are CAT displays of the same phenomena. Besides the display methods, the one other difference is the use of 50 trials per display instead of 20. Each display is a typical illustration of one of the seven different types of single unit discharges observed. The left column shows examples of driven discharge responses in which the neuron reacts to the stimulus with discharges for a short time followed by a period in which discharges are suppressed. Driven discharge responses are divided into two types, i.e. narrow-driven and broad-driven, characterized by the duration of discharge following the stimulus. The period is approximately 40 msec in the former and 70 msec in the latter. There is no definitive means of classifying these two types, this decision is based on the judgement of the experimenter. The upper histogram of the driven discharge response illustrates the narrow-driven type, and the middle histogram shows an example of broad-driven type. The bottom example is the driven type followed by a second period of suppression occurring, in this case, approximately 180 msec after termination of the first suppression period.

The right hand column of Fig. 6 contains examples of the non-driven reaction which is characterized by discontinuance of the spontaneous unit discharges in response to the stimulus. This suppression may appear in any one of four different manners, as shown from top to bottom respectively. The rapid-suppressive type shows complete suppression immediately upon stimulation. In the delayed-suppressive type the discharges entirely or substantially cease with some latency of response. The slight-suppressive type exhibits partial diminishing of discharges, with or without a short latency, after stimulation. Finally, in the double-suppressive type discharges are quelled completely upon stimulation with a second period of suppression, perhaps 230 msec, after normal discharge resumption. Latency of suppression is distinguished from driven discharge by continuation of the control discharge rate immediately after stimulation, whereas the driven discharge rate is very much higher than the control rate.

Measuring latency from the time of stimulation, the mean value for the narrow-driven type is 4.4 ± 2.3 msec (3—28 msec, N = 42). For the broad-driven type the mean value is 29.4 ± 7.7 msec (15—62 msec, N = 12). Inspection of Fig. 6 discloses that the latency of onset of inhibition is virtually zero for the suppression types, except the delayed-suppressive type. The delayed-suppressive type has an average latency of 19.2 ± 6.3 msec (11—80 msec, N = 15). The duration of inhibition varies from the longest value of 89 ± 6.7 msec for the broad-driven type, to 75 ± 4.3 msec for narrow-driven type, to 65 ± 4.9 msec for rapid-suppressive type, and down to 55 ± 3.8 msec for the delayed-suppressive type.

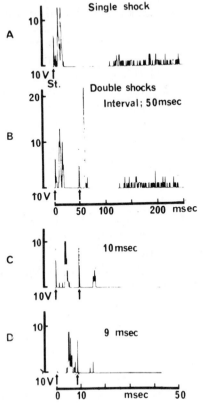

Inhibition of driven spike by double shock interval
Area 10 → LH

Fig. 7. A and B: time course of inhibition induced by double shocks to area 10 shown by PSTHs. C and D: inhibition of test driven discharges after the conditioning stimulation (9—10 msec).

Fig. 7 illustrates the inhibiting effect of one driven discharge on a second driven discharge as the time interval between conditioning stimulus and test stimulus is shortened. Fig. 7A shows the typical response of narrow-driven types to a conditioning stimulus, including the suppression period. Fig. 7B shows a test stimulus 50 msec behind the first. The driven responses occur, although such an occurrence is well within the suppression period of the first response. Normal discharges resume about 110 msec after the end of the first driven responses, not 110 msec after the second responses as might be expected. Fig. 7C and D show successively greater inhibition of the second driven response as the time interval between stimuli is diminished to 10 msec, being substantially diminished in C, and virtually disappearing in D. This inhibition time course is somewhat similar to that observed in the evoked potential shown in Fig. 4.

Depth effect

Table I lists the number of neurons exhibiting driven discharge, non-driven response, and no response as a function of recording site in the LH when stimulating the frontal cortex, area 10 (refer to Fig. 3). Driven discharges tend to appear more often in the dorsal third of the LH (47%), while non-driven occur more often in the ventral third (45%). Throughout the LH, neurons were tested which exhibited no response to frontal cortex stimulation. Most of these (48%) appeared in the ventral third. The variation of response type with depth is statistically significant ($P < 0.025$). These results are in agreement with the evoked potential results obtained in the same respective regions (Fig. 3). In the dorsal third of the LH, where most of the driven discharges are observed, there is a negative wave with superimposed evoked spikes followed by a positive wave. The negative wave is associated with driven unit discharges and the evoked spikes are extracellular evidence of unit discharges, while the positive wave is associated with inhibition. This negative-positive wave changes to a positive wave associated with inhibition in the ventral third of the LH where most of the non-driven discharges are observed.

Site effect

Table II summarizes the comparative results of stimulating areas 10 and 6 in the frontal cortex while recording from the LH. While stimulating area 10 the driven and non-driven responses were 48.6 and 30.1%, respectively, of 183 neurons tested. While stimulating area 6 the respective driven and non-driven responses were 13.3% and 27.8% of 180 neurons tested. These

TABLE I

Summary of patterns of poststimulus time histograms (PSTHs) as function of LH depth following stimulation of area 10 (driven type: $P < 0.025$)

Layer	Area 10 ⟶ LH		
	Driven	Non driven	No effect
Upper	42 ± 5.3	19 ± 6.2	17 ± 7.6
Middle	30 ± 5.0	13 ± 5.5	5 ± 5.0
Lower	18 ± 4.2	26 ± 6.5	20 ± 7.7
	N = 90 $P < 0.025$	N = 58	N = 42

TABLE II

Summary of driven, non-driven and no-effect types of PSTHs in the LH following stimulation of areas 10 and 6

Stimulation	Driven			Non-driven				No effects
	n–D	b–D	n–D+S	r–S	d–S	s–S	S+S	
Area 10 183 neurons in 54 tracts	31.1	13.7	3.8	10.4	14.8	4.4	0.5	
	48.6%			30.1				21.3
Area 6 180 neurons in 53 tracts	7.8	5.5	0	10.6	12.2	4.4	0.6	
	13.3			27.8				58.9

differences in single unit discharge response are in good agreement with the observed differences in evoked potential while stimulating the two different areas. A total of 78.7% of the neurons tested showed either driven or non-driven responses from area 10 stimulation and 58.9% showed no effects from stimulation of area 6. While area 10 was shown to have, by far, the greater number of connections with the LH, the total percentage of connections was sufficiently larger than 100% to suggest the existence of at least some LH neurons with simultaneous connections to both area 10 and area 6. Results of tests for the existence of convergence will be presented later.

Functional column structure

In Fig. 8 the schematic diagram in the lower right corner shows the LH with neurons having different functions arranged into columns in such a way that all neurons in one column are functionally of the same type, while those of a different type are in another column. The results presented in Fig. 8 and Table III verify the plausibility of this concept.

The group of three histograms of the CAT displays, T_1, shows responses from three different neurons to stimulation of area 10. Each neuron in this group displays non-driven responses. These three neurons were located by driving the recording electrode along the axis of the column (or tract) T_1 until a neuron emitting single unit discharges was discovered. Three such neurons were located along the axis of T_1, and no other neurons were detected by this method along this particular axis. These three neurons were at depths of 8.0 mm, 8.4 mm, and 8.6 mm from the surface of the cerebral cortex, as indicated by the depths shown in each of the three histograms. Thus, in the tract T_1 the only neurons in evidence were all of the same type. This procedure was repeated at each 0.1 mm distance for tracts T_2, T_3, T_4 and T_5 with the same results for all exept T_4 which produced two non-driven response type neurons and one driven response type neuron. This tract is referred to as mixed.

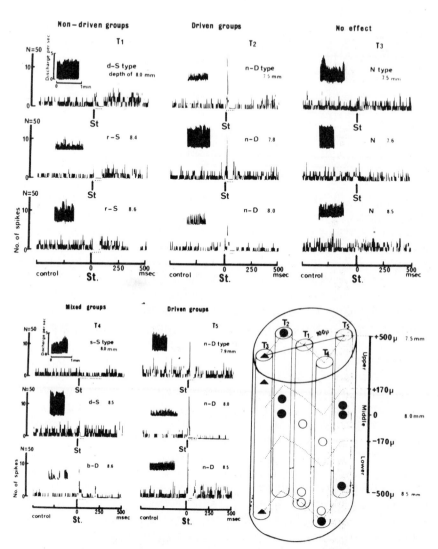

Fig. 8. An example of a functional column, observed in the patterns of LH PSTHs to the stimulation of area 10. Each inset record on the PSTHs shows discharges per sec of spontaneous unit discharge counted by a ratemeter and drawn by a pen recorder. Note that each of three neurons in T_1, T_2, T_3 and T_5 tracts of the LH show similar patterns of PSTHs following the stimulation of area 10. This functional column of PSTHs is summarized in the bottom schema. Solid circles, driven type; open circles, non-driven type; solid triangles, no effect type. St, stimulation. Each inset arabic numeral shows LH depth in mm from the surface of rat cerebral cortex. The upper and bottom edges of the LH are 7.5 and 8.5 mm respectively.

TABLE III

Summary of patterns of PSTH types in LH tracts following stimulation of areas 10 (54 tracts) and 6 (53 tracts)

Values obtained, compared with probability, were significantly greater for similar patterns of PSTH in each of four types (area 10: $P < 0.01$, area 6: $P < 0.025$). These results suggest the high probability of the existence of the functional columns in the LH shown in Fig. 6 as an example.

Stimulation	Driven	Non Driven	Mixed	No Effect
Area 10 54 tracts				
Obtained (%)	20.4	9.3	66.7	3.7
Probability(%)	11.5	2.8	84.8	0.9
				$P < 0.01$
Area 6 53 tracts				
Obtained (%)	1.9	7.5	60.4	30.2
Probability(%)	0.2	2.1	77.2	20.4
				$P < 0.025$

Repeating these procedures for 107 tracts, while stimulating from either area 10 (54 tracts) or area 6 (53 tracts) produced the results summarized in Table III.

From area 10 stimulation, 20.4% of the tracts were matched as containing only driven response type neurons, whereas the statistical probability if such matching were random is 11.5%. This probability of 11.5% is obtained from data shown in Table II. Since of the total population of neurons tested 48.6% were the driven response type, the probability that three located in one tract will all be the driven type is $(0.486)^3 = 0.115$. Because of the infrequency of tracts with four or five matched neurons they were treated in the data as having three. The other calculated probabilities were obtained in the same manner, using appropriate values from Table II.

The incidence of non-driven responses was 9.3% against a probability of 2.8%, of mixed responses 66.7% against 84.8% probability, and no-effect 3.7% against 0.9% probability. Similar results were obtained while stimulating from area 6. Altogether 363 neurons were checked by this method. The average number of neurons per tract was 3.4 with the actual number in any one tract ranging from three to five. Data from any tract which did not contain three or more neurons were eliminated.

These results constitute overwhelming evidence confirming the validity of the original hypothesis.

Convergence

As previously mentioned, the results of the tests relating site of stimulation to effects on single unit discharges suggested the possibility of convergence of neuronal pathways from both areas 10 and 6 on single neurons

TABLE IV

Summary of convergent impulses on the same LH neuron and the spontaneous unit activity following stimulation of areas 10 and 6 as shown by paired patterns of PSTHs

The numbers indicated by the solid triangles were found to be significantly greater than the probability shown in the respective brackets. n-D, narrow-driven; b-D, broad-driven; r-S, rapid-suppressive; d-S, delayed-suppressive types.

A \ B	n-D	b-D	r-S	d-S	N (No effect)
n-D	11▲ (5.1)	3▲ (2.7)	6 (6.3)	9▲ (6.6)	23 (31.3)
b-D	2 (2.3)	5▲ (1.2)	3▲ (2.8)	1 (2.9)	12 (13.8)
r-S	0 (2.0)	0 (1.0)	7▲ (2.4)	4▲ (2.5)	9 (12.0)
d-S	3▲ (2.9)	0 (1.5)	5▲ (3.5)	5▲ (3.7)	16 (17.4)
N (No effect)	1 (4.8)	1 (2.5)	0 (5.9)	3 (6.2)	44▲ (29.5)

within the LH. The following experimental results should reconcile this conjecture.

While recording from one neuron in the LH, areas 10 and 6 were alternately stimulated and the responses, if any, compared. A total of 173 LH neurons were tested (Table IV). Of these, 64 (37.0%) responded when either area 10 or area 6 was stimulated. This number was significant ($P < 0.01$), when compared to the random probability of such an occurrence. Of the 173 neurons, 65 responded to only one stimulus site compared with a statistical expectancy of 93.9, and 44 did not respond to any stimulation.

The probability of both stimuli producing, for instance, the narrow-driven type is $17/173 \times 52/173 \times 173 = 5.1$. Of the 64 neurons which responded to both stimuli, 28 responded with each showing the same type of response, compared with a probability that 12.4 neurons would so respond if the effect were random. These matched responses included all seven types of response.

The remaining instances of convergence (36) all displayed one type of response for area 10 stimulation matched with a different type of response for area 6 stimulation. Not all possible combinations of matching occurred. Missing were examples of rapid-suppression from area 10 coupled with any driven response from area 6, delayed-suppression from area 10 matched with broad-driven from area 6, and no effect from area 10 matched with rapid-suppression from area 6. In general it appears, from a superficial examination of the results, that there is a tendency for area 10 stimulation to yield driven discharge responses in an LH neuron while area 6 stimulation yields a non-driven type response in the same neuron, rather than vice versa.

The above results and observations, together with the previously observed fact that area 10 produces negative and positive wave sequences with evoked potential while area 6 produces predominantly positive waves, lead to the tentative conclusion that the type of single unit discharge may be a function of the origin of stimulation rather than a function of the responding neuron.

Fig. 9 illustrates one example of each of the seven types of matched convergence. Table IV, a tabulation of results, shows only four types of dis-

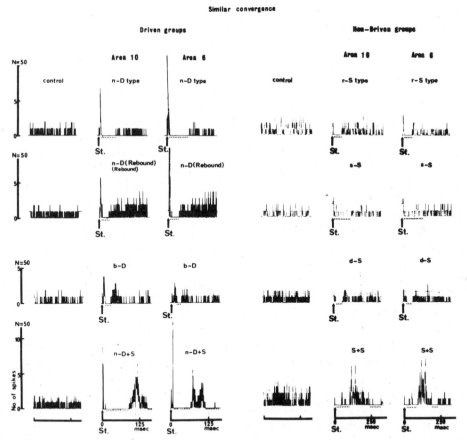

Fig. 9. PSTHs showing convergence of impulses on the same LH neuron with similar spontaneous unit discharge following the stimulation of areas 10 and 6. See Fig. 6 for abbreviations.

charge. The answer to this discrepancy is that in the table narrow-discharge plus second suppression examples are included with narrow-discharge types, double-suppression types are included with rapid-suppression types, and slight suppression types are included with delayed-suppression.

The question may arise as to whether the phenomenon observed is really convergence or simply the result of intersite stimulus current spread. If the phenomenon were, in fact, the result of such spread, then every neuron which responds to stimulation of area 10 would respond similarly to stimulation of area 6, and conversely. The occurrence of no-effect responses matched with driven or non-driven responses, or of one type of response matched with a different type of response should nullify any such objection. In addition, the evoked potentials, produced at a single observation site from alternate stimulation of areas 10 and 6, have a relationship, as previously discussed, which is consistent with the convergence concept in production of driven unit discharges. Furthermore, the nature of the evoked potentials is such as to preclude current spread as a factor.

DISCUSSION

From the results obtained we can summarize the frontal cortex-LH relationships and their connection with other cerebral areas, in a manner diagrammed in Fig. 10. The frontal cortex-LH pathway is conveyed through the medial forebrain bundle which passes through the preoptic region (Fig. 5). Axons from the dorsal half of the LH terminate mainly on the apical dendrites of the frontal cortex neurons and partly on the cell bodies (Fig. 1). Axons from neurons of the ventral half of the LH terminate principally on cell bodies (Fig. 1). In both cases the connections to the frontal cortex neurons are monosynaptic (Fig. 2). The calculated velocities of 2—4 m/sec indicate that the axons are thin myelinated fibers.

Neurons in the frontal cortex area 10 send axons to the dorsal half of the LH via excitatory (negative wave, corresponding to EPSP) and inhibitory (positive wave, corresponding to IPSP) pathways, and to the ventral half of the LH, predominantly via inhibitory pathways with synaptic terminations (Fig. 3). The large myelinated fibers, with conduction velocity of 14 m/sec, from the frontal cortex penetrate into the ventral half of the LH (Fig. 1). The rapid-suppressive type of non-driven response may be brought about by these axons. Recent studies with the electron microscope clearly indicate degenerated terminals on the soma membrane within the LH after lesion of area 10 (Yamamoto and Shibata, 1975). However, any direct synaptic contacts they may have with LH neurons, with inhibitory interneurons or the absence of contact are not yet clear.

Neurons in area 6 mostly send inhibitory synaptic signals to the entire LH. Pathways from areas 10 and 6 converge on individual LH neurons so that one LH neuron may respond to signals from either area 10 or 6 (Table IV).

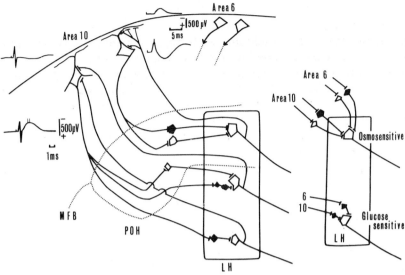

Fig. 10. Schematic circuitry between frontal cortex, areas 10 and 6, and LH. Evoked potentials at surface (upper) and 0.5 mm depth (lower) are shown by stimulation of the dorsal half of LH (right) and by that of the ventral half (left). Dorsal LH neuron axons mostly terminate on the apical dendrites and only partly on the soma. The ventral LH neuron axons terminate mostly at the soma. Frontal cortex neurons send axons to the dorsal and ventral half in different manners. Osmosensitive neurons mainly in dorsal LH; glucose-sensitive neurons, ventral LH. MFB, medial forebrain bundle; POH, preoptic hypothalamic area.

Conduction from the frontal cortex to the LH is slow, but lesion experiments show both afferent and efferent pathways through the preoptic region via the medial forebrain bundle (Fig. 5). This means that fiber diameters for conduction in both directions may be the same, and hence have the same conduction velocity. Therefore the efferent pathways from the frontal cortex might be multisynaptic thus accounting for the longer conduction time, since conduction time is consumed at each synaptic connection.

Anatomically and electrophysiologically, the pathways from the LH to the frontal cortex have been determined to be monosynaptic. Direct functional frontolateral hypothalamic connection in the monkey was first demonstrated by strychnine neurography (Ward and McCulloch, 1947). Anatomically the direct connection from the orbitofrontal cortex of the monkey to the lateral preoptic area and from the principal sulcus to the LH has already been shown (Nauta, 1972). The direct connection from the rabbit septal pellucidum to the lateral preoptic area and LH has also been shown to pass through the medial forebrain bundle (Zyo et al., 1963).

It has been definitely shown that LH neurons are capable of detecting the presence of, or discriminating the concentration of, certain endogenous chemical compounds such as glucose (Oomura et al., 1974), insulin (Oomura, 1973), free fatty acid (Oomura et al., 1975), etc. Consequently, results of the chemical analysis performed by the LH neurons are sent directly to the frontal cortex. In addition to the chemically produced information, the frontal cortex obtains information from other areas of the brain cortex where somatosensory, visual, olfactory or other sensory signals are processed. The frontal cortex then integrates not only the information received internally, but also information from outside after it is processed by other cortical regions. The results of the integration of information are then returned to the LH from whence they are sent to control precise motivational or alimentary behavior to be performed by the organism. There are many neuronal networks, each having a chemosensitive neuron at its head. Each chemosensitive neuron has a different threshold level for excitation by, for example, free fatty acid. The lowest threshold concentration of free fatty acid for firing a chemosensitive neuron in the LH is 1 mEq/liter (Oomura et al., 1975). Hence some neurons are fired as the concentration reaches a certain level, and some are not. As a network is activated its final output goes to the frontal cortex. That is the beginning of, for instance, hunger, which we are inclined to believe is initiated by free fatty acid. As more and more neurons activated by free fatty acid fire, the subject is motivated to behave in a manner intended to alleviate the hunger. Within the hypothalamus, only the LH begins to increase its firing rate 1.2 sec prior a bar-press for food (Ono et al., 1976). In the 0.6 sec period immediately preceding the bar-press, LH activity is suppressed. This is perhaps due to activity in the frontal cortex.

It has been ascertained that functional organization in the visual cortex (Hubel and Wiesel, 1965) and motor cortex (Asanuma et al., 1968) is arranged in columns. It has been generally believed that no such anatomical organizational pattern (Szentágothai, 1969) is associated with any part of the reticular formation of the midbrain. The LH, being part of the reticular formation (Morgane and Stern, 1974), was long assumed to also have no such organization. Also, the LH, having no histological layer structure, as has the cortex, was considered to have no such organizational pattern as well. A laminar form of functional organization of the LH was first discovered in the present experiment. In addition, a columnar form of organizational pattern, projecting through the laminae has been discovered. Thus the LH has not just one system of functional organization but two such interposed systems.

The significance of the existence of not just one, but two such intimately intersected systems is still not clear, and further study is required to ascertain its meaning and importance. According to Griffiths (1971), motivation is effected by not just one but many neuronal or functional units, each unit having all-or-none properties. It is conceivable that specific motivation may be produced by the group functioning of a multitude of neuronal units in a columnar grouping, with the form of motivation depending on the axial position of the involved neurons within the column.

Because of the chronological progress of the investigations, the first concept of organization within the LH was that it was laminar only. For instance, areas 10 and 6 converge on single neurons in a functional manner which is dependent on the axial position of the affected neuron within the LH. There is a spatial relationship between the effects produced by each area in the sense that area 10 appears to affect more neurons in the dorsal half of the LH while area 6 affects more neurons in the ventral half. There is a response oriented hierarchy of effects produced by area 10 which is dependent on the axial position of the affected neuron, while area 6 has no such effect. LH neurons which respond in a specific manner when area 10 or 6 is stimulated, tend to group into functional columnar arrangements according to their type of response. Within the hierarchical framework of their separate effects, areas 10 and 6 have effects on LH neurons in which one neuron responds to both areas. Some responses are identical for both areas, other responses are paired in various arrangements of a different type of response from each area.

Within the two independent but related systems that have been observed, a means of sorting, categorizing, and coding inter-regional reactions between the frontal cortex and the LH has begun to emerge. The frontal cortex is only one of the many sources of input to the LH including such things as blood chemistry (Oomura, 1973; Oomura et al., 1975), amygdaloid signals (Oomura et al., 1970), somatosensory, and proprioceptive signals (Marshall and Teitelbaum, 1974). Since it is possible to spatially sort out many of the different specific types of reactions between the LH and the frontal cortex, it seems to be completely reasonable that other signals reaching the LH can likewise be sorted and coded within the same two systems. Thus, peripherally initiated signals might be processed within the systems and appropriately joined to their respective counterparts from other regions.

It may be that information is arranged or coded generally by layer and then more finely organized within a column or columns. It may be that the column arrangement is a means of keeping bits of isolated, non-related information from creating mutual interference.

It is known that the LH receives information which it processes and then sends to the frontal cortex. Such information is then further processed and integrated with additional information, especially from peripheral regions. It is then sent back to the LH from where it is redispersed to its appropriate behavioral function terminal.

It is also quite conceivable that when more information is obtained, we will find that we are in reality dealing with one system, not two.

SUMMARY

Stimulation of the rat lateral hypothalamus while recording in the frontal cortex, or vice versa, revealed the following. Axons of LH neurons terminate directly on frontal cortex neurons and dendrites. Frontal cortex stimulation produced an excitation-inhibition sequence in many neurons in the dorsal half of the LH, but only inhibition in the ventral half. Antidromic frontal cortex spikes were obtained by stimulation of the ventral LH, but not from stimulation of the dorsal LH. Thus, the excitatory and inhibitory interneurons appear to be located outside the dorsal LH and within the ventral LH. Frontal cortex stimulation studies revealed a specific columnar structure within the LH, inferred from neuron response patterns.

These interconnections between the LH and frontal cortex indicate that the hypothalamus can report to the frontal cortex any changes in the organism's internal milieu. One-third of the LH neurons are known as chemosensitive neurons which can discriminate concentration of blood composition. Such mutual interrelationships between the frontal cortex and hypothalamus may provide for motivational feeding behavior.

Acknowledgements

We thank Prof. A. Simpson, Showa University for his invaluable advice and help for preparation of this manuscript.

This work was partly supported by Ministry of Education Grants 887010, 811002 and 844023 and DA-CRD-AFE-S92-73-G191.

REFERENCES

Asanuma, H., Stoney, Jr. S.D. and Abzug, C. (1968) Relationship between afferent input and motor outflow in cat motor sensory cortex. J. Neurophysiol., 31, 670–681.

Bruckmoser, P., Hepp-Reymond, M.-C. and Wiesendanger, M. (1970) Effects of peripheral, rubral and fastigial stimulation on neurons of the lateral reticular nucleus of the cat. Exp. Neurol., 27, 388–398.

Buser, P., Pouderoux, G. and Mereaux, J. (1974) Single unit recording in the caudate nucleus during sessions with elaborate movements in the awake monkey. Brain Res., 71, 337–344.

Eccles, R.M. (1955) Intracellular potentials recorded from a mammalian sympathetic ganglion. J. Physiol. (Lond.), 130, 572–584.

Griffith, J.S. (1971) Mathematical neurobiology. In An Introduction to Mathematics of the Nervous System. Academic Press, London, Chapter 8.

Hubel, D.H. and Wiesel, T.N. (1965) Receptive fields and functional architecture in two nonstriate visual areas (18 and 19) of the cat. J. Neurophysiol., 28, 229–289.

Huston, J.P. and Bureš, J. (1970) Drinking and eating elicited by cortical spreading depression. Science, 169, 702–704.

Izquierdo, I. and Merlo, A.B. (1966) Potentials evoked by stimulation of the medial forebrain bundle in rats. Exp. Neurol., 14, 144—159.

König, J.F.R. and Klippel, R.A. (1963) The Rat Brain. A Stereotaxic Atlas of the Forebrain and Lower Parts of the Brain Stem. Williams and Wilkins, Baltimore, Md.

Krieg, W.J.S. (1946) Connection of the cerebral cortex. J. comp. Neurol., 84, 222—323.

Leonard, C.M. (1969) The prefrontal cortex of the rat. I. Cortical projection of the mediodorsal nucleus. II. Efferent connections. Brain Res., 12, 321—343.

Lynch, G., Ballentine, P. and Campbell, B.A. (1971) Differential rates of recovery following partial cortical lesions in rats. Physiol. Behav., 7, 737—741.

Manning, F.J. (1973) Performance under temporal schedules by monkeys with partial ablation of prefrontal cortex. Physiol. Behav., 11, 563—569.

Marshall, J.F. and Teitelbaum, P. (1974) Further analysis of sensory inattention following lateral hypothalamic damage in rats. J. comp. physiol. Psychol., 86, 375—395.

Moorcroft, W.H. (1971) Ontogeny of forebrain inhibition of behavioral arousal in the rat. Brain Res., 35, 513—522.

Morgane, P. and Stern, W. (1974) Chemical anatomy of brain: circuits in relation to sleep and wakefulness. In E.D. Weitzman (Ed.), Advances in Sleep Research. Spectrum, Flushing, N.Y.

Nauta, W.J.H. (1972) Neural associations of the frontal cortex. Acta neurobiol. exp., 32, 125—140.

Ono, T., Oomura, Y., Sugimori, M., Nakamura, T., Shimizu, N. and Kita, H. (1976) Hypothalamic unit activity related to bar-press food intake in chronic monkey. In D. Novin (Ed.), Hunger: Basic Mechanisms and Clinical Implications. Raven Press, New York.

Oomura, Y. (1973) Central mechanism of feeding. In M. Kotani (Ed.), Advances in Biophysics, Vol. 5. Tokyo Univ. Press, Tokyo, pp. 65—142.

Oomura, Y., Ooyama, H., Yamamoto, T., Ono, T. and Kobayashi, N. (1969a) Behavior of hypothalamic unit activity during electrophoretic application of drugs. Ann. N.Y. Acad. Sci., 157, 642—665.

Oomura, Y., Ooyama, H., Naka, F., Yamamoto, T., Ono, T. and Kobayashi, N. (1969b) Some stochastical patterns of single unit discharges in the cat hypothalamus under chronic conditions. Ann. N.Y. Acad. Sci., 157, 666—689.

Oomura, Y., Ono, T. and Ooyama, H. (1970) Inhibitory mechanism of the amygdala on the lateral hypothalamic area in rats. Nature (Lond.), 228, 1108—1110.

Oomura, Y., Sugimori, M., Nakamura, T. and Yamada, Y. (1974) Glucose inhibition on the glucose-sensitive neurone in the rat lateral hypothalamus. Nature (Lond.), 247, 284—286.

Oomura, Y., Nakamura, T., Sugimori, M. and Yamada, Y. (1975) Effect of free fatty acid on the rat lateral hypothalamic neurons. Physiol. Behav., 14, 1—4.

Rolls, E.T. and Cooper, S.J. (1973) Activation of neurones in the prefrontal cortex by brain-stimulation reward in the rat. Brain Res., 60, 351—368.

Rolls, E.T. and Cooper, S.J. (1974) Anesthetization and stimulation of the sulcal prefrontal cortex and brain stimulation reward. Physiol. Behav., 12, 563—571.

Siegel, J. and Wang, R.Y. (1974) Electroencephalographic, behavioral, and single-unit effects produced by stimulation of forebrain inhibitory structures in cats. Exp. Neurol., 42, 28—50.

Siegel, A., Edinger, H. and Lowenthal, H. (1974) Effects of electrical stimulation of the medial aspect of the prefrontal cortex upon attack behavior in cats. Brain Res., 66, 467—479.

Szentágothai, J. (1969) Architecture of the cerebral cortex. In H.H. Jasper, A.A. Ward and A. Rope (Eds.), Basic Mechanisms of the Epilepsies. Little Brown and Co., Boston, Mass., pp. 13—28.

Tigner, J. (1974) The effects of dorsomedial thalamic lesions on learning, reversal, and alternation behavior in the rat. Physiol Behav., 12, 13—17.

Ward, A.A. and McCulloch, W.S. (1947) The projection of the frontal lobe on the hypothalamus. J. Neurophysiol., 10, 309—314.

Yamamoto, T. and Shibata, Y. (1975) Fronto-hypothalamic fiber connection in the rat. Pharmacol. Biochem. Behav., Suppl. 1,3, 15—22.

Zyo, K., Oki, T. and Ban, T. (1963) Experimental studies on the medial forebrain bundle, medial longitudinal fasciculus and supraoptic decussations in the rabbit. Med. J. Osaka Univ., 13, 193—239.

DISCUSSION

HORN: What happens to feeding behavior if you stimulate the frontal cortex?

OOMURA: Feeding behavior increases, also hyperphagia occurs.

PRIBRAM: Are you sure that the stimulated recorded elements are cells of frontal cortex and not the fibers of lateral hypothalamus?

OOMURA: Well, it is rather a difficult question. But from hypothalamus to cortex the conduction latency of the axons is of rather short duration, e.g. 1 msec, and also for acetylcholine it is 1 msec. In our case they were rather long latency elements, probably they are cells.

PURPURA: The fact is that you are able to study the effect of different inputs to the hypothalamus and it is surprising how the data that has originally been looked at in the ventromedial region with the amygdala from Gloor's laboratory, is now complemented quite a bit in the lateral hypothalamic zone. Now, how would you put together the differences between what Gloor sees with amygdala stimulation via the ventral pathway and the stria terminalis in relation to the VMH (ventromedial hypothalamus) area, and here (LH), because it is the integration in that system that we really ought to try to look at.

OOMURA: When we started these experiments, we were interested in reciprocal relationships between the ventromedial hypothalamus and the lateral hypothalamus. So we introduced two microelectrodes simultaneously into the ventromedial hypothalamus and the lateral hypothalamus and recorded the spontaneous discharge not only in an acute experiment but also in the chronic cat. Reciprocity actually occurs. This means that when the activity of a VMH neuron goes up, that of an LH neuron goes down. The amygdala, through the ventral amydalar pathway and the stria terminalis, also connects to the VMH cell. This was reported by Gloor and others. They also found interneurons just at the border of the ventromedial hypothalamic area. But in our case, we can not find these interneurons. We don't know why, we used the cat. We also made the lesion experiments or the Golgi-Cox experiments, but we could not find the degeneration fiber or the expansion of the fiber in the VMH. The LH neurons send axons up to the perifornical regions.

PURPURA: I must say that your suggestion of a collateral from the lateral hypothalamus all the way to the neocortex is as yet unproved anatomically.

OOMURA: Anatomically Nauta did some experiments.

PURPURA: From the lateral hypothalamus to the area 10 region?

OOMURA: Excuse me, Nauta did make only lesions in the cortex and found the terminals in hypothalamus.

PURPURA: That is right. The reason I bring it up is that I know that it has never been demonstrated, from the lateral hypothalamus to the cortex anyway. But now everybody is putting lesions in what they say is this medial forebrain system and in the region of projection zone of the dopaminergic system, and everybody is now saying that there are noradrenergic fibers all over the neocortex, as well as dopaminergic fibers, and I think one of the worries may be whether or not some of this system may in fact be what is being lesioned if the collateral is there. This is something you are to keep in mind. You don't believe that this is the case because the cells of that system are catecholaminergic. These cells of LH are not catecholaminergic, are they?

OOMURA: No, they are dopaminergic.

ALBE-FESSARD: Are they dopaminergic?

OOMURA: There are some adrenergic effects, but if the adrenaline is given through one of the microelectrodes it gives inhibition. The neurons are facilitated by stimulation of the globus pallidus.

PURPURA: But there is a great deal of work now to show that the noradrenergic activity produced by cannula injection induces eating.

OOMURA: That is right. This puzzles me.

PURPURA: It puzzles me, because those data from inplanted animals are very clear from several laboratories and the study at the Rockefeller University in particular is a very clear and precise study showing that catecholamines facilitate eating and drinking. Particular emphasis is on eating in lateral hypothalamic area.

OOMURA: No, I don't very much favor that data because they applied 10 μl or more from one cannula. In that case, the expansion of the drug will be more than 2 mm. So we do not know what happens in such gross applications.

PURPURA: But you know also that Ungerstedt's work shows that as soon as you block the system, the animal develops aphagia.

OOMURA: That is right. That is also very confusing.

PURPURA: Why? He has shown this in rat.

ALBE-FESSARD: There is no conversion.

PURPURA: You mean from the catecholamine to 6-hydroxydopamine?

OOMURA: You know, when we stimulate the substantia nigra we can get the facilitatory effect on the hypothalamic neurons. Then we apply dopamine through one of the multi-barrel electrodes. The neurons increase firing. So this is also contradictory to Ungerstedt's data.

PURPURA: Do you want to comment on that?

ALBE-FESSARD: In mouse you can block the satiety center and you can make the animal eat. It is a noradrenergic system which can be blocked.

PURPURA: Is this published now?

ALBE-FESSARD: I think it is.

PURPURA: I have not seen it.

10

FUNCTIONAL DEVELOPMENT OF INTRATHALAMIC AND RETICULOTHALAMIC SYNAPTIC PATHWAYS

DOMINICK P. PURPURA

Department of Neuroscience and Rose F. Kennedy Center for Research in Mental Retardation and Human Development, Albert Einstein College of Medicine, Yeshiva University, Bronx, N.Y. (U.S.A.)

INTRODUCTION

Intracellular studies of thalamic neurons in adult animals have disclosed several functionally different synaptic pathways linking intrathalamic nuclear organizations and reticulothalamic projection systems (Purpura, 1970 and 1972). Implication of these synaptic pathways in mechanisms of evoked synchronization and desynchronization of thalamic neuronal activity (Purpura, 1969) and in the modulation of relay transmission in specific thalamocortical projection systems (Purpura et al., 1966a) follows from a number of observations. First, low frequency (6—12/sec) stimulation of medial and intralaminar thalamic nuclei elicits prolonged EPSP-IPSP sequences in a large proportion of thalamic neurons during evoked electrocortical synchronization, i.e., recruiting responses (Purpura and Cohen, 1962). A major feature of this synchronizing activity is the prominence of prolonged (100—150 msec) IPSPs generated in thalamic neurons during thalamocortical recruiting responses (Feldman and Purpura, 1970). A second line of inquiry has established that intrathalamic internuclear synaptic pathways exhibit extraordinary frequency-specific responsiveness (Purpura and Shofer, 1963). This is evident in the observation that the transition from low to high frequency medial thalamic stimulation is accompanied by blockade, or inhibition of prolonged synchronizing IPSPs, and powerful increases in excitatory synaptic drives in thalamic neurons (Purpura and Shofer, 1963; Purpura et al., 1966a). These alterations in synaptic activities are associated with reticulocortical activation and electrocortical desynchronization (Purpura, 1969 and 1970). Attenuation of synchronizing IPSPs and moderate augmentation of excitatory synaptic activity in thalamic neurons is also observed during high frequency stimulation of brain stem reticular regions (Purpura et al., 1966a and b). Evidence has also been obtained that specific and non-specific (medial thalamic) nuclear organizations are linked by relatively short latency synaptic pathways which exert potent reciprocal excitatory and inhibitory effects on specific relay transmission and activity in non-specific projection nuclei (Desiraju and Purpura, 1970; Maekawa and Purpura, 1967; Purpura et al., 1965a).

The foregoing observations are relevant to problems of the functional organization of synaptic systems underlying sleep-wakefulness activities (Purpura, 1974b). The intracellular synaptic events observed during evoked electrocortical synchronization and desynchronization have their counter-part in spontaneous alterations in electrocortical activities in different behavioral states. In recent years there has been much interest in studies of the ontogenesis of these behavioral states (Clemente et al., 1972; Elling-son, 1972; Jouvet-Mounier et al., 1970; Shimizu and Himwich, 1968). These investigations have disclosed an orderly pattern of development of sleep-wakefulness activities in a number of altricial newborn mammals (Jouvet-Mounier et al., 1970; Shimizu and Himwich, 1968). A consistent finding has been the relative paucity of spindle wave electrocortical activity at birth with an increasing organization of spindle bursts and slow wave sleep during postnatal development.

In view of the important role of the thalamus in the generation of rhyth-mically recurring electrocortical activities, several questions may be raised concerning the development of these activities in immature animals. (a) What is the maturational status of inhibitory and excitatory intrathalamic synaptic pathways in the newborn animal? (b) Are there developmental alterations in the time-course and effectiveness of EPSPs and IPSPs in thalamic neurons that parallel the development of electrocortical synchronizing activities? (c) When do synaptic events underlying reticulothalamic activation develop, and how are they characterized? These questions have been explored in a series of ontogenetic studies carried out in the past few years with methods and techniques identical to those employed in intracellular studies of thalamic neurons in adult animals (see above). The present report summarizes the major findings of this investigation (Thatcher and Purpura, 1972 and 1973).

POSTNATAL DEVELOPMENT OF THALAMIC NEURONAL SYNCHRONIZATION

Low frequency medial thalamic (MTh) stimulation in neonatal and very young kittens does not elicit recruiting responses similar to those observed in adult animals. In agreement with studies of evoked cortical responses to thalamic stimulation in immature rabbits (DoCarmo, 1960) it is not possible to evoke typical long latency recruiting responses in young kittens. Rather, such stimulation generally produces a series of decrementing evoked cortical responses in young kittens during the first 7—10 days postnatally. By the end of the second week, however, low frequency MTh stimulation elicits recruiting activities. Spontaneous spindle bursts are then evident in electro-cortical recordings.

Despite difficulties in obtaining intracellular recordings from neurons of the immature feline brain it has been possible, in previous studies of neocortical and hippocampal neurons (Purpura et al., 1965b and 1968), to assess the properties of synaptic activities and spike potential character-istics in a wide variety of elements. It must be noted that thalamic neurons in neonatal and young kittens are even more 'fragile' than cortical neurons. Nevertheless, a number of consistent observations could be made on thalamic synaptic events in penetrations of over 250 cells. The majority of these neurons exhibited low resting potentials subsequent to traumatic impale-ment. This was especially the case for elements in neonatal kittens. Despite brief periods of intracellular or 'quasi-intracellular' recording it was possible to determine latency and duration characteristics of evoked IPSPs.

Low frequency (3.3/sec) MTh stimulation in young kittens elicited IPSPs in approximately 90% of impaled neurons widely distributed in the rostral thalamus. Reduction in discharge frequency was observed in a small proportion of cells in the absence of IPSPs. Examples of the characteristics of MTh-evoked IPSPs encountered in thalamic neurons of 1—3-day-old kittens are illustrated in Fig. 1. Only rarely were IPSPs preceded by clearly

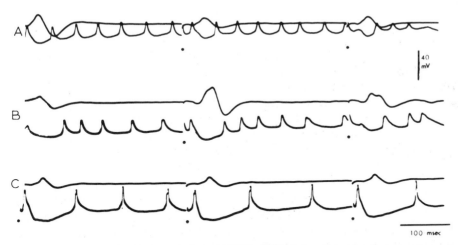

Fig. 1. Examples of characteristics of IPSPs evoked in thalamic neurons from 2- and 3-day-old kittens in response to low frequency (3.3/sec) medial thalamic (MTh) stimula-tion. A and C: from a 3-day-old kitten. B: from a 2-day-old kitten. In this and subsequent figures upper channel records are cortical surface response (negativity upwards). MTh stimuli indicated by dots. A: first three decrementing series of responses. B: alternating characteristics of cortical evoked responses during continued MTh stimulation. C: recorded during stabilization phase of cortically evoked response. IPSPs in these three cells ex-hibit variable duration. (From Thatcher and Purpura, 1973.)

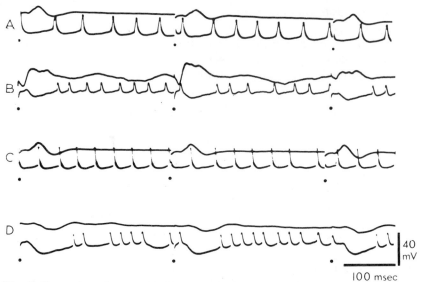

Fig. 2. Examples of synaptic events evoked in four different thalamic neurons by low frequency MTh stimulation during the course of experiments on 7-day-old kittens. A: a slight increase in the interval between discharges immediately after the MTh stimulus is the only effect detectable. B and D: short duration IPSPs are elicited by MTh stimulation in cells with partial spike potentials. C: cell unaffected by MTh stimulation. (From Thatcher and Purpura, 1973.)

defined EPSPs. However, this may have been due to relatively low membrane potentials subsequent to injury.

It is of interest that the general characteristics of IPSPs observed in the neonatal period were not significantly different in kittens 6—8 days old (Fig. 2). Thus, the mean latency of IPSPs during the first week postnatally was 14 msec and the mean duration was 50 msec. There was an equal probability of observing IPSPs with these characteristics in 3- and 8-day-old animals.

During the latter half of the second, and by the end of the third postnatal week, IPSPs with different characteristics were noted. In these older kittens (13—22 days) spike potentials (largely injury discharges) were considerably shorter in duration and larger in amplitude than in younger kittens. This reflects both the increasing tendency for more stable penetrations, and resistance to depolarizing inactivation secondary to membrane trauma. Examples of IPSP characteristics observed in 14- and 22-day-old kittens are shown in Figs. 3 and 4, respectively. The smoothly summating characteristics of the prolonged IPSPs observed in the older kitten (Fig. 4) are similar to those originally observed in adult animals (Purpura and Cohen, 1962; Purpura and Shofer, 1963). Comparison of the IPSP characteristics in 2—3-week-

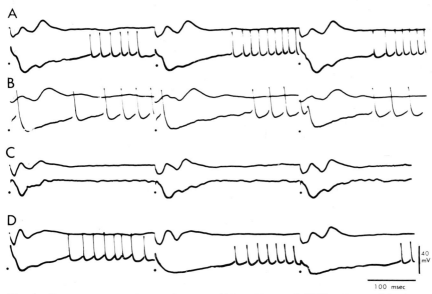

Fig. 3. Characteristics of long duration (80—160 msec) IPSPs observed in four different thalamic neurons from a 2-week-old kitten. Note that at this developmental stage injury discharges occur at a higher frequency and spike potentials are shorter in duration than in younger kittens. IPSPs in A and C have multiple components. (From Thatcher and Purpura, 1973.)

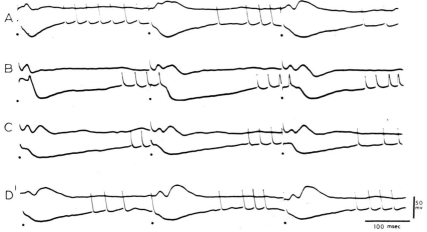

Fig. 4. Examples of IPSP characteristics observed in four different thalamic neurons from a 3-week-old kitten during low frequency MTh stimulation. Spike potential amplitude and duration are similar to spikes of thalamic neurons in adult animals. This display emphasizes the synchronizing features of the long duration IPSPs which limit spike discharges to the brief periods after IPSPs and just prior to the succeeding stimulus of the repetitive train. Note in particular that the IPSPs in B attain a duration of nearly 200 msec. In the other cells the IPSPs range from 100 to 150 msec. (From Thatcher and Purpura, 1973.)

old kittens with younger animals revealed the surprising finding of identical mean latencies. However, highly significant differences were observed in IPSP durations. Indeed, the mean duration of IPSPs in older kittens (2—3 weeks) was 127 msec, indicating more than a twofold increase in IPSP duration during the period of functional maturation of evoked recruiting responses. These observations point to an increasing capacity of thalamic inhibitory neurons to generate prolonged IPSPs in relay and other neurons as a major factor in the development of spontaneous spindle bursts and other synchronized electrocortical activities in the immature mammalian brain (Thatcher and Purpura, 1973).

DEVELOPMENT OF MTh-EVOKED DESYNCHRONIZATION OF THALAMIC NEURONAL ACTIVITY

The effects of high frequency (80/sec) MTh stimulation on intracellularly recorded synaptic activities of thalamic neurons in young (1-week-old)

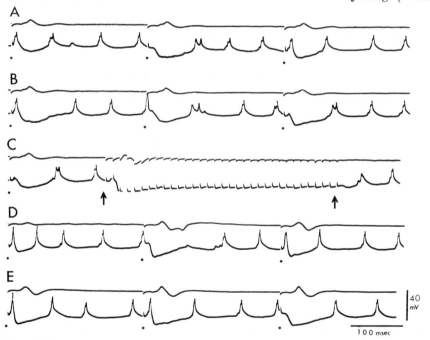

Fig. 5. Comparison of the postsynaptic effects of low (3/sec) and high (80/sec) frequency MTh stimulation observed in a thalamic neuron in a 3-day-old kitten. A—E: continuous recording. A and B: 3/sec MTh stimulation (dots) elicits prominent IPSPs. In C, between arrows, a period of high frequency MTh stimulation is introduced. Note summation of IPSPs and the attenuation of the IPSP elicited by the last stimulus of the repetitive train. D: resumption of low frequency stimulation (first dot) results in a markedly attenuated IPSP. Subsequent IPSPs are similar to IPSPs elicited prior to high frequency MTh stimulation. (From Thatcher and Purpura, 1972.)

and older kittens (2—3 weeks of age) were markedly different. In young kittens neurons that exhibited prominent IPSPs to low frequency MTh stimulation generally showed increases in membrane polarization during high frequency MTh stimulation (Fig. 5). It should be noted in Fig. 5 that the last stimulus of the high frequency repetitive train initiated an attenuated IPSP compared to the first stimulus (Fig. 5C). This attenuation persisted for 100—200 msec as indicated by the small IPSP observed upon resumption of the low frequency MTh stimulation (Fig. 5D). Thereafter IPSPs were similar to those elicited prior to the period of high frequency stimulation.

Entirely different effects of high frequency MTh stimulation were observed in thalamic neurons of 2—3-week-old kittens (Thatcher and Purpura, 1973).

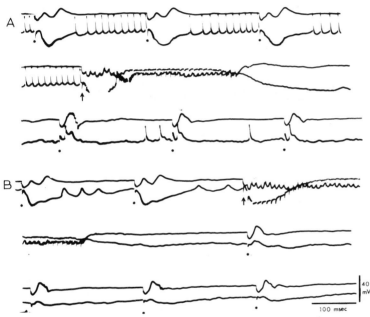

Fig. 6. Postactivation facilitation of EPSPs and attenuation of IPSPs in thalamic neurons from a 2-week-old kitten following high frequency MTh stimulation. A, upper set: low frequency MTh stimulation evokes IPSPs which are not preceded by EPSPs; middle set: onset of high frequency (80/sec) MTh stimulation (at arrow). IPSP is terminated by depolarizing shift in membrane potential; lower set: resumption of low frequency MTh stimulation several seconds later. In the postactivation period each stimulus elicits an EPSP and spike discharge, but IPSPs are not observed. Spontaneous discharges occur at variable times after the evoked EPSP. Note persisting change in evoked cortical potential in the postactivation period. B: recordings from a traumatized neuron in the same animal. Sequence of changes in evoked IPSPs, similar to that in A, occurs in the postactivation period. Towards the end of the lower set of records the EPSP induced by the prior period of high frequency stimulation becomes attenuated along with 'reappearance' of the prolonged IPSP. (From Thatcher and Purpura, 1972.)

This was seen particularly in respect to the cumulative actions of higher stimulus repetition rates. Long duration IPSPs were elicited in thalamic neurons in older kittens during low frequency MTh stimulation (Fig. 6A and B). A brief period of high frequency MTh stimulation produced, initially, a summated IPSP which was followed by a phase of sustained depolarization. Following cessation of high frequency stimulation there was a gradual recovery of membrane potential. Immediately thereafter low frequency MTh stimulation did not elicit prolonged IPSPs as in the period prior to high frequency MTh stimulation. Instead, during the postactivation period low frequency MTh stimulation elicited short latency EPSPs which triggered spike discharges (Fig. 6A). In other neurons, after loss of spike potentials, a similar transformation in synaptic events evoked by low frequency MTh stimulation was observed in the immediate postactivation period (Fig. 6B). Rapid attenuation of EPSPs and reinstitution of prolonged IPSPs occurred with continued low frequency MTh stimulation (Fig. 6B).

The findings of Figs. 5 and 6 permit the conclusion that at a time when synchronizing IPSPs exhibit functionally mature overt characteristics high frequency MTh stimulation is capable of activating parallel synaptic pathways which elicit sustained EPSPs in thalamic neurons. The consequences of this activation are seen in abrupt termination of prolonged IPSPs, a swamping effect of summated EPSPs and persistence of excitatory synaptic bombardment of thalamic neurons beyond the period of high frequency MTh stimulation. Evidently in the 2—3-week-old kittens excitatory synaptic drives initiated by high frequency MTh stimulation predominate and override IPSPs. In view of these observations it was important to determine whether brain stem reticular stimulation might also elicit different synaptic events in thalamic neurons in young and older kittens.

RETICULOTHALAMIC ACTIVATION

High frequency upper brain stem reticular formation (BSRF) stimulation in young kittens (1-week-old) produced synaptic effects in thalamic neurons that were identical to those observed following high frequency MTh stimulation (Fig. 7A). It was of interest that, at a time when prolonged low frequency MTh stimulation produced small IPSPs in thalamic neurons, superimposed BSRF stimulation augmented IPSPs (Fig. 7B).

Perhaps the clearest example of the combined synaptic effects of low frequency MTh stimulation and high frequency BSRF stimulation are to be seen in Fig. 8 from a 15-day-old kitten. Low frequency MTh stimulation produced a well-developed EPSP-IPSP sequence in this element (Fig. 8A). High frequency BSRF stimulation produced a prolonged summating IPSP, which, however, failed to block spontaneous discharges after the first 0.5 sec of stimulation (Fig. 8B). Minimal attenuation of the synchronizing IPSP was noted during early phases of BSRF stimulation (Fig. 8C). However, when

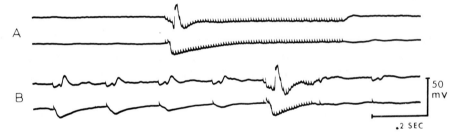

Fig. 7. Cortical surface (upper records) and intracellular recording (bursts) from a thalamic neuron in a 5-day-old kitten. A: high frequency upper brain stem reticular formation (BSRF) stimulation evoked a long duration IPSP. B: late phase of continued MTh stimulation and superimposed high frequency BSRF stimulation. The latter stimulation facilitates the MTh-induced IPSP. (From Homan, Shofer and Purpura, unpublished observations.)

the effects of such stimulation attenuated, low frequency MTh stimulation was still capable of evoking prominent IPSPs (Fig. 8D). These observations suggest little functional interaction within the inhibitory synaptic pathways involved in the production of MTh-induced IPSPs and BSRF-induced pro-

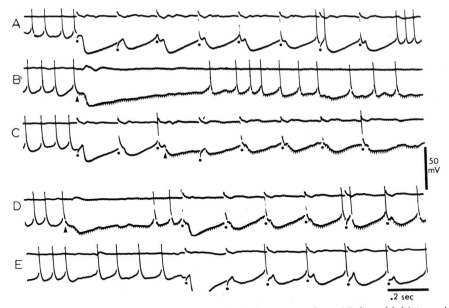

Fig. 8. Intracellular recording from a thalamic neuron in a 15-day-old kitten. A: low frequency MTh stimulation elicits prominent EPSP-IPSP sequences. B: high frequency BSRF stimulation (at arrow head) produces prolonged IPSP which attenuates after 0.5 sec. C and D: little interaction is observed between IPSPs evoked by two modes of stimulation. E: 10 sec after D. Recovery of MTh-evoked IPSPs. (From Homan, Shofer and Purpura, unpublished observations.)

longed IPSPs in thalamic neurons in the kitten. It is surprising that whereas high frequency MTh stimulation in the 2-week-old kitten elicits powerful excitatory drives in thalamic neurons *and* attenuation of the synchronizing IPSPs, high frequency BSRF stimulation produced only sustained relatively short latency IPSPs. Differences in the effectiveness of these two modes of thalamic neuronal desynchronization probably reflect the continuing and more prolonged maturation of brain stem influences on thalamic neuronal activity after the functional development of intrathalamic internuclear pathways.

DISCUSSION

The foregoing observations summarize the available data on the properties of intrathalamic synaptic pathways in the immature brain (Thatcher and Purpura, 1972 and 1973). Intracellular recording from thalamic neurons has provided evidence that inhibitory neurons have attained a level of functional maturity in the young kitten that parallels the development of inhibitory neurons in neocortex (Purpura et al., 1965b) and hippocampus (Purpura, 1969; Purpura et al., 1968) in the perinatal period. There is, however, one important difference. In the case of immature cortical neurons (Purpura et al., 1965b and 1968) evoked IPSPs are of long duration comparable to, if not greater than, IPSPs elicited in mature cortical neurons under similar conditions of examination (Purpura and Shofer, 1964; Purpura et al., 1964). IPSPs in thalamic neurons of neonatal and young kittens have a mean duration that is significantly shorter than the mean duration of IPSPs in 2—3-week-old kittens. After the third week such IPSPs exhibit all the characteristics observed in adult animals (Purpura, 1972). In view of the essential role of long duration IPSPs in generalized synchronization of thalamic neuronal activity (Purpura and Cohen, 1962), it follows that the functional maturation of intrathalamic internuclear events associated with thalamic neuronal synchronization consists primarily in an increase in the mean duration of IPSPs. The progressive augmentation in the capacity of internuclear pathways to elicit EPSPs in immature thalamic neurons represents a second feature of the maturational process of thalamic neuronal synchronization (Thatcher and Purpura, 1973).

Synaptic events observed following high frequency MTh stimulation also reflect the relative functional immaturity of thalamic internuclear excitatory synaptic pathways in young kittens. During the first postnatal week high frequency MTh stimulation elicits sustained inhibition of thalamic neuron activity. In kittens older than two weeks, a new synaptic event is added in the form of a powerful and sustained EPSP which may inactivate spike electrogenesis. This effect, and others, including the prominent post-activation attenuation of IPSPs and facilitation of short latency EPSPs, are similar to those observed in adult animals following high frequency

MTh stimulation (Purpura and Shofer, 1963). Thus the functional maturation of excitatory synaptic pathways during the second week heralds the capacity of thalamic neurons to exhibit powerful excitatory drives during MTh-evoked thalamic neuronal desynchronization and concomitant electrocortical activation.

The data indicating that two different effects are observed following high frequency MTh stimulation at different stages of postnatal development permit further analysis of the synaptic mechanisms underlying MTh-induced electrocortical activation in adult animals (Purpura and Shofer, 1963). It has been inferred from observations on the attenuation of synchronizing IPSPs in EPSP-IPSP sequences during the transition from low to high frequency MTh stimulation, that such attenuation results from an inhibition, or blockade, of inhibitory pathways generating the synchronizing IPSPs as well as augmentation of excitatory synaptic drives (Purpura and Shofer, 1963). The present study indicates that high frequency MTh stimulation does not activate pathways which are inhibitory to the interneuronal elements generating synchronizing IPSPs in thalamic neurons, at least in very young kittens. Thus, the thalamic neuronal events observed in older kittens and probably adult animals during high frequency MTh stimulation reflect the addition of EPSPs that override simultaneously elicited IPSPs.

The effects produced by high frequency MTh stimulation are undoubtedly complicated by involvement of mesencephalic and lower brain stem elements which have been shown to receive complex inputs from MTh regions (Mancia et al., 1974; Purpura, 1969). Intracellular data have also been obtained recently indicating reciprocal synaptic connections between MTh nuclei and mesencephalic and lower brain stem regions in adult animals (Mancia et al., 1971a, b and 1974). From the present studies it appears that upper brain stem stimulation in young kittens exerts a predominantly inhibitory action on rostral thalamic neurons through pathways which may not involve non-specific-specific internuclear projections underlying the production of synchronizing IPSPs. However, it must be noted that in adult animals disfacilitatory effects are observed in MTh neurons during high frequency mesencephalic stimulation (Mancia and Otero-Costas, 1973; Mancia et al., 1974). Further intracellular studies will be required in immature animals to define the involvement of thalamic disfacilitatory mechanisms in the operations of brain stem inputs to thalamic internuclear projection pathways.

It is of interest to consider whether observations on the discharge characteristics of thalamic neurons during low frequency MTh stimulation in young kittens can contribute information on the possible synaptic mechanisms underlying prolonged IPSPs. In none of the recordings obtained from immature thalamic neurons in the present study was there any indication that IPSPs were generated by repetitively active elements. This observation is consistent with previous studies of neocortical (Purpura et al., 1965b) and hippocampal (Purpura et al., 1968) neurons in newborn and young kittens. One explanation for this failure to encounter inhibitory interneurons in immature brain whose discharge characteristics could account for long duration IPSPs, is that such neurons may simply be too small and fragile to withstand close approach or impalement with the micropipettes employed in these studies. Alternatively, it may be argued that high frequency discharges of inhibitory interneurons may not be required to produce prolonged IPSPs in immature neurons if transmitter action is prolonged for various reasons (Purpura, 1972). To what extent morphogenetic changes in thalamic synaptic organizations may contribute to the developmental alterations in IPSPs during the first few weeks postnatally is not known. Electron microscope studies of thalamic elements in young kittens reveal complex synaptic arrangements and synaptic glomeruli by the third week (Purpura, 1974a), but the precise temporal pattern of development of these complex synaptic arrangements including dendrodendritic synapses remains for future investigation.

Extrapolation of the present intracellular data obtained in locally anesthetized-paralyzed young kittens to problems of the ontogenesis of sleep-wakefulness activities in intact animals may be justified solely on the grounds that it will probably not be possible to obtain similar data in the *behaving* kitten, at least with currently available microphysiological methodologies. It should be recalled that newborn kittens do not exhibit organized spindle burst activities to any significant degree until several weeks postnatally. Thus, studies of the ontogeny of sleep in kittens indicate that sleep spindles do not appear until 3—4 weeks (Shimizu and Himwich, 1968), i.e., at a time when the cerebral cortex has acquired all the ultrastructural features found in adult cats (Voeller et al., 1963). To the extent that the thalamus is the major source of afferent input to the cortex in the production of sleep spindles it follows that the functional immaturity of thalamic synchronizing mechanisms must contribute significantly to the delayed maturation of sleep spindle activity.

The present study reveals that electrical stimulation of thalamic nuclear organizations classically associated with the production of generalized electrocortical synchronization is capable of generating thalamic neuronal discharge synchronization 2—3 weeks postnatally in the kitten, but not earlier than this. Evidently 'spontaneous' operation of the thalamocortical synchronizing mechanism follows shortly thereafter. It is at the level of the thalamus where the effects of mesencephalic and brain stem reticular input systems appear to exert powerful synaptic actions in modulating electrocortical rhythms. In view of this it is not surprising that the development of reticulothalamic synaptic interactions should correspond to the periods of early maturation of sleep-wakefulness behavior in the kitten.

Acknowledgements

The author thanks Dr. Robert Thatcher, Dr. Richard Homan and Dr. Robert J. Shofer for permission to reproduce data obtained in collaborative studies.

This study was supported by NIH Grant NS-07512, NIMH Grant MH-6418 and a grant from the Alfred P. Sloan Foundation.

REFERENCES

Clemente, C.D., Purpura, D.P. and Mayer, F.E. (Eds.) (1972) Sleep and the Maturing Nervous System. Academic Press, New York.

Desiraju, T. and Purpura, D.P. (1970) Organization of specific-non-specific thalamic internuclear synaptic pathways. Brain Res., 21, 169—181.

DoCarmo, R.J. (1960) Direct cortical and recruiting responses in postnatal rabbit. J. Neurophysiol., 23, 496—504.

Ellingson, R.J. (1972) Development of wakefulness-sleep cycles and associated EEG patterns in mammals. In C.D. Clemente, D.P. Purpura and F.E. Mayer (Eds.), Sleep and the Maturing Nervous System. Academic Press, New York, pp. 165—174.

Feldman, M.H. and Purpura, D.P. (1970) Prolonged conductance increase in thalamic neurons during synchronizing inhibition. Brain Res., 24, 329—332.

Jouvet-Mounier, D., Astic, L. and Lacote, D. (1970) Ontogenesis of the states of sleep in rat, cat, and guinea pig during the first postnatal month. Develop. Psychobiol., 2, 216—239.

Maekawa, K. and Purpura, D.P. (1967) Intracellular study of lemniscal and non-specific synaptic interactions in thalamic ventrobasal neurons. Brain Res., 4, 308—323.

Mancia, M. and Otero-Costas, J. (1973) Nature of the midbrain influences upon thalamic neurons. Brain Res., 49, 200—204.

Mancia, M., Broggi, G. and Margnelli, M. (1971a) Brain stem reticular effects on intralaminar thalamic neurons in the cat. Brain Res., 25, 638—641.

Mancia, M., Grantyn, A., Broggi, G. and Margnelli, M. (1971b) Synaptic linkage between mesencephalic and bulbopontine reticular structures as revealed by intracellular recording. Brain Res., 33, 491—494.

Mancia, M., Margnelli, M., Mariotti, M., Spreafico, R. and Broggi, G. (1974) Brain stem-thalamus reciprocal influences in the cat. Brain Res., 69, 297—314.

Purpura, D.P. (1969) Interneuronal mechanisms in synchronization and desynchronization of thalamic activity. In M.A.B. Brazier (Ed.), The Interneuron, UCLA Forum in Medical Sciences. pp. 467—496.

Purpura, D.P. (1969) Stability and seizure susceptibility of immature brain. In H.H. Jasper, A.A. Ward and A. Pope (Eds.), Basic Mechanisms of the Epilepsies. Little, Brown and Co., Boston, Mass., pp. 481—505.

Purpura, D.P. (1970) Operations and processes in thalamic and synaptically related neural subsystems. In The Neurosciences II. Rockefeller University Press, New York, pp. 458—470.

Purpura, D.P. (1972) Intracellular studies of synaptic organizations in the mammalian brain. In G.D. Pappas and D.P. Purpura (Eds.), Structure and Function of Synapses. Raven Press, New York, pp. 257—302.

Purpura, D.P. (1974a) Development of synaptic substrates for drug actions in immature brain. In A. Vernadakis and N. Weiner (Eds.), Drugs and the Developing Brain. Plenum Press, New York, pp. 3—28.

Purpura, D.P. (1974b) Intracellular studies of thalamic synaptic mechanisms in evoked synchronization and desynchronization of electrocortical activity. In O. Petre-Quadens and J.D. Schlag (Eds.), Basic Sleep Mechanisms. Academic Press, New York, pp. 99—125.

Purpura, D.P. and Cohen, B. (1962) Intracellular recording from thalamic neurons during recruiting responses. J. Neurophysiol., 25, 621—635.

Purpura, D.P. and Shofer, R.J. (1963) Intracellular recording from thalamic neurons during reticulocortical activation. J. Neurophysiol., 26, 494—505.

Purpura, D.P. and Shofer, R.J. (1964) Cortical intracellular potentials during augmenting and recruiting responses. I. Effects of injected hyperpolarizing currents on evoked membrane potential changes. J. Neurophysiol., 27, 117—132.

Purpura, D.P., Shofer, R.J. and Musgrave, F.S. (1964) Cortical intracellular potentials during augmenting and recruiting responses. II. Patterns of synaptic activities in pyramidal and nonpyramidal tract neurons. J. Neurophysiol., 27, 133—151.

Purpura, D.P., Scarff, T. and McMurtry, J.G. (1965a) Intracellular study of internuclear inhibition in ventrolateral thalamic neurons. J. Neurophysiol., 28, 487—496.

Purpura, D.P., Shofer, R.J. and Scarff, T. (1965b) Properties of synaptic activities and spike potentials of neurons in immature neocortex. J. Neurophysiol., 28, 925—942.

Purpura, D.P., Frigyesi, T.L., McMurtry, J.G. and Scarff, T. (1966a) Synaptic mechanisms in thalamic regulation of cerebellocortical projection activity. In D.P. Purpura and M.D. Yahr (Eds.), The Thalamus. Columbia University Press, New York, pp. 153—172.

Purpura, D.P., McMurtry, J.G. and Maekawa, K. (1966b) Synaptic events in ventrolateral thalamic neurons during suppression of recruiting responses by brain stem reticular stimulation. Brain Res., 1, 63—76.

Purpura, D.P., Prelevic, S. and Santini, M. (1968) Postsynaptic potentials and spike variations in the feline hippocampus during postnatal ontogenesis. Exp. Neurol., 22, 408—422.

Shimizu, A. and Himwich, H.E. (1968) The ontogeny of sleep in kittens and young rabbits. Electroenceph. clin. Neurophysiol., 24, 307—318.

Thatcher, R.W. and Purpura, D.P. (1972) Maturational status of inhibitory and excitatory synaptic activities of thalamic neurons in neonatal kitten. Brain Res., 44, 661—665.

Thatcher, R.W. and Purpura, D.P. (1973) Postnatal development of thalamic synaptic events underlying evoked recruiting responses and electrocortical activation. Brain Res., 60, 21—34.

Voeller, K., Pappas, G.D. and Purpura, D.P. (1963) Electron microscope study of development of cat superficial neocortex. Exp. Neurol., 7, 107—130.

DISCUSSION

CHASE: There is an observation that the somatic reflex activity is facilitated during active sleep in the kitten. It is normally inhibited when the cat is in active sleep, whereas in wakefulness it is inhibited in the young kitten. The next observation is the effect of reticular formation stimulation, showing that one site of the reticular formation can lead to reflex facilitation during wakefulness and reflex inhibition during active sleep. It is also impossible to keep these young kittens in wakefulness, they can be aroused for a while and then they will go to active sleep state. Is it possible that any of these observations might relate to the effect of reticular stimulation on the thalamic system, as a kind of state-dependent phenomenon that might be related to the stage during which you stimulated?

PURPURA: We could not really look at these species and stimulate their reticular formation or the thalamus and say that we are stimulating in a state of normal active sleep. That will be fantastic. As it is, the kittens are exposed, they are depressed and they had a lot of volatile anesthetics to get them going. They are not in a natural state to look at. I would say that probably everything you have said has something to do with what I talked about and I think I have to leave it at that.

GILMAN: I want to ask you a similar question along similar lines that relates to your stimulation of the mesencephalic reticular formation. Probably you know that Hobson has some interesting data in which he recorded from the magnocellular portion of the pontine reticular formation. He has a nice correlation of unit activity with sleep states. My question is firstly whether the site of your stimulation bears any similarity to this region, and, secondly, why did you choose the site which you chose? Where were your electrodes?

PURPURA: There is no relationship to that work in terms of the kitten story that we were just talking about. The stimulation in the kitten is so prominent that the entire dorsolateral pontine tegmentum gets it and nobody is going to say that I am stimulating nucleus pontis oralis or caudalis or some other specific nucleus. I am saying that we are giving a large stimulation in order to get something upstream of any pathways running through, so I do not think there is any question about this.

GILMAN: Where is your electrode?

PURPURA: The electrode is at the level of the intercollicular region about 1.5 mm down from the central gray and about 1 mm from the midline. All of us seem to know that it is the dorsal pontine tegmentum, and beyond that it is one of the best places to stimulate the system in order to get a highly desynchronized cortex. Hobson's work has no relationship with anything we are doing because he is looking at units during natural sleep; and it is not the same region anyway.

11

CORTICAL INHIBITION DURING SLEEP AND WAKING

M. STERIADE

Laboratoire de Neurophysiologie, Département de Physiologie, Faculté de Médecine, Université Laval, Québec (Canada)

INTRODUCTION

Pavlov's suggestion (Pavlov, 1923) that 'internal inhibition' (i.e. decreasing responses to successive unreinforced stimuli) and sleep are two aspects of the same inhibitory mechanism, was revived from historical oblivion when sleep could no longer be exclusively regarded as a passive phenomenon, and active inhibitory processes were claimed to trigger and maintain it. The old pavlovian imagery of sleep as the result of mass cortical inhibition irradiating to the whole cerebrum is certainly untenable in view of the discovery, with the advent of unit recordings in behaving animals, that some sleep stages may be associated with increased neuronal firing (see monograph by Steriade and Hobson, 1976). Nonetheless, the core of Pavlov's theory on the causal relations between inhibition and sleep has been reactualized in an attempt by Moruzzi (1966) to introduce a doctrine based on the assumption that sleep is concerned with slow recovery events in those synapses where plastic changes occur during wakefulness as a consequence of learning or conditioning. Moruzzi's attractive hypothesis envisages the synaptic processes of interneurons as being involved in higher nervous activity, consequently suggesting that: "small interneurons are more strongly affected than the large neurons of the neocortical projection areas by these slow recovery processes", and concluding: "it would be impossible to deny that strategically placed interneurons or synapses may be inhibited during sleep" (Moruzzi, 1966; p. 377 and p. 378). This modern hypothesis on sleep and inhibition fits in well with Evarts' inference (Evarts, 1964), drawn from an analysis of discharge patterns in pyramidal tract (PT) neurons during the sleep-waking cycle, that recurrent inhibition and inhibitory cortical interneurons might be depressed during sleep. However, Moruzzi repeatedly pointed out that we have so far "no evidence that recurrent intracortical inhibition is depressed during sleep" (Moruzzi, 1966; p. 374) and "no direct information on the sleep behavior of small inhibitory interneurons" (Moruzzi, 1972; p. 9).

The lack of evidence on inhibitory processes and interneuronal apparatus persisted until very recently *. It is the aim of this report to summarize experimental work conducted during the last few years in collaboration with my colleagues on some of the unsolved problems concerning changes in inhibition during sleep and waking in motor, somatosensory and associative cortical neurons. Such a study exceeds the field of sleep mechanisms and function by throwing some light on changes in discriminatory processes related to sensorimotor and associative performances at different levels of vigilance.

TECHNIQUE

Details on the techniques employed in investigations using extracellular recordings in freely moving monkeys and encéphale isolé cats may be found in recent publications from our laboratory (Steriade, 1974; Steriade and Deschênes, 1974; Steriade et al., 1974a and b).

Briefly, in experiments conducted on macaque monkeys sitting in a primate chair, stimulating electrodes were inserted in the pes pedunculi (Fig. $1A_1$) and in the intermediate area between the rostral part of the thalamic ventrobasal (VB) complex and the posterior part of the ventrolateral (VL) nucleus (Fig. $1A_2$), for antidromic or/and synaptic activation of precentral neurons recorded from the arm area. The peduncular location for antidromic invasion of cortical output neurons was selected because in this region several millimeters separate the corticofugal fibers from the lemniscal pathway. In addition, to render as pure as possible the recurrent inhibitory effects in motor cortical neurons, an extensive lesion, destroying lemniscal fibers, was made in experiments on encéphale isolé cats anterior to the stimulating peduncular electrode (Fig. 1B). Identification of neurons recorded from the primary somatosensory (SI) area was possible by their antidromic and synaptic activation from the VB, the underlying white matter in a previously VB-lesioned preparation, and the ipsilateral pericruciate cortex. The input-output organization of neurons in parietal associative cortex (areas 5 and 7) was defined from synaptically and antidromically elicited discharges by stimulating the thalamic lateralis intermedius (LI), lateralis posterior (LP) and center médian (CM) nuclei.

METHODOLOGY

(I) An inevitable query is: have we the right to speak of inhibition without intracellular recordings and measurements of membrane conductance, as tested by injected current pulses? A definite negative answer may be valid for studies specifically directed to define the properties of synaptic pathways,

---

* The difficulties in accepting speculations on 'inhibition' from data obtained with mass evoked responses have been discussed elsewhere (Steriade et al., 1974a; Steriade and Hobson, 1976).

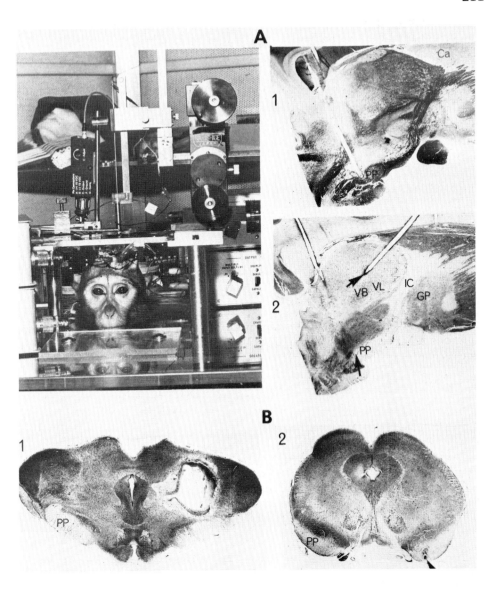

Fig. 1. Location of stimulating electrodes in experiments on chronically implanted, sitting *Macaca mulatta* (A) and encéphale isolé cat (B). A: sagittal sections stained with myelin (1) and Nissl (2) methods. Abbreviations: Ca, caudate nucleus; GP, globus pallidus; IC, internal capsule; PP, pes pedunculi; VL and VB, ventrolateral and ventrobasal thalamic nuclei. Arrows indicate stimulated points in the PP (two electrodes were inserted in this experiment) and in the intermediate area between VL and VB nuclei. B: frontal sections showing the stimulated point in the PP (arrow in B_2) and the mediolateral size of the lesion destroying the medial lemniscus (B_1) in front of the stimulated point. (Modified from Steriade, 1974 (A) and Steriade and Deschênes, 1974 (B).)

as in the usual investigations on the brain's wiring diagram. In our case, however, we must remember the still unsurmounted difficulties in maintaining an impaled neuron with a convenient membrane potential throughout different sleep-waking stages in a behaving preparation. Even in paralyzed preparations, an adequate study of intracellularly recorded activities during spontaneously occurring changes in the vigilance level is not yet available in the literature. I mean by 'adequate study' the identification of synaptic inputs and target structures of the recorded cell, the display of its background firing at least during one transition from EEG patterns of sleep to waking and vice versa, the investigation of synaptic and/or antidromic responsiveness during another sleep-waking transition, the study of inhibitory events by using paired stimuli to obtain information on the recovery cycle, and *all* these amusing procedures in the same neuron, over long enough periods of time to allow for statistical analyses of data.

Here are three main reasons justifying the above, seemingly exaggerated requirements for a study on neuronal activities during sleep and waking. (1) Neuronal identification by electrophysiological criteria is imperative, in view of different, even opposite, alterations undergone by various long axoned (fast- or slow-conducting) neurons and short axoned interneurons during various stages of sleep and waking (Steriade et al., 1972, 1974a and b; Steriade, 1973) (see Figs. 14—21). Moreover, differential synaptic responsiveness at various levels of vigilance has been found when dissociating in cat's motor cortex *simple* PT cells, driven purely by VL messages, from *complex* PT neurons, receiving convergent inputs from both VL and VB thalamic nuclei (Steriade et al., 1973). (2) The increased or decreased *spontaneous* firing in some neuronal classes is not necessarily associated with parallel changes in unit *responsiveness* to synaptic (Steriade et al., 1973) or antidromic (Steriade et al., 1974a) volleys. The study of mean rate and temporal patterns of spontaneous discharge must therefore be dissociated from the investigation of unit responsiveness, to prevent disruption of the background firing by testing shocks. (3) Waking, as well as sleep, are not continuous stable states associated with uniformly distributed single unit activities. During the short-lasting period of natural arousal and the excited wakefulness, the activity of some cortical output neurons may be oppositely altered when compared to the steady state of quiet wakefulness (Steriade et al., 1974a and b) (see Fig. 21). This imposes an investigation of nuanced phasic and tonic sleep-waking periods.

Confronted with such difficulties, sleep investigators are obliged, at least at present, to settle for extracellular studies during natural patterns of sleep and waking and to benefit from the available knowledge of synaptic mechanisms drawn from intracellular recordings performed during short periods of time in rather crude artificial conditions. I share the opinion expressed by Purpura in one of our previous symposia (Purpura, 1974) that such correlative studies are of redeeming value, each approach providing the other one with what both need: the knowledge of basic cellular mechanisms in a simplified model, and the disclosure of statistically analyzed fluctuations in cellular excitability correlated with behavior in an intact preparation. Let me stress the point that a study on excitatory-inhibitory sequences elicited during the natural sleep-waking cycle must employ very fine microwires allowing juxtacellular recordings for subtle detection of the various components of unitary discharge (e.g., the initial segment (IS) and somadendritic (SD) spikes (Brock et al., 1953)). This may give information, in a freely moving animal, on the changes in membrane polarization with transition from sleep to waking (Steriade and Deschênes, 1973; Steriade et al., 1974a) (see Fig. 13).

Two kinds of neuronal activities were tested in our experiments on changes in feedback and feedforward inhibition during sleep and waking. The first procedure measured the duration of the reduced or suppressed discharge period following an antidromic or orthodromic volley *. This was correlated with the duration of the focal slow positive waves simultaneously recorded by the microelectrode and presumably reflecting extracellularly summated hyperpolarizing potentials in the neuronal pool (see Fig. 7). The second and most important procedure concerned the probability of antidromically and/or orthodromically tested evoked discharge following a conditioning inhibitory volley setting in motion the recurrent or afferent collateral mechanism. This latter investigation analyzed the latency of inhibition (i.e., the shortest time interval between the conditioning stimulus and the first signs of inhibition, as measured by response to the testing stimulus), the efficacy of inhibition (estimated by the occurrence probability of the tested discharge), and the recovery curve. The same methodology was used and essentially the same results were obtained in experiments on monkey and cat.

Fig. 2A illustrates the method we used to test the feedback inhibition acting on antidromically elicited discharge in motor cortical PT neurons. (This was identical to the study of feedforward inhibition and to the tested orthodromic discharge.) The conditioning antidromic stimulus was applied to the pes pedunculi at the minimal voltage required to elicit inhibitory effects on the testing response; the latter was elicited by a shock to the same peduncular site, at the minimal voltage required to evoke 100% antidromic invasion (A_1). As usual, the intensity of the conditioning volley was higher than that of the testing one, but always submaximal for inhibitory effects so as to allow for their fluctuations during sleep and waking. The conditioning-testing combinations were then recorded, during both sleep and waking, at different time intervals (A_{2-5}), chosen according to the characteristics of the

---

* The necessity of using central (thalamic or radiation) stimuli when testing the reactivity of cortical synapses cannot be overemphasized. Using peripheral stimuli, which are certainly more natural, may obscure the results in view of competitive alterations occurring at various prethalamic relays.

214

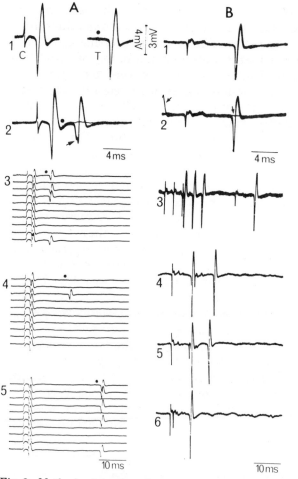

4 ms

4 ms

10 ms

10 ms

Fig. 2. Method of testing the latency, depth, and time course of recurrent inhibition acting on antidromically elicited discharges in cat's motor cortex. A and B show two different PT cells. A: the antidromic response latency (by stimulating the pes pedunculi), 1.65 msec. The conditioning volley (C) was delivered at 13 V, the minimal voltage required to elicit inhibitory effects on the testing response (T), which was evoked by a pulse of 5 V (dot), the minimal voltage required to evoke 100% antidromic invasion. A_2: C-T paired responses at an interval of 3.7 msec; note IS-SD break (arrow) and failure of the T response. A_{3-5}: 10-sweep sequences (with reduced spike amplitude) at C-T intervals of 6.6 msec, 14.3 msec and 27 msec, respectively; note failure of T response in 62% and 90% at 6.6 msec and 14.3 msec, respectively, and partial recovery beginning at 27 msec (failure of T responses in only 46%). These percentages have been computed from 50 T responses for each interval. B: unusually long latency (7 msec) of antidromic invasion (1), and collision with a spontaneous spike (arrow) which occurred 11 msec before (2). In B_3 (at lower sweep speed): the antidromic response was preceded at about 20 msec by a 3-shock train (with double intensity) applied through the same electrode in the pes pedunculi, to show the resistance to inhibition of the antidromic response in this particular unit. In B_{4-6}, the testing shock was preceded at 8.5 msec, 6.5 msec and 1.1 msec, respectively,

excitability cycle in each investigated neuron, as detected on the oscilloscope before recording for long periods on the tape. When the same intensity of stimulation was used for both the conditioning and the testing stimulation, which was often the case in the study of afferent inhibition of orthodromically elicited discharge, the probability of discharges evoked by the first shock in the pair could be considered as the control value for the testing discharge evoked by the second shock (see Fig. 10).

Since the conditioning volley inducing inhibitory effects was applied at intensities above the threshold for eliciting spike discharge, we should ask whether the effects are ascribable to true postsynaptic inhibitory influences mediated by local interneurons or to the cell refractoriness due to the hyperpolarizing afterpotential. This question could be answered in PT neurons which apparently lacked an inhibitory interneuronal apparatus, judging by their resistance to inhibition of the tested antidromic discharge even when a train of conditioning antidromic shocks was applied at very high intensities (Fig. 2B). In such cases, the duration of the refractory period usually proved not to be greater than 1.5—2 msec (Fig. $2B_{4-6}$), while antidromically elicited postsynaptic inhibition lasted for tens of milliseconds (Fig. $2A_{3-5}$, and other subsequent figures).

Finally, it must be emphasized that great care should be taken in choosing the intensity of conditioning and testing stimulations, especially when employing orthodromic volleys. In ideal experimental conditions, the use of several intensities (e.g., juxtathreshold, 25—40% suprathreshold, submaximal) may reveal different phenomena. All are 'true', even if apparently opposite with regard to the signs of alterations undergone by inhibitory events (see Fig. 3), but the investigator must be aware of the complex system he is studying, and this may be a source of fruitful analysis. Let us look at Fig. 3 depicting the effects of a conditioning arousing mesencephalic reticular (RF) train of pulses upon the responses evoked in an SI neuron by a shock-pair applied to the VB complex at two intensities, B being only 15% higher than A. Stimuli in the pair were of equal intensity in both A and B. While the excitability of this neuron was increased on reticular arousal from a control period of slow sleep in both A and B (as seen from increased responsiveness to the first shock in the pair), the afferent inhibition (triggered by the first shock and estimated from the response probability to the second, short-delayed stimulus in the pair) was differently affected on arousal, as a function of the intensity used. The reinforcement of inhibition (as reflected by failing responsiveness to the second shock) by a preceding RF stimulation

---

by a conditioning shock with double intensity. The second (test) response did not fail in this particular neuron at any of the intervals studied (some of them depicted in this figure), except for the interval of 1.1 msec (in B_6) which represents the refractory period of the unit. (Modified from Steriade and Deschênes, 1974 (A) and from unpublished experiment by Steriade and Deschênes (B).)

216

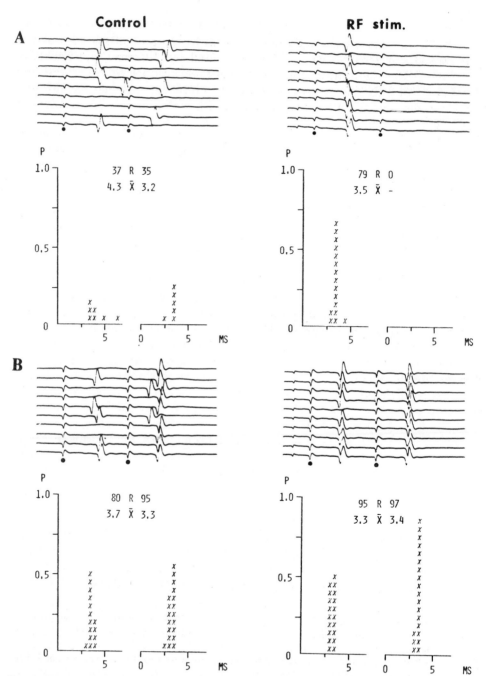

Fig. 3. Effects of reticular-elicited arousal on inhibitory events tested in cortical somatosensory neuron in cat. Two 6.8 msec-delayed shocks (dots) of equal intensity were applied to the thalamic VB complex: 12 V, 0.1 msec in A; 14 V, 0.1 msec in B. In both A

when using low intensity VB stimuli (A), as opposed to lack of significant reticular influences on unitary responsiveness to the second stimulus of the pair at higher intensity (B), may be explained by different, non-exclusive factors: (a) the RF-induced increase in neuronal responsiveness to the first shock is behind the increased activation on inhibitory interneurons through the recurrent collateral pathway, which, in turn, will diminish the occurrence probability of responses to the second stimulus in A; (b) if, at higher intensities of stimulation as in B, the percentage of responsiveness to the second shock in the control period is enhanced and the latency is shortened when compared with responses to the first shock, this is possibly due to a residual depolarization after the first discharge and/or to setting in motion the assembly of local cortical excitatory interneurons by collaterals of the afferent VB-SI volley. This depolarizing pressure may overwhelm the inhibitory effects triggered by the first shock and, therefore, mask the striking increase in inhibition elicited *at short delays* by RF stimulation in A. All of the above methodological details emphasize the need for judiciously using stimulus parameters and knowing the precise threshold of responses when reporting results on neuronal excitation and inhibition during various functional states.

(II) Another embarrassing question concerns the nature of electrophysiologically identified interneurons. These elements, whose sleep-waking behavior was only hypothesized (see Introduction) because of technical difficulties in picking up small sized units, have been recently recorded in our laboratory from thalamic nuclei (Steriade et al., 1971a and 1972; Steriade, 1973) and cortical areas (Steriade 1973 and 1974; Steriade and Deschênes, 1973; Steriade and Yossif, 1974; Steriade et al., 1974a and b), and the fluctuations in their spontaneous and evoked activities were studied during slow sleep, arousal and steady waking (see Figs. 16—19). They were recognized by several criteria: lack of antidromic invasion from different stimulation sites; exceedingly short modes (1.5—4.5 msec) and mean intervals (4.5—6.5 msec) in the interspike interval histograms of spontaneous firing, not only during slow sleep but also during waking, which is never seen in output neurons; and synaptic responses consisting of short or long, high frequency (300—800/sec) spike barrages. The outstanding finding was that the same interneurons recorded from the monkey's precentral cortex could be driven by both antidromic stimulation at the level of the pes pedunculi and by specific thalamic stimuli at latencies indicating monosynaptic excitation. The inter-

and B, left columns are taken from control periods of EEG synchronization, while right columns are from periods of EEG activation elicited by RF stimulation (the last shock of the reticular train of pulses may be seen at the extreme left of sweep sequences, preceding the first VB stimulus). Below the sweep sequences are poststimulus histograms depicting the distribution of responses to 100 testing shock-pairs. R, percentage responsiveness; $\overline{X}$, mean latency. Note especially different reticular effects on the second response of the pair by slightly increasing the intensity of stimulation. Full comments in text. Unpublished data by Steriade et al. (in preparation).

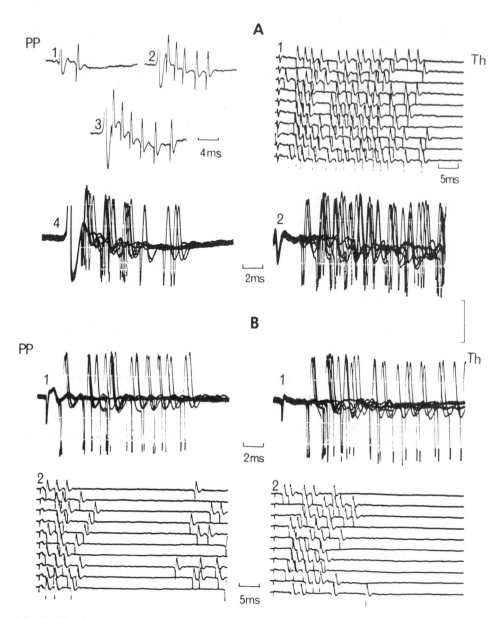

Fig. 4. Monosynaptic activation of monkey's precentral putative interneurons by antidromic pyramidal tract stimulation in the PP and by thalamic (Th) stimulation at the border between the VB and the VL nuclei. Only fast activities (175—10,000 Hz) are depicted in this figure. A and B: two different interneurons. Left column in both cases is PP stimulation; right column is Th stimulation. A: the PP testing shock was delivered in 2 and 3 at a double and triple intensity as the liminal one used in 1; the intensity for the superimposition of several traces in 4 (spikes depicted with double amplitude as that in 1—3) was the same as in 2. The same unit (A) was driven from the thalamus (Th); 10 suc-

neuron depicted in Fig. 4A discharged one spike at about 3.0 msec latency in response to a juxtathreshold peduncular (PP) shock and, by doubling and tripling the stimulation strength, it was driven with 5 and 6 spikes at 500—550/sec, the first discharge in the barrage occurring at latencies of 1.3 msec and 1.2 msec, respectively. Thalamic stimulation in the intermediate region between VB and VL nuclei elicited, in the same unit, bursts of 10—14 spikes at the same high frequency as evoked by PP shocks, with latencies of the first discharge in the barrage usually ranging from 2.2. to 3.5 msec, but occasionally exhibiting latencies as short as 1.5 msec. Similar latencies (longer with thalamic than with PP shocks), intraburst frequencies, and more numerous spikes within a barrage elicited by specific thalamic than by antidromic PP volleys, are shown in the other interneuron depicted in Fig. 4B. It discharged a burst of three spikes, at about 400—450/sec to a peduncular shock, the shortest latency of the first discharge being 0.9 msec, while it discharged 4—6 spikes at 400—450/sec to thalamic stimulation, the first group of discharges in the superimposition appearing at 2—2.3 msec latency. Such latency values indicate that these elements were *directly driven by both recurrent collaterals of fast PT fibers and by collaterals of specific thalamocortical axons.*

Most commonly, such interneurons are considered in the literature as inhibitory, especially when their high frequency barrage occurs in relation with a simultaneously recorded focal positive slow shift (Fig. 5), thus satisfying the natural need of investigators to put a finger on the progenitors of postsynaptic inhibition. But I have already stated elsewhere that this generalization may be a tenous inference in view of the complex, still unknown interactions between excitatory and inhibitory elements in the cortical interneuronal pools *, and I offered some experimental evidence that at least some of these units are excitatory and that they may exert a powerful depolarizing pressure on neighboring long-axoned cells and inhibitory interneurons (Steriade, 1974; Steriade and Yossif, 1974; Steriade et al., 1974a). Unfortunately there is no criterion to differentiate in the thalamus or the cerebral cortex inhibitory Golgi II cells from excitatory interneurons. Without a perfect morphological knowledge of the explored structure and unequivocal arrangements of the various interneuronal types, which is certainly not the case for neocortical areas, we must admit that intracellular studies hardly give more precise evidence on the nature of investigated internuncial cells than extracellular recordings. I would like to suggest an indirect

---

* See, for example, inverse correlation between interneuronal spike barrages and focal positive wave in Fig. 17: waking was associated with decreased number of discharges in the evoked burst, but with increased amplitude of the focal positive wave!

---

cessive sweeps (with reduced spike amplitude) and, below, superimposition of several traces. B: PP-evoked (left) and thalamically elicited (right) responses, depicted in the top superimpositions (1) and, below, in 10-sweep sequences (2). Vertical bar (at right): 0.8 mV for A, 2 mV for B. (Modified from Steriade et al., 1974a).

220

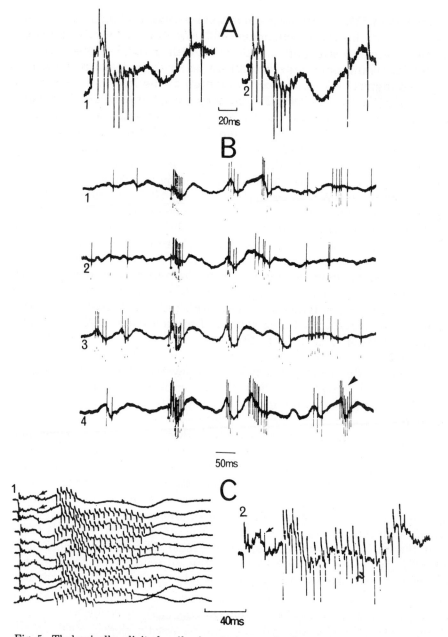

Fig. 5. Thalamically elicited spike bursts in monkey's precentral interneurons, and the relation of unitary responses with simultaneously recorded focal slow positive waves (band width between 1 and 10,000 Hz). A—C: three different units; recordings taken from slow sleep. A: a single thalamic VL shock (dot) elicited a burst of eight spikes at around 200/sec, superimposed on an initial slow negative wave and continued with the beginning of a long-lasting (80 msec), double positive wave; latencies of the first spike in

way of coping with the problem of inferring excitatory interneuronal activities from extracellular studies. If it were possible to infallibly recognize an output (relay) cortical cell by its antidromic invasion (or, less precisely, by the type of its orthodromic response consisting of single spike synaptic excitation), and detect a high frequency barrage following, by a few milliseconds, the antidromically elicited discharge, the second part of the response could be ascribable to activities in excitatory interneurons engaged in parallel by the testing volley, unless other 'unconventional' synaptic interactions are involved. If, furthermore, the early (antidromically or monosynaptically elicited) discharge undergoes differential alterations with changes in the vigilance state, as compared to those observed in the latter part of the unitary response (see Fig. 20), two pathways * with distinct behaviors have to be considered, the last one likely reflecting excitatory interneuronal activities.

The point is that by fulfilling the above-mentioned electrophysiological criteria, the putative interneurons recorded in our experiments proved to be a spectacularly homogenous population in their sleep-waking behavior, as far as the spontaneous firing and synaptic responsiveness were concerned. It is most probable that both types of interneurons (inhibitory *and* excitatory) were represented in our population sample. The discussion of data will consequently benefit from this univocal alteration.

RECURRENT AND AFFERENT INHIBITION DURING SLOW SLEEP AND WAKEFULNESS

(I) *The duration of suppressed spontaneous discharge* following an antidromic or orthodromic stimulation was two to four times longer during

---

* One might alternatively consider the possibility of two different sites of synaptic terminations.

---

the burst: 8 msec in 1, 2.5 msec in 2. Note the burst splitting in two groups of spikes in 2; note also progressive reduction in spike amplitude within the burst (leading in 2 to an abortive spike, the seventh in the burst) and recovery (after a period of 60 msec) of spontaneous firing with the initial spike amplitude. In B, four (1—4) samples of moving film showing the repetitive discharges elicited by a single shock (dot) to the specific VL-VB thalamic border area. The latency of the first spike in the burst varied between 1.8 and 3.5 msec. Note the close correlation between the evoked and even spontaneous (arrow in 4, among others) spike barrages and slow positive waves. C: the long variable (400—120 msec) duration burst evoked at 35—40 msec latency by a specific thalamic shock (dot) in $C_{1 \text{ and } 2}$ (large positive-negative spike) was preceded by a response consisting of a single spike discharge (small negative spike marked by arrows) occurring at a latency of around 20 msec; in 1, 10 successive sweeps with reduced spike amplitude to show the consistency of both short-latency and long-latency responses in the two units, and the good time relation of the long duration barrage with a focal slow positive wave. (From unpublished data (A) and modified from Steriade and Deschênes, 1973 (B) and Steriade, 1974 (C).)

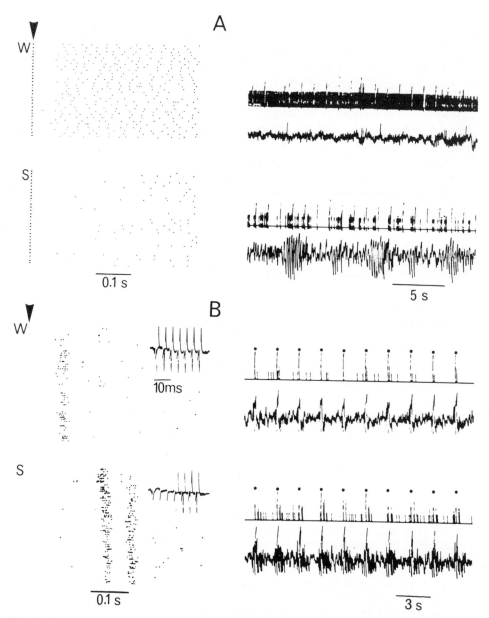

Fig. 6. Duration of neuronal silence following antidromic pes pedunculi stimulation during EEG patterns of waking (W) and slow sleep (S) in cat. Two PT cells (A and B; antidromic response latencies of 1.5 and 0.55 msec, respectively). Single shock (A, arrow) and 7-shock train at 250/sec (B) stimulation; the arrow in B indicates the last shock in the train. EEG synchronization (S) elicited in both cases by 1 mg/kg Surital i.v. Left-hand side: dotgrams with 30 (A) and 50 (B) sweeps. Right-hand side: ink-written records partially depicting the corresponding periods (upper trace: unit spikes; bottom trace: EEG

behavioral slow sleep compared to wakefulness in monkey, and during EEG synchronization compared to EEG desynchronization in cat *. This was constantly observed in output neurons (as recognized by their antidromic invasion) recorded from the motor cortex, SI and areas 5 and 7. Fig. 6 depicts this phenomenon for slow conducting (17 m/sec, in A) and fast conducting (45 m/sec, in B) PT neurons recorded from the precruciate gyrus in cat. The duration of neuronal silence following a single peduncular antidromic volley (in A) was about 65 msec during waking, while it was three times longer during slow sleep. When testing with a train of seven peduncular shocks (in B), a period of about 80 msec of neuronal silence during waking was followed by a rebound consisting of two to six high frequency spikes, while during slow sleep the suppressed firing lasted about 210 msec, it was followed by a rebound, another silence of 70 msec and a second rebound. As usual, longer periods of suppressed discharge during slow sleep were associated with decreased mean-rates of spontaneous firing (Fig. 6A). But it is interesting to note one of the exceptions (Fig. 6B), in which the duration of the first period of neuronal silence was longer during slow sleep (and the inhibition was cyclic, as seen from the two postinhibitory rebounds), in spite of increased background firing.

Simultaneous recording of the focal slow waves with the unitary all-or-none activity may give indications on changes of membrane polarization in the recorded pool of neurons during sleep and waking. The slow positive component, likely reflecting extracellularly summated hyperpolarizing potentials of neighboring units, lasted between 100 and 200 msec during slow sleep, and was faithfully associated with arrest of firing in the single unit under observation (Fig. 7, S). The subsequent negativity was superimposed by spike clusters, suggesting the postinhibitory excitation (see especially Fig. 7, D). Such events, which were absent during wakefulness (Fig. 7, W), were observed especially when studying the transition from waking to slow sleep in the behaving monkey. Rhythmic (8—12/sec) positive-negative waves and the associated changes in unit discharges could be elicited

---

* For the sake of simplicity, I will refer to 'light' or 'slow sleep' and 'waking' or 'wakefulness' whenever comparing periods of EEG synchronization with periods of EEG desynchronization in encéphale isolé cats, being understood that complete behavioral observations were possible only in chronically implanted monkeys and that 'slow sleep' and 'waking' in cats were simply estimated from patterns of EEG rhythms and pupillary signs.

---

waves). In B, the 7-shock trains with their antidromic response are indicated with dots on the ink-written records; note the irregular, smaller amplitude of the big deflections during S (compared with W), indicating the decreased probability of antidromic invasion during S; the lack of antidromic responses occurred during S at the first three to four shocks in the train, as seen in the inserts with original spikes. Note that the more prolonged cessation of spontaneous discharges following antidromic stimuli during S in both cells was related with opposite changes induced by EEG synchronization on the mean rate of their background firing; striking decrease during S in neuron A, increase during S in neuron B. (From Steriade and Deschênes, 1974.)

224

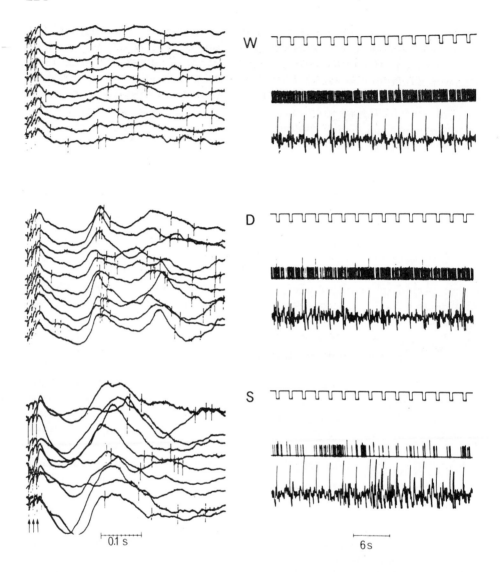

Fig. 7. Changes in afferent inhibition induced in monkey's precentral cortex by VL thalamic stimulation (a train of three shocks, arrows) during the steady state of wakefulness (W), drowsiness (D), and behavioral sleep with EEG slowing (S). In each of these three functional states (W, D, S) 10-sweep sequences depicting successive unitary and focal slow wave activities elicited by the VL shock-train. Note increased VL-elicited inhibition during D and S compared to W, inferred from both spontaneous firing and patterns of slow waves; postinhibitory rebound during D. Especially note that rhythmic inhibitory-excitatory sequences occurred during D in spite of no significant changes in the background firing of the cell and in the EEG gross waves. See text. (Modified from Steriade et al., 1974b.)

in precentral neurons by specific thalamic stimulation, particularly at the very onset of drowsiness, with transient periods of closing and reopening of the eyes (Fig. 7, D). Progressively longer periods of suppressed firing associated with progressively larger amplitude focal positive slow waves could be observed when studying the transition from waking to drowsiness and, thereafter, to slow sleep (Fig. 7, S). Such events could precede the clearcut EEG signs of sleep and the decrease in the mean rate of firing in the unit under observation by 1—2 min. The fact that at the initial stage of sleep, during drowsiness, cyclic inhibitory-excitatory sequences may be seen as a first electrographic sign, without alteration in the mean rate of discharge or in

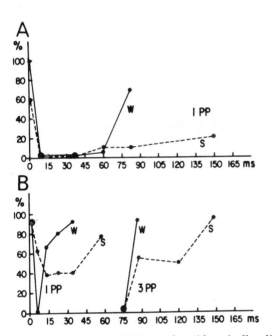

Fig. 8. Recurrent inhibition of antidromically elicited discharges during EEG patterns of waking (W) and slow sleep (S) in cat. A and B are two different PT units (antidromic response latencies of 3.8 msec and 1.5 msec respectively). The testing antidromic shocks were preceded by a single shock or 3-shock trains to the pes pedunculi (PP), as indicated in each graph (1 PP or 3 PP); in B, both conditioning procedures were used. Testing PP shock was delivered at the same intensity as the conditioning one in A, and it was at 60% of the intensity used for the conditioning stimulation in B. Note in A the deep inhibition during both W and S below a 60 msec interval, and faster recovery during W; note also the decreased probability of the test antidromic response during S compared to W. Note in B the much longer inhibition with 3 PP conditioning shocks than with a single one; when a single PP shock was used to elicit inhibition, this was deeper during W than during S in this particular neuron; with both conditioning procedures (1 PP and 3 PP), the recovery was slower during S. Computations were made from responses to 50 stimuli. Control responses to testing shocks (without conditioning inhibitory stimulation) appear at time 0. (Modified from Steriade et al., 1974b.)

gross EEG waves (see Fig. 7, D), may suggest that powerful inhibitory mechanisms favor the falling into sleep before any reduction in the excitatory drive.

(II) The analysis of spontaneous discharges needs to be completed by an investigation on *cellular responsiveness*. The conditioning procedures which were used to determine the effectiveness and the time course of recurrent and afferent collateral inhibitory mechanisms are exposed above (Methodology).

Fig. 8 shows the effects of feedback inhibition (elicited by stimulating the pes pedunculi in a preparation with lesioned medial lemniscus) on antidromically elicited discharges in two slow conducting (7 m/sec in A, 16.5 m/sec in B) PT cells recorded from the motor cortex in cat. Computations to establish the probability of the testing antidromic spike at different time intervals were made from responses to 50 stimuli. The graphs show the percentage probability of the testing response (ordinate) at various intervals following the conditioning shock (abscissa). Percentages of testing response occurrence without conditioning inhibitory stimulation appear at time 0. The testing shock was delivered at the same intensity as the conditioning one in A, and it was at 60% of the intensity used for the conditioning inhibitory stimulation in B. Conditioning peduncular stimulation consisted of one shock in A, and it was delivered with both one shock and a train of three shocks in B. As expected, an inhibitory shock-train induced a delayed recovery of the testing response during both slow sleep and waking, compared to that seen following a single conditioning shock (B). Some differences become evident when comparing the depth and time course of inhibition elicited by a single peduncular shock in neurons A and B: (a) equal, very deep inhibition during both waking and slow sleep at delays up to 60 msec in A, and deeper inhibition during waking, compared to sleep, at delays shorter than 15 msec in B; (b) faster recovery in B than in A during both functional states; (c) decreased probability, during slow sleep, of the control testing response in A (see percentages at time 0), contrasting with lack of differences between waking and sleep in B. In spite of these variations, which only slightly indicate the complexity seen in PT cells, one general finding has to be emphasized which proved to be valid not only for the motor cortex, but also for SI and parietal associative areas: the time up to almost complete recovery was roughly two or even three times longer during slow sleep than during waking, and the return to control values was slowly progressive during sleep which contrasted with sudden recovery during waking. The same type of phenomenon (i.e., faster recovery during waking) was found when comparing in the same neuron the alterations undergone by antidromically and by orthodromically evoked testing discharge following a conditioning stimulation setting in motion the recurrent collateral mechanism (Fig. 9).

The study of changes in afferent inhibition during sleep and waking offered similar results. Fig. 10 depicts a fast (50 m/sec) precentral PT neuron,

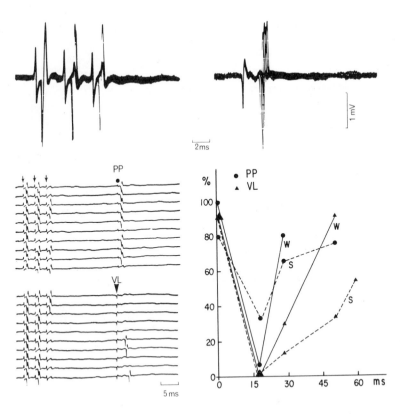

Fig. 9. Recurrent inhibition of antidromically and synaptically elicited discharges during EEG patterns of waking (W) and spontaneously occurring slow sleep (S) in cat. Top: antidromic responses (0.7 msec latency) to a 3-shock train at 320/sec (left superimposition), and synaptically elicited discharges (latency: around 2.0 msec) in the same fast PT cell by stimulating the thalamic VL nucleus (right superimposition). Below: two 10-sweep sequences depicting the effect of conditioning antidromic 3-shock train (small arrows) to the pes pedunculi (PP) on the antidromic PP-elicited and synaptic VL-induced response; both sequences were taken from periods of W, at an interval of around 27 msec (26.5 msec in the case of VL stimulation), to show the much greater resistance to inhibition of the antidromically elicited spike. At right, the graph shows the inhibitory effects of the 3-shock train to the peduncle on the test antidromic response at intervals of 18 and 27 msec during W and S, and at 50 msec only during S; and effects of the same conditioning stimulation on the test VL-induced response at 18, 27 and 50 msec during W and S, and at 60 msec only during S. The intensity of the testing PP and VL shock was about 45% of that used for conditioning PP shocks. In 10-sweep sequences and the above superimposition: inhibition of antidromic responses to the second and especially third shocks in the conditioning train. Note in graph (computation from responses to 50 stimuli) the decreased probability of the antidromic PP test (control) response during S (80%) compared to W (100%); deeper inhibition during W of antidromically elicited spike at 18 msec interval and shorter recovery during W; deeper inhibition of synaptically elicited discharges compared to antidromically elicited ones at the same intervals; faster recovery of synaptically elicited responses during W compared to S, as was also the case when testing with antidromic volleys. (From Steriade and Deschênes, 1974.)

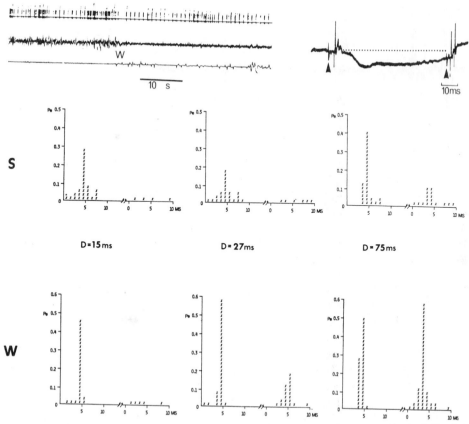

Fig. 10. Thalamically elicited inhibition of orthodromic discharges in a PT neuron during steady waking (W) and slow sleep (S) in monkey. The pattern of thalamically evoked orthodromic discharges in this cell is depicted at the top (right) at an interval of 75 msec between a pair of shocks. The conditioning thalamic stimulus at the VB-VL border (left part in histograms) preceded the testing shock (delivered through the same electrode, with the same parameters) by 15, 27 and 75 msec. These three delays were studied in three different sleep-waking cycles (arousal elicited by the experimenter). Symbols in post-stimulus histograms: Pe, probability of discharges evoked at latencies indicated in milli-seconds on the abscissa (100 stimuli); D, delays between conditioning and testing shocks. At the top (left) is an example of awakening in one of the three sleep-waking cycles. Comments in text. (Modified from Steriade and Deschênes, 1974.)

which could be synaptically activated at short latency from the VB-VL border in monkey. Three intervals (15 msec, 27 msec and 75 msec) between a pair of thalamic stimuli of equal intensity were studied in this cell during three natural sleep-waking cycles. The similarities between the analyzed vigilance states are reflected by the similarly increased synaptic respon-siveness to the first shock in the pair during waking compared to slow sleep (The occurrence probability of the first response in the pair can be considered as the control value for responses tested by the second shock.) As in the case of recurrent inhibition, two major findings are disclosed by the poststimulus histograms in Fig. 10: (a) a deep inhibition of the short-delayed (15 msec) testing response during both slow sleep and waking; (b) faster recovery during waking; the recovery was partial at a delay of 27 msec when the orthodromic response was still profoundly inhibited during sleep; and a postinhibitory facilitation can be seen during waking at the 75 msec interval (see also oscilloscopic trace at the top), when the testing response had only partially recovered during slow sleep.

The general conclusion can be drawn that *deep or complete inhibition had already developed during both waking and slow sleep at time intervals of 5—15 msec after a conditioning, antidromic or orthodromic, stimulation.* It seems, therefore, that regardless of the variations in the vigilance state, powerful inhibition follows the initial excitation of cortical neurons. Inhibition appears to affect the region of the axon hillock and the adjacent somatic membrane, as shown by complete failure of antidromic invasion, as well as the region of the dendritic tree, judging by the suppression of specific orthodromic discharges. *The time course of recovery from deep inhibition seen at short delays following the conditioning stimulus was the main difference between slow sleep and wakefulness.* This time course was invariably characterized by faster recovery during waking compared to slow sleep. Taking into consideration that inhibitory mechanisms subserve a fine control of cortical performances, the deep and short recurrent and afferent inhibition seen during wakefulness shows that this state provides a neuronal organization leading to accuracy in the analysis of excitatory inputs and to ability in following rapidly recurring activity.

EFFECTS OF RETICULAR-ELICITED AND NATURAL AROUSAL ON INHIBITORY EVENTS

In many respects, the short-lasting period of arousal from slow sleep was associated with alterations in inhibitory phenomena which were very similar to those observed during the steady state of wakefulness: improved responsiveness and reduced duration of inhibition when compared to prior periods of synchronized sleep. There were, however, some additional aspects resulting from experiments on the behaving monkey, in which natural arousal was accompanied by removal of inhibition seen during slow sleep, but paradoxically associated in some neuronal classes with a simultaneous striking decrease in the mean rates of spontaneous discharge. This may offer some clues to a better understanding of the complex mechanisms underlying the transitional period from sleep to wakefulness.

The arousal reaction induced by brief trains of high frequency pulses to the mesencephalic reticular formation in encéphale isolé cats significantly reduced, and in some instances abolished, the period of suppressed spon-

230

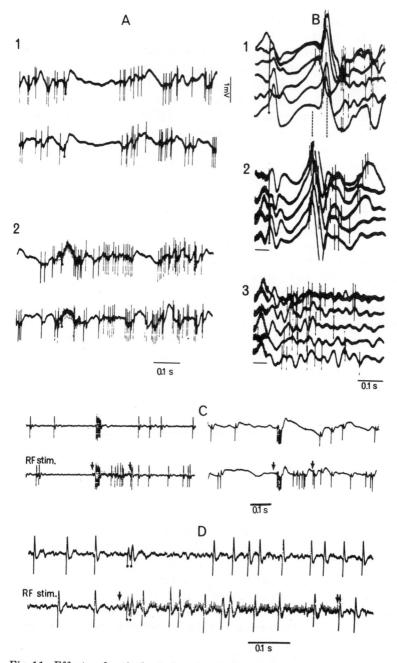

Fig. 11. Effects of reticular-induced arousal on inhibition of spontaneous discharges in anterior suprasylvian neurons (A and B) and precruciate PT cells (C and D). A: suppression of spontaneous firing following a single shock (dot) to the thalamic LI nucleus (1), and erasure of this thalamically elicited silent period by applying a brief train of high

taneous firing which followed an afferent or antidromic inhibitory stimulation. This is shown in Fig. 11 for two anterior suprasylvian neurons (A and B) and two precruciate PT cells (C and D). In all these cases, the suppression of spontaneous discharges following specific thalamic stimulation (A, B and D) or antidromic PT volleys (C) lasted about 150—200 msec during control periods of EEG synchronization, while this period of silenced firing was reduced to less than 100 msec (A and C) or completely abolished (D) when the inhibitory stimulation was associated with an arousing reticular stimulation.

Another way of appreciating the reduced duration of inhibitory events during arousal is to measure the latency of the postinhibitory rebound during EEG patterns of slow sleep and during reticular-elicited EEG activation (Kitsikis and Steriade, 1974). The sweep-sequences in Fig. 11B represents a simultaneous recording of a single unit and focal slow waves from suprasylvian area 7. In the top sequence (B_1), from a period of slow sleep, a shock to the thalamic LI nucleus first evoked a short-latency, depth-negative slow wave, reflecting summated depolarizing potentials in the neuronal pool recorded by the microelectrode. This early excitatory field response was followed by a long-lasting depth-positive component of about 100—150 msec, which is commonly ascribed to summated hyperpolarizing potentials. The long duration slow positivity, which was associated with silenced firing in the unit under observation, was followed by a huge depth-negative component, the so-called rebound phenomenon, reflecting postinhibitory excitation in the pool of neurons. The rebound was unfailingly superimposed by spike discharges of the recorded unit. In B_2 a 50 msec pulse-train to the reticular formation preceded the testing thalamic shock and changed the EEG patterns of slow sleep into EEG activation. The salient feature was that during reticular arousal the duration of the long-lasting hyperpolarizing wave was considerably reduced, and that the latency of the postinhibitory rebound was shortened by about 60—70 msec from light sleep to arousal. Comparing the dashed lines, roughly representing the peak

frequency pulses to the mesencephalic reticular stimulation (2). B: latency shortening of LI-elicited postinhibitory excitation (1) by applying a conditioning, arousing reticular stimulation (horizontal bar, 2), and the effects of the reticular shock-train alone (3). Comments in text. C (left and right columns are recordings with bandwidths of 50—10,000 Hz and 1—700 Hz, respectively): a train of 7 PT shocks at 320/sec evoked antidromic spikes without failure at 1.2 msec latency, followed by inhibition lasting about 200 msec; the slow negative shift associated with abolition of spontaneous discharges may be regarded in this juxtacellular record as reflecting the hyperpolarizing potential of this unit; reticular stimulation (between arrows; lack of shock artifacts in the right column are due to attenuation of high frequency components) strikingly reduced the duration of the inhibitory period following antidromic invasion and increased the mean rate of discharge. D: suppression, during reticular stimulation, of the inhibitory period elicited in a PT neuron by VB stimulation. (From experiments by Steriade et al., in preparation (A and B) and modified from Steriade et al., 1971b.)

latencies of the rebound during EEG synchronization and activation patterns, gives a good idea of the reticular effect. It is worthwhile looking at the events induced by the reticular shock-train alone (in B_3). After an early, depth-negative (depolarizing) wave, the single unit was constantly activated in a latency range of 100 msec. This cell activation suggests that the reduced duration of the inhibitory wave and the reduced latency of the postin-hibitory rebound in B_2 are due to cutting off the inhibition by a strong excitatory drive of reticular origin. It therefore seems difficult to explain the postinhibitory rebound exclusively on the basis of the preceding inhibition. An additional mechanism, such as a powerful excitatory impingement, has to be envisaged in the triggering of the rebound phenomenon.

The excitatory effect of arousal was further seen when studying cellular responsiveness to antidromic volleys during periods of slow sleep compared to periods of EEG activation elicited by reticular stimulation. A good example is the precruciate PT cell in Fig. 12, which was driven without failure by 250/sec antidromic shocks during waking (A), and then, when the animal fell into slow sleep (B), the neuron progressively exhibited unresponsiveness to testing stimuli. High frequency mesencephalic reticular stimulation changed the EEG patterns of slow sleep into EEG activation and fully restored the unit responsiveness to PT antidromic volleys (C). This was observed in both fast and slow conducting PT neurons, and was also valid for corticothalamic neurons recorded from motor, somesthetic and parietal associative areas, as recognized by their antidromic invasion to stimulation of VL, VPL or LI-LP nuclei, respectively.

Increased antidromic responsiveness was also found during natural arousal, compared to prior periods of slow sleep, in the behaving monkey *. Even when the number of antidromic responses to a shock-train did not vary as a function of the vigilance state, significant alterations could be observed in the pattern of antidromic spikes, with IS-SD splitting during slow sleep and with complete or partial recovery on arousal and during subsequent steady waking. In some precentral neurons, very long recording periods permitted the observation of identical changes in antidromic invasion during several sleep-waking cycles in the chronically implanted monkey. The antidromic invasion of the fast PT cell depicted in Fig. 13A showed a pronounced IS-SD break observed in the first antidromic response during sleep (arrows in 1 and 2; compare with spontaneous spikes, S, without notches), while this spike fragmentation was scarcely or not at all visible in antidromically elicited responses following arousal. The soma invasion was accelerated by 0.08 msec during waking compared to sleep, as measured by the peak latency of the

---

* It must be emphasized that in view of the high safety factor of antidromic invasion in PT neurons (Phillips, 1956; Krnjević et al., 1966) care has to be taken in delivering juxta-threshold testing stimuli allowing fluctuations of cell responsiveness according to the vigilance state.

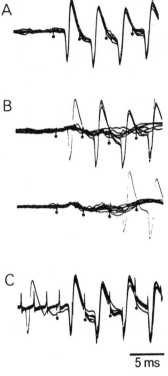

Fig. 12. Facilitation of antidromic invasion during reticular-elicited arousal in cat. Antidromic responses of a precruciate PT neuron to a 4-shock train during EEG patterns of waking (A), depressed responsiveness during progressively developing EEG patterns of slow sleep (B), and recovery of full antidromic responsiveness during subsequent arousal induced by high frequency reticular stimulation (C). Unpublished data by Steriade, Apostol and Wyzinski.

antidromic spike (compare in 2 and 4 the two superimposed antidromic responses marked by dots in the lower beam). The partial (IS) spike evoked by the second antidromic shock was not, however, susceptible to changes from sleep to waking. The antidromic invasion of the fast PT cell on Fig. 13B was tested with a train of three shocks at 110/sec. The first antidromic response to the first stimulus in the train showed during sleep an IS-SD break (arrows in 1 and 2), and progressive accentuation of the splitting phenomenon in responses to subsequent stimuli in the train. From the very beginning of arousal and during subsequent steady waking, the first antidromic spike fully recovered, with no sign of an IS-SD break and acceleration of the soma invasion (the peak latency of the spike was shorter by 0.08 msec during waking than during slow sleep); the subsequent antidromic spikes in the train showed during waking a clearcut diminution in their still present IS-SD break (see superimpositions 3 and 4) compared to slow sleep (superimpositions 1

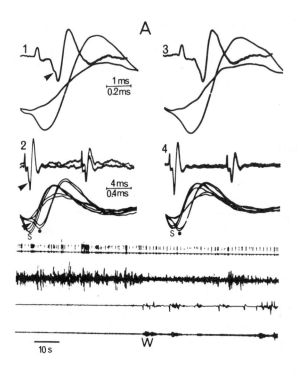

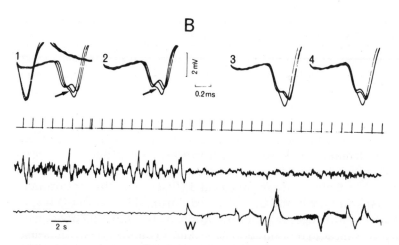

Fig. 13. Patterns of antidromic invasion of precentral PT neurons during behavioral slow sleep and waking. A and B are two fast PT cells (antidromic response latencies: 0.55 msec in A, 0.5 msec in B). Neuron A: superimpositions of two sweeps with responses to paired antidromic volleys (separated by 9.5 msec) are shown during slow sleep (2) and wakefulness (4); above, at faster speed, the detailed configuration of the antidromic response to the first shock during sleep (1) and waking (3). In both cases, 1-3 and 2-4, the upper beam was triggered at a predetermined time before the first shock while the lower beam

and 2). Similar changes in the pattern of antidromic invasion with arousal from sleep were seen in this neuron when testing with a train of five shocks at 350/sec during another transition from sleep to waking (see Fig. 9A in Steriade et al., 1974a). It must be stressed that facilitation of antidromic invasion during awakening occurred in the monkey's fast PT neurons in spite of the fact that these elements exhibited on arousal a spectacular arrest of spontaneous firing. This paradoxical association is discussed below.

COMMENTS ON POSSIBLE MECHANISMS, WITH PARTICULAR EMPHASIS ON UNDERLYING INTERNEURONAL ACTIVITIES

Two aspects of the above results will be discussed with additional experimental arguments: (I) the increased antidromic responsiveness on *arousal*, as seen in a particular neuronal class (fast PT cells of monkey) which showed arrest of firing during the same functional state, and (II) the mechanism underlying the shorter time required during *steady waking* (compared to slow sleep) for full recovery from inhibition of tested spontaneous or evoked unitary activities.

(I) When trying to correlate the facilitation of antidromic responsiveness during arousal with the changes in spontaneous firing, the unorthodox observation was made that fast (conducting at above 40 m/sec) precentral PT cells in the monkey stopped firing on natural arousal from sleep *. Fig. 14 shows

---

* This could not be seen during reticular-elicited arousal in the encéphale isolé cat, an experimental condition which induced increased mean rates of spontaneous discharge in both slow *and* fast PT cells (Steriade et al., 1973).

---

was triggered by spontaneous and antidromically elicited discharges. In 1 and 3 the two traces in the lower beam represent the full antidromic response to the first shock and the IS spike in response to the second shock (not appearing on the upper beam); in 2 and 4 traces in the lower beam represent three spontaneous discharges in both 2 and 4 (S), the full antidromic spikes (marked by dots) evoked by the first shock in two successive stimulations as depicted in the superimposition of the upper beam, and the two IS spikes in response to the second shocks. Below, the four ink-written traces represent unit activity (including discharges evoked by 0.75/sec antidromic stimuli); EEG waves; ocular movements and electromyogram; awakening reaction in W. The IS-SD break in the antidromic response to the first shock can be seen during sleep (arrows in 1 and 2), in spite of the fact that spontaneous spikes (S) do not have such notches. The lack of IS-SD fragmentation is visible during waking (3 and 4). No changes occurred between sleep and waking in the IS spikes in response to the second shocks. Neuron B: superimpositions at the top represent antidromic responses to a train of three shocks at 110/sec during sleep (1 and 2) and waking (3 and 4); sweeps triggered by both the shock artifacts and the spontaneous discharges. Arrows indicate the IS-SD break of the first antidromic response in the train during sleep; note that spontaneous discharges (in 1) do not exhibit such notches. Note also full recovery of the first spike in the train and diminution in the IS-SD break of successive responses during waking compared with sleep. (Modified from Steriade et al., 1974a.)

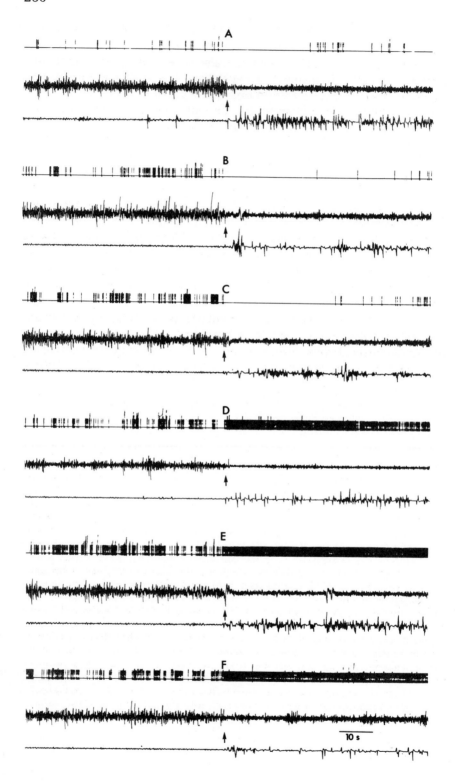

the contrast between the behavior of fast and slow PT neurons during one minute following spontaneous or elicited arousal, compared with their behavior throughout one minute preceding slow sleep. The sudden increased firing of slow PT cells from the very beginning of arousal (D—F) could be spectacularly differentiated from the neuronal silence in fast PT cells. The fast PT neurons then resumed their spontaneous discharges, but at a lower level compared to prior sleep. This decreased mean rate of discharge in fast PT cells, compared to slow sleep, was seen only in the period immediately following arousal, lasting about 3—60 sec. It sometimes continued for longer when the experimenter actively prolonged the orienting reaction of the initial arousal by continuously keeping the animal very alert. This opposite behavior in the two PT neuronal classes could also be seen when phasic periods of increased vigilance occurred during the transition from quiet waking to slow sleep. As demonstrated in Fig. 15 depicting the drowsiness stage, brief periods of spontaneous or elicited awakening reactions (indicated by eye opening and desynchronization of EEG rhythms) were closely associated with a decreased firing rate in fast PT neurons (A and B) and an increased firing rate in slow PT units (C and D). The above described differentiated behavior of fast and slow PT neurons characterized exclusively the short-lasting arousal and the phasic periods of increased vigilance due to orienting reactions. As reported below (see Fig. 21), unlike the transient period of arousal, the *steady* state of quiet waking was characterized, in variance with Evarts' (1965) data, by similarly increased mean rates of discharge, compared to slow sleep, when the two (fast and slow conducting) PT neuronal populations were analyzed (Steriade et al., 1974a).

As far as the arrest of firing in fast PT cells on arousal is concerned, one might envisage at first sight a postsynaptic inhibition exerted on the fast PT neuronal membrane by ascending influxes of the reticular arousing system or by inhibitory interneurons set in motion during the dramatic increase of spontaneous firing in slow PT cells on arousal. This possibility can be discarded in view of data showing increased antidromic responsiveness and

Fig. 14. Opposite changes in background firing of fast and slow PT neurons on behavioral arousal from slow wave sleep. Six different units. A—C: fast PT cells with antidromic response latencies of 0.3, 0.4, and 0.5 msec, respectively. D—F: slow PT neurons with antidromic response latencies of 1.4, 1.7, and 2.5 msec, respectively. The three ink-written traces represent, from top to bottom, unit spikes (displayed on the oscilloscope and used to deflect the pen of the EEG machine; each deflection exceeding the common level represents a group of several high frequency discharges); EEG rhythms recorded from the perirolandic region, and eye movements. In A—E, arousal was induced by the experimenter who entered the monkey's room (arrows); in F, spontaneously occurring arousal (arrow). Note the grouped discharges and spike clusters interspersed with periods of silence during sleep, the neuronal silence on arousal from slow sleep, lasting 25 sec (A), 28 sec (B), and 33 sec (C) in fast PT cells and the increased mean rate of discharge in slow PT neurons from the very beginning of arousal. (From Steriade et al., 1974a.)

238

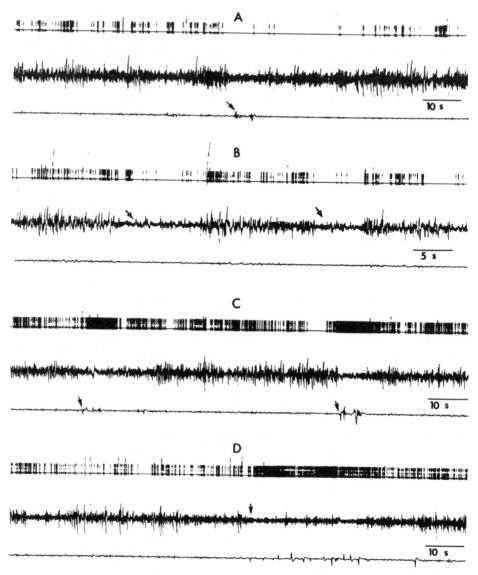

Fig. 15. Spontaneous discharges of fast and slow conducting PT neurons during drowsiness and transient periods of increased vigilance in monkey. A and B: two fast conducting PT cells, both with antidromic response latency of 0.5 msec. C and D: two slow conducting PT neurons, with antidromic response latencies of 0.9 msec and 3.6 msec, respectively. All the records were taken from periods of drowsiness, subsequent to the steady state of quiet waking, when the animals intermittently closed and reopened their eyes. Note that short periods of spontaneously occurring EEG desynchronization during the stage of falling into sleep, without (B) or with opening of the eyes (A, arrow) were associated in fast PT cells with an obvious decrease in the mean rate of discharge; also that similar transient periods of increased vigilance occurring during drowsiness, either spontaneous

development from split to unbroken spikes on arousal (Fig. 13). Such findings provide evidence that arousal is *not* associated with postsynaptic inhibition of fast PT cells, but, contrariwise, with the removal of inhibitory mechanisms acting on these elements during synchronized sleep. It is actually known from intracellular studies on spinal motoneurons (Coombs et al., 1955) that the IS-SD break occurs in relation with an increase of membrane polarization induced by injecting current. Removal of inhibition during arousal is in line with some findings at the thalamic VL level, showing blockade of medial thalamically evoked IPSPs (Purpura, 1970) and reduced amplitude and duration of antidromically evoked inhibitory field potentials (Bremer, 1970; Steriade et al., 1971a and 1972) during reticular arousal.

Another way of accounting for the arrest of firing in fast PT cells on arousal may be a sudden disfacilitation of these elements. This disfacilitation may result from removal, during arousal, of powerful depolarizing pressure exerted by cortical excitatory interneurons. Some stellate cells, especially those known from Ramón y Cajal's designation as "cellules à double bouquet dendritique", are likely involved in the vertical spread of excitation along the dendritic shaft of medium sized and large PT cells, as indicated by the columnar concept (Colonnier, 1966). In particular the large PT cells, with a much lower membrane resistance than that of small PT neurons (Takahashi, 1965), might require a source of powerful excitation to be set in motion. This can be secured by the repetitive discharges of local excitatory interneurons, which are particularly active during slow sleep (Steriade, 1974). In this case, the association of arrest of firing with increased antidromic responsiveness in fast PT neurons on arousal may be ascribed to a combination of disfacilitation (removal of depolarizing pressure from excitatory interneurons) and disinhibition (inhibition of inhibitory interneurons). If this would be the case, we expect that both excitatory and inhibitory interneurons would be inhibited on arousal from sleep.

In spite of the difficulties in dissociating inhibitory from excitatory interneurons, the fact that no exception could be observed in the behavior of putative short-axoned cells on arousal from sleep allows me to state that the changes observed in interneuronal activities may apply to both (excitatory and inhibitory) classes of internuncial elements. Without exception, behavioral arousal was associated in monkey with a striking reduction or complete arrest of spontaneous firing in electrophysiologically identified precentral interneurons (Fig. 16). Concerning their synaptic responsiveness, this was also strikingly depressed on arousal compared to the period of preceding

---

(with opening the eyes, arrows in C) or induced by the experimenter (by switching off a background noise, arrow in D; note also appearance of eye movements) were associated in slow (C and D) PT neurons with a dramatic increase in the mean rate of discharge; and that high frequency bursts of discharges occurred in close time relation with EEG spindle sequences (big deflections, especially visible in B). Unpublished data by Steriade, Deschênes and Oakson.

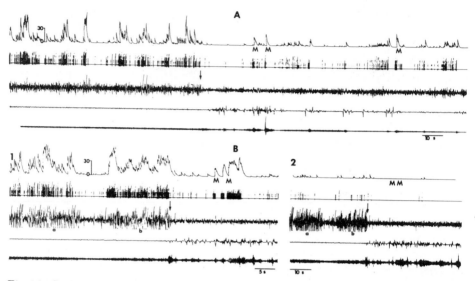

Fig. 16. Spontaneous firing of monkey's precentral interneurons during transition from behavioral slow sleep to waking. The five ink-written traces in A and B represent, from top to bottom: the integrated unit activity (figures on the ordinate indicate numbers of spikes per second), unit spikes (displayed on the oscilloscope and used to deflect the pen of the EEG machine, deflections exceeding the lowest level represent bursts of high frequency discharges), EEG focal waves recorded by the same microelectrode and adequately amplified, eye movements and EMG. Neuron A was driven by pes pedunculi stimulation with a barrage of 3—4 spikes at 500/sec, the shortest latency being 2 msec. In B: two simultaneously recorded interneurons (a negative spike and a biphasic, positive-negative spike). The unit discharging the negative spike was driven by peduncular stimulation with a barrage at 300/sec at a latency of 2.2 msec. 1 and 2 represent the same period of sleep-waking transition, at different time scales. In B_1, discharges of both interneurons are depicted while in B_2 only the positive-negative spike deflected the pen of the EEG machine. Arousal marked by arrows. M shows animal movements. Note striking depression of interneuronal spontaneous activity on arousal from slow sleep; the inhibition of spontaneous firing can also be seen during a transient period of EEG desynchronization during sleep (between a and b in B_1), before the awakening of the animal. (Modified from Steriade et al., 1974a (A) and unpublished experiment by Steriade, Deschênes and Oakson (B).)

slow sleep; high frequency spike barrages usually consisted of five to seven discharges during sleep, while they were replaced during arousal by single or double spike excitation (Fig. 17), sometimes occurring at longer latencies than those seen during slow sleep (Fig. 18). The phasic inhibition of interneuronal discharges was further found in our laboratory at the level of somatosensory and parietal associative cortices during reticular-elicited arousal in encéphale isolé preparations (Fig. 19).

When trying to infer changes in excitatory interneuronal activities from their reflection in neighboring cells (see Methodology), an elective suppres-

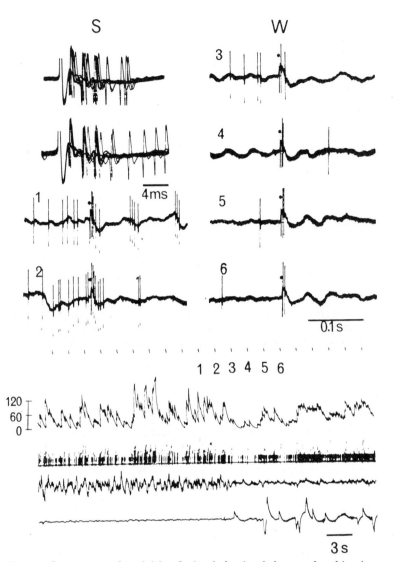

Fig. 17. Interneuronal activities during behavioral sleep and waking in monkey. Same pre-central interneuron as depicted in Fig. 4A. Single shocks were applied to the pes pedunculi during slow sleep (S) and wakefulness (W). The top superimpositions in S represent unitary responses preceding those depicted in samples 1 and 2 of moving film. Oscilloscopic recordings 1—6 correspond to stimulation periods indicated by the same figures on the below depicted ink-written traces (representing, from top to bottom: testing shocks, integrated unit activity, unit spikes, EEG waves and eye movements). Spontaneous awakening of the animal, as seen from EEG activation and ocular movements. Note that decreased evoked and spontaneous interneuronal firing on arousal from sleep is very similar to that seen in another interneuron of the next figure (Fig. 18) depicting the effect of an arousal reaction elicited by the experimenter. From unpublished data of Steriade and Deschênes.

242

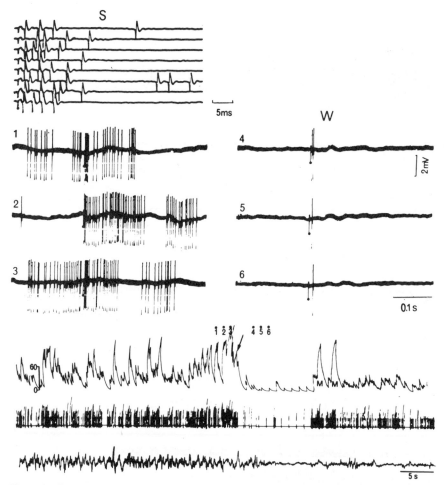

Fig. 18. Changes in synaptic responsiveness of an interneuron recoreded from monkey's precentral motor cortex during transition from slow sleep (S) to waking (W). Arousal elicited by the experimenter (marked by arrow on the ink-written trace indicating the intergrated unit activity). Same unit as that depicted in Fig. 4B. Single shocks applied to the pes pedunculi. Left column: an 8-sweep wavegram and three samples of moving film, both taken from the period of S preceding the arousal. Right column: three other samples of moving film, immediately after arousal. Figures on the oscilloscopic traces (1—6) correspond to those indicated on the ink-written record. At the bottom the three ink-written traces indicate: the integrated unit activity (figures on the ordinate represent number of spikes per second), unit spikes and EEG perirolandic rhythms. Note: constant barrages consisting of 3—5 spikes evoked by peduncular stimulation during S, at latencies indicating monosynaptic excitation (see text corresponding to Fig. 4B for latencies and intraburst frequencies); progressive reduction in the intraburst number of spikes leading to two and then to one single discharge, and progressive lengthening of latencies on arousal (4—6); this was associated with silence of spontaneous firing for about 10 sec; the striking decrease in unitary activity preceded the gross EEG signs of low voltage fast rhythms. (From Steriade et al., 1974a.)

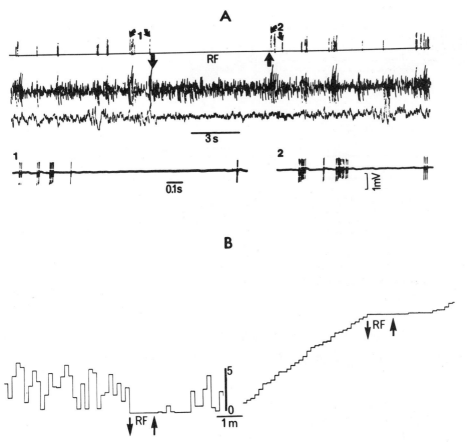

Fig. 19. Effects of reticular-elicited arousal on spontaneous firing of cortical interneurons recorded from SI (A) and area 7 (B). The ink-written traces in A represent: unit spikes (periods 1 and 2, between small oblique arrows, correspond to those in the below depicted oscilloscopic traces), focal slow waves recorded by the microelectrode, and surface EEG waves. Note complete suppression of bursting firing during high frequency stimulation of the mesencephalic reticular formation (RF). The same suppressing effect of RF stimulation can be seen for the suprasylvian interneuron in B; it is illustrated in both forms of sequential mean rates (left) and cumulative histogram (right). Note the aftereffect of RF stimulation. Unpublished data of Steriade et al. (A) and Steriade, Kitsikis and Oakson (B).

sion of such repetitive discharges was seen to occur during EEG arousal. Fig. 20 shows the changes in synaptic responsiveness of a somatosensory cortical neuron during EEG patterns of slow sleep and EEG activation. This unit exhibited primary discharges to specific VB stimuli and was also driven, with corresponding longer latency, by medial lemniscus stimulation. Following this initial excitation, seen in the single-spike responses, the cell discharged during slow sleep a burst of several spikes at 500—600/sec, which, judging

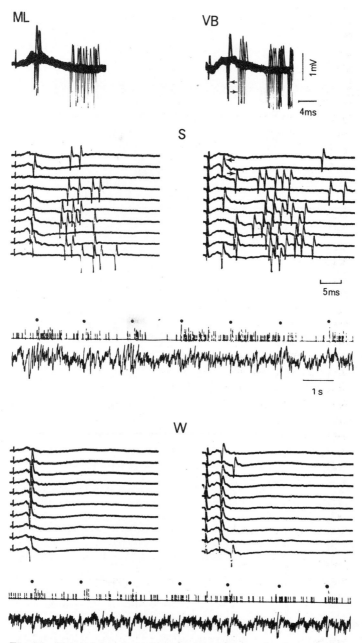

Fig. 20. Changes in two types of evoked discharges in a cortical somatosensory neuron during EEG patterns of slow sleep (S) and waking (W) in the encéphale isolé cat. The neuron was modulated by stimulating both the medial lemniscus (ML) and the thalamic VB nucleus, with similar patterns of activity. Superimpositions of several responses are shown at the top, and ten successive sweeps in wavegrams (with reduced spike amplitude)

from the short latency (about 5 msec after the early discharge), probably represented a reflection of the activity in excitatory interneurons engaged by collaterals of the specific VB-cortical axons. During EEG patterns of arousal, the high frequency burst disappeared completely, while the initial discharge was facilitated. On the basis of this evidence, one might conclude that the synaptic responsiveness of the unit under observation was facilitated on arousal, but, on the other hand, the activity in the collateral excitatory pathway (inferred from the late repetitive burst) was suppressed during the same functional state. The same conclusion was reached from depression, during arousal, affecting preferentially, or even exclusively, the interneuronally linked unit discharges evoked by VL in PT neurons (see Figs. 9 and 10 in Steriade et al., 1973).

(II) The faster recovery from inhibition, as seen in PT cells during steady wakefulness compared to slow sleep, can be reasonably ascribed to powerful excitation overwhelming inhibitory processes by limiting the duration of antidromically or orthodromically elicited IPSPs. This was actually observed when analyzing the fluctuations in the spontaneous firing of cortical output neurons with transition from sleep to the steady state of waking. In contrast with decreased firing electively seen in fast PT cells during brief periods of arousal or phasic orienting reactions (see again Figs. 14 and 15), the subsequent state of quiet wakefulness was characterized by similarly increased firing rates in both slow and fast PT neurons (Fig. 21). (We may conceive that the decreased firing rate, during waking, as reported by Evarts (1965) in large PT units, was due to alertness in his preparations.) The increased mean rate of spontaneous discharge in precentral fast and slow PT neurons during waking compared to drowsiness and slow sleep is mainly ascribable to changes, during the sleep-waking cycle, in the incoming influxes acting on the source of the cortical outflow. The most powerful excitatory input arises in the VL thalamus. Thus, the increased firing rate of PT cells during waking may be viewed as a direct consequence of dramatic increase in thalamic VL neuronal activities (Steriade et al., 1969, 1971a and 1972). Since VL-fugal fibers contact preferentially fast PT neurons, it is not surprising to find that the spontaneous discharge of large sized PT cells was higher during wakefulness than during slow sleep.

Shorter inhibition during wakefulness must be essentially considered as being due to increased excitation along the major thalamocortical input during this state, since the synaptic responsiveness of interneurons inter-

---

are depicted during both S and W. The ink-written records show in each functional state: the unitary discharges (first trace) and EEG waves (bottom trace); VB shocks indicated by dots. VB stimulus resulted during S in two groups of short latency discharges (indicated by two arrows), followed after a few milliseconds by a high frequency spike burst. Note during EEG desynchronization (W) the increase in the probability of firing of early (single spike) evoked discharges and disappearance of subsequent repetitive spikes. Unpublished observations by Steriade et al., in preparation.

246

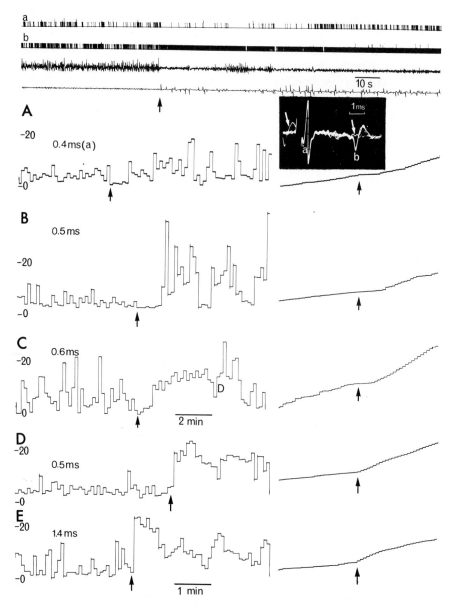

Fig. 21. Sequential mean rates (left) and cumulative histograms (right) of four fast-(A—D) and one slow (E)-conducting PT cells during slow sleep, arousal (arrows), and subsequent steady state of quiet waking. Figures on the ordinate indicate number of spikes per second; 10 sec (A—C) and 5 sec (D and E) bins. Antidromic response latencies indicated in each case at left. In A, the fast conducting PT cell, a, was simultaneously recorded with the slow conducting PT cell, b, (see collision phenomenon in the insert depicting antidromically elicited discharges in both neurons; arrows indicate a spontaneous discharge of the b unit and corresponding lack of its antidromic response). The ink-

calated in the recurrent and afferent collateral pathways did not exhibit major differences between *steady states* of slow sleep and waking, the evoked discharges being even more concentrated at early peaks during waking (see poststimulus histograms in Fig. 15 of Steriade et al., 1974a). This again emphasizes that inhibition of interneuronal activities is confined to the short-lasting period of arousal.

Further experimentation with intracellular recording and morphological identification of cortical interneurons in simpler preparations is certainly necessary to disclose the intimate synaptic operations which were suggested by our experiments on behaving animals.

Acknowledgements

I am indebted to the following collaborators for their skillful and creative work: M. Deschênes, Anne Kitsikis, G. Oakson and G. Yossif.

Supported by grants from the Medical Research Council of Canada (MT-3689) and the Ministère de l'Education du Gouvernement du Québec.

REFERENCES

Bremer, F. (1970) Inhibitions intrathalamiques récurrentielles et physiologie du sommeil. Electroenceph. clin. Neurophysiol., 28, 1—16.
Brock, L.G., Coombs, J.S. and Eccles, J.C. (1953) Intracellular recording from anti- dromically activated motoneurons. J. Physiol. (Lond.), 122, 429—461.
Colonnier, M.L. (1966) The structural design of the neocortex. In J.C. Eccles (Ed.), Brain and Conscious Experience. Springer, New York, pp. 1—23.
Coombs, J.S., Eccles, J.C. and Fatt, P. (1955) The electrical properties of the moto- neurone membrane. J. Physiol. (Lond.), 130, 291—325.
Evarts, E.V. (1964) Temporal patterns of discharge of pyramidal tract neurons during sleep and waking in the monkey. J. Neurophysiol., 27, 152—171.
Evarts, E.V. (1965) Relation of discharge frequency to conduction velocity in pyramidal tract neurons. J. Neurophysiol., 28, 216—228.
Kitsikis, A. and Steride, M. (1974) Arousal effects on evoked inhibition in parietal associa- tive neurons. Proc. XXVIth. Int. Congr. Physiol., Vol. XI, p. 207.

written records at the top represent: spontaneous firing of separated discharges of units a and b, EEG waves and ocular movements. Note: increased firing of unit b from the very beginning of arousal (arrow); much lower mean rate of discharge in unit a during the first minute following arousal (compared to sleep) but, afterwards, during steady waking, in- crease of its firing rate over the value seen during sleep, as can also be observed in the below-depicted sequential mean rate. Similar events in B. In C, a period of drowsiness (D) occurred 4 min after arousal; note disorganization of the tonic firing seen during the prior steady waking. The fast PT cell in D (0.5 msec latency) was one of five exceptions from 31 analyzed fast PT neurons which increased the mean rate of discharge from the beginning of arousal. (Modified from Steriade et al., 1974a.)

248

Krnjević, K., Randić, M. and Straughan, D.W. (1966) An inhibitory process in the cerebral cortex. J. Physiol. (Lond.), 184, 16—48.

Moruzzi, G. (1966) The functional significance of sleep to particular regard to the brain mechanisms underlying consciousness. In J.C. Eccles (Ed.), Brain and Conscious Experience. Springer, New York, pp. 345—379.

Moruzzi, G. (1972) The sleep-waking cycle, Ergebn. Physiol., 64, 1—165.

Pavlov, I.P. (1923) 'Innere Hemmung' der bedingten Reflexe und der Schlaf - ein und derselbe Prozess. Skand. Arch. Physiol., 44, 42—58.

Phillips, C.G. (1956) Intracellular records from Betz cell in the cat. Quart. J. exp. Physiol., 41, 58—69.

Purpura, D.P. (1970) Operations and processes in thalamic and synaptically related neural subsystems. In F.O. Schmitt (Ed.), The Neurosciences, Second Study Program. Rockefeller Univ. Press, New York, pp. 458—470.

Purpura, D.P. (1974) Intracellular studies of thalamic synaptic mechanisms in evoked synchronization and desynchronization of electrocortical activity. In O. Petre-Quadens and J. Schlag (Eds.), Basic Sleep Mechanisms. Academic Press, New York, pp. 99—122.

Steriade, M. (1973) Short-axoned cells in the motor thalamocortical system during sleep and waking. In P.J. Morgane and W.C. Stern (Eds.), Neural Systems and Circuitry Concerned with Sleep-Waking Behavior. Univ. of Calif. Brain Information Service, Los Angeles, Calif., pp. 47—59.

Steriade, M. (1974) Interneuronal epileptic discharges related to spike-and-wave cortical seizure in behaving monkeys. Electroenceph. clin. Neurophysiol., 37, 247—263.

Steriade, M. and Deschênes, M. (1973) Cortical interneurons during sleep and waking in freely moving primates. Brain Res., 50, 192—199.

Steriade, M. and Deschênes, M. (1974) Inhibitory processes and interneuronal apparatus in motor cortex during sleep and waking. II. Recurrent and afferent inhibition of pyramidal tract neurons. J. Neurophysiol., 37, 1093—1112.

Steriade, M. and Yossif, G. (1974) Spike-and-wave afterdischarges in cortical somatosensory neurons of cat. Electroenceph. clin. Neurophysiol., 37 633—648.

Steriade, M. and Hobson, J.A. (1976) Neuronal activity during the sleep-waking cycle. In G.A. Kerkut and J.W. Phillis (Eds.), Progress in Neurobiology. Pergamon Press, Oxford.

Steriade, M., Iosif, G. and Apostol, V. (1969) Responsiveness of thalamic and cortical motor relays during arousal and various stages of sleep. J. Neurophysiol., 32, 251—265.

Steriade, M., Apostol, V. and Oakson, G. (1971a) Control of unitary activities in the cerebello-thalamic pathway during wakefulness and synchronized sleep. J. Neurophysiol., 34, 389—413.

Steriade, M. Wyzinski, P., Deschênes, M. and Guérin, M. (1971b) Disinhibition during waking in motor cortex neuronal chains in cat and monkey. Brain Res., 30, 211—217.

Steriade, M., Wyzinski, P. and Apostol, V. (1972) Corticofugal projections governing rhythmic thalamic activity. In T. Frigyesi, E. Rinvik and M.D. Yahr (Eds.), Corticothalamic Pathways and Sensorimotor Activities. Raven Press, New York, pp. 221—272.

Steriade, M., Wyzinski, P. and Apostol, V. (1973) Differential synaptic reactivity of simple and complex pyramidal tract neurons at various levels of vigilance. Exp. Brain Res., 17, 87—110.

Steriade, M., Deschênes, M. and Oakson, G. (1974a) Inhibitory processes and interneuronal apparatus in motor cortex during sleep and waking. I. Background firing and responsiveness of pyramidal tract neurons and interneurons. J. Neurophysiol., 37 1065—1092.

Steriade, M., Deschênes, M., Wyzinski, P. and Hallé, J.Y. (1974b) Input-output organization of the motor cortex and its alterations during sleep and waking. In O. Petre-Quadens and J. Schlag (Eds.), Basic Sleep Mechanisms. Academic Press, New York, pp. 143—200.

Takahashi, K. (1965) Slow and fast groups of pyramidal tract cells and their respective membrane properties. J. Neurophysiol., 28, 908—924.

DISCUSSION

BESSON: Have you any information about the unit activity in paradoxical sleep?

STERIADE: I do not have data on paradoxical sleep. Our monkeys are very vigilant and we have troubles in studying them even in slow sleep. Perhaps I have seen one PT neuron during the paradoxical phase of sleep, no more and I do not have data for that.

PURPURA: I think we have a little cultural lag in one thing. It has taken years to go from the concept of a IA inhibitory neuron just being interpolated, to recognizing from the work of the Swedish group that the IA inhibitory neuron is a magnificent integrating machinery and such neurons analogously called Renshaw cells and everything. I think what you have done is shown that the cortical inhibitory interneuron is possibly collaterally activated and most probably is also being afferently effected through the thalamus and other interneurons, and so is a very complex machinery which is probably going to turn out to be much more complicated than the IA interneuron where it has taken maybe 20 years to find out that it is not just another relay pathway but is a central focus of the organization of the spinal cord. I think these interneurons in the cortex are going to turn out to be the same thing that you have.

STERIADE: The complication also comes out from the fact that we still do not have any precise criteria to differentiate between excitatory and inhibitory interneurons. I do not know why all these bursting neurons are called inhibitory. I call them inhibitory because I need to put a finger on the progenitors, but I suppose all these are not necessarily very small cells. The important point is that they discharge in bursts. Why would 'la cellula de double bouque' found by Cajal not be the bursting neuron? And this is an excitatory neuron, but we don't have evidence for that.

PURPURA: You think that it is a double bouquet cell?

STERIADE: I mean 'la cellula double bouque' is an excitatory interneuron which may also discharge in bursts. It is a small neuron and in general small sized neurons tend to discharge in bursts, like the small and slow PT neurons have membrane properties different from large sized fast conducting PT neurons.

PURPURA: No, you have to be careful with that because we used to think that about interneurons in the spinal cord and then Likhovsky lit up the IA interneurons. It is an impossibly big neuron, dendrites extending for an extensive area. One should be careful in correlating size, speed of conduction, etc.

STERIADE: Yes.

KUBOTA: How are you sure that you are recording from fast conducting axons?

STERIADE: Because they responded with a short latency to pes peduncular stimulation.

KUBOTA: What is the latency?

STERIADE: 0.9 msec. If you consider minimum delay and the synaptic delay of about 0.4 msec, that is fast conducting.

KUBOTA: What is the intensity of the stimulus?

STERIADE: We usually employ about 0.05 to 0.2 mA and a pulse duration of about 0.1 msec, and in this instance a physical spread of the current is no more than 1.5 mm. So I suppose it is impossible in any case that the current spread from pes penduculi to the lemniscal fibers because such a latency precludes another synaptic delay in the VPL. This can only be by antidromic activation of PT-fibers and then synaptic activation of the interneuron with such a very short latency. In any case, by stimulating the VPL or VL the latency was always longer, which was about 2 msec.

PURPURA: That is fast.

STERIADE: It is too fast to come through the thalamus. I do not know whether the thalamus elicits a monosynaptic response but the pes penduculi certainly elicits a monosynaptic response to the contralateral cortex.

GILMAN: I have observed your demonstration of seizure in some of those recordings. Do I understand that they occur spontaneously?

STERIADE: These are spontaneously occurring. There is a paper published recently in the EEG Journal about such interneurons in which we demonstrated that such interneurons exhibited very powerful activity during drowsiness when the monkey began to sleep reopening and reclosing the eyes.

GILMAN: Have you seen any manifestations of the seizure begin, too?

STERIADE: No. The experiments were not designed originally to detect manifestations of so-called impairment of consciousness. We detected such seizure on the magnetic tape of the record and it was a chance observation.

GILMAN: So what do you mean by seizure.

STERIADE: By seizure I mean an electrographic pattern of spikes and waves which outlasts the stimulation and tonic movement of eyelids.

GILMAN: Oh, do they?

STERIADE: Yes, they did. And they are expressed as tonic ocular movements and not phasic eye movements as in alerting reaction with a tonic eye opening. But we do not have any other signs of seizure.

GILMAN: There is a problem in finding a seizure there.

STERIADE: They are focal seizures which were very poorly reflected in the cortical surface. This emphasized that it was a circumscribed focus in the depth.

KUBOTA: According to Evarts' data, fast PT cells have enhanced discharge in slow sleep. But, your data is different.

STERIADE: I do not want to mention Evarts' data. I discussed his data in a paper which will be published in the Journal of Neurophysiology. I can tell you that in his experiments, he remarked that fast conducting PT neurons are less active during wakefulness and slow conducting ones are more active during wakefulness. Now, as a curiosity in his first paper in 1964, there was no mention made about antidromic response latencies. All his 40 PT neurons were more active during wakefulness than during sleep. Most probably he recorded from both slow and very fast, for they are much easier to record. Then, in a subsequent paper in 1965, he observed this discrepancy between fast conducting and slow conducting neurons. I ascribed this difference to some other reason in his preparation because he did not analyze the difference between orienting reaction and quite wakefulness. He analyzed the so-called stable state of slow sleep. I suppose his stage of wakefulness was in fact an aroused or an excited wakefulness.

DESIRAJU: I want to suggest that you clarify more about comparing your data with that of Dr. Evarts. You have already made some comments. Unfortunately not many people have worked on the motor cortex and the Evarts' data is still the classic data quoted everywhere. As you have been contributing a lot on the motor cortex, what do you think? The reason why I am putting this question is that I am always puzzled if Evarts or somebody suggests that the pattern is random, random in the sense of uniformly distributed, in wakefulness and is very clustered in slow sleep, and it is much further clustered in paradoxical sleep. This is in Evarts' 1964 paper and in 1965 he differentiated some neurons, particularly the fast conducting ones as identified by this way, as discharging more slowly (except during movements) in wakefulness than in sleep, when they discharge more, whereas it is the other way round for the small neurons. In other words, the 'large' neurons remained inactive in wakefulness and they became more active in slow sleep, but he does not show data on them in paradoxical sleep. I have always been curious about the nature of the neuron of the dramatic picture of 1964 which is quoted in so many textbooks. Can you comment on this? Can we generalize it to the whole cortex? We have to look into it.

STERIADE: I suppose the picture by Evarts concerning the distribution of interspike intervals is true, and we found the same. The point is the difference between the mean height of discharge. It is very difficult to understand why Evarts did not mention in his paper of 1965, his paper of 1964. I mean in Table I in the paper of 1964 he analyzed 40 neurons. All these neurons had increased mean height of discharge from sleep to waking. It may be reasonable to consider that he recorded especially large sized, I mean, fast conducting, PT neurons. Why he found one year later that fast conducting ones are less active, is still a mystery for me. I ascribe his finding to an increased excitation of the animal. I found that during excitation when I move the finger the animal is motionless and the fast PT neuron has a very low activity. Now when the animal is still motionless and is quiet in excitation the PT cell discharges rapidly. I do not know why but it is so.

ALBE-FESSARD: Have you any idea as to where these interneurons are in your explanation?

STERIADE: We do not have accurate estimations of the depth, because we are not entering that perpendicular to the cortex. The chamber was implanted in stereotaxic plane. I have no indication of the depth. I can only say that such interneurons were below the entry point of the muscular afferents, I mean below 0.5 mm. I do not know more.

ALBE-FESSARD: Near to PT cells?

STERIADE: Yes in clusters. We have about 40 interneurons in perhaps seven or eight groups as has been found in the VB.

12

REORGANIZATION OF NEURONAL DISCHARGES IN THE CEREBRAL CORTEX THROUGH CHANGING STATES OF CONSCIOUSNESS

T. DESIRAJU*

Department of Physiology, All India Institute of Medical Sciences, New Delhi 110016 (India)

INTRODUCTION

Knowledge on the neuronal mechanisms of consciousness is required to understand the basis of mental functions of not only the perceptual, but also the expressive processes which can not be manifested in the absence of the conscious state. An organism without consciousness has little chance of survival in nature. Nevertheless, a considerable proportion in the life of mammals is spent in sleep — a reversible state of unconsciousness and altered consciousness — whose biological value is yet unknown.

Consciousness, if assumed in the simplest way to be an elementary sense of awareness of the environment and of self, is evident even in primitive vertebrates which do not have a well developed cerebral cortex. However, enlargement of the cerebral cortex in the course of evolution of primates is probably one of the most important factors which may have contributed to the uniquely enlarged dimensions of conscious mental processes endowed in man. Consciousness in man is not only a mere awareness, but is also an advanced state of perception and an understanding (of relationships between the states of environment and of self) based on comparisons of current information with previously developed frames of references acquired by experience under restriction of inherited limits, and finally leading to manifestations of realistic and purposeful responses or actions and to the formation of additional frames of references for future use.

The problem of the formation of codes or transmission of signals of the cerebral cortex and associated subsystems of the brain required for the maintenance and expression of acts of consciousness has been investigated for a few years only. Experimental ablations of large areas of the cerebral cortex

* Present address: Neurophysiology Research Unit of ICMR, National Institute of Mental Health and Neurosciences, Bangalore — 560027, India.

in animals may not result in a total loss of consciousness but in derangements of volitional functions. However, a fully decorticated non-human mammal or a human can not be expected to discharge conscious behavioral reactions to contingencies of the environment in a manner to ensure unaided survival. The normal operational modes underlying consciousness involve interactions among the cerebral cortex, the thalamus, and special regions of the reticular formation, being keyed by signals originating in sensory receptors due to changes in external and internal environments, and also modulated by chemical signals of certain endocrine secretions and other metabolites directly permeable into the brain. The transmission of some of such input signals can, in turn, be influenced and gated by the output products of interactions which are influenced by the signals. Under these principles of brain function the thalamocortical operations have a great significance in the mechanisms of regulation of sleep and consciousness.

In this paper, patterns of changes found in the neuronal activitiy of the cerebral cortex as correlated to states of sleep and wakefulness are discussed to reflect not only the states of the thalamocortical system during the cycle of natural sleep and wakefulness, but also the principle of unit function reorganization in communications of the brain. Although the state of the cerebral cortex in different states of consciousness (as in natural cycles of sleep and wakefulness) has been a subject of investigation for a long time, impulse discharges of neurons in the cortex of primates have so far been studied only in the motor cortex (Evarts, 1967), parietal association cortex (Desiraju, 1972b and c) and frontal association cortex (Desiraju, 1973c). In discussing the significant properties of primate cortical areas, data reported in the literature on non-primate cortex, and also data on synaptic relations in feline thalamus, are given consideration to widen the scope of interpretation and perspective of the data available on the primate cortex *.

METHODS

Recordings of unit activity were made in (free to move) rhesus monkeys (of 3—4 kg weight) seated in a primate chair (Fig. 1). The monkeys were prepared to carry chronically implanted electrodes (EEG, EOG, EMG of neck nuchals) and a pedestal to hold a microelectrode driver device. Most of the monkeys were also implanted with stainless steel bipolar focal stimulating electrodes in the thalamus. Some monkeys also had cannulae in the cerebral ventricles or other areas of the brain for aiding in injecting chemicals or for guiding microelectrodes to depths (Desiraju, 1972a and 1973b).

Macroelectrode data recordings were made on an eight-channel ink-writing electroencephalograph (Grass, U.S.A.). Data on single units were collected

---

* The data on feline thalamus was collected while working in the laboratory of Professor Dominick P. Purpura, Albert Einstein College of Medicine, New York, N.Y., U.S.A.

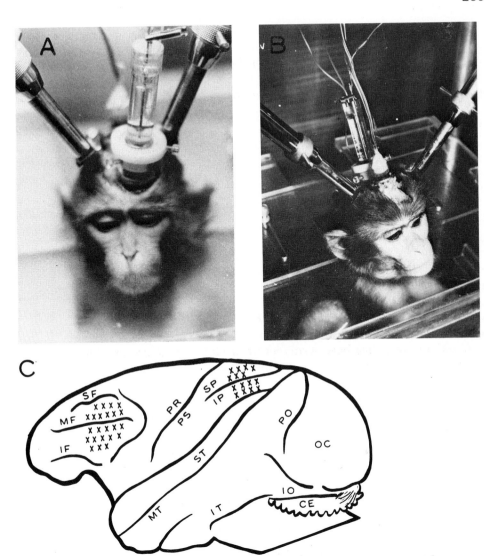

Fig. 1. Monkeys seated during recording sessions, with implanted aids for recording impulses of neurons of frontal association cortex (A) and parietal association cortex (B). The plug connecting macroelectrodes and the hydraulic drive for connecting microelectrode and the restraining clamps are visible in the photographs. The areas of cortical gyri which have been explored with microelectrodes are indicated by crosses in C. CE, cerebellum; IF, inferior frontal; IO, inferior occipital; IP, inferior parietal; IT, inferior temporal; MF, middle frontal; MT, middle temporal; OC, occipital; PO, preoccipital; PR, precentral; PS, postcentral; SF, superior frontal; SP, superior parietal; ST, superior temporal.

from the parietal association cortex and the dorsolateral prefrontal association cortex (Fig. 1). Microelectrode recordings of impulse discharges of units were not only displayed on an oscilloscope, from which they were photographed at intervals, but were also transformed into replicas as Schmitt trigger pulses and recorded continuously on one of the channels of the ink-writer simultaneously with the corticogram of the same and other areas of the cortex and with EOG and EMG. Thus, recorded information was available firstly, to study alterations of unitary discharges during several hours through the changing states of sleep-wakefulness cycles of conscious behavior and, secondly, to draw inferences on relationships between patterns of electrocorticograms and neuronal discharges of impulses. The criteria for division of the monkey's sleep-wakefulness cycle into different states have been described previously (Desiraju, 1972b).

Records of impulse discharges obtained in several epochs under the states of behavior were examined for alterations of frequencies, and differences among them were assessed by using both parametric and non-parametric statistical procedures. Interspike intervals of representative records were manually measured and their relative frequencies in the total number of a given epoch were plotted in histograms. Poisson predictions of each ordinate were calculated by using the formula

$n = N \cdot t/T \cdot \exp(-t/T)$ (Fatt and Katz, 1952).

Recording sites of the cortex were noted on the basis of stereotaxic coordinates of the electrode carrier pedestal, readings on microelectrode drive, and postmortem histology of sections stained with thionin and Luxol fast blue. Additional clues on the depth in the prefrontal cortex were also available in some monkeys from the nature of the potentials recorded while the electrode was being lowered in the cortex as the dorsomedial thalamic nucleus was simultaneously stimulated (Desiraju, 1973b).

RESULTS AND DISCUSSION

Properties of discharge patterns of association areas of the cerebral cortex

Consistent relationships have been found between behavioral states of sleep and discharge transformations of certain neurons of the association cortex of both parietal and frontal lobes of the primate brain (Fig. 2). The direction of change of unit discharges in the sleep-wakefulness cycle was found to be not the same for different units. These patterns of changes can be distinguished into at least four broad categories (types I to IV) in the association cortex (Table I).

The type I unit discharge alterations were frequently noted in the frontal association cortex (Figs. 3 and 4). The type II unit patterns were found in the frontal association cortex as well as the parietal association cortex (Figs. 5—7). The type III unit patterns (Fig. 8) were, so far, observed in the frontal cortex whereas the type IV units were observed in both frontal and parietal cortices.

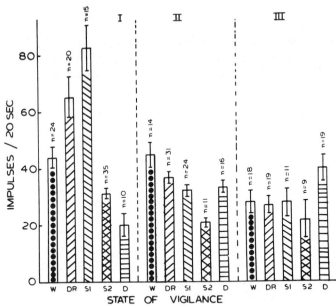

Fig. 2. Mean discharge frequencies of impulses of three types of units (I, II and III) of frontal association cortex during quiet and relaxed wakeful state (W), drowsy state (DR), early part of slow wave sleep (S_1), late or well developed part of slow wave sleep (S_2) and REM sleep (D).

TABLE I

Patterns of mean frequencies of impulses discharged by different categories of neurons in the association cortex (parietal and dorsolateral prefrontal areas) during different states of sleep, expressed in relation to the fequency (****) of the respective category during the quiet wakeful state

State of behavior	Category of units according to sequence of change of discharge frequency of impulses of neurons			
	I	II	III	IV
(1) Non-REM sleep states (i) Drowsy state (DR)	******	***	****	****
(ii) High voltage slow wave EEG state (light) (S_1)	*****	**	****	****
(iii) High voltage slow wave EEG state (deep) (S_2)	**	*	****	****
(2) REM sleep state	*	****	*****	****

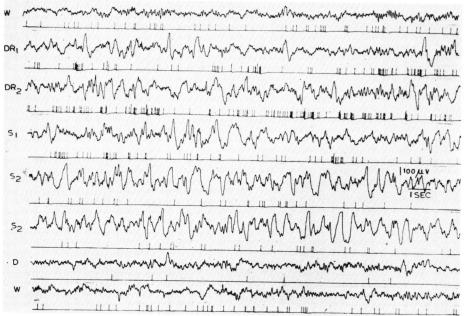

Fig. 3. Impulse discharge pattern of a type I unit of frontal association cortex during the cycle of wakefulness-sleep-wakefulness. In each pair of traces the upper one represents the electrocorticogram and the lower one the impulse replicas recorded simultaneously from the same area of cortex. Note increase of impulse discharge during drowsy state (DR) and marked decrease of discharge during REM sleep (D). Impulses in each epoch of 20 sec: W, 50; DR_1, 79; DR_2, 136; S_1, 64; S_2, 32; S_2, 26; D, 7; W, 40. (From Desiraju, 1973c.)

Some information is also available about differences of input organization of the I and II categories of units in the frontal cortex. The type II units were identified as the neurons responding with short latency (4—9 msec) excitatory effects to specific thalamocortical projection influences which evoked an 'augmenting' type of electrical discharge (Fig. 9). The type I units were not clearly influenced by specific thalamic stimulations. Some of them were found to be excited by stimulations of the rostral non-specific thalamus at the fringe of the ventralis anterior magnocellularis, centralis intermedialis and paracentralis which evoked a 'recruiting' type of electrical discharge (Fig. 10).

Fig. 4. Impulse discharge pattern of a variation of type I unit of prefrontal cortex (A), and interspike interval histogram of a similar unit (B). The broken line histograms represent Poisson expectations. $\overline{X}$: mean interspike interval; $\overline{OX}$: standard error; R: reciprocal of interval; N: number of intervals analyzed; F: mean frequency of spikes; T: duration of record analyzed. The last bar in each histogram represents the fraction of intervals longer than 1267 msec duration. Impulses in each epoch of 20 sec in A: W, 61; S_1, 89; S_2, 60; S_3, 57; S_4, 36; D, 32; W, 58. The gradual decrease of discharge through early slow sleep (S_1) and late slow sleep (S_2, S_3 and S_4 traces) is illustrated in A.

A

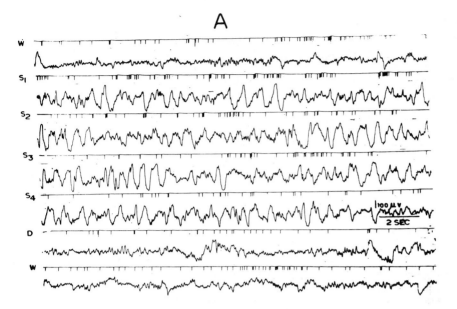

B

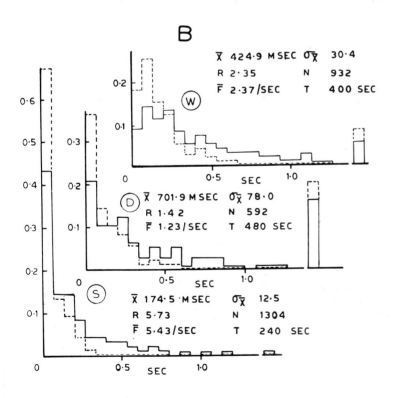

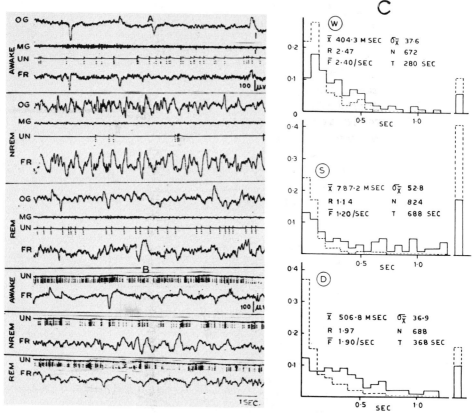

Fig. 5. Impulse discharge patterns of two type II units of prefrontal cortex, a slow firing one (A) and a fast firing one (B). Note low level of discharge during slow sleep (NREM) and high level of discharge during REM sleep. Interspike interval histogram of a type II unit is represented on the right (C). Abbreviations as in Fig. 4. Frequency (per sec) of impulses: A, awake 2.5, NREM 0.65, REM 2.25; B, awake 16.5, NREM 10.5, REM 15.8. (From Desiraju, 1973c (A and B).)

The type I and type II units were not found to be segregated, but could be detected even at close proximities in the cortex (layers IV—VI). However, in the upper levels (about layer II) of the cortex, type I units were found to be more common.

Grouping of impulses in dense clusters or bursts during slow sleep was more obvious in unit discharges of the prefrontal cortex (particularly of the type I units in drowsy state) than of the parietal cortex (Desiraju, 1972b, c and 1973c).

The nature of the change in discharge pattern of category I units of the prefrontal cortex is opposite to that of the category II units of prefrontal or parietal areas during states of drowsiness and of paradoxical sleep (Fig. 11).

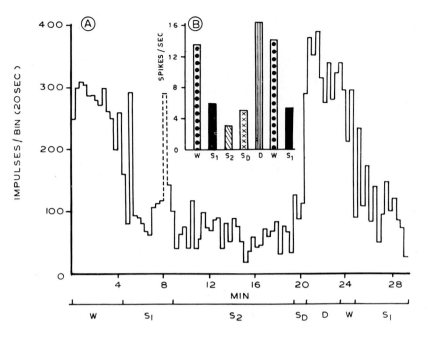

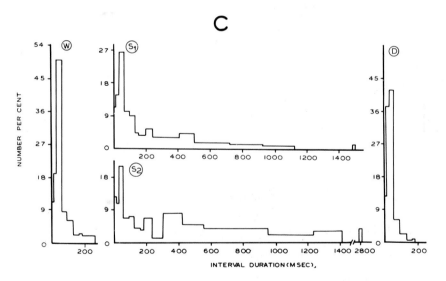

Fig. 6. Discharge periodicity of impulses in successive 20 sec epochs (A) and mean frequencies (B) of a parietal association cortex unit (type II) through states of sleep-wakefulness cycle. The interspike interval histogram of such a unit is given in C. (From Desiraju, 1972c.)

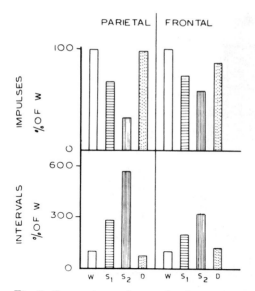

Fig. 7. Comparison of mean levels of impulse discharges of type II units of parietal and frontal association cortices. Note that the degree of reduction of discharge during S_2 is more in parietal than in frontal cortex.

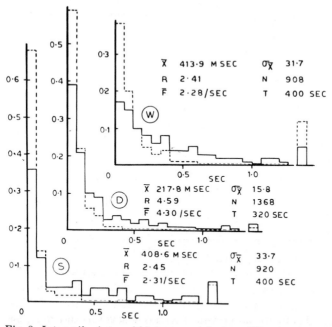

Fig. 8. Interspike interval histograms of a type III unit of prefrontal cortex. Note increase in mean discharge frequency or reduction of mean interspike interval during D sleep. Abbreviations are as in Fig. 4.

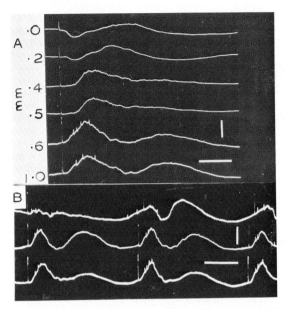

Fig. 9. Laminar field potentials recorded at indicated depths in prefrontal cortex (A) evoked by stimulations of nucleus medialis dorsalis thalami and a sequence of augmenting response (B) recorded in depth (0.6 mm) of the cortex. Note the unitary discharges evoked by the stimulation. Such units followed the type II sequence of changes illustrated before. Time bar in A is 20 msec and in B is 40 msec. Amplitude bars represent 1.5 mV. (From Desiraju, 1973d.)

However, such an inverse correlation between type I and type II unit discharges was not present during late slow wave EEG sleep.

The nature of the change of discharges of the I and II units was also opposite with respect to reactions of the wakeful state. Mean discharge frequencies of I units underwent a decrease and of II units an increase during movement periods of wakefulness (Desiraju, 1972b and 1973c). The two categories also showed the interesting change in inverse directions during psychoactive periods of alert wakeful state without body movements. When an attentive or orienting reaction (not accompanied by body movements, as judged from the apparent behavior of the monkey as well as by the neck electromyogram) was evoked in the monkey by the experimenter staring suddenly into the eyes of the monkey or by any novel alteration in the monkey's purview, the ongoing rate of discharge of impulses was decreased (up to 50%) transiently for some seconds in the parietal association cortex (II units), whereas such psychoactive stimuli evoked a several-fold increase of unit discharge of the type I units of the prefrontal cortex (Desiraju, 1972b and 1973c). The stimuli quickly lost effect on repeating a few times.

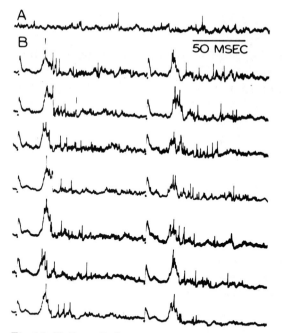

Fig. 10. Unitary discharges recorded at a depth of 0.6 mm, associated with recruiting type of potentials evoked in prefrontal cortex by stimulations of rostral non-specific thalamic nuclei. A: spontaneous activity. B: evoked responses. Such units followed the type I sequence illustrated before. (From Desiraju, 1973e.)

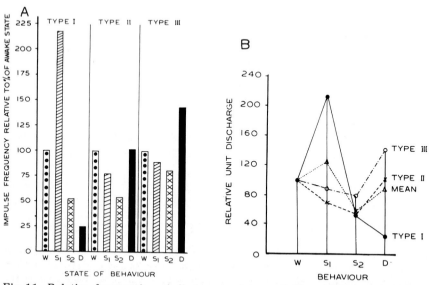

Fig. 11. Relative frequencies of discharges of types I, II and III units during successive states of the wakefulness-sleep cycle (A), and their extrapolation on common time scale (B). Note the mean which can reflect the resultant functional state of population of units with respect to each state of behavior, subject to assumptions made in the text.

Such discharges were not like the shortest latency specific projection activities in specific cortex due to sensory stimuli. These observations suggest that transmission of cortical neuronal signals of conscious psychosomatic function are probably related to several underlying factors, including legislation and execution of production or inhibition of movements of muscles, psychological components related to emotion, motivation, attention, novelty, expectation of outcome, and other higher aspects.

The functional alteration of an area depends on at least two processes: (1) change in discharge pattern restricted to a particular subpopulation of neurons and (2) change in activity of the whole population due to relatively interdependent changes among subpopulations of the area. If it is assumed that the three main categories of units (I, II and III) which undergo alterations of impulse discharges with respect to states of sleep-wakeful behavior are represented in equal proportions in a population of neurons (in this case the dorsolateral prefrontal cortex is considered), the mean number of impulses discharged by the whole population per unit time will be more during light slow sleep and less during deep slow sleep, and about similar during paradoxical sleep relative to quiet wakeful state (Fig. 11). On the other hand,

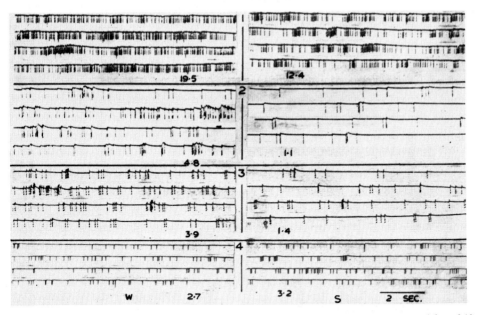

Fig. 12. Four examples of patterns of change in unit discharges concomitant with a shift from wakeful state (W) to slow sleep state (S). A discharge of 20 sec is illustrated in four traces for each state. Small number under each set of traces represents mean frequency. Note high frequency tonic discharge of W changes into low frequency and phasic pattern during S (unit I), whereas low frequency unit discharges of W may change into either lower frequencies (units 2 and 3) or a higher frequency (unit 4) during S.

if any of the categories of units is disproportionately represented or activated, the population discharge pattern of the area can be modified accordingly. These possibilities have to be kept in mind when changes in EEG or behavior are evaluated.

The pattern of discharge in a behavioral state was sometimes predictable from the level of frequency of discharge in a preceding state of behavior. The classification of units according to the discharge rates of quiet wakeful state suggested that the type I units are of a low frequency (less than 7/sec) class and the type II units are of both high and low frequency classes (Fig. 12). Units with a much higher frequency (>15/sec) were always found to follow the sequence of the type II category. Thus, units of high frequency can be predicted, from records of wakeful state, to follow the type II sequence in states of sleep, and units of low frequency can not be predicted as to which of the patterns (types I to IV) of sequences they may show during sleep.

Some units of the prefrontal cortex were found to be active during wakefulness and they became silent after a few episodes of sleep. Initially it was thought that the silence of the units was due to dislocation of the relation of the recording electrode to the unit, but after making the possible checks and repeated observations under good experimental conditions no electrode dislocation was suggested and it was realized that the postsleep quiescence was a unique behavior of some units of the prefrontal cortex. Whether these units reflect some mechanism of satiation of a drive serving sleep function is as yet difficult to state, although the suggestion is positive.

Comparison of the properties of unit discharges of association cortex and of primary cortex

(A) Primate brain
'Medium' sized (size assumed on the basis of conduction velocity) pyramidal tract (PT) neurons of the precentral gyrus were found to discharge in bursts during slow sleep and even more phasically during REM sleep in contrast to the uniform discharge patterns of the quiet wakeful state (Evarts, 1967). The patterns of large PT neurons, particularly during REM sleep, are not well known. These units and also non-PT neurons were reported to be more active during slow sleep than during the quiet wakeful state (Evarts, 1967).

The most important difference between the association cortex and the motor cortex is the absence of the intensely phasic and bursting pattern of discharge of units in the former during REM sleep. The second most important revelation is the finding of very low rates of discharge of a considerable proportion of prefrontal cortex units (type I) during REM sleep.

There are also some similarities between association and primary cortices. The sequence of changes of frequencies of discharges (in the progression of the behavioral cycle) of medium sized PT neurons is similar to the sequence of type II units of the association cortex. The behavior of large PT neurons and non-PT neurons of the motor cortex is somewhat similar to the behavior of type I association cortex neurons during early slow sleep. Burst formations of impulses are present in discharges of both motor cortex and association cortex during slow wave sleep stages.

Discharge frequencies of large PT units were augmented during movement periods, whereas discharges of type I units of the prefrontal cortex were retarded and those of type II units of the parietal cortex were augmented. On the other hand, stimulations with novel stimuli, which evoked psychic responses but not body movements, were accompanied by augmented unit discharges of type I units of the prefrontal cortex and retardation of discharges of type II units of the parietal cortex, respectively. The principle of psychic influence on unit discharges is also implicit but not clearly enunciated for units of the motor cortex of the primate.

(B) Non-primate brain

Units of the middle suprasylvian gyrus of cat discharge with frequencies which are similar during the alert state and the wakeful state, with a rate lower than this by about 22% during slow sleep and a rate higher by about 100% during REM sleep (Noda and Adey, 1970). This pattern is somewhat similar to that of type II units of the primate association cortex, but the degree of decrease in slow sleep is much less and the degree of increase in REM sleep is much higher for cat's cortex.

There are differences in the observations of different authors on the visual cortex. Units of the visual cortex of cat discharge at about equal frequencies during quiet wakefulness and slow sleep, and at very high rates during paradoxical sleep and during wakeful periods of visual stimulation (Evarts, 1967). Surprisingly, very few of the unit discharges of the visual cortex were found to be related to PGO waves of REM sleep (Kasamatsu and Adey, 1973), but most of the unit discharges of REM sleep occurred during episodes of eye movements or body movements (Hobson and McCarley, 1971). Slow units underwent an increase whereas fast units underwent a decrease of discharges during slow sleep (Hobson and McCarley, 1971). However, they all were reported to discharge at high rates during REM sleep. The visual cortex unit discharges which are not found to undergo reduction during slow sleep stage, but to undergo an increase in REM sleep (Evarts, 1967) are in a way comparable to the type III category of prefrontal units which discharge without decrement during any stage of sleep and only undergo some increment during the REM stage. The reciprocal projections between the peristriate cortex and the prefrontal cortex may provide some basis for this similarity. However, contrary to other units of the visual cortex, either the type III units or other categories of units of the association cortex of monkey or of cat are seldom found to discharge in close temporal correlation to eye movements of REM sleep or of wakefulness.

The hippocampus which is an archicortex shows, in cat, a remarkably rhythmic theta EEG during REM sleep. Surprisingly, the patterns of unit discharges and the theta waves from the cortex have not been found to be well correlated (Noda et al., 1969). The patterns of discharge frequencies of the hippocampal units seem to be approximately similar to the behavior of type II units of the association cortex of monkey. The origin or operational mechanism of the huge theta waves of the EEG during REM sleep in cat is yet to be resolved.

Large and recurring EEG waves possibly reflect not the spike discharges but the rhythmic occurrence of IPSPs or long duration summations of fields of PSPs in the dendrites of pyramidal neurons. This was hypothesized to explain delta waves in the neocortex and the lack of correlation between the waves and unit discharges which were decreased (Desiraju, 1971a, 1973c and 1974).

Discussion on units of augmenting and recruiting thalamocortical subsystems of the association cortex

The type I units of the prefrontal cortex were found to be not excited but rather slightly inhibited or unaffected by stimulations of the dorsomedial thalamus during the wakeful state. On the contrary, the type II units were evoked to discharge impulses and also the corticogram was markedly altered by the stimulations. Further, the stimulations could not evoke alterations of the corticogram (Fig. 13) during slow sleep in which there was also a reduction of frequency of spontaneous unit discharge. These correlations suggest that the excitatory influences of specific thalamic projections in the cortex are dampened during slow sleep, resulting in a decrease of firing of impulses of a category of neurons (type II) in the cortex. The data also suggest that the concomitant mechanism for augmentation of the discharges of type I units is either activated or disinhibited. As the type I units could be (in the instances tested so far) activated during 'recruiting' potentials, it appears that the operation of a recruiting system is the likely mechanism for enhanced discharges of type I units during drowsy or early slow sleep stages. Later, the recruiting excitation mechanism also is possibly dampened, as the discharges of type I units also undergo reduction through the late slow sleep stage of high amplitude delta EEG.

The inference is that the neurons (types I and II) of the association cortex whose discharges undergo reduction during deep slow sleep are elements closely linked to the augmenting and recruiting thalamocorticothalamic subsystem, whereas other types of neurons of the cortex whose discharges are not altered even in deep slow sleep and whose discharges are maintained on as much an average activity in sleep as in the quiet wakeful state, may be elements which are more closely related to other subsystems whose functions are awaiting understanding.

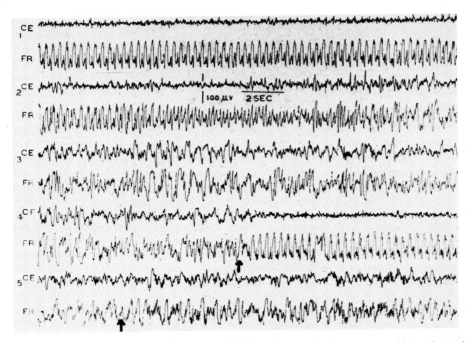

Fig. 13. Effect of background state of EEG and consciousness on prefrontal cortical rhythms evoked by stimulations of nucleus medialis dorsalis thalami. CE: electrocorticogram of precentral gyrus; FR: electrocorticogram of prefrontal cortex. Stimulation is during wakeful state (set 1) and through drowsy state (sets 2 to 4). At arrow in set 4, the monkey is awakened by which restoration of response resulted, as in set 1. Set 5 is recorded under Nembutal anesthesia, the arrow demarcates record into parts before and after onset of stimulation. (From Desiraju, 1973b.)

Although the behavior of type II units may generally reflect the properties of a specific thalamocortical division of the system in sleep-wakefulness cycle, whereas the behavior of type I units may reflect properties of changes in non-specific thalamocortical division of the system in the behavioral cycle, 'critical' interactions and gatings between the two divisions probably occur in the construction of codes related realistically to consciousness about self and about environment.

Thalamic and other controls on reorganization of cortical neuronal activities of conscious and subconscious functions of wakefulness and sleep

Having observed some properties of cyclic alterations of cortical impulse codes correlated with the fundamental alterations of conscious behavior, it is impelling to consider the possible role of thalamic and corticocortical afferent and efferent subsystems and pathways underlying the observed alterations of the cortical codes.

270

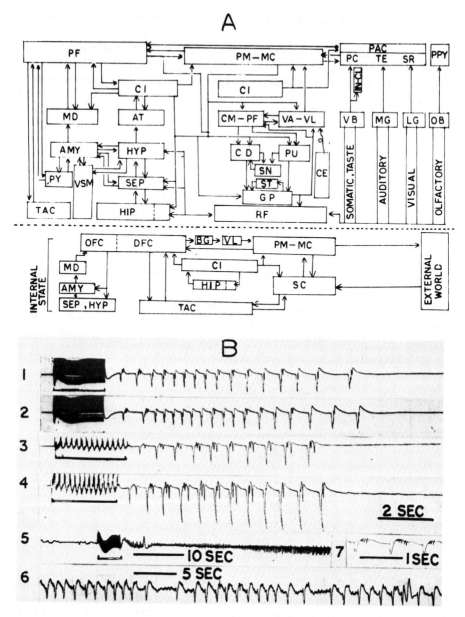

Fig. 14. Principal relationships of frontal and parietal association cortices in primate (A), and nature of electrical discharges evoked after a brief period of direct stimulation of an area of association cortex (in suprasylvian gyrus in cerveau isole cat) devoid of neuronal connections with the rest of the brain in situ (B). Traces 1 to 4 are from acutely isolated slabs, and 5 to 7 are from chronically isolated (12 weeks) slabs. The discharges of chronic slabs were highly prolonged, lasting hours. Abbreviations for this and subsequent figures: AMY, amygdala; AT, anterior thalamic nuclei; BG, basal ganglia; CD, caudate; CE, cere-

The thalamus can play an important role in relating and regulating interoceptive and exteroceptive information that is meaningful in the realm of subconsciousness and consciousness. It (VB, VL-VA, pulvinar, LP, etc.*) is a vital station for transmission of not only sensory information about the external world but also of motor information based on signals received from basal ganglia and the cerebellum to the cortex. In addition, the thalamus (DM, anterior nuclei, and medial and intralaminar nuclei) is also concerned with the formation and transmission of codes of information between the old and new cortical subsystems to relate events of psychosomatic functions with respect to internal and external worlds in the spheres of intellectual, affective, alimentary, autonomic and visceral adaptations (Fig. 14).

Lesions of the thalamus result in insomnia (Villablanca and Salinas-Zeballos, 1972). Stimulations of the thalamus have been studied for a long time (Jasper, 1954; Hess, 1957) and the effects, on the whole, can be summed up (Desiraju, 1971a) as suggesting that they have powerful influence on not only the electrocorticogram but also behavior; the low frequency stimulations facilitate EEG slow waves and hypnogenic behavior, whereas the high frequency stimulations facilitate EEG desynchronization and attentive or alert behavior. Isolation of the cortex from thalamic and intercortical pathways frees the cortex from spindling and other cortical rhythms of the normal electrocorticogram (Desiraju, 1966). However, when directly stimulated the isolated area can give slow waves as afterdischarges whose durations are longer in chronically isolated slabs than in acutely isolated slabs (Fig. 14). Stimulation of some areas of the cerebral cortex in humans is known to evoke altered conscious responses of a psychic nature (Penfield, 1969). A great deal of neurological discussion on the role of the cortex and the thalamus on consciousness and behavior has taken place to explain the spread of disturbances generated in cortical foci to other critical areas of the brain and the regeneration of paroxysms. Any significant alteration of mental state or behavior probably involves coordinated changes in intercommunication of

---

* For abbreviations see legend to Fig. 14.

---

bellofugal projection, CI, cingulate gyrus; CM-PF, nucleus centrum medianum and parafascicularis; DFC, dorsolateral prefrontal cortex; GP, globus pallidus; HIP, hippocampus; HYP, hypothalamus; IN-CL, insulaclaustrum; LG, lateral geniculate; MD, nucleus medialis dorsalis thalami; MG, medial geniculate; OB, olfactory bulb; OFC, orbitofrontal cortex; PAC, parietal association and peristriate cortices; PC, postcentral cortex; PF, prefrontal cortex; PM-MC, premotor and motor cortex; PPY, prepyriform cortex; PU, putamen; PY, pyriform cortex; RF, reticular formation; SC, sensory cortex; SEP, septum; SN, substantia nigra; SR, striate cortex; ST, subthalamus; TAC, temporal association cortex; TE, auditory cortex; VA-VL, nucleus ventralis anterior and lateralis; VB nucleus ventrobasal complex; VSM, visceral sensorimotor nuclear areas.

codes in extensive areas of brain. However, lesions in certain small areas of the brain stem may result in alterations of consciousness or even in coma. Such observations on the effects of lesions and of some drugs or chemicals indicate that the thalamocortical system has to operate conjointly with the rest of the brain, particularly the brain stem reticular system, including mid-brain connections at an intercollicular level and of the monoaminergic neuronal loci (Desiraju, 1971b and 1973a; Jouvet, 1974).

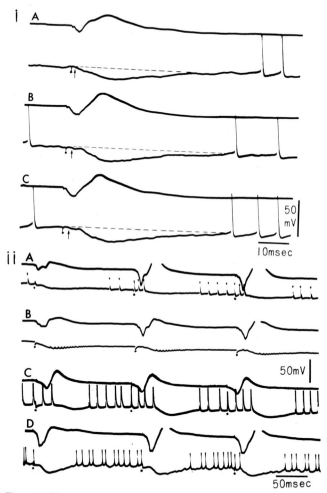

Fig. 15. Examples of simple varieties of intracellularly recorded synaptic influences resulting in neurons of non-specific thalamus during stimulations of specific thalamic nuclei (VL-VA). In each pair, upper trace is pericruciate corticogram and lower trace the intracellular record of thalamic neuron. This, and the following eight figures (Figs. 15—23), are from experiments on encephale isole cats. Note onset (arrows) of short latency powerful IPSPs (i) as well as long latency IPSPs (ii). Four neurons are represented: i; ii A, B; ii C; ii D. (From Desiraju and Purpura, 1970b (i) and Desiraju and Purpura, unpublished (ii).)

One of the most important advances made in recent years to new knowledge on forebrain physiology is the revelation of a 'reciprocal control' mechanism between specific thalamic and general (non-specific) thalamic subsystems (Desiraju et al., 1969; Desiraju, 1970 and 1971a; Desiraju and Purpura, 1970b). It was found that experimental alterations of activity induced in one subsystem resulted in alteration of impulse discharge mechanisms in the other subsystem. Further, the effects of stimulation of a specific thalamic subsystem on the neuronal excitations or inhibitions of the general thalamic subsystem (Figs. 15 and 16) were found to be relatively

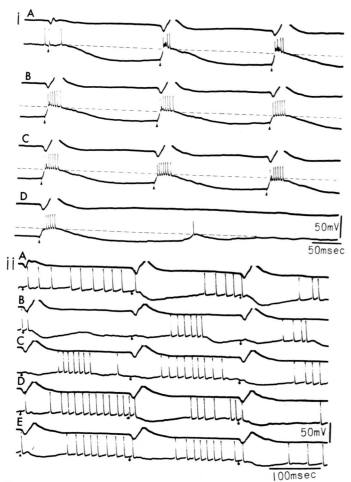

Fig. 16. Examples of complex varieties of rhythm generating synaptic potentials in neurons of non-specific thalamus generated during stimulations of specific thalamus. Note in i rhythmic EPSPs and IPSPs which also summate to hyperpolarize the neuron; and in ii the establishment of a cyclic phase relation of a complexly timed sequence of response to the sequence of the stimulus. (From Desiraju and Purpura, 1970b.)

even more powerful than the effects of the latter on the former (Fig. 17). However, the influence of the general thalamic subsystem seems to be more effective at the level of the specific thalamus than in cortex. In other words, the intrathalamic reciprocal control mechanisms between specific and general thalamic subsystems and a relatively parallel intracortical provision for inter-action of specific and general thalamic projection activities within the cortex, together provide an important integratory mechanism in the fore-brain to establish suitable patterns of activity of cerebral cortical areas.

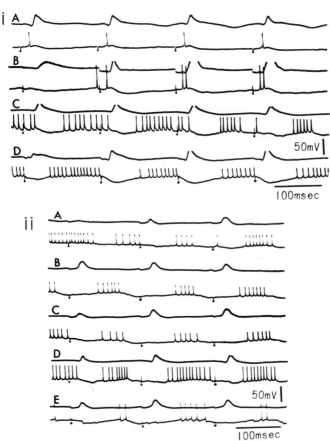

Fig. 17. Examples of varieties of synaptic mechanisms generated in neurons of specific thalamic nuclei (VL-VA) during stimulations of non-specific thalamus. The four neurons in i illustrate EPSP-IPSP sequences which have relatively simple temporal relations to stimuli. The three more neurons (A—C; D; E) in ii illustrate the generation of complex rhythmic discharge of impulses in specific thalamic neurons during cortical recruiting responses or stimulations of non-specific thalamus. (From Desiraju and Purpura, unpub-lished.)

The intrathalamic reciprocal mechanism would be engaged and conditioned firstly by the operation of inputs of specific and non-specific thalamic subsystems (Figs. 18—22) and, secondly, by the corticofugal influences (Fig. 23). The corticofugal influences are known to traverse via relatively direct projections and also via basal ganglia relays which project to both specific (Figs. 18, 19 and 22) and general thalamic subsystems (Figs. 20 and 21). Thus, the alterations of cortical neuronal discharge patterns of impulses can occur according to changes of the states of sleep-wakeful behavior accompanying general shifts in synaptic operations of the complex forebrain interactions, while keeping relationships with those of the rest of the brain as well.

The highly enlarged prefrontal cortex of primates occupies part of a more

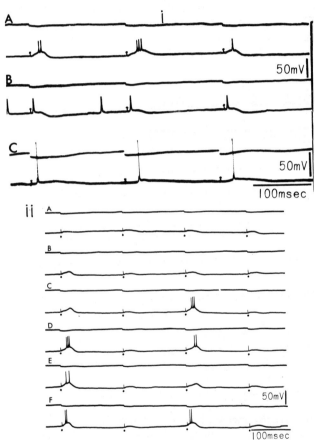

Fig. 18. Examples of varieties of modifications introduced in specific thalamic (VL-VA) synaptic transmission by outflows of basal ganglia. The relatively simple stimulus-response relationships of three neurons are illustrated in i and a sequence of complexly modulated EPSP (suppressed or facilitated alternately) generation in another variety is illustrated in ii. (From Desiraju and Purpura, unpublished.)

complex system than the specific cortical areas (Desiraju, 1975). The dorso-lateral sector of the prefrontal cortex and the orbital side of the prefrontal cortex have interconnections directly with all other major cortical sub-systems (parietopreoccipital, temporal and limbic cortical), and also cortico-fugal or corticopetal or subcortical connections with amygdala, septum, hy-pothalamus, midbrain tegmentum on one hand and with dorsomedial thala-mus and basal ganglia on the other (Fig. 14). Thus, the prefrontal cortex has a close relationship with mechanisms serving in both conscious and subcon-scious states of brain function, and with subsystems regulating not only the homeostasis of the internal environment but also the larger homeostasis of behavior of the organism in the external environment in a realistic and meaningful manner.

Although the prefrontal cortex is in a complex association system, the fundamental principles of intrathalamic reciprocal control mechanisms and the thalamocortical relationships enunciated above may probably be, in prin-ciple, applicable for the prefrontal cortex also. It has been recently estab-

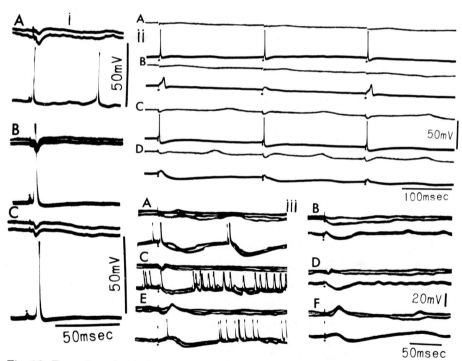

Fig. 19. Examples of varieties of influences of cerebellofugal projections (i three neurons; ii C, D; iii C, D), basal ganglia projections (ii A, B; iii A, B) and non-specific thalamic projections (iii E, F) on responses of neurons of specific thalamic nuclei (VL). ii and iii represent one neuron each to illustrate differences and similarities of responses to con-verging inputs originating in different sources. (From Desiraju and Purpura, unpublished.)

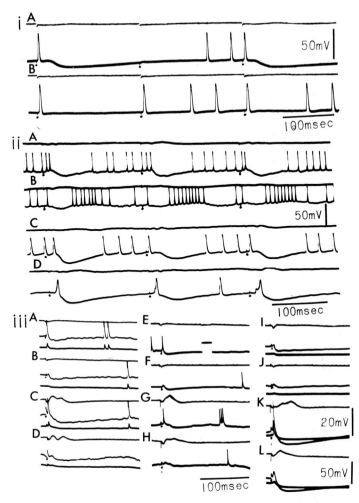

Fig. 20. Varieties of synaptic potentials which can be evoked in neurons of non-specific thalamus by pallidofugal (four neurons: i A, B; ii A; B; C, D) cerebellofugal and cortico-fugal pathways (three neurons in iii: A—D; E—H; I—L; traces AB, EF and IJ are cerebellar effects and the rest are corticofugal effects). (From Desiraju and Purpura, unpublished.)

lished electrophysiologically that the dorsomedial thalamic nucleus indeed satisfies the criteria of a relay nucleus or specific thalamic nucleus to the primate prefrontal cortex (Desiraju, 1973b and d) and that the rostral medial thalamus (in the vicinity of VA magnocellularis) as a zone of non-specific thalamus for the cortex (Desiraju, 1973e and 1975). Anatomical reports earlier suggested corticofugal pathways to this area of thalamus. An additional point of significance is that the prefrontal cortex can modify the

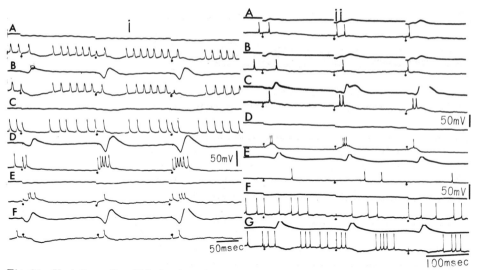

Fig. 21. Varieties of pallidofugal and reciprocal engagements of non-specific thalamic neurons (i) and specific thalamic neurons (ii). The three non-specific thalamic neurons (A; B; C, D; E, F) are influenced by both pallidal and specific thalamic stimulations, the nature of effects being different. The three specific thalamic neurons (A—C; D, E; F, G) illustrate responsiveness to either inputs or to both. Neuron A—C is influenced by both; neuron D, E is influenced only by pallidum and not medial thalamus; neuron F, G is influenced (complex relation) only by medial thalamus and not by pallidum. (From Desiraju and Purpura, unpublished.)

motor system function by way of influences through the basal ganglia. The interactions among the basal ganglia, cerebellum, substantia nigra, specific (VL) and general thalamic nuclei and sensorimotor cerebral cortex are being investigated intensively (Purpura et al., 1964; Desiraju and Purpura, 1969 and 1970a; Steriade, 1974).

The great scope of such adaptive operations in the subsystems of primary cortical and association cortical mechanisms makes it very difficult to accept any simplistic theories on mechanisms of alterations of cortical neuronal activity in the cycle of sleep and wakefulness. Further, any scheme trying to account for the transformation of neuronal discharges in sleep-wakefulness cycles should also be able to explain (1) the sequential nature of awake-slow sleep-REM stages of behavior, (2) the facility in the system to revert from any stage to any of its preceding stages, (3) the easy recurrence of awake-slow sleep stages, and (4) the criticality of the onset of the REM state which is relatively sudden and always follows, and not precedes, slow sleep state. Sleep is an altered state of not only consciousness but also of all other centrally integrated adaptations including posture and voluntary muscle control, perception, and other neural and endocrine functions. So little is now known

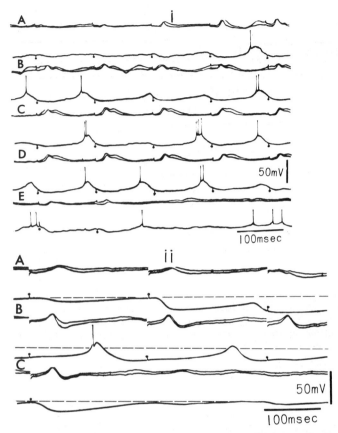

Fig. 22. Examples of generation of oscillating high amplitude and long duration synaptic potentials in neurons of specific thalamus during stimulations of medial thalamus (i), and medial pallidum (ii) during which the corticogram exhibits slow waves. (From Desiraju and Purpura, unpublished.)

of the brain, that it is difficult as yet to distinguish the causes and effects in complexly interlinked and mutually influencing subsystems and derive inferences on the respective role of each subsystem in what appears to be a vital neurological mechanism, encompassing most parts of the brain underlying the control of a deliberate lapse of consciousness with an inherent danger to life of self due to considerable loss of contact with the external environment. Recurring periods of rest or inactivity of the motor system may ensure considerable conservation of cellular processes of the body and may thereby slow aging and prolong survival of the individual and propagation of the species. Further, a consideration of the complex relations and properties of impulse discharges suggests that the programming of neuronal activities of the brain in sleep may be not only for neuronal rest or for a

280

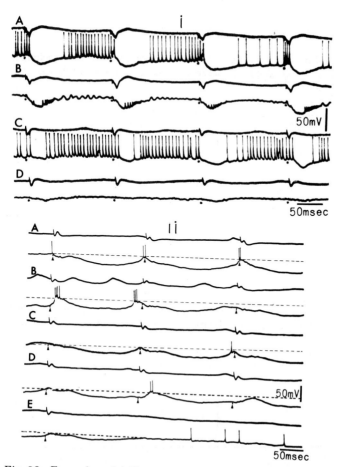

Fig. 23. Examples of influences of specific corticofugal (anteror sigmoid) and specific thalamic (VL-VA) subsystem on neurons of non-specific thalamus. In i the effects of stimulations of VL (traces A, B) and cortex (traces C, D) are given. In ii is given the sequence of a complex response of another neuron to stimulation of cortex resulting in a sustained IPSP and also oscillating PSPs during cortical slow waves. (From Desiraju and Purpura, unpublished.)

state of some purposeful release of neuronal activity, but also to support possible mechanisms in the homeostatic regulation of mental health.

Acknowledgement

The author was supported by the Indian Council of Medical Research.

REFERENCES

Desiraju, T. (1966) Stimulus-response relationship in the production of afterdischarges and their spread from intact cerebral gyri to neuronally isolated slabs. Electroenceph. clin. Neurophysiol., 21, 345—354.

Desiraju, T. (1970) Organization and synaptic properties of neurons of the thalamic reticular system. Bull. All India Inst. med. Sci., 4, 59—66.

Desiraju, T. (1971a) Neural integrations in the substrate for sleep and vigilance. Curr. Mod. Biol., 4, 1—11.

Desiraju, T. (1971b) Effects of stimulations and lesions of monoamine neuronal systems on sleep and wakefulness in monkey. In Proc. Int. Union Physiol. Sci., XXVth Congress, Munich, Vol. IX. p. 139.

Desiraju, T. (1972a) Cortical neuron discharge patterns and their relationships to sleep function and electroencephalogram. Annals Indian Acad. med. Sci., VIII, 219—228.

Desiraju, T. (1972b) Transformations of discharges of neurons of parietal association cortex during sleep and wakefulness in monkey. J. Neurophysiol., 35, 326—332.

Desiraju, T. (1972c) Discharge properties of neurons of the parietal association cortex during states of sleep and wakefulness in the monkey. Brain Res., 47, 69—75.

Desiraju, T. (1973a) Effect of intraventricularly administered prostaglandin E_1 on the electrical activity of cerebral cortex and behavior in the unanesthetized monkey. Prostaglandins, 3, 859—870.

Desiraju, T. (1973b). Electrophysiology of the frontal granular cortex. I. Patterns of focal field potentials evoked by stimulations of dorsomedial thalamus in conscious monkey. Brain Res., 58, 401—414.

Desiraju, T. (1973c) Electrophysiology of the frontal granular cortex. II. Patterns of spontaneous discharges of impulses of neurons in the cortex through states of sleep and wakefulness in the monkey. Brain Res., 63, 19—29.

Desiraju, T. (1973d) Mechanisms for control of neural activity of the cerebral association cortex. I. The occurrence of augmenting potentials in the frontal granular cortex during stimulations of the nucleus medialis dorsalis. Neurology (Bombay), XXI, 145—151.

Desiraju, T. (1973e) Mechanisms for control of neural activity of the cerebral association cortex. II. The occurrence of recruiting type of potentials in the frontal granular cortex during stimulations of medial thalamus. Neurology (Bombay), XXI, 152—158.

Desiraju, T. (1974) Cortical unit activity in sleep. In Proc. Int. Union Physiol. Sci., XXVIth Congress. New Delhi, X. pp. 190—191.

Desiraju, T. (1975) Neural ·mechanisms of afferent projections in the organization of dorsolateral prefrontal cortex. In S. Kondo, M. Kawai, A. Ehara and S. Kawamura (Eds.), Proc. Symp. Fifth Congr. Int. Primatol. Soc., 1974. Japan Science Press, Tokyo, pp. 423—443.

Desiraju, T. and Purpura, D.P. (1969) Synaptic convergence of cerebellar and lenticular projections to thalamus. Brain Res., 15, 544—547.

Desiraju, T. and Purpura, D.P. (1970a) Antidromic responses and 'recurrent' IPSPs of thalamic VL neurons. Fed. Proc., 29, 323.

Desiraju, T. and Purpura, D.P. (1970b) Organization of specific-nonspecific thalamic internuclear synaptic pathways. Brain Res., 21, 169—181.

Desiraju, T., Broggi, G., Prelevic, S., Santini, M. and Purpura, D.P. (1969) Inhibitory synaptic pathways linking specific and nonspecific thalamic nuclei. Brain Res., 15, 542—543.

Evarts, E.V. (1967) Unit activity in sleep and wakefulness. In G.S. Quarton, T. Melnechuk and F.O. Schmitt (Eds.), The Neurosciences. Rockefeller Univ. Press. New York, pp. 545—556.

Fatt, P. and Katz, B. (1952) Spontaneous subthreshold activity at motor nerve endings. J. Physiol. (Lond.), 117, 109—128.

Hess, W.R. (1957) The Functional Organization of the Diencephalon, 1949. Translation, J.R. Hughes (Ed.), Grune and Stratton, New York.

Hobson, J.A. and McCarley, R.W. (1971) Cortical unit activity in sleep and waking. Electroenceph. clin. Neurophysiol., 30, 97—112.

Jasper, H.H. (1954) Functional properties of the thalamic reticular system. In E.D. Adrian, F. Bremer and H.H. Jasper (Eds.), Brain Mechanisms and Consciousness. Oxford Univ. Press, New York, pp. 374—401.

Jouvet, M. (1974) The interaction between monoaminergic neurons in the control of the sleep-waking cycle. In Proc. Int. Union Physiol. Sci., XXVIth Congress. New Delhi, X. pp. 192—193.

Kasamatsu, T. and Adey, W.R. (1973) Visual cortical units associated with phasic activity in REM sleep and wakefulness. Brain Res., 55, 323—331.

Noda, H. and Adey, W.R. (1970) Changes in neuronal activity in association cortex of the cat in relation to sleep and wakefulness. Brain Res., 19, 263—275.

Noda, H., Manohar, S. and Adey, W.R. (1969) Spontaneous activity of cat hippocampal neurons in sleep and wakefulness. Exp. Neurol., 24, 217—231.

Penfield, W. (1969) Consciousness, memory, and man's conditioned reflexes. In K.H. Pribram (Ed.), On the Biology of Learning. Harcourt, Brace and World, New York, pp. 127—168.

Purpura, D.P., Shofer, R.J. and Musgrave, F.S. (1964) Cortical intracellular potentials during augmenting and recruiting responses. II. Patterns of synaptic activities in pyramidal and nonpyramidal tract neurons. J. Neurophysiol., 27, 133—151.

Steriade, M. (1974) Thalamo-cortical relations during slow sleep. In Proc. Int. Union Physiol. Sci., XXVIth Congress, New Delhi, X. pp. 194—195.

Villablanca, J. and Salinas-Zeballos, M.E. (1972) Sleep-wakefulness, EEG and behavioral studies of chronic cats without thalamus: the 'athalamic' rat. Arch. ital. Biol., 110, 383—411.

DISCUSSION

CHASE: When you say wakefulness, was the animal moving or was it quiet wakefulness?

DESIRAJU: The wakefulness wherever I have mentioned it is quiet wakefulness. I am not now discussing the moving state of wakefulness.

CHASE: In one of the patterns shown by you, the neurons show an increase of discharge in the drowsy state, and subsequently show a decrease. The cortex appears to be having there a mu rhythm, the sensory motor rhythm or a mm rhythm, the inhibitory rhythm which is correlated to the lack of movement. I am just wondering whether there is any relationship between the lack of movement and the inhibitory cortical rhythm, the sensory motor cortical rhythm or mu rhythm as Gastaut has described, and the lack of it and the increase of cortical activity, so that when the rhythm is present there is inhibition. I am thinking that perhaps when the mu rhythm is not present, it maybe starts the increased firing from wakefulness during progression into sleep.

DESIRAJU: I do not know. The mu rhythm is not clear in this cortex during either quiet wakeful state or deep delta sleep, when unit firing is low.

STERIADE: The mu rhythm was observed in cat and does not correspond to the area Dr. Desiraju is working on. He is working on the prefrontal cortex.

CHASE: The presence of the rhythm reflects the activity of the thalamocortical system. I am just wondering whether these units might be correlated whether the rhythm is in that area or not, and whether the presence, or not, of that rhythm in two states during wakefulness can be explained as the mu rhythm state when the animal is awake, but inhibiting the units, and the wakefulness state, when there is no inhibition.

DESIRAJU: Well, I have no comment.

STERIADE: The mu rhythm starts from the thalamus at VL and VPL and extends to the central motor cortex.

DESIRAJU: This thalamus and this cortex are entirely different from the sensorimotor cortex. That is why I took much time to first describe the thalamocortical relationship of the prefrontal cortex. I do not know yet whether we can extrapolate on this the mu rhythm mechanism of the sensorimotor cortex.

CHASE: What I am saying is that the waking state is not a simple state.

DESIRAJU: It is not a simple state.

ALBE-FESSARD: Are some of these cells driven by movement of the eyes?

DESIRAJU: No. The area of the cortex under recording was deliberately kept a little forward from the arcuate sulcus. In all of these units, blinks or eye movements seldom drive impulse discharges. Eye movements either of the wakeful state or of the paradoxical sleep state are not found to have a close correlation with alterations of impulse discharges. This area is about 5 mm in front of the eye zone of the frontal cortex.

OOMURA: You said you did not find any units which decreased discharge frequency during paradoxical sleep.

DESIRAJU: No, I said I did find a decrease of discharge for one group of units. In fact, that was the surprise finding I had, two years ago not now.

OOMURA: At that time, I also observed, in the hypothalamus (ventromedial nucleus) of cat during sleep, that the frequency of firing increased but later the frequency of firing decreased.

PURPURA: That is in two areas.

DESIRAJU: Is that related primarily to the hunger and satiety states?

OOMURA: I observed this in sleep during hunger and also satiety.

13

PHYSIOLOGICAL STUDIES OF ATTENTION AND AROUSAL

GABRIEL HORN

Department of Anatomy, University of Bristol, The Medical School, Bristol BS8 1TD
(Great Britain)

An animal's capacity to respond to an event in the external environment and the type of response the animal gives vary over a wide range. The response a sleeping animal emits to an intense stimulus is generally to wake up, although the threshold for wakening varies with the state of sleep. I do not wish to argue that the transition from sleep to wakefulness is either physiologically or behaviourally simple: only that the overt responses emitted by the sleeping animal are relatively restricted. In contrast, the waking, alert animal may respond in a variety of specific, often complex ways to external events and may learn their characteristics. When those external events contain many sets of sensory stimuli to which the animal *could* respond, it selects and responds to only a limited number of them. From this highly responsive, critically reacting, attentive state of behaviour during which information can be stored — that state which, in humans, is referred to as 'conscious' — to that of deep sleep, which represents a kind of physiological unconsciousness, there exists a whole spectrum of behavioural states. An animal does not translate, as it were, from one extreme of this spectrum to the other instantaneously, the animal that wakes from sleep is not immediately analysing the shape of objects in the fields of vision, selectively taking in and storing information, critically analysing and responding to sensory stimuli, behaving, that is, as in the attentive state described above. In humans the time taken to achieve this state after sleep may take seconds, minutes or hours depending on circumstances and the individual and there is no good evidence of which I am aware to suggest that a comparable transition period does not exist for other mammals. A similar argument is probably valid for the transition from relaxed wakefulness to that of the fully attentive state (Horn, 1965a and b). If this is correct, then the fully developed state of attentive behaviour is different from the two transitional states although the word 'aroused' is commonly used to describe them all; the animal that is attentive and responding selectively is aroused, so is the animal which gives an orienting response when, in a state of relaxed wakefulness, it is presented with a novel stimulus, and so is the animal that has just been awakened from sleep. The point is that the attentive state is a highly specific one. In contrast, the aroused state is not specific: through common usage, the term has come to be applied to a number of behavioural states (see, for example, Andrew, 1974).

When human subjects attend to visual stimuli the alpha rhythm, if present, is frequently blocked (Berger, 1969a; Adrian and Matthews, 1934). This observation might suggest that during attention to vision, signals have access to the visual cortex in a way they do not have when the subject attends to, say, a sound. Such an hypothesis has been put forward, in one form or another, several times in the present century (Tello, 1904; Foerster, 1929a; Adrian, 1944 and 1954; Hernández-Peón et al., 1956; Berger, 1969b) and appeared to receive dramatic support from the observations of Hernández-Peón and his colleagues (Hernández-Peón, 1956 and 1957). In one of a series of experiments these workers used a flash of light as a 'probe' stimulus to test the sensitivity of the visual cortex: the flash-evoked potential recorded in the relaxed cat was compared with that recorded when the cat was aroused by an acoustic stimulus (Hernández-Peón et al., 1957). The amplitudes of the late components of the cortical response to the flash were reduced when the sounds were presented.

To what extent do the above observations on the human electroencephalogram (EEG) and those on the cat give unequivocal support to the hypothesis that the transmission of signals to the visual cortex is blocked during attention to an acoustic stimulus? Since the early studies of Berger (1969a) and Adrian and Matthews (1934) it has become clear that alphablocking can be induced in a variety of ways and one would be hard-pressed to argue that visual attention is common to them all (see, for example, Evans and Mulholland, 1969). So, whilst the hypothesis may be correct, the evidence of these studies is ambiguous. There is also ambiguity in interpreting the work on the cat. When an animal is aroused by a novel stimulus the EEG becomes desynchronised over widespread areas of the cerebral cortex (Rheinberger and Jasper, 1937; Moruzzi and Magoun, 1949). When this happens the evoked response to a sensory probe stimulus is commonly reduced. If a sound is used to arouse the animal (Bremer, 1954), the evoked response recorded at the auditory cortex, to an acoustic probe stimulus (click), is reduced (Fig. 1). Similarly (Horn, 1960), if the stimulus used to arouse the cat is visual, flash-evoked potentials recorded at the visual cortex are reduced (Fig. 2A): the response to this stimulus is also reduced if the cat is aroused by an acoustic stimulus (Fig. 2B). The reduction in amplitude of the flash-evoked potentials which occurs when the cat is alerted by an acoustic stimulus is consistent with the transmission blockade hypothesis: the reduction in amplitude of the potentials evoked by the probe stimulus which occurs when this is in the same modality as the alerting stimulus is not consistent with this hypothesis in a correspondingly simple way. As with the

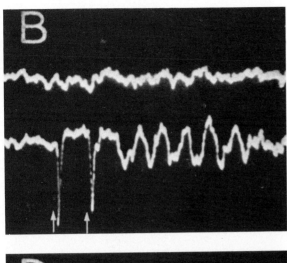

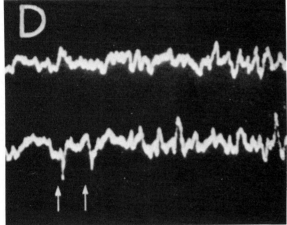

Fig. 1. Reduction of the evoked response to a click recorded at the auditory cortex of the cat during arousal from sleep (encéphale isolé preparation). The upper trace of each figure was recorded from the middle suprasylvian gyrus and the lower trace from the middle ectosylvian gyrus. In B the animal was drowsy. In D the cat had just been awakened by a voice call. The arrows indicate presentation of the clicks which were separated by an interval of 50 msec. The length of the arrows in D correspond to 200 μV on all traces. (After Bremer, 1954.)

human EEG studies, one would be hard-pressed to argue that these changes in amplitude of the evoked potentials are exclusively related to attention (Horn, 1965a and 1975a; Näätänen,1967).

When auditory or visual stimuli are used to assess the sensitivity of the respective pathways in freely moving animals, a number of technical difficulties may be encountered which complicate the interpretation of results. In particular, the position of the head, and hence of the sense organs, may not

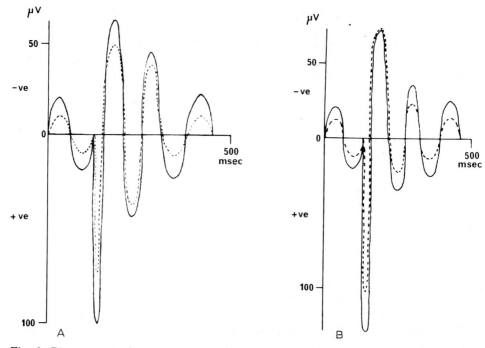

Fig. 2. Diagrammatic representation of mean evoked response to flash recorded at the visual cortex of 5 unanaesthetised cats. The first and last waves represent the mean duration and amplitude of waves in the 500 msec preceding the primary wave and following the secondary wave of the response, respectively. The continuous lines represent the control responses recorded when the cats were relaxed, the broken lines represent the responses recorded during arousal. Differences in amplitude are only shown if significant ($P < 0.02$). A: cat watches mouse. B: cat aroused by acoustic stimulus. (After Horn, 1960.)

be fixed in respect of the stimulus source, and various peripheral control mechanisms may operate (for example, changes in the diameter of the pupil, contraction of the middle ear muscles) to modify the amount of energy ultimately impinging on the sense receptors. In such experiments these relatively trivial factors may adequately account for an observed change in the size of an evoked potential. In the absence of any control for these factors, such experiments are unlikely to give satisfactory evidence that transmission in sensory pathways is subject to central control, a notion that is implicit in the hypothesis that we have been considering. Some evidence for the central control of afferent transmission is, however, available. For example, Malcolm et al. (1970) monitored transmission through the lateral geniculate nucleus (LGN) of cats by measuring the response of the nucleus to shocks delivered to the optic tract. The shocks were delivered when the cat was relaxed and when it was alert. They found that the responsiveness of neurones in the LGN increased during arousal. Horn and Wiesenfeld (1974) obtained similar results. Thus transmission in the visual pathway does appear to be subject to central control and this control process is thrown into operation during arousal. However, if we are to determine whether or not transmission to the visual cortex varies with the state of attention, it is essential to study sensory transmission in behavioural situations that would generally be agreed to satisfy the criteria of attention in order to distinguish any effect which might be specific to this form of behaviour from any that might be attributable to other types of behaviour (for example, the orientation reaction, or transitional states of arousal). Such dissociation is difficult to achieve in experiments which involve an animal switching its attention from one stimulus to another. Fortunately, however, there are now agreed to be several aspects of attentiveness. One of these, vigilance, has been studied extensively in human subjects within the general theoretical framework of attention (Mackworth, 1956; Broadbent, 1958; Moray, 1970; Poulton, 1970).

In a vigilance task the subject is required to attend in order to detect a signal whenever it occurs. In a recent series of experiments (Horn and Wiesenfeld, 1974; Wiesenfeld and Horn, 1974), six cats were trained to perform such a task. Each cat was trained to press a pedal on the floor of the training box (Fig. 3). There then followed an interval of time after which a stimulus was presented. If the cat pressed a panel when the stimulus was present, the cat was rewarded with food. In one series of experiments the waiting interval, which followed the pedal press, was of fixed duration; in the other series the waiting interval was of variable duration. The duration of the fixed interval was constant for a given animal, but varied from cat to cat within the range of 2.5 to 3.0 sec. In the variable interval schedule the durations of the waiting interval ranged from 1 to 3.5 sec (five cats) and 0.8 to 2.8 sec (one cat). The intervals were presented in a quasirandom fashion to make it difficult for the cat to predict when the stimulus would appear, and so to ensure that the cat was alert if it were to achieve a high rate of success in detecting the stimulus. If the cat pressed the panel before the stimulus appeared, it received no food reward for that trial. The cat then had to press the pedal to initiate the next trial in order to obtain the reward. The timing of the stimulus was arranged in such a way there was a 1 in 6 chance of it occurring after the shortest waiting interval (usually 1 sec). If the stimulus had not occurred then there was a 1 in 5 chance of it occurring after the next waiting interval (usually 1.5 sec). If the stimulus had not occurred then, there was a 1 in 4 chance of it occurring after the next waiting interval (usually 2.0 sec) and so on, such that if the stimulus had not occurred at 3.0 sec there was a probability of 1 that it would occur 3.5 sec after the pedal had been pressed. Thus the probability of occurrence of the stimulus increased with the lapse of time following pedal press. Two stimuli were used: a small spot of light or a tone. These were thus four experiments using the

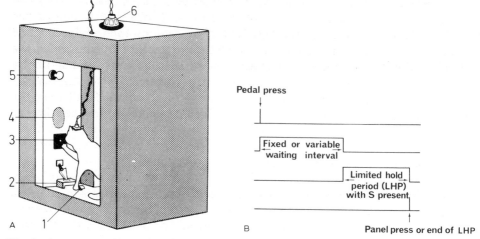

Fig. 3. Apparatus and behavioural sequence. A: apparatus with door removed. 1, pedal which was pressed by the cat to initiate a trial; 2, food dish; 3, hinged panel. If this was pressed in the presence of the stimulus (S) a reward (1 to 2 ml of a suspension of tinned cat food in milk or water) followed immediately. Illustrated on the panel is the small spot of light that was S in the fixed and variable interval visual schedules; 4, speaker used in the fixed and variable interval auditory schedules when S was a 4 kHz tone; 5, box light that was only on during the initial behavioural training; 6, speaker used to deliver 70 dB (re 2×10^{-4} dyne cm^{-2}) masking white noise continuously. All sides of the box, except the door and the front panel were covered with 2 cm thick expanded polystyrene to further attenuate extraneous sounds. The pedal (1) was close enough to the front of the box for the cat to press it without moving backwards. All cats were trained to press the pedal with the left paw and the panel with the right; so that they were able to stand in one place during the whole trial. B: sequence of events in each trial. Read from above downwards, left to right. S stayed on until either the panel was pressed, after which food was delivered, or the end of the limited hold period (LHP). This period was 3 sec for four cats and 5 sec for two. These values were determined by assessing the behaviour of each cat during initial training; shorter periods increased the number of errors and disrupted performance. (After Horn and Wiesenfeld, 1974.)

two different types of interval and the two different stimuli: fixed interval auditory and fixed interval visual, variable interval auditory and variable interval visual. The cats were all initially trained on a fixed interval schedule, the tone being used as stimulus for three of them and the light spot for the remainder. When this experiment was completed, the cats were trained on the variable interval schedule using the same stimulus. The cats were then trained on the variable interval schedule in which the stimulus of the other modality was substituted. Finally, the cats worked on the remaining fixed interval schedule, though data from one cat on this schedule was not available. After a cat had reached criterion (80% correct responses) the light in the training box was extinguished and all data collected with the animal working in darkness.

The latency of response following the onset of the stimulus was measured for each waiting interval in the variable interval schedules. For all cats on the variable interval visual schedule, and for five of them on the variable interval auditory schedule, it was found that the latency to respond decreased as the length of the waiting interval increased. That is, the cats responded more quickly to the stimulus as the probability of occurrence of the stimulus increased. There was no evidence that one task was more difficult than the other. For one thing no more errors (pressing the panel before the stimulus was present) were made when the stimulus was a light spot than when it was a tone. For another, there were no significant differences between the latencies to respond to the stimuli in the two schedules.

In general these results are similar to those obtained from human subjects required to respond to a stimulus the probability of occurrence of which is varied. In such experiments it is found that, within limits, the time taken to respond to the stimulus decreases as the probability of the stimulus occurring increases (Klemmer, 1956; Näätänen, 1970; Stilitz, 1972). Such results have been interpreted in terms of expectancy. This is measured as the probability that a stimulus will occur at a given point in time provided that the stimulus has not already occurred (Audley, 1963; Thomas, 1970; Stilitz, 1972): expectancy increases as stimulus probability increases with a corresponding reduction in reaction time. Deese (1955) suggested that an observer's level of expectancy determines his vigilance level. Deese used the term 'vigilance' to mean a high state of readiness to respond to an event (Head, 1926). If Deese's suggestion is correct, the vigilance of the cats should have increased with the length of the waiting interval. The observed results are consistent with this prediction.

The level of vigilance must necessarily be inferred from the observed behaviour: so there can be no certainty that the level of vigilance, or attentiveness, varied with the duration of the waiting interval. It is not, however, implausible that such was the case. Were there any changes in the capacity of the visual pathways to transmit signals as the length of this interval increased?

During the waiting interval the optic tract was shocked once and the response of the LGN and visual cortex recorded through implanted electrodes. The time at which a shock was delivered varied from one trial to the next. The responsiveness of the LGN and visual cortex did not vary during the waiting interval in either of the fixed interval schedules or in the variable interval schedule in which the stimulus was a spot of light. However, in the variable interval schedule in which the stimulus was a tone, the responsiveness of the visual cortex to the thalamocortical input declined as the length of the waiting interval increased (Fig. 4). No changes were observed at the LGN or in the presynaptic component of the cortical response.

A shock to the optic tract is a relatively crude stimulus with which to monitor the sensitivity of the visual pathways, but it has certain merits. In the first place, the same stimulus can be delivered irrespective of the

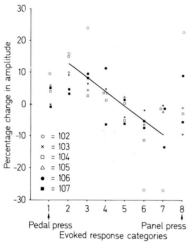

Fig. 4. Mean percentage change in the amplitude of a postsynaptic (C_5) component of the cortical response to a shock applied to the optic tract. The responses were recorded from cats during performance of the variable interval schedule when a 4 kHz tone was the stimulus. The symbols on the left hand side of the graph refer to the corresponding cats, numbered 102 to 107. Twenty five responses were recorded at the time of the pedal press, and at various times in between (Evoked response categories). The mean amplitude of C_5 for each of the eight categories of evoked response was calculated for each cat and standardised against the overall mean of the eight categories from that cat. This was done for each of the six cats. The percentage deviation of each of these mean values from the grand mean for all cats was computed. These deviations are plotted against evoked response category. The correlation coefficient for the regression fitted to data from categories 2—7 was $r = -0.66$ ($P < 0.001$). The slope was $B = -4.46 \pm 0.88$ (S.D.) which was significantly ($P < 0.001$) different from zero. (After Horn and Wiesenfeld, 1974.)

position of the cat's head or eyes. Secondly, the response of the LGN and visual cortex to the optic tract shock can be recorded simultaneously. Thirdly, the physiological bases of the field potentials evoked by the shock and recorded at these two sites are well understood. The response of the LGN contains two waves, respectively the t and r waves. The t wave measured in the present study is generated by activity in the terminals of fast conducting optic tract fibres and the r wave by activity in fast conducting postsynaptic neurones in the LGN (G.H. Bishop and O'Leary, 1940; P.O. Bishop and McCleod, 1954; P.O. Bishop and Evans, 1956; Fukada, 1973). The first component (C_1) of the cortical response to the shock is due to activity of fibres in the optic radiation, and the fifth (C_5) is due to activity in postsynaptic neurones in the visual cortex (Marshall et al., 1943; Chang and Kaada, 1950; G.H. Bishop and Clare, 1952; Malis and Kruger, 1956; Bremer and Stoupel, 1956; Schoolman and Evarts, 1959). The two responses are illustrated in Fig. 5. If there is a change in amplitude of a component of these responses during the performance of a behavioural task, it is possible to

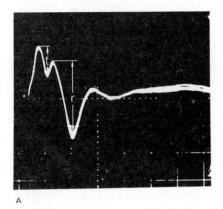 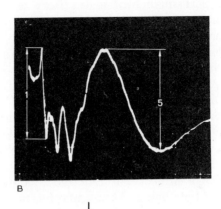

Fig. 5. Responses to shocks applied to the optic tract. A: LGN responses to five single shocks to optic tract, superimposed. The presynaptic wave is labelled t and the post-synaptic wave, r. Scale, 1 mV and 0.5 msec. B: maximal cortical response to a single optic tract shock. Components 1 and 5 are labelled. Scale, 200 μV and 2 msec. In both figures positivity at the recording electrode is represented as an upward deflection of the trace. (After Horn and Wiesenfeld, 1974.)

infer the anatomical locus of the change. The results of the electrophysiological studies provide evidence of a change in the responsiveness of the visual cortex, but not of the LGN, during attention to an auditory stimulus. No changes at any anatomical level were observed during the performance of the variable interval task in which the animal was waiting to respond to a spot of light.

How are the electrophysiological changes related to vigilance? In the fixed interval schedules the cats, after training, need not have attended to the stimulus to obtain a reward, but simply pressed the panel a set time after having pressed the pedal. There may not have been any changes in the level of vigilance during the performance of these tasks; so, it is interesting to find that there were no changes in transmission through the LGN or visual cortex. In the variable interval schedules the cat did not know exactly when the stimulus would appear. However, the longer the interval that elapsed after the cat had pressed the pedal, the higher was the probability that the stimulus would occur. The implication of the studies is, therefore, that as the level of vigilance for the occurrence of the auditory stimulus increased, the responsiveness of the visual cortex declined. The physiological significance of these studies has been discussed in detail elsewhere (Horn and Wiesenfeld, 1974; Horn, 1975b). The point I wish to emphasise is that a differential change in the responsiveness of the visual cortex to an afferent input occurred during the performance of an auditory task, but not during the performance of a visual task. The two tasks appear to have been balanced for difficulty so there are no grounds for supposing that the animals were aroused to different extents. The selective change in transmission appears to be related to the animals' level of vigilance and, by inference, level of attention.

A prediction from these results is that when a subject is required to detect or discriminate an auditory stimulus in a task requiring a high level of attentiveness, the performance of a visual detection task, particularly one involving moving stimuli (Horn and Wiesenfeld, 1974), should deteriorate. I am not aware of such an experiment having been conducted on animals or on human subjects but Suboski (1966) performed a similar experiment in which a subject was required to detect a stationary stimulus. The subject faced four lights. At irregular intervals three of them lit up. The fourth came on 67 msec after the first three. The light that was delayed changed randomly from trial to trial and the subject had to detect which had been delayed on each trial. The subject had also to detect a 560 Hz tone lasting 67 msec. The tone was superimposed on white noise. The two tasks were either undertaken as completely separate tasks or were run concurrently. When they were run concurrently the tone, when it occurred, sounded during the 67 msec when only the three lights were on. In this condition the tone was presented during half of the 67 msec intervals selected at random. The subjects had to detect the presence and absence of the tone and to detect which light was missing at the same time. Both tasks were sufficiently difficult for the subject to make errors even when the tasks were presented separately. There was, however, a marked increase in the number of errors on the visual tasks when the tasks were run concurrently.

A possible explanation for this effect is that when the subject was required to detect the presence of absence of the tone, the visual threshold increased, so reducing the probability of detecting the occurrence or position of the fourth light. The putative change in threshold could be brought about in at least two ways depending on whether the tone was or was not present in the 67 msec interval when only three lights were on. If the tone was present, the threshold change may have been brought about through sensory interaction. Horn and Venables (1964) measured the threshold of fusion of paired light flashes by determining the longest interval between two flashes of light reported as one and not as two. A weak electric shock was delivered to the skin, or a click was delivered through headphones 200 msec before the first of the two light flashes. The threshold of fusion was increased compared to the threshold measured when the flashes were unaccompanied by the additional stimulus. It was suggested that the change in threshold might be accounted for by an influence on neurones in the visual pathways of impulse activity evoked by the heteromodal stimulus (see, for example, Lömo and Mollica, 1962; Jung et al., 1963; Horn, 1963 and 1965b), a kind of masking affect. In the experiments where the tone was absent (Suboski,

1966), an explanation in terms of sensory interaction cannot be invoked to account for a change in the visual detection threshold. A more plausible explanation is to be found in the results described in the present study — a reduction in the responsiveness of the visual cortex during high levels of vigilance for an auditory stimulus — when the optic tract was shocked before the tone was sounded.

If the evocation of a perceptual or overt behavioural response depends on exciting certain groups of neurones, it may be that, for the response to be maintained, the input to such cells must also be maintained, and closing the pathways to such cells may be a necessary condition for the perceptual rejection of a stimulus (Horn, 1965a). The putative assembly of cells must receive input from the sensory pathways. It is possible that reduction of the sensitivity of the visual cortex to activity evoked by a visual stimulus may reduce the likelihood of that activity gaining access to the postulated system of neurones. If this system is 'engaged' by a non-visual input, or by the expectation of one, then attenuation of the output from the visual cortex might reduce the likelihood of the animal being distracted by a visual stimulus. Such a notion is in advance of our present physiological knowledge. Nevertheless, the problems posed by the phenomenon of attentive behaviour exist and a solution to them, expressed in terms of the activity of neurones, and of the interactions between groups of neurones in the behaving animal, will continue to be sought. Neurones with some of the properties expected of cells in the postulated assembly (Horn, 1965a) exist in the superior colliculus (Horn and Hill, 1964 and 1966; Harutiunian-Kozak et al., 1971; Cynader and Berman, 1972; Oyster and Takahashi, 1975) and the suggestion (Horn, 1965a) that they play an important role in attentive processes has received support from recent work (Goldberg and Wurtz, 1972; Rizzolatti et al., 1974; Updyke, 1974; Goodale and Murison, 1975).

In an experimental situation, attention is commonly studied by using two or more stimuli competing for a response, or the subject performs a vigilance task and waits for the occurrence of a stimulus. A feature which is common to these experiments is that, not unexpectedly, external stimuli are used. However, the subject may perform tasks of mental arithmetic or experience visual images, and such mental activities, difficult though they may to be study, are presumably important sources of competition for the neural apparatus underlying attentive behaviour. Certainly a subject engaged on such mental activity may be inattentive to many external stimuli. The neural mechanisms of visual imagery and visual hallucinations have not yet systematically been investigated (see, for example, Jung, 1973), nor is it easy to see how this may be accomplished, although studies using hallucinogenic drugs (see, for example, Horn and McKay, 1973), of dreaming associated with rapid eye movement sleep (Dement and Kleitman, 1957) and studies in which visual images are elicited by electrically stimulating the cerebral cortex of the exposed human brain during neurosurgical operations (Foerster,

1929b; Penfield and Rasmussen, 1952; Brindley and Lewin, 1968) are yielding promising results. A problem that is relevant in the present context is how the subject distinguishes an event occurring in the field of vision from visual imagery, when a perceptual event is not accompanied by a corresponding event in the field of vision. Now, the superior colliculus receives input directly from the optic tract and also from the visual cortex. Is it possible that an event is classified as occurring in the external world if there is an input to cells in the superior colliculus from both the optic tract and the cortex, and classified as visual imagery if the cells receive input from the cortex but not from the optic tract? Once again, such an hypothesis goes beyond the neurophysiological data. But the problem is one which must surely be analysed if the functions of the central nervous system in the behaving subject are comprehensively to be understood.

SUMMARY

The difficulties encountered in studying the neurophysiological events associated with attentive behaviour are discussed in the context of experiments that enquire whether or not transmission in the visual pathways changes when an animal attends to an auditory stimulus. Evidence is presented which suggests that the responsiveness of the visual cortex declines during high levels of vigilance to an acoustic stimulus. This finding is related to the results of certain psychophysical experiments on human subjects. Some of the many problems that remain to be solved are briefly discussed.

REFERENCES

Adrian, E.D. (1944) Brain rhythms. Nature (Lond.), 153, 360—362.
Adrian, E.D. (1954) The physiological basis of perception. In E.D. Adrian, F. Bremer and H.H. Jasper (Eds.), Brain Mechanisms and Consciousness, Blackwell, Oxford, pp. 237—248.
Adrian, E.D. and Matthews, B.H.C. (1934) The Berger rhythm: potential changes from the occipital lobes in man. Brain, 57, 355—385.
Andrew, R.J. (1974) Arousal and the causation of behaviour. Behaviour, 51, 135—165.
Audley, R.J. (1963) Decision models in reaction time. In Psychophysics and the Ideal Observer, Proc. 17th Int. Congr. Psychol., North-Holland Publishing Co., Amsterdam.
Berger, H. (1969a) Über das Elektrenkephalogramm des Menschen. Zweite Mitteilung. J. Psychol. Neurol. (Lpz.), 40, 160—179.
(English translation in Electroenceph. clin. Neurophysiol., Suppl. 28, 75—93.)
Berger, H. (1969b) Über das Elektrencephalogramm des Menschen. Dritte Mitteilung. Arch. Psychiat. Nervenkr., 94, 16—60.
(English translation in Electroenceph. clin. Neurophysiol., Suppl. 28, 95—132.)
Bishop, G.H. and Clare, M.H. (1952) Site of origin of electric potentials in striate cortex. J. Neurophysiol., 15, 201—220.

Bishop, G.H. and O'Leary, J.S. (1940) Electrical activity of the lateral geniculate of cats following optic nerve stimuli. J. Neurophysiol., 3, 308—322.

Bishop, P.O. and Evans, W.A. (1956) The refractory period of the sensory synapses of the lateral geniculate nucleus. J. Physiol. (Lond.), 134, 538—557.

Bishop, P.O. and McLeod, J.G. (1954) Nature of potentials associated with synaptic transmission in lateral geniculate nucleus of cat. J. Neurophysiol., 17, 387—414.

Bremer, F. (1954) The neurophysiological problem of sleep. In E.D. Adrian, F. Bremer and H.H. Jasper (Eds.), Brain Mechanisms and Consciousness, Blackwell, Oxford, pp. 137—162.

Bremer, F. et Stoupel, N. (1956) Interprétation de la réponse de l'aire visuelle à une volée d'influx sensoriels. Arch. int. Physiol., 64, 234—250.

Brindley, G.S. and Lewin, W.S. (1968) The sensations produced by electrical stimulation of the visual cortex. J. Physiol. (Lond.), 196, 479—493.

Broadbent, D.E. (1958) Perception and Communication. Pergamon Press, London.

Chang, H.T. and Kaada, B. (1950) An analysis of primary response of visual cortex to optic nerve stimulation in cats. J. Neurophysiol., 13, 305—318.

Cynader, M. and Berman, N. (1972) Receptive-field organization of monkey superior colliculus. J. Neurophysiol., 35, 187—201.

Deese, J. (1955) Some problems in the theory of vigilance. Psychol. Rev., 62, 359—368.

Dement, W. and Kleitman, N. (1957) The relation of eye movements during sleep to dream activity; an objective method for the study of dreaming. J. exp. Psychol., 53, 339.

Evans, C.R. and Mulholland, T.B. (1969) (Eds.) Attention in Neurophysiology, Butterworth, London, 447 pp.

Foerster, O. (1929a) quoted by Berger, H. (1931).

Foerster, O. (1929b) Beiträge zur Pathophysiologie der Seebahn under der Sehspäre. J. Psychol. Neurol. (Lpz.), 39, 463—485.

Fukada, Y. (1973) Differentiation of principal cells of the rat lateral geniculate body into two groups: fast and slow. Exp. Brain Res., 17, 242—260.

Goldberg, M.E. and Wurtz, R.H. (1972) Activity of superior colliculus in behaving monkey. II. Effect of attention on neural responses. J. Neurophysiol., 35, 560—574.

Goodale, M.A. and Murison, R.C.C. (1975) The effects of lesions of the superior colliculus on locomotor orientation and the orienting reflex in the rat. Brain Res., 88, 243—261.

Harutiunian-Kozak, B., Dec, K. and Dreher, B. (1971) Habituation of unitary responses in the superior colliculus of the cat. Acta neurobiol. exp., 31, 213—217.

Head, H. (1926) Aphasia. Cambridge University Press, London.

Hernández-Peón, R., Scherrer, H. and Jouvet, M. (1956) Modification of electrical activity in cochlea nucleus during 'attention' in unanaesthetised cats. Science, 123, 331—332.

Hernández-Peón, R., Guzman-Flores, C., Alcarez, M. and Fernandez-Guardiola, A. (1957) Sensory transmission in visual pathway during 'attention' in unanaesthetised cats. Acta neurol. lat.-amer., 3, 1—8.

Horn, G. (1960) Electrical activity of the cerebral cortex of the unanaesthetised cat during attentive behaviour. Brain, 83, 57—76.

Horn, G. (1963) The response of single units in the striate cortex of unrestrained cats to photic and somaesthetic stimuli. J. Physiol. (Lond.), 165, 80—81P.

Horn, G. (1965a) Physiological and psychological aspects of selective perception. In D. Lehrman, R.A. Hinde and E. Shaw (Eds.), Advances in the Study of Behaviour, Vol. 1. Academic Press, New York, pp. 155—215.

Horn, G. (1965b) The effect of somaesthetic and photic stimuli on the activity of units in the striate cortex of unanaesthetised unrestrained cats. J. Physiol. (Lond.), 179, 263—277.

298

Horn, G. (1975a) Attention and the orientation response. In M.R. Kietzman, S. Sutton and J. Zubin (Eds.), Experimental Approaches to Psychopathology. Academic Press, New York, pp. 187—195.

Horn, G. (1975b) Does transmission in the visual pathway vary when an animal attends to an auditory or a visual stimulus? In R. Galwin (Ed.), Sensory Physiology and Behaviour. Plenum Press, New York, pp. 25—40.

Horn, G. and Hill, R.M. (1964) Habituation of the response to sensory stimuli of neurones in the brain stem of rabbits. Nature (Lond.), 202, 296—298.

Horn, G. and Hill, R.M. (1966) Responsiveness to sensory stimulation of units in the superior collicus and subjacent tectotegmental regions of the rabbit. Exp. Neurol., 14, 199—223.

Horn, G. and McKay, J.M. (1973) Effects of lysergic acid diethylamide on the spontaneous activity and visual receptive fields of cells in the lateral geniculate nucleus of the cat. Exp. Brain Res., 17, 271—284.

Horn, G. and Venables, P. (1964) The effect of somatic and acoustic stimuli on the threshold of fusion of paired light flashes in human subjects. Quart. J. exp. Psychol., 16, 289—296.

Horn, G. and Wiesenfeld, Z. (1974) Attentive behaviour in the cat: electrophysiological and behavioural studies. Exp. Brain Res., 21, 67—82.

Jung, R. (1973) Visual perception and neurophysiology. In R. Jung (Ed.), Handbook of Sensory Physiology, Vol. VII/3A: Central Processing of Visual Information, Part A. Springer, Berlin, pp. 1—150.

Jung, R., Kornbuber, H.H. and da Fonseca, J.S. (1963) Multisensory convergence on cortical neurones. Neuronal effects of visual, acoustic and vestibular stimuli in the superior convolutions of the cat's cortex. In G. Morozzi, A. Fessard and H.H. Jasper (Eds.), Brain Mechanisms, Progr. Brain Res., Vol. 1. Elsevier, Amsterdam, pp. 207—234.

Klemmer, E.T. (1956) Time uncertainty in simple reaction time. J. exp. Psychol., 51, 179—184.

Lömo, T. and Mollica, A. (1962) Activity of single units in the primary optic cortex in the unanaesthetised rabbit during visual, acoustic, olfactory and painful stimuli. Arch. ital. Biol., 100, 86—120.

Mackworth, N.H. (1956) Researches on the Measurement of Human Performance. Med. Res. Council Special Report No. 268, H.M.S.O., London, 156 pp.

Malcolm, L.J., Bruce, I.S.C. and Burke, W. (1970) Excitability of the lateral geniculate nucleus in the alert, non-alert and sleeping cat. Exp. Brain Res., 10, 283—297.

Malis, L.I. and Kruger, L. (1956) Multiple response and excitability of cat's visual cortex. J. Neurophysiol., 19, 172—186.

Marshall, W.H., Talbot, S.A. and Ades, H.W. (1943) Cortical response of the anaesthetised cat to gross photic and electrical afferent stimulation. J. Neurophysiol., 6, 1—15.

Moray, N. (1970) Attention: Selective Processes in Vision and Hearing. Hutchinson, London.

Moruzzi, G. and Magoun, H.W. (1949) Brain stem reticular formation and activation of the EEG. Electroenceph. clin. Neurophysiol., 1, 455—473.

Näätänen, R. (1967) Selective attention and evoked potentions. Ann. Acad. Sci. fenn. A5, 151B, 1—226.

Näätänen, R. (1970) The diminishing time-uncertainty with the lapse of time after the warning signal in reaction-time experiments with varying fore-periods. Acta psychol. (Amst.), 34, 399—419.

Oyster, C.W. and Takahashi, E.S. (1975) Responses of rabbit superior colliculus neurones to repeated visual stimuli. J. Neurophysiol., 38, 301—312.

Penfield, W. and Rasmussen, T. (1952) The Cerebral Cortex of Man. Macmillan, New York.

Poulton, E.C. (1970) Environment and Human Efficiency. Thomas, Springfield, Ill., 328 pp.

Rheinberger, M. and Jasper, H.H. (1937) Electrical activity of the cerebral cortex in the unanaesthetised cat. Amer. J. Physiol., 119, 186—196.

Rizzolatti, G., Camarda, R., Grupp, L.A. and Pisa, M. (1974) Inhibitory effect of remote visual stimuli on visual responses of cat superior colliculus: spatial and temporal factors. J. Neurophysiol., 37, 1262—1275.

Schoolman, A. and Evarts, E.V. (1959) Response to lateral geniculate radiation stimulation in cats with implanted electrodes. J. Neurophysiol., 22, 112—129.

Stilitz, I. (1972) Conditional probability and components of RT in the variable foreperiod experiment. Quart. J. exp. Psychol., 24, 159—168.

Suboski, M.D. (1966) Bisensory signal detection. Psychon. Sci., 6, 57—58.

Tello, F. (1904) Disposición macroscópica y estructura del cuerpo geniculado externo. Trab. Lab. Invest. Biol. Univ. Madrid, 3, 39—62.

Thomas, E.A.C. (1970) On expectancy and average reaction time. Brit. J. Psychol., 61, 33—38.

Updyke, B.V. (1974) Characteristics of unit responses in superior collicus of the *Cebus* monkey. J. Neurophysiol., 37, 896—909.

Wiesenfeld, Z. and Horn, G. (1974) The effects of eye movement and dark-adaptation on transmission through the visual pathways of unrestrained cats. Brain Res., 77, 211—219.

DISCUSSION

STERIADE: I suppose your later findings are entirely due to the measurement of wave 5 only. I would ask you why only wave 5? Because we know that waves 3 and 4 also reflect postsynaptic changes. Wave 5, in fact, is on the envelope of descending 3, 4 and 5 waves. Why do you measure only 5 as reflecting postsynaptic activity? You know all the findings in the literature agree that the response would enhance during geniculocortical transmission.

HORN: You have raised two points. Let me answer first why we measured wave 5 envelope and wave 1. Because we are measuring by hand and we have no computer system, and because it is clear that wave 5 is universally postsynaptic and, whereas there is some doubt about other waves and we prefer something unequivocal, we chose that.

STERIADE: There are doubts about wave 2, but no doubts about waves 3 and 4.

HORN: No doubts about wave 5?

STERIADE: No doubts.

HORN: That is the reason, and no doubt on that score. Now the other question that you raise: are our results in agreement? The answer is that our results are not in disagreement with results in the literature, because what you say I agree with. If you stimulate the geniculate-calcarine radiation, then it is, by-and-large, agreed that you do get enhancement with desynchronization of the cortical response. But there is also the most peculiar of the results if you stimulate the optic radiation, you get a very different picture. And the pictures you can get from stimulating the optic radiation and the optic tract do appear to be rather consistently different. In the paper that has just appeared we discussed this. Our results do not disagree with the basic results obtained on stimulating the optic tract. The paradox is why should it be the geniculocalcarine radiation stimulation which gives the result in one way, whereas the optic tract stimulation gives the result in another way. And that is interesting. It is there, it has got to be studied.

STERIADE: The postsynaptic activity of the visual cortex is certainly enhanced. This comes from several observations. You mentioned that the flash-evoked response decays. It decays just when you observe the first reaction when you differentiate the first component and late components which are certainly describable as postsynaptic cortical events. You know that Evarts has mentioned that the chronically implanted cat gave responses to photic stimuli with an 18 msec latency and the cortical potentials are enhanced in arousal. I observed the same by stimulating the reticular formation, and the so-called postfinal waves are electrically decreased over the first negative waves, which means that, in fact, the subcortical events are enhanced. Evarts, in his 1963 paper, finds that the latency of single unit responses increases from 5 or 10 to 68 msec, which fits well with what I observed, with the so-called postfinal waves being in exactly the same latency range by stimulating the reticular formation.

HORN: You know there is some difficulty. It is very difficult to relate what goes on at the single unit level and what goes on at the evoked responses level. This is certainly my experience with evoked responses to flashes and if the EEG is desynchronized by-and-large, the evoked responses the early components, which are called the late waves we are talking about (an evoked response to a flash of light may have a latency of about 24 msec) and even the late components, in fact particularly the later components, of responses are virtually eliminated when the animal is in the desynchronized state.

STERIADE: That means you are considering the slow components. When you considered the fast components, about 50% of them are after the fast afterdischarge and not the slow afterdischarge, and the fast afterdischarges are electrically enhanced. I worked with evoked responses, and Evarts has worked with unit responses.

KUBOTA: There is a paper by Suzuki and others published in Physiology and Behaviour. He observed depression of wave 4 evoked by flash stimulation in the lateral geniculate when the lever is pressed. So, I wonder if the depression of the wave you have observed may be related to the lever pressing.

HORN: I think that is impossible because the experiment is rather well balanced in the sense that it is a variable proviso during the same behavioral operations. The only difference is that the animal is waiting to have the auditory stimulus in one case and the visual stimulus in the other case, and it is only when the stimulus is an auditory one that you can get any change in the evoked response. Now, notice also that the shocks to optic tracts are given when there is no stimulus: no auditory stimulus present, and no visual stimulus. The animal has been waiting for it. It is only in one case that you get this reduction. It seems to me that if these reductions were related in any way to motor activity, it ought to go in the same way in both the cases, and it does not.

KUBOTA: I should like to point out a similar thing with prefrontal units investigated by Sakai in my laboratory. He first gives a light stimulus and then lever pressing. Many units show activity before the light onset and the unit frequency goes up until the light onset, and that lever pressing is coupled to light onset. You see this activity related to expectation may be so important.

HORN: Yes, it is a problem. I mentioned that we used a variable interval situation. The animal did not know when the stimulus was going to come. But when the animal did know, we did a series of experiments where the interval between the pedal and the panel pressing was fixed and here, if anywhere, the animal did know when the stimulus was going to come on, and in fact under these conditions during the waiting interval when the animal knew, there was no change in transmission at all. It was only when the interval was variable and when the stimulus was going to come, but I think even there the animal does not know when. We can not interpret these results.

ASRATYAN: I have some questions concerning the behavioral aspects of this paper. First of all, tell me whether the animal was satiated before the experiment; how much did you give to your cats to eat? Satiation of the animal changes the animals' lever pressing. Have you noticed such changes? Did you study the effect of satiation of the animal before experimentation?

HORN: Yes, the animal won't work unless it is hungry.

ASRATYAN: But don't you try to satiate before experiments?

HORN: We do.

ASRATYAN: Yes, of course, he is getting some more meat after pressing. And in your control, satiated animal experiment how much food did you give him first and how did he subsequently work?

HORN: Very interesting. He won't give any attention to the lever.

ASRATYAN: Why is this interesting? Because one could not only relate these changes to the light, to the lever pressing, but also by activation of an alimentary center or other sources. It is very important to answer.

HORN: I don't think so for explaining the results, because once again the real need for food is the same to the variable interval in the visual or the auditory stimulus experiments. So the degree of hunger, presumably, and the degree of the motor activity was mostly identical in the experiments under comparison.

ASRATYAN: Second question. You have some changes in the expectation as the electrical response increased or decreased. You measured the latency and so on, but what concerns the threshold of intensity of stimulation? Have you some changes in threshold as a measure of the level of excitability of the structures?

HORN: Well, we did measure the current which was drawn by the electrodes and there was no change in the current drawn by the stimulating electrodes. But of course, if there are changes in the lateral geniculate or visual cortex in the sense that it changes threshold, the response under one condition is large and then you give the same stimulus, same shock, and the responses are suppressed to the threshold.

ASRATYAN: Then I want to say that you have a point of view which is advocated by some of us. We are able to see that all changes in the cortical point of signal stimuli are also determined by inborn, vitally active signals, in our case by alimentary centers. For example, we have conditioned reflexes to a light and to a flash far from the food box, at quite different places. When we are giving the light signals it elicits orienting reflex. The dog turns his head to the place of the light. And then we give food pieces. This is an unconditioned reflex. The animal is eating and when finished, we take away the food box. You can see that the animal wants more food pieces and turns his head towards that lamp. Thus, he turns his head, firstly when we switched on the lamp and the second time when he completed eating. We studied electrophysiologically the optical cortex from which we recorded the evoked potential. We found that as the conditioned reflex is elaborated excitability of the same point of the cortex from where we registered evoked potentials was increased. We measured this by means of estimating threshold levels. We explained this not only on the basis of a forward conditioning formed between the optical cortical point of signal stimulus and a point of inborn vitally important alimentary reflex, but also, even, on a new backward connection. I do not know what is in the neuronal structures, maybe we have mobilized the reticular formation or some other structures. For me this is a scheme, but we cannot say that this inborn vitally important center for unconditioned reflex can change the functional state of the signals. The animal is trying to actively search for the biologically important signals while increasing their sensitivity by lowering threshold. That is what is biologically very important. This is an explanation. But the fact is that we recorded when the animals can not eat and are looking towards the signals, once when signal is given and again when eating is finished. Thus, we used electrophysiological methods to make clear what happens in the structures the stimulus signals when acting as a signal. These data revealed some forward conditioning and, again, some backward conditioning between cortex and alimentary centers. When we satiated our animal, we could not notice such a threshold difference after eating. So I am asking you what about that in your experiments? You could say that not everything is similar in both our experiments, but much similarity could be established as I will tell you further. In your case, too, it seems that there is a motor point to lever pressing. In our case also there are motor points for lifting of the legs for the lever and there is the food or alimentary center. This, in our terminology, is a primary reflex and in your case, also, you first of all trained the animal to press a pedal for getting food and then trained with the light as a secondary stimulation. In our experiments we asked the possibility to see if there is a two-way conditioned reflex. In your case the flash and the lever pressing are secondary and the decisive role is played by the food reflex. Changes in this alimentary center alters the very important biological reflex and this reflex is transmitted to the motor and to the optical systems by means of backward conditioning. So, our explanations of your results are different. I am not now paying attention to the neural substrates which are involved. I am interested mainly from the point of view of physiological mechanisms and the biological importance of these.

14

EXECUTIVE FUNCTIONS OF THE FRONTAL LOBES

KARL H. PRIBRAM

Department of Psychology, Stanford University, Stanford, Calif. 94305 (U.S.A.)

INTRODUCTION

The subject of this symposium concerns the mechanisms of transmission of signals necessary for conscious behavior to occur. Implicit in framing the question in this fashion is a view of the nervous system as a processor of input signals, signals which constitute information for the organism. This 'information processing' view of neuronal mechanisms finds considerable support in the current experimental and theoretical literature on brain function.

My purpose here is to emphasize a complementary view of the brain mechanisms coordinate with consciousness. My view stresses the fact that, while signal transmission does, of course, occur, the essential mechanism involved in the production of awareness is the pattern of local graded potential changes, the depolarizations and hyperpolarizations which occur at synaptic junctions and in dendritic networks.

Further, I want to present evidence that what, an organism becomes aware of is related as much to the internal activities of its brain as it is due to the external situation that ordinarily provides the contents of awareness. This process by which an organism becomes conscious of selected aspects of a situation is usually called attention. Thus my presentation falls into two parts: one, a brief description of the brain state presumably coordinate with awareness; and two, a more detailed description of the attentional control processes that organize this state.

THE HOLOGRAPHIC HYPOTHESIS

At a recent meeting of the European Brian and Behavior Society Weiskrantz and Warrington (1974) presented the remarkable case history of a patient who had sustained an occipital lobe operation with its consequent hemianopia. However, Weiskrantz and Warrington were able to train this patient to respond accurately to the location of objects in the hemianopic field and to discriminate among fairly complex patterns presented in the 'blind' portion of the field. The object placement was identified by the patient's pointing to it and the discriminations were performed by depressing an appropriate button. What is so remarkable about this case history is that the patient insisted that he was *un*aware of the stimuli to which he was responding, stating that he was only guessing on the basis of some vague feeling of what an appropriate response might be. Yet his performance was in the range of 85—90% correct.

These observations suggest that, in man at least, structured conscious awareness may be dependent on the integrity of his cerebral cortex, a view, by the way, which was practically universally held in neurological circles toward the end of the 19th century (see, for example, Pribram and Gill, 1976). This view does not, of course, deny that the more global determinants of conscious states are regulated by core brain structures, thalamus, mesencephalic reticular formation and the like. What the Weiskrantz and Warrington observations point to is that the experiencing of detail in awareness is a function of the integrity of the cortex.

The involvement of the cortex in the structuring of awareness is also suggested by the experiments of Libet (1966) who showed that electrical excitation of the postcentral cortex of man leads, after several seconds, to a state of awareness of the part of the body represented in the cortex being excited. I have elsewhere (Pribram, 1971) taken especial note of the fact that several seconds of excitation are necessary and that this suggests that some sort of brain state must become established before structured awareness can occur. The Weiskrantz and Warrington observations make it plausible that this state is in fact cortical.

What is the nature of this cortical state? In this presentation I want only to mention my hypothesis which has been detailed elsewhere (Pribram, 1966 and 1971; Pribram et al., 1974). This hypothesis suggests that at any moment, a state composed of the microstructure of local junctional and dendritic (pre- and postsynaptic) potentials is the neural mechanism coordinate with structured awareness. Bennett presents in this volume (Chapter 16) a detailed and excellent review of the composition of such slow potential states in receptor organs and Purpura (Chapter 10) has once again presented evidence (see also Purpura, 1958 and 1969; Purpura and Yahr, 1966) that similar processes occur at the cortex. Because a wave-mechanism description of the microstructure of such states is plausible (slow potentials are wave forms) and has proved fruitful (Pribram, 1975), I have suggested that the mathematics of optical information processing (i.e., of holography) be used to describe these states. The strong form of this hypothesis suggests that the input channel is, at its cortical termination, composed of narrowly tuned channels (i.e., is akin to a Fourier hologram) and this strong form of the hypothesis is being tested at both the neural and psychophysical levels for the visual mechanism in several laboratories (Pollen et al., 1971; Glezer et al.,

1973; Pollen and Taylor, 1974; Stromeyer and Klein, 1974, 1975a and b; Pollen and Ronner, 1975).

Given that the terminations of the input systems in the cerebral cortex are important to structured awareness, the question remains as to how the state of the cortex becomes structured. Obviously, the input per se is largely responsible. However, there are a series of experimental results which indicate that other processes, more central in origin, also play a crucial role. I will here review the evidence that relates the functions of the frontal cortex to these more centrally organized processes, although I could use the functions of the inferotemporal cortex (Pribram, 1974) or hippocampus (Pribram and McGuinness, 1975) just as readily. As noted earlier, the neural processes that organize the structure of awareness are usually subsumed under the rubric 'attention' and Horn, in his paper in this symposium (Chapter 13 and also Horn, 1970), has introduced the issues involved in his admirable presentation. His suggestions are compatible with those presented in a somewhat more comprehensive review that distinguishes three separate neural attentional systems (Pribram and McGuinness, 1975). Since these overall views of the issues are available, I prefer here to summarize in somewhat greater detail recent experiments on the primate frontal cortex as they relate to the problems of attention and awareness.

THE INPUT-OUTPUT RELATIONSHIPS OF THE FRONTAL CORTEX

The major themes of the research of the past decade have been (a) to discover the critical input-output relationships between frontal (eugranular) cortex and the rest of the brain; (b) to subdivide the frontal (eugranular) cortex into functional subunits; and (c) to reach some better understanding of the functions affected by frontal resections and stimulations.

The input-output relationships between frontal eugranular cortex and other brain structures have been assessed by making resections or stimulations in most other brain locations to see whether such manipulations influence the performance of delay tasks. Manipulations of most brain structures do not affect such performances (Pribram, 1954).

A major puzzle to investigators derives from the fact that the input to frontal cortex from subcortical structures derives almost exclusively from the nucleus medialis dorsalis of the thalamus, an intrinsic nucleus (i.e., one which derives its subcortical connections largely from other thalamic structures). Yet resections or stimulations of this thalamic nucleus do not, as a rule, disturb delay task performance (Chow, 1954; Peters et al., 1956). By contrast, when the limbic formations are invaded, e.g. the amygdala, hippocampus and cingulate cortex, the performance of some, though not all, delay tasks becomes markedly deficient (Pribram et al., 1952 and 1962; Pribram and Fulton, 1954). The only other brain structures consistently involved in influencing delay task performance are the head of the caudate nucleus and

306

related parts of the globus pallidus and, in the thalamus, the centrum medianum. (See for instance early experiments by Rosvold: Rosvold and Delgado, 1953; and by Pribram: Migler, 1958; reviewed and extended by Rosvold and Szwarcbart, 1964; and Rosvold, 1972.)

These results suggest that the frontal eugranular cortex has special functional affinities with the limbic forebrain and with parts of the basal ganglia. This suggestion is supported by the finding that the head of the caudate nucleus and the amygdala respond with extremely large electrical potential changes when the frontal eugranular cortex is stimulated (Pribram, unpublished results) and anatomical techniques have shown major connections to these structures (Kemp and Powell, 1970; Whitlock and Nauta, 1956).

Thus, the involvement of the frontal cortex in delay tasks is not a function of input to that cortex but of the complex relationships among the structures of the frontolimbic forebrain and especially between these and the output functions of the amygdala and the caudate nucleus of the basal ganglia (Fig. 1).

Recent research has also emphasized the diversity of the functions of the frontal cortex anterior to the motor regions. Though generally related to delay tasks, the type of task influenced by limited resections differs depending on whether dorsal, ventral or orbital cortex is resected or stimulated (see, for example, early experiments by Blum, 1949 and 1952; by Mishkin, 1957; and by Pribram et al., 1966a; and more recent studies by Passingham, 1974; and by Oscar-Berman, 1975). In general, these studies suggest that spatial delay tasks are affected by dorsal cortex manipulation; that visual

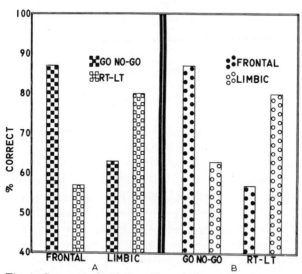

Fig. 1. Comparison of the effect of frontal and limbic lesions on A: go no-go and right-left alterations; comparison on the basis of lesion locus, and B: comparison on the basis of task (darkened circles represent the frontal group; open ones the limbic group).

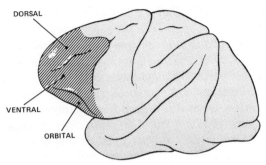

DORSAL

VENTRAL

ORBITAL

Fig. 2. Outline of monkey brain indicating dorsal, ventral and orbital frontal regions of the cortex.

delayed matching is related to the ventral frontal regions, and that successive, go/no-go tasks suffer most when orbitofrontal cortex is manipulated. What more general functions each of these subcategories of delay tasks represents is at present unclear and considerably more work is necessary to untangle the various variables that now confound interpretation of these nonetheless reliable results (Fig. 2).

Somewhat more headway has been made in understanding the functions represented by the general category of delay tasks. Such understanding may, or course, have to be revised when a clearer view is obtained of the meaning of the subcategories. But, at the same time, elucidating the meaning of the subcategories may well depend on first understanding the overall problem.

Delay tasks, by definition, represent short-term memory processes: the subject is asked to perform on the basis of cues not present at the time performance is sought but present some short interval (seconds to minutes) previously. But the locus of the disturbance produced in the short-term memory process by frontal lesion can be due to: (1) improper encoding of the cue, an attentional and/or intentional deficiency; (2) a rapid decay of an encoded trace, a consolidation impairment; or (3) confusion at the time of response, a retrieval deficit. Behavioral analysis has ruled out the trace-decay and retrieval deficit hypotheses (Pribram, 1961), and this conclusion has been amply substantiated by the results of electrical stimulation of the frontal eugranular cortex during the performance of delay tasks: the monkeys fail a trial when the stimulation to the frontal cortex occurs during the time of cue presentation and immediately (a few milliseconds) thereafter (see, for example, Stamm and Rosen, 1973), but not when such stimulations are made during the delay period per se or at the time when response is demanded. Thus, the role of the frontal cortex in short-term memory has so far been shown to involve attention and encoding appropriate to the intended behavior, not trace decay or retrieval per se.

THE FRONTAL CORTEX, ATTENTION AND INTENTION

There is a good deal of additional evidence that *attention* to input (arousal) and *intention*, readiness or set to respond (activation), are both regulated by the frontolimbic formations of the forebrain. This evidence is the subject of the recent review mentioned above (Pribram and McGuinness, 1975) which identifies three separate but interacting frontolimbic systems. One system centers on the amygdala and deals with phasic *arousal* of the organism to a novel, surprising input. A second system centers on the head of the caudate nucleus and related basal ganglia and tonically *activates* the brain, readying the organism for intended behavior. The third system centers on the hippocampus and coordinates arousal and activation, making it possible to maintain behavior in the face of distraction or to shift from one state of readiness to another without undue disruption (Fig. 3).

It is tempting to relate the three frontal subsystems to the three frontolimbic mechanisms. The hypotheses might, therefore, be fruitfully entertained that the orbital cortex is primarily related to the amygdala arousal system; the dorsal frontal cortex to the caudate readiness system; and the ventral frontal cortex to the hippocampal coordinating mechanism. The anatomical connections and physiological results obtained from stimulating these frontal subdivisions make the orbital and dorsolateral parts of the proposal plausible (Pribram et al.,1950; Kaada et al., 1949; Pribram and McLean,

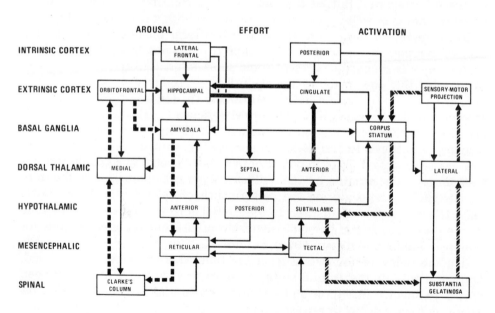

Fig. 3. Highly oversimplified diagram of the connections involved in the arousal (amygdala), activation (basal ganglia), and effort (hippocampal) circuits.

1953; Nauta, 1964). Behavioral results obtained from resections of the dorsal and the orbital areas also support the hypotheses (Rosvold, 1972; Pribram et al., 1966a). With regard to the ventral frontal cortex, however, the effects on delayed matching from sample need to be tested with hippocampal resections. Other evidence (i.e., the fact that spatial delayed response remains unaffected by hippocampal lesions: Mishkin and Pribram, 1954) suggests that this correlation may not, in fact, occur. It is more likely that the known anatomical connections between the hippocampal system and the medial frontal and cingulate cortex (Pribram and Fulton, 1954) will be the substrate of the arousal-activation coordinating system and that the ventral frontal cortex has yet another function related to the temporal isocortex with which this part of the frontal lobe is heavily connected (Mettler, 1935; von Bonin and Bailey, 1947; Jones, 1974). The temporal isocortex deals with selective attention (Rothblat and Pribram, 1972; Pribram et al., 1975) via connections to the putamen, the remaining basal ganglion of the corpus striatum (Reitz and Pribram, 1969; Buerger et al., 1974). In short, the functions of the ventral frontal cortex remain in doubt: they may relate to the hippocampal circuit, but are more likely to tie into a temporal lobe isocortex-putamen system which raises the unanswered question of the possible circuitry involved.

In recent years a few new facts have confirmed earlier findings and extended them. The new data concern two related domains: (1) the problem of orienting reactions to novel stimuli and therefore the organism's distractibility; and (2) the importance of the frontal eugranular cortex in organizing sets or contexts that regulate the organism's behavior. Again, these domains can be conceptualized in terms of attention and intention, respectively.

As noted earlier, frontal lobe resections interfere dramatically with the autonomic nervous system components of the orienting reaction. This effect of the lesion is coupled to an increased behavioral response to novelty: a failure to habituate to repetitions of a novel stimulus in both man and monkey (Luria et al., 1964; Pribram, 1973; Grueninger and Grueninger, 1973). The failure to habituate to an orienting stimulus is reflected in increased distractibility, which in monkeys is especially evident when spatial distractors, i.e. changes in the placement of cues, are involved (Grueninger and Pribram, 1969). This finding suggests that, contrary to the more common interpretation, frontal resections influence the response to spatial cues by *dis*inhibition: the common view is that dorsolateral frontal lesioned monkeys can no longer respond to spatial input; the more recent data suggest that the spatial input is responded to, but a failure in processing (ordinarily evidenced by habituation) is responsible for the observed deficit in behavior. For example, in a recently completed experiment (Brody, 1975) monkeys were taught to press a panel *next to* another that was marked by being lighted green. Both normal and frontally lesioned monkeys learned to do this readily until the marked panel was shifted among 16 placements from trial to trial. Now only the normal monkeys were able to perform the task, the frontal lobe-lesioned animals failing completely.

Taken together with the finding that interruption of the efferent connections of the frontal cortex are responsible for the lesion effects, the question is raised as to how the efferents work. Electrophysiological experiments by Lindsley and his students (especially Skinner) and Clemente and his group have traced inhibitory pathways in cat and monkey from frontal cortex, through midline diencephalic pathways to the mesencephalic reticular formation (Skinner and Lindsley, 1973; Sauerland and Clemente, 1973). The relationship needs now to be investigated between these pathways and the efferent connections from frontal cortex to the basal ganglia, spelled out via anatomical and behavioral techniques reviewed above. As noted, we were able to distinguish a separate neural system that deals with orienting (an arousal system centering on the amygdala) which includes these frontodiencephalic-reticular inhibitory pathways (Pribram and McGuinness, 1975). Cutting the pathways or resecting the cortex of their origin ought to be *disinhibiting* and the behavioral result using spatial distractors is therefore in consonance with the electrophysiological data.

According to this view, then, the distractibility due to frontal lesions is due to disinhibition of the ordinary control exercised by the frontal cortex.

In another set of experiments we tried to place the effects of frontal lesions in a somewhat more general framework. The delayed response test is similar in many respects to a task used to trace the development of intelligence in the infant by Piaget. In fact, delayed response was invented by Hunter at the University of Chicago shortly after World War I in order to determine whether children and animals could hold ideas in mind. In Piaget's work the task is called an 'object constancy' problem (Piaget, 1954; Table I).

TABLE I

Stages in the development of the object concept

Stage	Time	Description
Stages 1 and 2	0—4 months	sucking reflexes; transient images primary circular reactions
Stage 3	4—10 months	interrupted prehension; secondary circular reactions
Stage 4	10—12 months	coordination of secondary schemas; retrieval of hidden object
Stage 5	12—18 months	sequentional displacements
Stage 6	18—24 months	invisible displacements

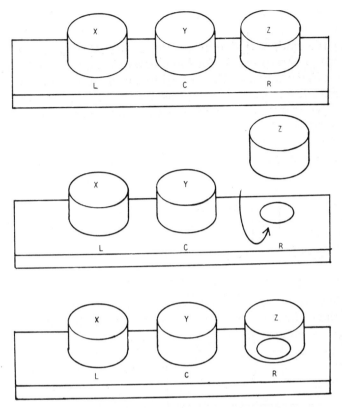

Fig. 4. Diagram showing delayed response type problem which illustrates Stage 4 of Piaget's object constancy paradigm.

In a just completed study (Anderson et al., 1976) we were able to show that frontally lesioned monkeys do in fact have difficulty when first faced with the object constancy task. In full view of the monkey a grape was hidden under one of three inverted baskets on a tray which was then pushed forward to allow the animal to lift the appropriate basket. This is a very rudimentary form of the delay task and I found many years ago that patients with ongoing pathology in frontal tissue (but not lobotomized patients) fail even this simple task (Figs. 4 and 6).

But we were not content with this result. On the basis of some of the findings reviewed above, the hypothesis had been constructed that much of the difficulty experienced by monkey and man after frontal resections was due to a failure to develop appropriate sets or contexts within which behavior could become arranged. The object constancy-delayed response task (really the old-fashioned shell game) was therefore complicated so that the baskets were moved about (without lifting them) after the placement of the grape, all within view of the monkey. The baskets were conceived as the

312

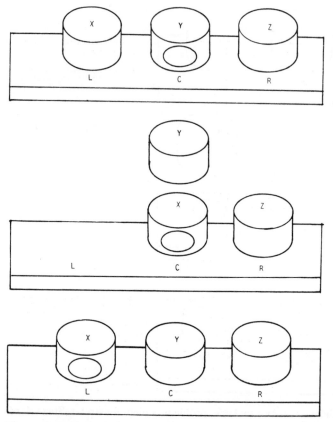

Fig. 5. Diagram showing delayed response type problem which illustrates context-dependency paradigm described in text.

context within which the grape was hidden. Whereas the object constancy problems (there was a series of them) were finally mastered by the frontally lesioned monkeys, albeit with a deficit, the context problems were *never* performed correctly, despite the fact that for normal monkeys these problems proved to be as easy as the object constancy versions (Figs. 5 and 7).

We initially interpreted these results as showing that two separate frontal lobe functions had been tapped by the experiment: one dealing with object constancy and the other with context processing. However, we learned that Bower had shown that the reason infants were defective in the object constancy situation was that they were distracted by the contextual cues within which the object became hidden (Bower and Wishart, 1972).

These results, therefore, again point to a disinhibiting role of frontal lesions which leave the organism more distractible. The results suggest additionally that distractibility interferes primarily with the establishment (perhaps by habituation) of a stable set or context within which novel stimuli

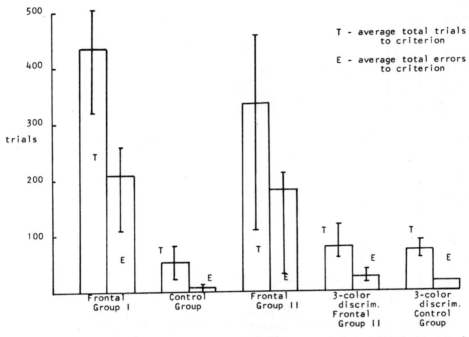

Fig. 6. Bar graph showing results obtained in the active search for vanished object problem (Piaget's Stage 4).

can be processed, so that behavior can become appropriate to the situation at hand.

A final experimental result bears on this interpretation regarding the relationship between frontal eugranular cortex and the importance of context in determining appropriate perceptions and behavior. Warren McCulloch used to enjoy startling his audiences with readings (accompanied by sonorous intonations) and picturizations of the Marzy Doates (Mares eat oats) type:

INMUDEELSARE
INCLAYNONEARE
INPINETARIS
INOAKONEIS

TO	O	TI
EM	O	UL
ES	O	TO

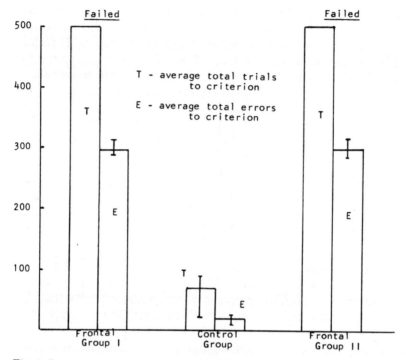

Fig. 7. Bar graph showing results obtained in the transient context modification problem.

were two of his favorites. I wondered whether, in the absence of an established context, the world of the frontal lobe-lesioned monkey looked somewhat like the McCulloch presentations. In fact, I had devised a match task in 1946 to test just this possibility on lobotomized patients. Instructions were given primarily non-verbally by showing the subject how to pick up the alternate match in regularly spaced series of three rows of twelve matches.

```
1 1 1 1 1 1 1 1 1 1 1 1
1 1 1 1 1 1 1 1 1 1 1 1
1 1 1 1 1 1 1 1 1 1 1 1
```

Then the following array was presented and the subject asked to do the same thing he had just done with the regularly spaced series:

```
11 111 1 1111 11
111 11 11111 1 1
11111 1 1 1 111 1
```

Unfortunately I found that many control subjects, as well as the lobotomized patients had difficulties in performing this task.

With monkeys the following test was devised as a modification of the delayed alternation procedure: ordinarily the delay interval between responses is kept constant. A peanut or grape is alternately placed in one of two inverted baskets but not in view of the monkey. Thus the task goes: R (right basket) 5 sec, L (left basket) 5 sec, R 5 sec, L 5 sec, R 5 sec, etc. The modification entertained on the basis of McCulloch's readings was to alter the equal spacing of the delay period into an unequal spacing: R 5 sec, L 15 sec, R 5 sec, L 15 sec, R 5 sec, etc. Behaving according to prediction, the frontal lobe-lesioned monkeys failed the equal spaced task but were practically indistinguishable from unoperated controls in their performance of the unequally spaced task (Fig. 8).

Milner (1971 and 1974) has shown a somewhat similar effect for frontal patients using a test where 'temporal tagging' (rather than the spatial 'tagging' I had tried earlier) is used. A ready interpretation of these results would be that frontal lesions interfere with the temporal organization, the 'parsing', of input so that it makes sense: becomes meaningful. A time tag, such as unequal spacing, would provide the necessary cues to parsing by the frontally lesioned subject which the normal organism ordinarily can supply to some extent himself.

In a not yet completed automated replication of the monkey experiment, a further control procedure was inserted. Each day the 5-15 spacing was

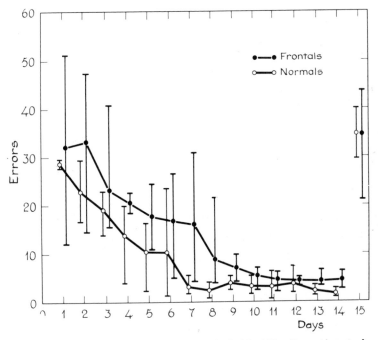

Fig. 8. Results obtained in the modified (5—15) alternation task referred to in text.

reversed so that on Monday the monkey was tested on R 5 sec, L 15 sec, R 5 sec, L 15 sec, R 5 sec, etc., while on Tuesday the order would be R 15 sec, L 5 sec, R 15 sec, L 5 sec, R 15 sec, etc. Again, the frontally resected monkeys are performing essentially as did their unoperated controls (although they cannot maintain a criterion performance as readily as do the controls; see also Pribram et al., 1966b) while doing more poorly on the equally-spaced alternation task (Anderson, Leong and Pribram, in preparation).

For both the operated and unoperated monkeys, this version of the unequally spaced alternation was extremely difficult. This, together with the results relating frontal cortex to spatial context already reviewed, raises the question as to whether temporal tagging is in fact the critical variable or whether temporal tagging is only one of several potent determiners of context. Another way of stating this question is to ask whether perhaps the frontal cortex is involved in the categorizing of relationships, much as the posterior intrinsic cortex is involved in the categorizing of properties. Of course, the possibility remains that different classes of categorization (e.g., temporal and spatial) are dependent on different portions of the frontal eugranular cortex and this possibility needs now to be tested.

In short, the current experimental results confirm and extend earlier ones in suggesting that the frontal eugranular cortex ordinarily serves to inhibit the distracting effects of novel inputs by processing the input (via habituation) in terms of an established context with controls what is attended and intended.

CONCLUSION: THE RELATIONSHIP OF FRONTAL LOBE FUNCTION TO THE TRANSMISSION OF SIGNALS IN THE NERVOUS SYSTEM

With respect to the concern of this symposium, I draw the following conclusion from the results reviewed. The fashion today is to consider brain function in terms of information processing. Usually implicit in these formulations — though occasionally made explicit (for example as by Gibson, 1966) — is the assumption that the information being processed 'resides in' the *input* to the brain, even in the *world* from which the senses derive their input.

The data on frontal lobe function reviewed here, while not denying the importance of input, do focus our attention on a currently neglected aspect of brain function: its spontaneous activity, its generative capacities. True enough, the spontaneous neural rhythms become initially programmed by input (unless the programs are pre-established, i.e. innately given) but they are then maintained as central states by memory mechanisms that serve as the context within which subsequent input becomes processed. Our search for the routes taken by information processing need not, therefore, necessarily come up with an input → central processor → output paradigm. Rather, as demonstrated here for frontal lobe function, and elsewhere (Pribram,

1971 and 1974) for other parts of the brain, a more practical and realistic

paradigm is central processor $\underset{\searrow \text{output.}}{\overset{\nearrow \text{input.}}{}}$

The emphasis in this paradigm becomes the organization of central brain states which control input and output rather than the transmission of signals from receptors to effectors. The change in view is comparable to that in chemistry where analysis of simple one-way reactions gave way to the analysis of reciprocally interacting thermodynamic systems. We therefore must, for instance, begin to look in the nervous system for variables (e.g., time constants) similar to rate-limiting reactions studied by biochemists. Thus we may come to understand that neural inhibition is an organizing process, not one which necessarily leads to the inhibition of perception and behavior: the neural disinhibition resulting from frontal lesions described here results in perceptual and behavioral disorganization (disruption of context) which may in the same animal be manifested as increased distraction (behavioral disinhibition) or perseveration (behavioral inhibition), depending on the situation in which the monkey is studied (Pribram et al., 1964). The task ahead is to formulate additional currently feasible neurophysiological experiments which can detail the mechanism by which the frontal cortex organizes the context — categorizes the relationships — within which behavior occurs.

Acknowledgements

This work was supported by NIMH No. MH 12970-09 and NIMH Career Award No. MH15214-13 to the author.

REFERENCES

Anderson, R.M., Hunt, S.C., Vander Stoep, A. and Pribram, K.H. (1976) Object permanency in frontalized and normal monkeys (*Macaca fascicularis*). Neuropsychologia, in press.

Blum, R.A. (1949) The nature of delayed response deficit in relation to the locus and character of prefrontal extirpations in primates. Unpublished Ph.D. dissertation, Yale University.

Blum, R.A. (1952) Effects of subtotal lesions of frontal granular cortex on delayed reaction in monkeys. Arch. Neurol. Psychiat. (Chic.), 67, 375—386.

Bonin von, G. and Bailey, P. (1947) The Neocortex of *Macaca mulatta*. University of Illinois Press, Urbana, Ill.

Bower, T.G.R. and Wishart, J.D. (1972) The effects of motor skills on object performance. Cognition, 1, 165—172.

Brody, B.A. (1975) The role of spatial and sequential factors in determining the deficit in problem solving after frontal and parietal cortex lesions in monkeys. Ph.D. Thesis, in preparation.

Buerger, A.A., Gross, C.G. and Rocha-Miranda, C.E. (1974) Effects of ventral putamen

318

lesions on discrimination learning by monkeys. J. comp. physiol. Psychol., 86, 440—446.

Campbell, F.W. (1974) The transmission of spatial information through the visual system. In F.O. Schmitt and F.G. Worden (Eds.), The Neurosciences Third Study Program. MIT Press, Cambridge, Mass., pp. 95—103.

Chow, K.L. (1954) Lack of behavioral effects following destruction of some thalamic association nuclei. Arch. Neurol. Psychiat. (Chic.), 71, 762—771.

Gibson, J.J. (1966) The Senses Considered as Perceptual Systems. Houghton-Mifflin Co. Boston, Mass.

Glezer, V.D., Ivanoff, V.A. and Tscherbach, T.A. (1973) Investigation of complex and hypercomplex receptive fields of visual cortex of the cat as spatial frequency filters. Vision Res., 13, 1875—1904.

Grueninger, W.E. and Grueninger, J. (1973) The primate frontal cortex and allassostasis. In K.H. Pribram and A.R. Luria (Eds.), Psychophysiology of the Frontal Lobes. Academic Press, New York, pp. 253—290.

Grueninger, W. and Pribram, K.H. (1969) The effects of spatial and non-spatial distractors on performance latency of monkeys with frontal lesions. J. comp. physiol. Psychol., 68, 203—209.

Horn, G. (1970) Changes in neuronal activity and their relationship to behavior. In G. Horn and R.A. Hinde (Eds.), Short-term Changes in Neural Activity and Behavior. Cambridge University Press, Cambridge, pp. 567—606.

Jones, E.G. (1974) The anatomy of extrageniculostriate visual mechanisms. In F.O. Schmitt and F.G. Worden (Eds.), The Neurosciences Third Study Program. MIT Press, Cambridge, Mass., pp. 215—227.

Kaada, B.R., Pribram, K.H. and Epstein, J.A. (1949) Respiratory and vascular responses in monkeys from temporal pole, insula, orbital surface and cingulate gyrus. A preliminary report. J. Neurophysiol., 12, 347—356.

Kemp, J.M. and Powell, T.P.S. (1970) The cortico-striate projection in the monkey. Brain, 93, 525—546.

Libet, B. (1966) Brain stimulation and conscious experience. In J.C. Eccles (Ed.), Brain and Conscious Experience. Springer-Verlag, New York, pp. 165—181.

Luria, A.R., Pribram, K.H. and Homskaya, E.D. (1964) An experimental analysis of the behavioral disturbance produced by a left frontal arachnoidal endothelloma (meningioma). Neuropsychologia, 2, 257—280.

Mettler, F.A. (1935) Corticifugal fiber connections of the cortex of Macaca mulatta. The frontal region. J. comp. Neurol., 61, 509—542.

Migler, B. (1958) The effect of lesions to the caudate nuclei and corpus callosum on delayed alternation in the monkey. Master's thesis, University of Pittsburgh, Pa.

Milner, B. (1971) Interhemispheric difference in the localization of psychological processes in man. Brit. med. Bull., 27, 272—277.

Milner, B. (1974) Hemisphere specialization: scope and limits. In F.O. Schmitt and F.G. Worden (Eds.), The Neurosciences Third Study Program. MIT Press, Cambridge, Mass., pp. 75—89.

Mishkin, M. (1957) Effects of small frontal lesions on delayed alternation in monkeys. J. Neurophysiol., 20, 615—622.

Mishkin, M. and Pribram, K.H. (1954) Visual discrimination performance following partial ablations of the temporal lobe: I. Ventral vs. lateral. J. comp. physiol. Psychol., 47, 14—20.

Nauta, W.J.H. (1964) Some efferent connections of the prefrontal cortex in the monkey. In J.M. Warren and K. Akert (Eds.), The Frontal Granular Cortex and Behavior. McGraw Hill, New York, pp. 28—55.

Oscar-Berman, M. (1975) The effects of dorsolateral-frontal and ventro-lateral orbitofrontal lesions on spatial discrimination learning and delayed response in two modalities. Neuropsychologia, 13, 237—246.

Passingham, R.E. (1974) Delayed matching in rhesus monkeys with selective prefrontal lesions. Paper presented at the 6th Annual Meeting of the European Brain and Behavior Society, Sept., 1974.

Peters, R.H., Rosvold, H.E. and Mirsky, A.F. (1956) The effect of thalamic lesions upon delayed response-type tests in the rhesus monkey. J. comp. Psychol., 49, 111—116.

Piaget, J. (1954) The Construction of Reality in the Child. Ballantine, New York.

Pollen, D.A. and Ronner, S.F. (1975) Periodic excitability changes across the receptive fields of complex cells in the striate and parastriate cortex of the cat. J. Physiol. (Lond.), 245, 667—697.

Pollen, D.A. and Taylor, J.H. (1974) The striate cortex and the spatial analysis of visual space. In F.O. Schmitt and F.G. Worden (Eds.), The Neurosciences Third Study Program. MIT Press, Cambridge, Mass., pp. 239—247.

Pollen, D.A., Lee, J.R. and Taylor, J.H. (1971) How does the striate cortex begin the reconstruction of the visual world? Science, 173, 74—77.

Pribram, K.H. (1954) Toward a science of neuropsychology (method and data). In R.A. Patton (Ed.), Current Trends in Psychology and the Behavioral Sciences. University of Pittsburgh Press, Pittsburgh, Pa., pp. 115—142.

Pribram, K.H. (1961) A further experimental analysis of the behavioral deficit that follows injury to the primate frontal cortex. Exp. Neurol., 3 , 432—466.

Pribram, K.H. (1966) Some dimensions of remembering: steps toward a neuropsychological model of memory. In J. Gaito (Ed.), Macromolecules and Behavior. Academic Press, New York, pp. 165—187.

Pribram, K.H. (1971) Languages of the Brain: Experimental Paradoxes and Principles in Neuropsychology. Prentice-Hall, Inc. Englewood Cliffs, N.J.

Pribram, K.H. (1973) The primate frontal cortex — executive of the Brain. In K.H. Pribram and A.R. Luria (Eds.), Psychophysiology of the Frontal Lobes. Academic Press, New York, pp. 293—314.

Pribram, K.H. (1974) How is it that sensing so much we can do so little? In F.O. Schmitt and F.G. Worden (Eds.), The Neurosciences Third Study Program. MIT Press, Cambridge, Mass., pp. 249—261.

Pribram, K.H. (1976) Holonomy and structure in the organization of perception. In Proceedings of the Conference on Images, Perception and Knowledge, University of Western Ontario, May, 1974, in press.

Pribram, K.H. and Fulton, J.F. (1954) An experimental critique of the effects of anterior cingulate ablations in monkeys. Brain, 77, 34—44.

Pribram, K.H. and Gill, M.M. (1975) Freud's 'Project for a Scientific Psychology': Preface to Contemporary Cognitive Theory and Neuropsychology. Basic Books, New York.

Pribram, K.H. and MacLean, P.D. (1953) A neuronographic analysis of the medial and basal cerebral cortex: II. Monkey. J. Neurophysiol., 16, 324—340.

Pribram, K.H. and McGuinness, D. (1975) Arousal, activation and effort in the control of attention. Psychol. rev., 82, 116—149.

Pribram, K.H., Lennox, M.A. and Dunsmore, R.H. (1950) Some connections of the orbito-fronto-temporal, limbic and hippocampal areas of Macaca mulatta. J. Neurophysiol., 13, 127—135.

Pribram, K.H., Mishkin, M., Rosvold, H.E. and Kaplan, S.J. (1952) Effects on delayed-response performance of lesions of dorsolateral and ventromedial frontal cortex of baboons. J. comp. physiol. Psychol., 45, 565—575.

Pribram, K.H., Wilson, W.A. and Connors, J.E. (1962) The effects of lesions of the medial forebrain on alternation behavior of rhesus monkeys. Exp. Neurol., 6, 36—47.

Pribram, K.H., Ahumada, A., Hartog, J. and Roos, L. (1964) A progress report on the neurological process disturbed by frontal lesions in primates. In J.M. Warren and K. Akert (Eds.), The Frontal Granular Cortex and Behavior. McGraw-Hill, New York, pp. 28—55.

Pribram, K.H., Lim, H., Poppen, R. and Bagshaw, M.H. (1966a) Limbic lesions and the temporal structure of redundancy. J. comp. physiol. Psychol., 61, 365—373.

Pribram, K.H., Konrad, K. and Gainsburg, D. (1966b) Frontal lesions and behavioral instability. J. comp. physiol. Psychol., 62, 123—214.

Pribram, K.H., Nuwer, M. and Baron, R. (1974) The holographic hypothesis of memory structure in brain function and perception. In R.C. Atkinson, D.H. Krantz, R.C. Luce and P. Suppes (Eds.), Contemporary Developments in Mathematical Psychology. Freeman, San Francisco, Calif., pp. 416—467.

Pribram, K.H., Day, R.U. and Johnston, V.S. (1975) Selective attention: distinctive brain electrical patterns produced by differential reinforcement in monkey and man. In D.I. Mostofsky (Ed.), Behavior Control and Modification of Physiological Activity, in press.

Purpura, D. (1958) Discussion. In M.A.B. Brazier (Ed.) The Central Nervous System and Behavior. Josiah Macy, Jr. Foundation, New York, pp. 1—9.

Purpura, D. (1969) Stability and seizure susceptibility of immature brain. In H.H. Jasper, A.A. Ward and A. Pope (Eds.), Basic Mechanisms of the Epilepsies. Little, Brown and Company, Boston, Mass.

Purpura, D. and Yahr, M.D. (1966) The Thalamus. Columbia University Press, New York.

Reitz, S.F. and Pribram, K.H. (1969) Some subcortical connections of the inferotemporal gyrus of monkey. Exp. Neurol., 25, 632—645.

Rosvold, H.E. (1972) The frontal lobe system: cortical-subcortical interrelationships. Acta neurobiol. exp., 32, 439—460.

Rosvold, H.E. and Delgado, J.M.R. (1953) The effect on the behavior of monkeys of electrically stimulating or destroying small areas within the frontal lobes. Amer. Psychologist, 8, 425—426.

Rosvold, H.E. and Szwarcbart, M.K. (1964) Neural structures involved in delayed-response performance. In J.M. Warren and K. Akert (Eds.), The Frontal Granular Cortex and Behavior. McGraw-Hill, New York, pp. 1—15.

Rothblat, L. and Pribram, K.H. (1972) Selective attention: input filter or response selection? Brain Res., 39, 427—436.

Sauerland, E.K. and Clemente, C.D. (1973) The role of the brain stem in orbital cortex induced inhibition of somatic reflexes. In K.H. Pribram and A.R. Luria (Eds.), The Psychophysiology of the Frontal Lobes. Academic Press, New York, pp. 167—184.

Skinner, J.E. and Lindsley, D.B. (1973) The nonspecific mediothalamic-frontocortical system: its influence on electrocortical activity and behavior. In K.H. Pribram and A.R. Luria (Eds.), Psychophysiology of the Frontal Lobes. Academic Press, New York, pp. 185—234.

Stamm, J.S. and Rosen, S.C. (1973) The locus and crucial time of implication of prefrontal cortex in the delayed response task. In K.H. Pribram and A.R. Luria (Eds.), Psychophysiology of the Frontal Lobes. Academic Press, New York, pp. 139—153.

Stromeyer, C.F. III and Klein, S. (1974) Spatial-frequency channels in human vision as asymmetric (edge) mechanisms. Vision Res.

Stromeyer, C.F. III and Klein, S. (1975a) The detectability of frequency modulated gratings: evidence against narrow-band spatial frequency channels in human vision. Vision Res.

Stromeyer, C.F. III and Klein, S. (1975b) Adaptation to complex gratings: on inhibition between spatial frequency channels. Vision Res., submitted for publication.

Weiskrantz, L. and Warrington, E.K. (1974) 'Blindsight': residual vision following occipital lesions in man and monkey. Paper presented at the 6th Annual Meeting of the European Brain and Behavior Society, Sept. 1974.

Whitlock, D.G. and Nauta, W.J.H. (1956) Subcortical projections from the temporal neocortex in Macaca mulatta. J. comp. Neurol., 106, 183—212.

DISCUSSION

HIGHSTEIN: Is not the hemianopia different in occipital and frontal lesions?

PRIBRAM: I think the valid point is irrespective of the frontal lobe lesion which gives rise to a very different kind of hemianopia than, let us say, occipital lobe lesion. But the point here is that in one patient reported by Weiskrantz and Warrington there is a dissociation very much as there is in the split brain patient I think of right hemisphere blocking. The verbal report of awareness, I must say, is very operational, it is dissociated from the discriminatory instrumental response, and you see that dissociation may begin to have at least one loop around the problem of what we report to each other on the cerebral context of awareness.

HIGHSTEIN: What cortical lesions are you dealing with?

PRIBRAM: Most of us are dealing with lesions restricted to the occipital cortex and, of course, in the monkey studies it is the same thing.

GILMAN: Along the same lines is Sprague's experiment in which a cat lost discriminatory power after occipital lesions in the hemianopic field, but regained it again after lesions in the contralateral geniculate?

PRIBRAM: No, it is colliculus.

GILMAN: It indicates that it is present whether or not there is an occipital lesion. I think the Highstein point a good one. One has to be careful in dealing with patients who are hemianopic, because many of them have either cortical blindness and retain vision which they recognise, or they can have an agnosia in which they are able to see things but not perceive things. But the data you have mentioned is solid, neurologically.

RAMAMURTHI: I would like to ask a question and to make a remark. You said the input connections of the transcortical connections do not affect the function of the frontal cortex.

PRIBRAM: I did not say that. I said for the tests we have performed.

RAMAMURTHI: This is what we have also learnt in psychosurgery, that the ancient days of prefrontal lobotomies which knock off all the input connections do not give the results, whereas a precise orbital frontal cortex lesion we now make delivers the goods. Secondly, you were talking about the attention that does not concentrate or stay in one point. I do not exactly understand what you said. Did you say that it was dependent on the amygdala connections, or what?

PRIBRAM: No, what I said was that three neural systems are involved. One of them is the amygdaloid nucleus and another is the posterior part of the putamen and the hippocampus.

RAMAMURTHI: That scheme is meaningful in psychosurgical procedures in the human and lesions in the amygdala for certain. Your scheme was facinating, also, from our concept of psychosurgical procedures of arousal, effort and activation. For instance, we make cingulum lesions in obsessions with excellent results. So I think perhaps we may provide neurosurgically or psychosurgically some support for the table that you have made.

PRIBRAM: Well, I hope so. You remember that lesions were tried many years ago in the head of the caudate nucleus and you get the full blown syndrome as you do with frontal lobotomy. The only afferent connections known at that time to the frontal cortex were from the dorsomedial thalamic nucleus, we made lesions in the afferent paths and the effects were not produced. That is very good I think, the efferent paths are important. All I am saying is that here is a little tip of a handle to hang on to the problem of awareness.

PURPURA: I am going to give a silly sentence. When I leave a blank you answer it. I, Karl Pribram, believe that the role of the frontal lobe is to ...

PRIBRAM: ... act as an executor to the rest of the brain. It sets up a programme or a context in which all the other activity takes place, a programme that has all the executive functions of the brain.

15

PARTICULAR AND GENERAL MECHANISMS OF THE CEREBRAL
MAINTENANCE OF MENTAL ACTIVITY IN MAN, AND PROSPECTS
OF THE PROBLEM

N.P. BECHTEREVA

Institute of Experimental Medicine, Leningrad (U.S.S.R.)

Clinical-anatomical comparisons which started the objective investigation
into the structural-functional organization of the human brain (Broca, 1861;
Wernicke, 1874), while gathering and analyzing facts, originated localization-
istic ideas of the cerebral maintenance of functions (with all their practical
virtues and theoretical imperfection) and simultaneously provided ground
for one of the most fruitful fields of psychology: neuropsychology. Analysis
of the contemporary state, and prospects of the development of neuropsychology may be found in a number of works, including Luria (1975) and
Pribram (1971).

Neuropsychology, rich in filigreed psychological approaches, uses more
and more actively the opportunities offered by neurosurgical and neurological clinics, as well as human brain physiology. However, data on cerebral
lesions or on the changes of electric activity recorded from the scalp, provide
a psychologist with considerably less evidence compared with the brain's
actual abilities.

Until very recently, the possibilities of physiologically studying the cerebral maintenance of mental processes were relatively limited. An exception
rather than the rule for the vast amount of neurophysiological studies of
higher functions in man, by their thorough theoretical approach and fruitful
results, is the data obtained by Livanov and his colleagues, completely summarized in 1972 (Livanov, 1972), on the role of spatial synchronization of
biopotentials in the mechanisms of mental processes, as well as Adey's (1970)
data on reflection in the biopotentials of fine characteristics of different brain
conditions during mental activity, or Grey Walter's (1965, 1966, 1967, 1971
and 1973) data on the possibility of estimation of the readiness for action
by the brain bioelectric activity, and the data obtained by some others.

Evolution of the neurophysiology and neuropsychology of man's mental
activity has only proved possible during the latest decade on the ground of
opportunities provided by the clinical use of the implanted electrodes

324

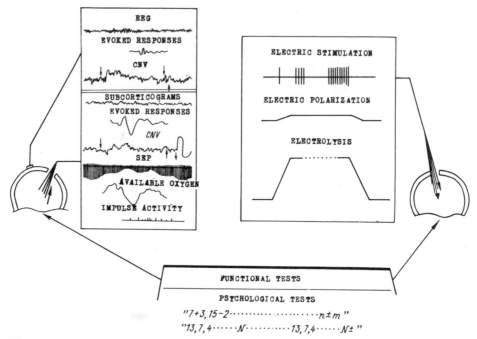

Fig. 1. Scheme illustrating the complex method of investigation into cerebral structural-functional organization. CNV, contingent negative variation; SEP, slow electric processes.

method (Bechtereva, 1965, 1966 and 1974) and by use of the microelectrode technique during stereotaxic surgery (Livanov and Raeva, 1972). The multipoint long-term contact with the human brain determined the necessity and possibility, for diagnostic and therapeutic purposes, of recording various electric processes occurring in limited areas of the living brain and organism in normal physiological and disease conditions of rest and activity, and during spontaneous and willed activities of patients. A rational programme of such studies has been summarized in the form of the complex method for brain studies (Fig. 1). While using this method for diagnosis and treatment of different patients, valuable data started to gather on the interrelationships between the structure and the function of the human brain on particular and general mechanisms of its activity, and on the intricacy and level of organization of neural processes and phenomena.

Point-limited electric procedures (stimulation, electropolarization, electrolysis) enabled the observation of a wide range of changes occurring in a patient's mental state. On the basis of these data, the charts of cerebral maintenance of emotional-mental responses and states are being drawn and completed (Fig. 2) (Bechtereva, 1974; Smirnov, 1966, 1970, 1972 and 1974; Sem-Jacobsen, 1968).

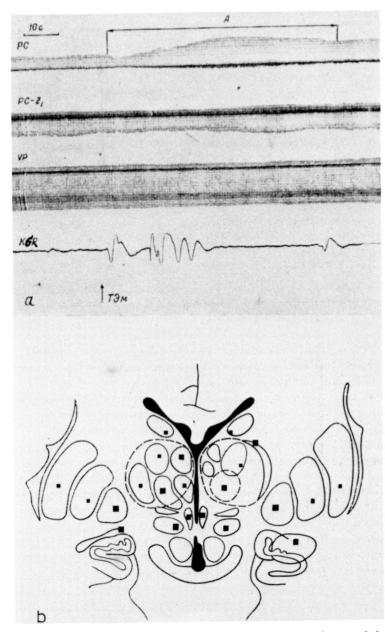

Fig. 2. Examination of the brain emotiogenic areas. a: change of the slow electric processes (SEPs) during emotiogenic tests. T3M, emotiogenic test; KGR, skin galvanic response: PC, pedunculi cerebri; VP, posterior ventral thalamic nucleus; Z$_i$, zona incerta. b: scheme of the brain. Black squares mark the areas in which changes of SEP during emotiogenic tests were observed. Major squares mark the areas in which the SEP changes were more obvious and frequent, and small squares the areas in which the SEP changes were rare and not pronounced.

The stimulation of some brain areas was found to entail such changes of its mental conditions as could further provide ground for behavioural responses. Thus, for instance, repeated electric stimulation of the thalamic reticular nucleus at its border with the ventrolateral nucleus evoked a sexually coloured emotional state, and entailed formation of a behavioural response. A therapeutic effect on the parkinsonian signs of the patient resulted out of the electrical procedures, while the stimulation-bound side effect of behavioural sexual response was suppressed by psychotherapeutic means. The psychotherapeutic communication with the patient was successful enough to prevent formation of a negative emotional behavioural response in spite of a very distinct fear, almost awe, arising in the patient during each stimulation of the rostral portions of the brain stem.

Analysis of the results showed that the conditioned reflex determining these behavioural responses could be established on the basis of reinforcement resulting from activation (evoked electrically) of an emotiogenic structure which was obviously *significant enough* within the system maintaining emotions for causing the activation of *this whole system*. The conditioning occurs rather rapidly, though *not instantaneously*. There are reasons to suppose that embedding of the matrix of a behavioural response in the memory of these cases proceeds in an ordinary way of retention of a conditioned reflex as a biologically significant reinforcement. This response is more or less extinguishable, particularly because of the conscious correction at any stage of its formation and retention, although it would be natural to assume that in this kind of response, and the possibility of the influence of volition upon it, a considerable role may be played by specific features of the patient's personality.

The emotional-mental responses also occurred during electrical procedures in other subcortical structures. However, the behavioural responses either did not develop at all or were transient (Smirnov, 1972 and 1974; Sem-Jacobsen, 1968). Admittedly, along with the effect of the preventive psychological training of the patient, the minor significance of the stimulated areas as the links of the emotions-maintaining system has its say too.

During electrical stimulation of the brain, a third type of reaction was also revealed, resembling the first one by formation of a behavioural response. In this third case the responses are formed on stimulation of other brain areas practically *instantaneously* and, once formed, do not yield to psychotherapeutic correction. In Smirnov's (1974) opinion, these responses closely resemble the imprinting phenomenon. They are qualitatively different, by the pattern of their formation and retention, from the responses occurring with repeated stimulations and yielding to conscious correction. Thus, on stimulation of the area located at the border between the ventromedial thalamic portion and the brain stem rostral portion, a response of the phobia type occurred. This response could be abolished by the stimulation of an area within the thalamic centre median. Stimulation of an area within the reticular thalamic nucleus resulted in a forcible laughter response which could be suppressed by stimulation of the brain stem reticular formation area.

The virtual possibility of either gradual or instantaneous formation of behavioural responses opens intriguing prospects for the therapy of otherwise incurable diseases of a stable pathological condition (Bechtereva, 1974; Bechtereva and Bondarchuk, 1968).

The emotional-mental displays of electrical effects on the brain, exerted via implanted electrodes, were observed, amongst others, by Bechtereva (1965, 1966 and 1974), Bechtereva et al. (1963), Smirnov (1963, 1966, 1970, 1972 and 1974), Sem-Jacobsen (1963) and Delgado (1970). Their analyses presented in a new way the mechanisms of speech, body image, the structural-functional organization of emotions, and intellectual-mnestic activity. On the ground of these data, Delgado (1970) states that the electrical stimulation provided a possibility of observing mental processes (emotions in particular) 'from within' the brain. One might probably agree with that, bearing in mind, however, that the electrical effects on the brain enable one to study mental states and responses, but what changes occur in the brain in the course of maintaining mental activity, and how, still proves to be rather complicated.

Recordings of electrosubcorticogram revealed in the patients the development of pathological activity in the brain in different clinical reactions (Hodes et al., 1954; Heath, 1954). Kambarova (1974, in Bechtereva et al., 1975) noted in an epileptic patient spikes in the amygdala during evoked negative emotional response. The phenomenon proved regular, reproducible, and indicated, apparently, the role of this structure in the maintenance of emotional responses and, particularly, its role in the complex of emotional disturbances of this grave epileptic patient. However, neither these kinds of findings, nor studies of the electroencephalogram (electrosubcorticogram) provided progress in the investigation of the cerebral system for the maintenance of mental functions, or of the particular or general mechanisms of their structural-functional and neurophysiological maintenance.

Virtually new data on the events 'within' the brain were obtained when studying the patterns of slow electric processes (SEP) and other slow physiological processes in the brain (PO_2, local blood flow, impedance), as well as the impulse activity of neuronal populations. Of great importance was the juxtaposition of recordings of cerebral physiological processes and the dynamics of the peripheral displays: the muscle tone, the state of the capillaries, SGR, and others. Recordings of cerebral physiological processes during changes in the patient's state depending on, or irrespective of, the disease, and during spontaneous and willed activity, made it possible to obtain a vast amount of evidence indeed concerning the events 'within' the brain: the cerebral maintenance of functions both in normal and pathological conditions.

While studying physiological events occurring in the brain during psychological tests, the data on the structural-functional organization of mental processes were essentially widened, and the hypothesis was advanced (Bechtereva et al., 1967; Bechtereva and Gretchin, 1968) describing the maintenance of mental activity in man, involving the rigidly participating links and the secondary flexible links recruited with regard to alterations in the environment or in the inner milieu. It has also been suggested that the relatively great number of flexible links is a specific feature of the system serving the more complicated functions, particularly special human functions. The main factors of reliability of the cerebral system maintaining mental functions include the apparatus of the flexible links, the polybiochemical character of the system, and the assembly character of organization (Bechtereva, 1974), while the mechanism of optimization includes the apparatus of errors detection (Bechtereva and Gretchin, 1968). Studies by Iliukhina (1973) deciphered the systematic basis of the structural-functional mechanisms of the E-wave phenomenon and the readiness for action, while a number of other works showed the cerebral spatial-temporal dynamics of physiological parameters during the simplest intellectual-mnestic activity (Gretchin, 1972; Matveev, 1972; Trohatchev, 1971). New data were also obtained on the formation of the slow negative potential shift in subcortical structures within the range of relatively small values (25—100 μV) of a bioelectric signal during verbal operations: construction of words out of syllables, and associative uniting of words into an idea (Bundzen, Iliukhina, Malyshev). Raeva showed changes of the impulse activity, mainly of the activation type, during psychological tests in a number of neuronal populations of the subcortical structures.

Recording of physiological parameters while studying the human brain made it possible to resolve the *neurophysiological essence* of the changes occurring in the brain during fulfillment of different functions, including emotional-mental ones.

On the basis of a vast amount of findings a kind of an 'alphabet' of emotions was evolved (Fig. 3) (Smirnov and Speransky, 1972).

The simultaneous study of the cerebral (slow electric processes) and extracerebral (SGR) parameters of emotional states made it possible to distinguish the components of the non-specific activation and of the emotional-activation proper (Grekova, 1974). The regularity of the initial development of the unspecific activation seems to corroborate Lindsley's (1957) hypothesis of the role of the reticular formation in the development of emotional responses. This, however, needs further study and, apparently, some model observations using pharmacological differentiation of the closeness of connection between the non-specific and the emotionally-bound activations.

A fact drawing attention to its seemingly phenomenological interest consisted of electrical shifts of different direction revealed in many subcortical structures when experiencing different emotions (Bechtereva et al., 1967 and 1975; Bechtereva and Gretchin, 1968; Avramov and Smirnov, 1968). The

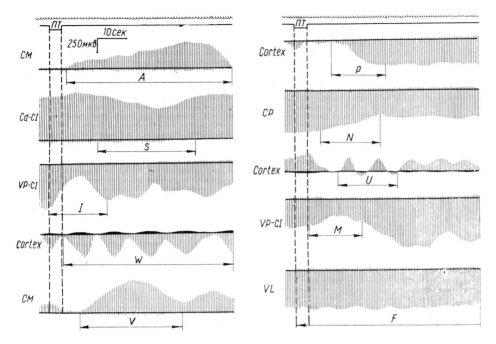

Fig. 3. Typical components of the SEP responses to physiological effects activating attention and emotional behaviour. High amplitude complex components — waves: A, application wave; S, cellar wave; I, I-wave, W, W-wave; V, V-wave. High amplitude non-complex components of the shift: P, positive; N, negative shift of SEP. Low amplitude non-complex components: U, wave undulation; M, monotonous waves (oscillations); F, the background activity to the response. NT, test; CM, n. centrum medianum; Cd-Ci, n. caudatus-capsula interna; VP-CI, n. ventralis post-capsula interna; CP, globus pallidus; VL, n. ventralis lateralis.

later data confirmed this and revealed the negative shifts of slow electric processes in the brain during different emotions. A thorough analysis of this event, considering the experimental data on physiological significance of the sign of the slow electric potential shift (Aladjalova, 1969; Russinov, 1969) suggested that active participation of a brain area as a link of the system maintaining emotional responses is associated with the negative shift of electric potential. The rather infrequent cases of increasing electrical negativity during some negative emotional experiences can be understood when considering the prevalence of positive emotional responses observed during electrical procedures.

Having accepted such an explanation of the data obtained, it would be logical to suggest a neurophysiological scheme of successive development of emotions of different types as follows. Any emotional experience is associated with developing negativity in those brain areas which are the links of the system of its maintenance. When developing another emotion against this

cerebral background, not merely an activation (expressed in electrical negativity) of areas representing the links maintaining this particular emotion occurs, nor a preservation of the active condition in those areas which are non-
specifically participating in this particular emotional response, but also the
development of an electrical positive shift, the development of *slow electric
processes of the opposite sign in those areas which have been negative* during
the former emotion, occurs. These phenomena are quite obviously displayed
when recording the slow electric processes. Such cerebral dynamics demands,
apparently, not only time but energy expenditures too. A negative emotional
state against the background of a positive one or, more generally, the development of any other state against the background of a preceding different
one, accounts to a major extent for the inertia of emotional responses. The
above phenomena can be regarded from another standpoint too. Probably,
these processes are the neurophysiological bases of the empirically founded
thesis of a *defensive role of the positive emotions' optimal level with regard
to negative emotions* with all their somatic consequences.

Neurophysiological study of human emotions made it possible to elucidate yet another, also previously empirically founded, phenomenon as pic-
turesque as to be even expressed in the figure of speech: 'there is but one
step from love to hate', and such others. It has been long known that the
development and sustenance of a strong positive emotion, especially in an
unbalanced person, can evoke without any reason, or with objectively negligible reasons, an obvious negative emotion. Study of slow electric processes
showed that in some cases one can note a 'spontaneous' alteration of their
sign correlated with the patient's emotional state (Avramov and Smirnov,
1968).

No doubt it would be primitive mechanistic to imagine that such an alteration of emotional states during strong and/or sustained emotional responses
of an unbalanced person can be accounted for just by changes of the slow
electric process in the brain. The intrinsic basis of all brain phenomena, including these ones, involves the finest biochemical processes. However, it
would be equally unjust to disregard the role of the observed bioelectrical
processes, in this case of the slow electric processes in the brain. The brain
electrical processes were shown in numerous studies (Livanov, 1962; Aladjalova, 1962; Bechtereva, 1966 and 1974) not only to be an epiphenomenon
but also to possess a controlling function in the brain mechanisms. Hence,
the data on the patterns of slow electrical processes should be considered
not only when deciphering the brain current neurodynamics but also the
general principles of its activity. The data on the patterns of slow electrical
processes in the brain can be used as the 'indication for action', i.e. for a
necessary pharmacological or electric therapeutic (correcting) interference.
One of the forms of such interference used by us for therapy involved electrical stimulation of the brain and electrical micropolarization (Bechtereva
et al., 1972; Shandurina, in Bechtereva et al., 1975) both of them changing

considerably the spatial-temporal dynamics of the slow electrical processes (data obtained by Iliukhina, 1975).

Evidence on the general and particular principles and mechanisms of the structural-functional maintenance of intellectual-mnestic processes, and the contemporary possibilities of mathematical and instrumental analysis of physiological data made it possible to analyze the problem of cerebral maintenance of mental activity in man and the principles and the concrete forms of verbal signals coding in the human brain. The importance of this question is that the deciphering of the verbal code alone can actually open the way to investigation into the laws and mechanisms of the mental activity proper.

The question of the possibility of the words-code revealing impulse activity in the brain was raised five years ago (Bechtereva, 1971) and was found in the impulse activity of neuronal populations. The impulse activity was analyzed in such a way as to distinguish the functionally united groups of neurones: assemblies, their spatial-temporal dynamics and interrelationships, the independence and dependence on the signal changes of the current frequency, and the structure of the impulse activity in neuronal groups: forms of impulses, etc. The methodical approach has been described by Bundzen et al. (1973) and is being continuously perfected according to the more and more complicated character of the tasks to be solved. The technical basis for the analysis is provided by an analog and digital computer technique with added standard and modified auxiliary blocks (the Minsk-32 computer, Didak-4000, M-6000, etc.) (Fig. 4).

Activity of neuronal populations which had been found, by means of the preliminary integrated recording of the impulse activity (Matveev, 1971), to participate in the structural-functional maintenance of mental activity, was analyzed. The main results of these studies were the revealing of the acoustic (Bechtereva et al., 1971) and of the semantic codes (Bechtereva and Bundzen, 1974a) in the impulse activity of the brain neuronal populations, and the dependence of the bioelectrical code's dynamics on the long-term memory basis. Coding of verbal signals in the impulse activity of neuronal populations of the human brain was shown to be reflected by a readjustment of the neurones' firing rate, by the appearance of spikes grouped in a certain way, by a certain form of spikes, and by a change of interrelationships between adjacent neurones and between neuronal populations located in different brain areas representing elements of the system maintaining the given intellectual-mnestic activity. An important control of the existence of this code of words turned out to be the finding of a phonetic code (Perepelkin, 1974) and of a code of word-composing syllables (Gogolitsyn, 1974a).

At first, words are coded in the brain in complex acoustic signals. The impulse activity of neuronal populations undergoes a readjustment respective to the acoustic characteristics of the words (Fig. 5) (Bechtereva et al., 1971). The dynamics in time of the occurring pattern is subordinate to the state of the long-term memory. The pattern is preserved in the impulse activity at the

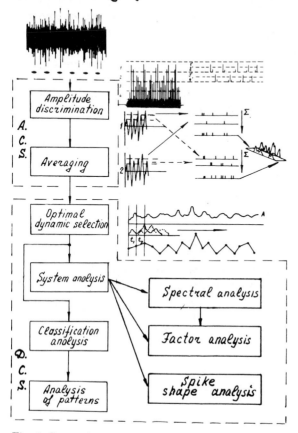

Fig. 4. Succession of operations for the complex analysis of the multiunit activity. A.C.S. and D.C.S. are analog and digital computer systems.

presentation of an unfamiliar word, though in a discrete form in every given neuronal population (Bundzen and Kaplunovsky, 1974; Gogolitsyn, 1973). One of the mechanisms of this discreteness probably involves the reverberation process. In this case the occurring pattern has at least three main physiological functions: the function of coding of the incoming signal, the function of formation of the long-term memory basis, and the function of control over the output signal, i.e. the reproduced word. Stability of the occurred pattern is sustained by the test-bound motivation and absence of inhibiting influences from the long-term memory basis. When presenting a familiar word, the motivation provides premises for the occurrence of a controlling signal, while extinguishing the primarily occurring pattern. The new controlling pattern is derived from activation of the long-term memory engram

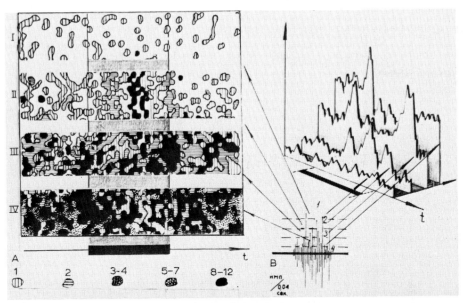

Fig. 5. Chronogram of the impulse activity of a human brain neuronal population in analogue expression (A), and graphic representation of patterns of the current frequency function registered within the four discrimination windows (I, II, III and IV — the ordinate) on ten-fold presentation of the word "khor" (B). Abscissa: time (epoch 40 msec). Vertical hatching, one pulse in 40 msec; horizontal hatching, 2 pulses in 40 msec; transversal hatching, 3—4 pulses in 40 msec; dotted areas, 5—7 pulses in 40 msec; blackened area, 8—12 pulses in 40 msec. Vertical lines, the start and the cessation of the verbal signal.

which inhibits the first pattern when 'having recognized' the word (Bechtereva and Bundzen, 1974b). The dependence of the controlling code's neurodynamics on the long-term memory was convincingly shown in studies with learning the Russian meaning of foreign words (Gogolitsyn, 1974b). In this case transformation of neurodynamics is revealed as well as the appearance of neurodynamics specific for the tests with familiar words. Interesting findings in these studies were obtained in such test modifications when, knowing the meaning of a foreign word, the subject was made to reproduce alternatively either Russian or foreign words. The neurodynamics could change in such a way that at least the acoustic coding of Russian and foreign words seemed to occur (or to be able to occur) in different neuronal populations. In the first case, when keeping in memory the pattern formed at the moment of the word presentation, and in the second case the controlling pattern, apparently both reflect the sensorimotor structure of the word-response, while the initially occurring pattern is mainly the sensory image of the presented word. Differences between the controlling and the initial patterns were shown in tests with presentation of familiar words, but until now only the differences between sensory elements of these patterns have been presented objectively. Study into the relative weight of the sensory and motor elements in the controlling pattern is one of the future tasks of investigation of the controlling signal.

Study of the semantic neurodynamic code has been fulfilled on the ground of psychology's traditional methods based on using the commonness

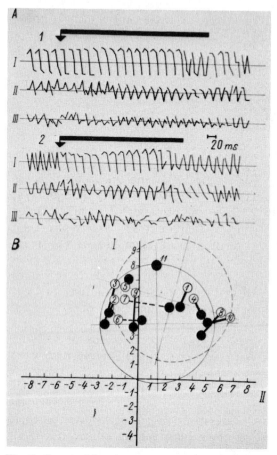

Fig. 6. Compositional types of the neural code for the word "tree" (A_1) and the word "fir (tree)" (A_2), extracted by means of the dynamic factor analysis of the multiunit activity, and the differentiation of the code types (B) of the concrete verbal signals from the semantic field "tree". In A, I, II and III are factorial structures profiles. Arrows denote the moments of verbal signals reproduction. B: axes correspond to the values of the first (I) and second (II) factors. Black circles, distribution of the compositional patterns, exposed during reproduction of the verbal signals meaning different trees by means of the second-order factor analysis; white circles, distribution of the concrete trees, calculated by means of the factor analysis of the Osgood's test results. 1, birch-tree; 2, fir-tree; 3, pine-tree; 4, maple-tree; 5, spruce; 6, mango; 7, larch; 8, lime-tree; 9, boabab; 10, oak-tree; 11, 'tree'.

of meaning of different words (Osgoods's test, 1953) (Fig. 6). Physiologically objective presentation of the commonness of meaning of different words belonging to one semantic field has been until recently fulfilled using the 'peripheral' signs of physiological readjustments in the organism (Luria and Vinogradova, 1970). When differentiating between acoustic and semantic codes, it is essential to consider the differences in the acoustic characteristics of words belonging to one semantic field and, respectively, their semantic nearness. Neurophysiological studies of the acoustic and semantic codes showed that the readjustment of interrelationships between neuronal groups and populations, formation and transformation of the assemblies, is, apparently, the universal kind of the 'chief' brain code; all the other types of neurodynamic readjustments playing an auxiliary role (Bechtereva and Bundzen, 1974b). These brain mechanisms of codes of words can be deciphered by using the factor analysis in its different modifications, as it reveals in the best way the readjustment of interrelationships among the brain structural-functional elements (Kaplunovsky, 1972 and 1974). The mutually complementing factor analysis of current frequency in the distinguished neuronal assemblies (Kaplunovsky, 1972 and 1974) and the factor analysis of spectres of the neuronal populations' multiunit activity (Gogolitsyn, 1974b) made it possible not only to show the presence of a similar factor structure in words of a common semantic field, but also to reveal certain brain mechanisms of interaction between the word-elements of this field. Thus, the elements of a common factor structure were revealed in the code of names of different trees and their 'anatomical components'. On the other hand, neurophysiological analysis revealed the grouping of factors for trees reflecting their geographical, seasonal, and other (height etc.) characteristics. The words 'forest' and 'foliage' were noted in the code of different trees and the words 'furniture' and 'trees' immediately after presentation of the very first generalized words. Hence it is quite comprehensible that even now, at the very beginning of neurophysiological study of the semantic code, the prospects for revealing both the type and the individual laws of thinking in man, are being opened. The first steps in this regard involve the deciphering of mechanisms of the simplest logical operations of the generalization type and, as shown above, of the neurophysiological mechanisms of the individual neuropsychology of generalizations (Fig. 7).

Naturally, extensive further work is demanded for studying the neural code. One of the nearest tasks of this problem is the study of the interrelationship between acoustic and semantic coding. The first basic data in this field may be considered the findings made during the fine study of discrete and mutually interrelated neurodynamics of the acoustic code in the form of readjustment of the current frequency, and of the spatial-temporal code during the interaction of the initial or the 'acoustic' pattern with the long-term memory and formation of the controlling code. It proved possible to reveal a type of spatial-temporal code, delayed in time from the

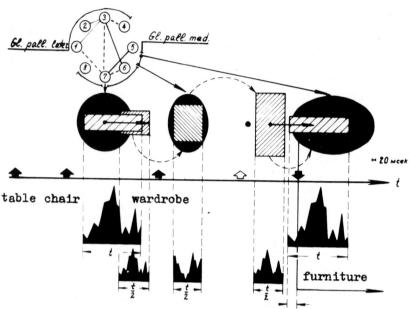

Fig. 7. The reorganization of the code types during associative logical operations in neuronal populations of the striopallidal system. 1—8 are neuronal ensembles, separated within the population. Continuous and dashed lines denote the direction and the strength of interconnections between the ensembles characterizing the compositional type of the code for the word 'furniture'. Arrows and ellipses point to the moments in time (t) of the appearance of the given type of neuronal ensembles interaction. Temporal analysis time bin, 20 msec. Large arrowheads pointing upwards denote the moments of verbal signals (table, chair, wardrobe) presentation, and those pointing down the moment of response (furniture). The positions of rectangles with different kinds of shading correspond to the moments of exposure of controlling code with time dimension (t) equal to the length of the verbalization process and reduced two-fold (t/2). In the lower part of the figure the profiles of the controlling code elements are presented. Vertical shading, code profiles projections of the time axis and the moments of exposure of compositional code. Dashed curves unite the moments of exposure of the reduced controlling code. Black dot, the moment of exposure of the autonomous code.

acoustic code, which appears in the current frequency on presentation of a word, and precedes an analogous code at the word reproduction. During the retention of the word in memory both types of code can be revealed in different proportions, the code's compression, scanning, and invertion being noted. There are some reasons to suppose that this delayed and preceding spatial-temporal code is associated already with semantic coding, though of course quite a few objections can be made here.

In the mechanisms of acoustic and semantic coding, the element of interaction of the input signal with the long-term memory, and the activation of the engram during the process of retrieval, are very important. One of the phenomena observed when studying the neural code: appearance of a certain form of impulses, by the conditions of its occurrence seems to correspond to the neurophysiological display of this mechanism. The time of its appearance and its obviousness is clearly dependent on the words frequency index and it does not occur with quasiwords (Bundzen in Bechtereva et al., 1973; Bundzen, 1974). Admittedly, an activation of the membrane structures responsible for the changes and stabilizing of the action potentials' form, underlies this phenomenon. However, having accepted this, it is necessary to assume further that not the cortex alone but the subcortical structures as well are responsible for the storage of activated engram of the long-term memory. This phenomenon has been observed in the thalamic associative nuclei.

The study of the brain mechanisms of the words coding makes it possible to suggest the scheme of this information processing as follows. The initial coding of words, proceeding according to the laws of coding of complex acoustic signals, is independent of the semantic meaning of these words. The occurring acoustic code is further directed to the long-term memory summed up in result of the subject's individual experience, which activates it or forms it if necessary. At the acoustic coding level, with regard to a number of additional factors, a preliminary selection, or filtration of information is possible (Iliukhina et al., 1974). The activation of the long-term memory leads to the formation of a new operative unit in the brain: the semantic code, able to be the basis for other much more complicated mental processes. If the verbal realization of a mental process is necessary, the controlling code is formed in the brain. In the absence of a corresponding basis in the long-term memory, the functions of the controlling code may be fulfilled by the initial acoustic code which has been formed in the brain on presentation of an unfamiliar word.

The direct study on the human brain opened the really excellent prospects for study of the cerebral mechanisms of mental activity. Much depends on time, adequate clinical-physiological symbioses, and on confluence with neuropsychology. However, at this stage of investigation, not only the possibilities and prospects but also the absolute and relative limits of the human study should be ascertained.

The implanted electrodes method in man is used, and should be used, exclusively for therapeutic and diagnostic purposes and not for solving the scientific problems.

Contemporary psychosurgery, according to clinical indications, involves extirpation of various emotiogenic areas in emotional disturbances (Petrie, 1952; Heath, 1972; Heath et al., 1968; Laitinen, 1972; Obrador et al., 1974). It is also quite possible to form desirable behavioural responses using a combination of electrical stimulation of emotiogenic areas with any other chosen method.

However, the matter is far from that simple. At the level of 'human' studies, their physiological methodical possibilities being equal in principle to those of experiment, and their psychophysiological possibilities being, naturally, even greater, a 'legitimate obstacle' for the brain studies arises in the form of medical and ethical problems. The choice of areas for implantation of electrodes is governed narrowly with regard to the patient's interests. However, due to the widening of the range of diseases treated with stereotaxic methods, the number of cerebral structures which are the stereotaxic targets is enlarging. In the gravest forms of epilepsy, even one of the most dangerous areas for interference and one especially significant for the physiology of emotions, the hypothalamus, has become such a target in some clinics. It is true that very few take the risk of interfering with this area in man, being well aware of the probability of development of various dystrophic complications. Quite reasonable is the caution with regard to the brain stem structures as well. Electrodes are also being implanted into some cortical areas in epilepsy, and visual and hearing prosthetic appliances are being implanted (Brindley and Lewin, 1968; Brindley, 1973; Michelson, 1971; Simmons et al., 1965). And still, considering specifics of these diseases, there are no reasons to suppose that in the near future it will prove possible, without disregarding the limitations of a medical-ethical character, to obtain a long-term contact with a large enough number of different brain areas. Therefore, when compared with experiments in animals, studies of the human brain lack rather much in the *possible completeness of the brain examination.* Obtaining the necessary data is possible in principle, but this process cannot be accelerated as much as physiology wishes it.

In brain and behavioural physiology Olds' experiments are well known (Olds and Milner, 1966). Like many other rationally organized experiments, they made it possible to introduce the essential quantitative component into the behavioural aspect of the study. Similar kinds of studies in man are but the domain of science fiction (Crichton, 1972).

Naturally enough, the ascertainment of the observed emotional displays during diagnostic stimulation needs to be repeated. Repeated stimulation of these areas for diagnostic purposes is inadmissible. The therapeutic electric stimulation of emotiogenic areas would seem to provide a greater opportunity for observation of the dynamics of the results. However, the therapeutic stimulation should only be carried out according to the indications of emotional disturbances, i.e. to the primordial disturbance in the activity of the system which maintains emotions and where repetition of stimulation, in the case of improvement, leads to alteration of the response quality.

Neither of the possibilities opened up by recording the physiological parameters during emotiogenic tests are limitless in the case of study of the cerebral maintenance of emotional responses. An animal may, and sometimes should, be put under the most complicated emotiogenic situation (for the interests of man). *The emotiogenic tests for patients should be chosen extremely cautiously, particularly those which evoke a negative emotion!*

When speaking of limitations in human brain physiology one should not forget that these physiological studies of the human brain, enriched by the possibility of human communication, make it possible to unveil a number of facts. The interpretation of these facts based on the experimental studies has been rather disputable; for example, the Olds' experiments did not actually permit one even to approach the interpretation of the subjective equivalent of behaviour.

How does the matter stand here with the animal experiments and the human studies? The first paper on the dependence of at least one type of neural code of words on words' acoustic characteristics appeared as a result of studies in man (Bechtereva et al., 1971). This was followed by quite comparable data on the acoustic code of words in the cat brain (Walker and Halas, 1972). Because of this, the findings in man concerning the possibility of coding the acoustic characteristics of words began to represent if not the general biological regularity, at least a common enough brain mechanism.

Are there in brain physiology any problems, questions, or aspects where the experiment stays always and in principle primordial? Probably there are, and this involves first of all the study of the neurophysiology of many behavioural responses.

Delgado is working at the present time in an institute in Madrid where the diagnosis and treatment of epileptic and some other patients are carried out under his guidance using the possibilities of implanted electrodes and telemetry. However, neither the most modern techniques of his studies, nor the possibilities provided by a wide range of patients enabled him to do without experiment when he encountered the task of studying the neurophysiological mechanisms of maintaining the hierarchy in a population of highly organized animals.

The behavioural hierarchy and its willed readjustment achieved by influencing the cerebral modulating structures are being experimentally studied in quite a few countries (Ploog, 1970). The tasks of such studies vary rather widely from sociological to purely neurophysiological.

The example of Delgado making this kind of study in a colony of monkeys on the Bermudas is only demonstrative of important possibilities spreading beyond experiment.

The list of limitations for the study of the physiology of higher nervous activity in man, if one is to include all particular variants, could probably occupy many pages. It is certainly unnecessary for the present paper elucidating, first of all, the contemporary ideas of the human brain mechanisms. It is important to emphasize that the possibilities of human brain physiology have been extremely enlarged, particularly during the last two decades. Physiological studies being combined with the 'human' contact help to penetrate deep into those cerebral mechanisms which can only indirectly be judged upon proceeding from experiment. Still, one should keep in mind the fact that the physiology of the human brain will have to lean upon experimentation in animals.

REFERENCES

Adey, W.R. (1970) In The Neurosciences. Rockefeller University Press, New York, pp. 224—243.
Aladjalova, N.A. (1962) Slow Electric Processes of The Brain.
Aladjalova, N.A. (1969) In Slow Electric Potentials of the Nervous System. Tbilisi, p. 236.
Avramov, S.R. and Smirnov, V.M. (1968) Vop. fiziol., 3, 62—76.
Bechtereva, N.P. (1965) In Rol Glubokikh struktur mozga tcheloveka v mekhanizmakh patologitcheskibh reaktsiy. pp. 25—30.
Bechtereva, N.P. (1966) In Glubokie struktury mozga tcheloveka v norme i patologii. pp. 18—21.
Bechtereva, N.P. (1974) Neurophysiological Aspects of Mental Activity in Man. Meditsina.
Bechtereva, N.P. and Bondartchuk, A.N. (1968) Vop. Neirokhir., 3, 39—44.
Bechtereva, N.P. and Bundzen, P.V. (1973) In S. Bogoch (Ed.), Biological Diagnosis of Brain Disorders, Vol. 3, p. 24.
Bechtereva, N.P. and Bundzen, P.V. (1974a) In Memory and the Trace Processes. Pushchino na Oka. p. 253.
Bechtereva, N.P. and Bundzen, P.V. (1974b) In Int. Annual Nauka i Tchelovetchestvo. Znanie, pp. 21—31.
Bechtereva, N.P. and Gretchin, V.B. (1968) Int. Rev. Neurobiol., 11, 239—246.
Bechtereva, N.P. Gratchev, K.V., Orlova, A.N. and Yatsuk, S.L. (1963) Zh. Nevropat. Psikhiat., 63, 3—8.
Bechtereva, N.P., Bondartchuck, A.N., Smirnov, V.M. and Trohatchev, A.I. (1967) Physiology and Pathophysiology of the Human Deep Brain Structures, Meditsina.
Bechtereva, N.P., Bundzen, P.V., Matveev, Yu. K. and Kaplunovsky, A.S. (1971) Fiziol. Zh. (Leningr.), 57, 1745—1761.
Bechtereva, N.P., Bondartchuk, A.N., Meliutcheva, L.A. and Smirnov, V.M. (1972) Vop. Neirokhir., 1, 7—12.
Bechtereva, N.P., Bundzen, P.V., Keidel, W.D. and David, E.E. (1973) Fiziol. Zh. (Leningr.), 59, 1785—1802.
Bechtereva, N.P., Kambarova, D.K. and Pozdeev, V.K. (1974) In Catecholamines and Behaviour, Vol. 1. Plenum, New York, pp. 109—166.
Bechtereva, N.P., Kambarova, D.K., Smirnov, V.M., Tchernigovskaya, N.V. and Shandurina, A.N. (1975) Amer. Psychol., in press.
Brindley, G.S. (1973) In Handbook of Sensory Physiology, Vol. 7/3. Springer, Berlin, pp. 583—594.
Brindley, G.S. and Lewin, W.S. (1968) J. Physiol. (Lond.), 196, 479—493.
Broca, P. (1861) Bull Soc. Anthrop., 2, 1861; 6, 1861; 6, 1861. Cited in Luria, A.R. (1962) Higher Cortical Functions of Man and their Disorders in Focal Brain Lesions.
Bundzen, P.V. (1974) Self-organization of information-controlling functions of the human brain. Doctoral thesis.
Bundzen, P.V. and Kaplunovsky, A.S. (1974) Probl. fiziol. patol. 5, 80—108.
Bundzen, P.V., Gogolitsyn, Yu.L., David, E.E., Kaplunovsky, A.S. and Perepelkin, P.D. (1973) Fiziol. Zh. (Leningr.), 59, 1803—1810.
Crichton, M. (1972) The Terminal Man. London.
Delgado, J.M.R. (1970) In Physiological Correlates of Emotion. New York, pp. 189—204.
Gogolitsyn, Yu.L. (1973) Mat. V Vseosiuzn. konf. po neirokibernetike. Rostov on Don, p. 68.
Gogolitsyn, Yu.L. (1974a) Mat. II Vsesoiuzn. konf. po biol. i med kibern.
Gogolitsyn, Yu. L. (1974b) In memory and the Trace Processes. Pushchino na Oka, pp. 255—257.

Grekova, T.I. (1974) Probl. fiziol. Patol., 5, 274—285.

Gretchin, V.B. (1972) Clinical Neurophysiology. Nauka, pp. 494—530.

Grey Walter, W. (1953) The Living Brain. London.

Grey Walter, W. (1965) Brit. J. physiol. Opt., 22, 1—9.

Grey Walter, W. (1967) Electroenceph. clin. Neurophysiol., 23, 489.

Grey Walter, W. (1971) Biol. Psychiat., 3, 59—69.

Grey Walter, W. (1973) In K.H. Pribram and A.R. Luria (Eds.), Psychophysiology of the Frontal Lobes. New York, pp. 109—122.

Heath, K. (1954) In Studies in Schizophrenia. Cambridge, Mass., pp. 151—156.

Heath, R.G. (1972) J. nerv. ment. Dis., 154, 3—18.

Heath, R.G., John, S.B. and Fontana, C.J. (1968) In N. Klin and E. Laska (Eds.), Computers and Electronic Devices in Psychiatry. New York, pp. 178—189.

Hodes, R., Heath, R.G. and Miller, W.H. (1954) In Studies in Schizophrenia. Cambridge, Mass., pp. 157—195.

Iliukhina, V.A. and Khon, Yu.V. (1973) Fiziol. Zh. (Leningr.), 59, 1811—1824.

Iliukhina, V.A., Kaplunovsky, A.S. and Perepelkin, P.D. (1974) In Memory and the Trace Processes. Pushchino na Oka, pp. 269—271.

Kaplunovsky, A.S. (1972) In Samoreguliatsia neirofiziol. mekhanizmov integrat. i adaptivn, deyat. Mozga. p. 47.

Kaplunovsky, A.S. (1974) In Memory and the Trace Processes. Pushchino na Oka, pp. 271—272.

Laitinen, L.V. (1972) Lancet, 1, 472.

Lindsley, D.B. (1957) Psychophysiology and Motivation. Nebraska,

Livanon, M.N. (1962) In The EEG Studies of the Higher Nervous Activity. AN SSSR, pp. 174—185.

Livanov, M.N. (1972) The Spatial Organization of the Brain Processes. Nauka.

Livanov, M.N. (1972) Raeva S.N. DAN SSSR, 6, 507—509.

Luria, A.R. (1975) Physiology of Man, 1 (in press).

Luria, A.R. and Vinogradova, O.S. (1970) Cited in A.I. Leontiev (Ed.) Osnovy toerii rechevoy deyatelnosti. Nauka, 1974.

Matveev, Yu.K. (1971) In A.I. Trohatchev (Ed.), Impulse Activity of the Human Brain. Meditsina, pp. 132—140.

Matveev, Yu.K. (1972) Fiziol. Zh. (Leningr.), 58, 1341—1346.

Michelson, R.P. (1971) Arch. Otolaryng., 93, 317—323.

Obrador, S., Delgado, J.M.R. and Martin-Rodriguez, J.C. (1974) Emotional Areas of the Human Brain and their Programmed Stimulation for Therapeutic Purposes. In press.

Olds, J. and Milner, B. (1966) In C.R. Evans and A.D.R. Robertson (Eds.), Brain Physiology, Butterworths, London, pp. 51—64.

Osgood, Ch.E. (1953) Method and Theory in Experimental Psychology. Oxford Univ. Press, New York.

Perepelkin, P.D. (1974) In Memory and the Trace Processes, Pushchino na Oka, p. 277.

Petrie, A. (1952) Personality and the Frontal Lobes: An Investigation of the Psychological Effect of Different Types of Leucotomy, London.

Ploog, D. (1970) In The Neurosciences. Rockefeller Univ. Press, New York. pp. 349—361.

Pribram, K. (1971) Language of the Brain. Prentice-Hall, Englewood Cliffs, N.J.

Russinov, V.S. (1969) The Dominanta. Meditsina.

Sem-Jacobsen, C.W. (1968) Depth Electrographic Studies of the Human Brain and Behaviour.

Simmons, F.B., Epley, J.M., Guttman, N., Frishkopf, L.S., Harmon, L.D. and Zwicker, E. (1965) Science, 148, 104—106.

Smirnov, V.M. (1966) Vop. Fiziol., 3, 85—95.

Smirnov, V.M. (1970) Vestn. AMN SSSR, 1, 35—42.

Smirnov, V.M. (1972) In 1 Vsesoiuzny Siezd Neirokhir. Vol. 5. pp. 166—199.

342

Smirnov, V.M. (1974) Probl. Fiziol. Patol., 5, 252—273.
Smirnov, V.M. and Gratchev, K.V. (1963) In Electrofiziologiya nervnoi sistemy. Rostov on Don.
Smirnov, V.M. and Speransky, M.M. (1972) Vop. Fiziol., 3, 21—38.
Trohatchev, A.I. (1971) Impulse Activity of the Human Brain. Meditsina.
Walker, J. and Halas, E. (1972) Physiol. Behav., 8, 1099—1105.
Wernicke, C. (1874) Der Aphasische Symptomenkomplex. Breslau.

DISCUSSION

PHILLIPS: It seems that you have shown that these different functional levels of activity, that is to say, the recognition of an object that gives the acoustical code related to the name of it and the generalization of the name, say, from chair and table to furniture, all take place in the same grouping of cells in the brain which you recorded from via the same electrodes at the same time. Is this correct? If so, it is extremely interesting that we could have these hierarchical levels of functions in the same place and not in different places. Were all the records taken from the globus pallidus?

BECHTEREVA: No. Thank you very much for your question. There are at least three levels of codes which I talked about. The first level is acoustical coding when the word is not a word but just is a convert signal, the second level is semantic coding when the word is a word in the brain, and thirdly the intellectual activity, the enunciation, and so on when the brain is dealing with the word doing something with the word. Until now we have investigated what the effects are in subcortical structures and some cortical structures. We investigated 2000 points in the brain. We were able to record not only neuronal activity but also other physiological events to find out structural-functional relations of brain. I can tell you that there is a strange phenomenon in some parts, where it is impossible even to find acoustical code of the native and foreign language in the same neuronal population. Sometimes we find that there are different rays of the system, that is, different structures are responsible for the same process, for example for coding of native and foreign languages. I can also tell you, for instance, that the electrical equivalent of the readout of the long-term memory is in the association nuclei of the thalamus. We find a semantic code in some other places of the subcortex. Thus, in most places we find either the acoustical code or the semantic code, but there are places where in the same neuronal population we have found acoustic as well as the semantic code. But a neuronal population is a very big group, and there are many functionally united groups. So, if we actually speak about one place of the brain, there are thousands of neurons, and all the brain is not the same. But in most cases there are different places where we find the acoustical code, the general code and the word code. What was surprising was that we did find all three together in some places.

PHILLIPS: Was it in the dominant hemisphere or equally in both the hemispheres and in the subcortex?

BECHTEREVA: I fear I should not speak about the difference now, when we are not sure of the difference. But, according to the results of electrical stimulations of the brain, we know that to interfere with speech is much easier by stimulating the dominant hemisphere than the subdominant hemisphere. But in this phenomenon, we have no data and we have no statistically significant proof, but we have seen that the record of the word appears more often in the dominant hemisphere, although I cannot stress this.

STERIADE: Did you emphasize that you prefer to record multiunit activation? Do all these neurons you are recording behave similarly, or do you observe some of the effects in one way and the other in another way, and so on?

BECHTEREVA: I think my third or fourth slide would give the technique which we used for extracting the information from the neuronal activity. If all the neurons behave in the same way, we did not need such a complex method. Most certainly different groups of neurons of the same neuronal population can behave quite differently and also the same group can behave in opposite ways in opposite types of behavior. For instance, in the same area there can be excitation and inhibition in nearby groups of neurons. But usually it is not as simple as that; we do find the functional unitable groups of neurons. We can find them by recording and discriminating amplitudes or the spike shapes which change configurations in time. Only then we can find this code and in finding this code we find out that even in the functionally unitable group of neurons not all the neurons behave in the same way.

BUCHWALD: I wonder if you would tell us some of the technical aspects and methods of your recording, and how many electrodes?

BECHTEREVA: There are from 36 to 70 electrodes at a time and the registration can be as long as many months. We can record neuronal activity, without any harm to the patient, virtually on every day. We have developed a kind of method to compensate for brain movements, which is a real technical problem, and for extracting information from the findings.

BUCHWALD: Are the electrodes fixed?

BECHTEREVA: Yes, certain electrodes are fixed. We have at least two kinds of technique. We introduce a bundle of electrodes through one hole on the skull and the electrodes are fixed just at the outside of the hole. In the second technique, the electrodes are introduced into the brain through different holes. The electrodes are of 50—200 μm in diameter and are connected in bundles of 6—10 electrodes, each one ending lower or higher than the other, the distance between them being 2—5 mm depending on the task. The electrodes are glued and isolated to a depth to the very tip of 1 mm with neutral plastin.

BUCHWALD: It is interesting that single unit recording can be done with large electrodes.

BECHTEREVA: Actually, not only we but many people now receive from the brain multiunit activity with 50 μm electrodes. We are not alone in the world.

PHILLIPS: Adrian was the first to use enamel wires for recording.

BUCHWALD: How do you record single unit activity?

BECHTEREVA: We register multiunit activity, but we can extend our technique to extract even the activity of a single unit in some cases. How do we do that, I have explained before.

PURPURA: I would assume that in the epileptic patients you had many electrodes around the temporal lobe areas. You are recording, therefore, some kind of semantically related activities in your testing. Hopefully, from the experimental standpoint, one would have had some epileptic phenomena, seizure activity, at the same time as during a particular run of an experiment. Or was this never a coincidence? Did you ever see at the time that you were making language tests epileptic activity within the area that you were recording from? Now, if that is the case, why should there be any influence of the disease process, let us say, on the characteristic of the code of discharge? I think this is an absolutely fundamental observation if one can relate the appearance of a disturbance in the electrical activity with a disturbance in the patterns of the multiunit activity. This would account for some failures of semantic recognition or failure on the part of the patient to comprehend that you have asked questions or asked him to perform in a certain linguistic way. Did you ever see any interaction of this nature?

BECHTEREVA: Thank you very much for mentioning this very topic. We did not investigate those cases. We tried to have our data about the brain code of words belonging to words as pure as possible. And so, when we have the epileptogenic discharges we did not read the data. I am pleased that I now understand the value of this, and we shall do it sometime later. We have the traces so it is possible for us to do that analysis, and when we do we will try to compare data from different kinds of diseases and different types of patients just to be sure that what we are seeing after our treatment of the data is really not an artifact of, for instance, parkinsonism and so on. So that is for our future. We shall do that.

16

TRANSMISSION AT RECEPTOR SYNAPSES

MICHAEL V.L. BENNETT

Division of Cellular Neurobiology, Albert Einstein College of Medicine, Yeshiva University, New York, N.Y. 10461 (U.S.A.)

INTRODUCTION

In what have been termed primary receptors, the initial sensory transduction is mediated by the afferent nerve fiber itself. In the so-called secondary receptors, which are restricted to vertebrates, the initial transduction is carried out by neuroepithelial cells that transmit synaptically to the afferent fibers. Secondary receptors include receptors of taste and of the vestibular, auditory and lateral line systems (acousticolateralis receptors). There is some evidence that Merkel's disks (Patrizi and Munger, 1966) and carotid body receptors (Eyzaguirre et al., 1970) are also of this kind. Rods and cones of the retina are usually not considered secondary receptors, but have a number of similar properties. The primary subject of this paper are electroreceptors which are modified receptors of the lateral line system (Bennett, 1971a and b; Szabo and Fessard, 1974). They have largely lost their mechanical sensitivity and have become specialized for sensing electric fields. In several cases these adaptations allow the processes of transmission at their synapses to be studied with particular ease. Electroreceptors, which have independently evolved in a number of different groups of fishes, attracted attention because of the extraordinarily high sensitivities that some of these fishes exhibit in behavioral experiments (Lissmann, 1958; Lissmann and Machin, 1958). For example, skates (Rajidae) are able to detect gradients of 0.01 μV/cm, which is astonishing to the electrophysiologist in terms of the noise he ordinarily deals with (Kalmijn, 1971 and 1974). It can also be given some concreteness when it is viewed as the gradient provided by the voltage of a single flashlight cell spread over the distance between Miami and Boston (or, in honor of the hosts for the symposium, Delhi and Madras).

Analysis of the mechanisms of electroreception has removed some of the mystery. Although the absolute sensitivities are high and they are not

346

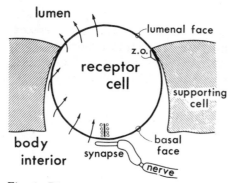

Fig. 1. Diagram of a receptor cell. The zonula occludens (z.o.) indicated on the right seals off extracellular space between receptor and supporting cells and divides the receptor cell membrane into lumenal and basal faces. The arrows show direction of current flow on the left side of the cell when the ampullary lumen is made negative. Current is inward through the basal face and outward through the lumenal face. The afferent synapse is shown as having a presynaptic ribbon with associated vesicles. (From Obara and Bennett, 1972.)

to be ascribed to faults in the conditioning techniques, they are high partly because of accessory tissues that channel current flow and cause a significant fraction of the voltage drop across the entire fish to be developed across a few receptors that are appropriately oriented and placed. The membrane mechanisms, although very voltage sensitive, are unlikely to be qualitatively different from those of other receptors of the acousticolateralis system or even of some interneuronal synapses.

As would be expected if spatial information were to be obtained, the electroreceptors are distributed widely over the body. Being derivatives of the lateral line system they are innervated by the eighth cranial nerve. The receptor cells themselves have an important feature that fits them for their function. They are joined at their apical margins by occluding junctions that prevent current flow through the intracellular clefts (Fig. 1), and they lie surrounded by a high resistance epithelium. These features maximize the voltage drop across the receptor cells. The occluding zonules divide the surface of the receptor cell into lumenal and basal faces. The synapses with the afferent fibers are on the basal face. As in other acousticolateralis receptors the electroreceptor synapses have a presynaptic dense body or ribbon which may be involved in moving vesicles to the release sites. If the outside of the body or the lumenal side of the receptor cell is made negative, some current flows through the cell out of the fish's body. This current is outward through the lumenal face and tends to depolarize it; this current is inward through the basal or presynaptic face and tends to hyperpolarize it. Stimuli of the opposite polarity have opposite actions. The effects of a given polarity of current will be important to remember in the course of the discussion.

Two functional classes of electroreceptors have been described previously in freshwater teleosts: (1) phasic, AC, high frequency or tuberous receptors, and (2) tonic, DC, low frequency or ampullary receptors (Bennett, 1965, 1967, 1971a and b; Szabo and Fessard, 1974). These findings will be briefly summarized, and then more recent data from marine fishes will be considered.

PHASIC RECEPTORS

Phasic receptors are found in mormyrids and gymnotids, which are freshwater electric fish from Africa and South America respectively. These receptors are termed tuberous because the receptor cells lie in a cavity in the epidermis without an obvious canal connecting to the exterior. The cells at the edge of the cavity are joined by occluding junctions to a flattened layer of cells that appears to provide the main resistive barrier of the skin. They are overlain by a loose plug of cells as well as the outer mucous secreting portion of the epidermis, but the high degree of electrical sensitivity of some of these receptors suggests that there is little voltage drop across the overlying tissue.

The operation of phasic receptors is straightforward. The lumenal face of the receptor cell is inexcitable. The basal face is regeneratively responsive to depolarizing stimuli and, depending on the type, generates an 'all-or-none' action potential or a graded response. As in many other excitable tissues responses to termination of hyperpolarizing stimuli are also seen. The combination of stimulus and response either causes the presynaptic secretory membrane to release transmitter, or is transmitted electrotonically, and leads to the generation of impulses in the postsynaptic afferent fiber. The strength of the stimulus may be coded in the afferent discharge in the usual ways, by changing the probability, number, and latencies of the impulses (Scheich and Bullock, 1974).

Phasic receptors are only sensitive to AC or high frequency stimuli because the outer face of the receptor cells acts as a blocking capacity, and DC potentials applied across the epithelium do not appear across the basal face of the receptor cells. In most cases the receptor cells protrude into the overlying cavity and have their outer face markedly increased by microvilli. Since specific areal capacitance of biological membranes varies little from about 1 μF/cm^2, it appears that the function of the surface proliferation is to increase the capacitative admittance of the outer face. The specific resistance of this membrane is difficult to measure because of the parallel pathways through the skin, but it need not be extraordinarily high compared to several other biological membranes in order to account for the observed DC insensitivity. Phasic receptors are sensitive primarily to the frequencies present in the electric organ discharge and they are presumably important in electrolocation and, as has been recently established in a number of species, in communication via electric signals (Scheich and Bullock, 1974).

Transmission at some phasic receptors appears to be chemically mediated, as suggested by multiple impulse discharges in response to a brief presynaptic depolarization and the presence of an irreducible synaptic delay. In one receptor transmission appears to be electrical, as indicated by a short latency, the occurrence of antidromic invasion from nerve to receptor cell and insensitivity to high magnesium, low calcium solutions (Steinbach and Bennett, 1971). A second phasic receptor appears on morphological grounds to have electrical synapses: there are close appositions that are probably gap junctions between receptor cell and afferent fiber (Srivastava, 1972). At* one chemically transmitting receptor transmission was shown to be blocked by high magnesium low calcium solution (Steinbach and Bennett, 1971). This finding suggests that by analogy with conventional synapses transmitter release is mediated by calcium influx through electrically excitable channels that are opened by the stimulus. A further indication of calcium involvement is that the electrical responses of phasic receptors are insensitive to tetrodotoxin (TTX), although this toxin blocks the electric organs, muscles and nerves to the receptors themselves (Zipser and Bennett, 1973). Calcium channels are insensitive to TTX as far as is known. The TTX insensitivity of the receptor responses may mean that the receptor responsiveness was achieved in the course of evolution by an increase in the relative number of electrically sensitive calcium channels of the kind that mediate transmitter release in ordinary acousticolateralis receptors.

TONIC RECEPTORS

Tonic electroreceptors are found not only in the teleost electric fish, but also in the non-electric catfish (and, on morphological evidence only, in the paddle fish, *Polyodon* (Jørgensen et al., 1972)).

The tonic receptors have receptor cells in an ampulla at the central end of a canal that opens directly to the exterior, hence the term ampullary. They are sensitive to low frequencies and there is a tonic discharge in their afferent fibers that is modulated up and down by low frequency stimuli of appropriate polarity; hence the terms tonic, DC, and low frequency (Fig. 2, inset). Several lines of indirect evidence suggested that transmission from receptor cells to afferent fibers is chemically mediated. In short: (1) the discharge in response to a brief stimulus can long outlast the stimulus; (2) such an afterdischarge cannot be blocked by a strong inhibitory stimulus, and (3) there is a synaptic delay of about 1 msec. The tonic discharge was ascribed to tonic excitation mediated by tonic release of transmitter from the receptor cell. Stimuli were presumed to act directly on the presynaptic secretory membrane to increase the ongoing release of transmitter; outside or lumen-positive stimuli, which depolarize the secretory membrane, being excitatory, and outside negative stimuli, which hyperpolarize the secretory face, being inhibitory. The input-output relation of these cells was found

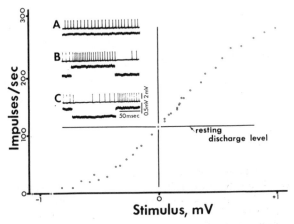

Fig. 2. Responses of a tonic receptor of the gymnotid *Gymnotus*. Inset: upper trace, impulses in the afferent nerve fiber; lower trace, stimulating potential applied externally at the receptor opening. A: resting tonic discharge. B: excitation by an outside-positive stimulus; there is some accommodation during the stimulus and a silent period after its end. C: inhibition by an outside-negative stimulus; there is accommodation during the stimulus and rebound after its end. Graph: for the same receptor, the average impulse frequency during a stimulus of about 100 msec duration is plotted against stimulating voltage, outside-positive stimuli to the right. For small stimuli of either sign the input-output relationship is linear. A large change in impulse frequency is produced over a stimulus range of ± 1 mV. (From Bennett, 1971a.)

to be quite linear for small signals of either sign (Fig. 2), a property which confirms that an ongoing process is modulated rather than that there are separate processes for stimuli of opposite polarity. Furthermore, since no obvious electrical response could be recorded external to the receptors (other than the nerve impulse) it was presumed that the receptor cells were reasonably linear, and in a more recent study intracellular recording from the receptor cells showed little responsiveness (Bennett, 1971b).

Given the data that transmission at phasic receptors requires calcium and that there is an electrically excitable calcium response, it seems likely that there is a similar mechanism at tonic receptors. A likely hypothesis is that in the absence of applied stimulation some calcium channels in the basal face are open, to account for the resting release of transmitter. These channels are closed by hyperpolarization of this membrane. Depolarization of the basal membrane opens more calcium channels and more calcium flows inward where it (somehow) increases transmitter release. To be sure, inward calcium flux should depolarize the receptor cell and cause regeneration, but if there were sufficient potassium or chloride channels in parallel, the non-linearity could be negligible. The linearity would, however, be achieved at the expense of sensitivity. The absence of obvious calcium responses in the receptor cells would be somewhat analogous to the squid

350

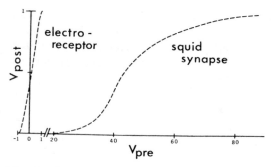

Fig. 3. Comparison of input-output relations inferred for the receptor synapse and measured for the squid giant synapse. (From Kusano, 1970.) The abscissa is the voltage in the presynaptic terminal or the voltage applied across the receptor cell and largely developed across the basal face. (From Bennett, 1971b.) The ordinate is the PSP amplitude normalized with respect to its maximum value. The relation for the receptor is much steeper (the scale of the abscissa is changed) and is shifted to the left so that there is a maintained PSP in the absence of stimulation.

giant synapse where electrical effects of calcium activation in the presynaptic terminal are ordinarily obscured by much larger conductances associated with sodium and potassium responses (Katz and Miledi, 1969).

Although transmission at the electroreceptor synapse can now be explained in terms of the same mechanisms as operate at the more widely known synapses, some differences should be noted. The relation between pre- and postsynaptic potential can be inferred from the stimulus response relation (Fig. 2). On the assumption that the PSPs in the receptors are of ordinary size (as has been measured directly in the marine receptors, see below), one can draw an input-output relation for the receptor synapse normalized with respect to maximum amplitude (Fig. 3). When this relation is compared to that for the squid synapse, two important differences are obvious. The slope is much greater for the receptor; that is, a larger proportional change in output is obtained for a smaller presynaptic potential. Also, the relation is shifted towards more negative voltages for the receptor, to the point where there is an output in the absence of an applied stimulus. The origin of these differences will be considered further below.

TONIC RECEPTORS OF MARINE FISH

The foregoing picture of the operation of tonic receptors of freshwater teleosts (which has been somewhat clarified with the aid of hindsight) was greatly strengthened by data obtained from electroreceptors of marine fish, specifically the ampulla of Lorenzini of the skate *Raja* (Clusin and Bennett, 1973 and unpublished; Clusin et al., 1975; Obara and Bennett, 1972), and the electroreceptor of the marine catfish *Plotosus* (Akutsu and Obara, 1974; Obara, 1974; Obara and Oomura, 1973). The receptors of *Plotosus* have long canals like those of *Raja* and have been considered by some to be an ampulla of Lorenzini. I would rather have restricted the term to elasmobranch ampullae because of the functional differences between the elasmobranch and teleost lines that are described below, but I suspect this nomenclatural nicety has already been precluded by other workers. The important characteristics of these receptors for experimentation is that they have long canals and that the canal and afferent nerve can be isolated for external recording and controlled external stimulation, and the ampulla can be isolated for application of external solutions.

Both receptors are tonic. The *Plotosus* receptor operates in essentially the same way as the receptors of freshwater teleosts. Outside or lumen-positive stimuli depolarize the presynaptic (basal) face of the receptor cell and lead to acceleration of the nerve discharge: lumen-negative stimuli lead to deceleration. In this case there is direct evidence for maintained activation of calcium channels in the basal face without application of stimuli (see below).

In the skate the sensitivity for stimuli in the physiological range is of the opposite polarity; as has been known for some time lumen-negative stimuli increase the afferent discharge and lumen-positive stimuli decrease it (Murray, 1965 and 1967). It turns out that there is a calcium response in the lumenal face that is partially activated in the *in situ* condition. Depolarization of the lumenal face by a lumen-negative stimulus turns on calcium channels to the extent that a net inward current flows through the lumenal membrane. This current flows outward through the basal membrane, depolarizing it and causing it to release more transmitter. Conversely lumen-positive stimuli close calcium channels in the lumenal face. Thus they decrease the inward current through this face and lead to a hyperpolarization of the basal face and reduced secretion of transmitter. As would be expected, strong stimuli can override the responsiveness of the lumenal face. Strong lumen-positive stimuli cause enough current to flow inward through the lumenal membrane that the basal membrane is hyperpolarized. Strong lumen-negative stimuli cause enough outward current through the lumenal membranes that the basal membrane is hyperpolarized.

One can think of two simple mechanisms whereby a population of electrically excitable calcium channels in one membrane of a receptor cell could be somewhat activated in the absence of applied stimuli. The resting membrane potential of the activated face (basal in *Plotosus*, lumenal in *Raja*) might be low enough to turn on these channels. Alternatively, the opposite face of the receptor cell might have a lower resting potential, and thereby might depolarize the activated face. In other words given the difference in potential between the two faces, current would flow along the canal and back around the exterior pathway and through the cell into the canal lumen again. The face with the lower resting potential would be hyper-

352

polarized. The face with the higher resting potential would be depolarized enough to turn on some calcium channels. The latter possibility now has been demonstrated for both *Raja* and *Plotosus*. In each case the canals can

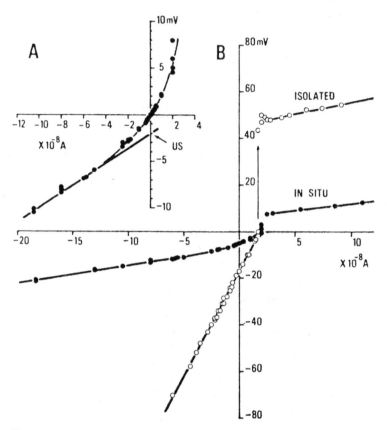

Fig. 4. Voltage-current relationships of the *Plotosus* receptor. In the electrically isolated condition (B, open circles) there is a lumen-negative resting potential of about 17 mV. The voltage-current relationship is linear for lumen-negative displacements (hyperpolarizing the basal face) and small lumen-positive displacements. Larger lumen-positive displacements cause a jump in potential to a large lumen-positive potential and a new linear region of the voltage-current relationship that results from maximal calcium activation. In the in situ condition (filled circles, see diagram in Fig. 6A) the resting potential is reduced to about 5 mV lumen-negative. The voltage-current relation is non-linear for small displacements in either direction (higher gain in A with resting potential omitted). Evidently calcium is partially activated as a result of current flowing along the in situ canal. Lumen-negative stimuli greater than about 6 mV (hyperpolarizing the basal face) turn off calcium activation and bring the receptor into a linear region of the voltage-current relation. (The slope is less than for the isolated ampulla because of the shunting provided by the canal and external current path.) Lumen-positive stimuli (depolarizing the basal faces) bring the receptor into the linear region in which calcium is maximally activated. (From Obara, 1974.)

be isolated for a sufficient length for the resistance along the exterior to be greatly increased either by drying or by washing with non-electrolyte solutions. When the receptor epithelium of *Plotosus* is electrically isolated in this way, the lumen goes about 10 mV negative to the body interior (which is external to the basal face), and the spontaneous activity in the nerve virtually stops. Evidently the lumenal face has a less inside-negative resting potential than the basal face. For small polarizations of either sign the electrically isolated epithelium behaves quite linearly (Fig. 4, open circles). For somewhat larger depolarizations there is a slight bend upward in the curve and for very slightly larger stimuli a threshold is reached and the potential goes upward to reach a long lasting plateau (Fig. 5). The amplitude of the plateau is affected by calcium solutions bathing the lumenal face, as predicted by the Nernst relation (Akutsu and Obara, 1974). The plateau is very long lasting but can be terminated by an adequate stimulus in the opposite direction. In a number of other tissues calcium channels show very slow inactivation (see, for example, Baker et al., 1971; Katz and Miledi, 1969), so the long duration of the response is not surprising.

In the ampulla *in situ* and prior to isolation the current-voltage relationship for small stimuli is non-linear with an upward concavity (Fig. 4, filled circles). Evidently the reduction in resting potential due to short circuiting by the canal brings the basal membrane into the voltage range in which calcium is being activated. (The higher gain measurements in Fig. 4A have removed the resting potential.) Further depolarization turns on more calcium channels, causing the current-voltage relation to curve upwards, but then the relationship becomes linear again as calcium activation is maximal. Hyperpolarization turns off calcium channels, and the current-voltage relationship approaches the linear region it exhibits for voltages more lumen-negative than about 6 mV from the resting potential.

The effects of depolarization on calcium conductance are confirmed by the nerve discharge. In the shunted condition there is a tonic nerve discharge ascribable to the tonic calcium activation (Fig. 5A). In the isolated condition the nerve discharge is virtually abolished. Nerve activity is not evoked until the potential reaches the range where calcium channels are activated (Fig. 5B).

The absence of a well defined threshold in the shunted ampulla is readily explained. In a preparation exhibiting a threshold for a brief pulse (which may be defined as a point of unstable equilibrium (cf. Bennett et al., 1970)) inward calcium current equals the sum of the outward currents through the basal face and through the lumenal face and down the canal. A small increment in potential causes more calcium activation and development of a net inward current and a full sized response. A small decrement in potential reduces calcium activation and the current becomes net outward and the potential returns to the resting level. The larger the current through the basal faces, the more calcium must be activated to reach threshold. In the electrical-

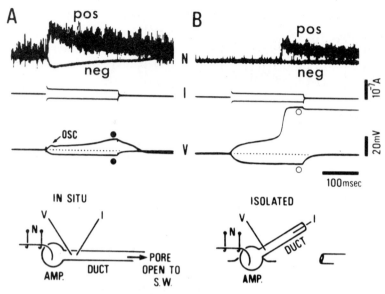

Fig. 5. Responses of the *Plotosus* receptor in situ and electrically isolated. N (upper traces), recording from the afferent nerve; two superimposed sweeps with a lumen-positive stimulus (pos) and a lumen-negative stimulus (neg). I (middle traces), currents applied to the receptor. V (lower traces), potentials in the lumen recorded positive upwards. The insets diagram the recording conditions (AMP is ampulla, DUCT is the canal, S.W. is seawater). A: in the in situ condition a lumen-positive stimulus evokes a small oscillation (OSC) at the onset and a slower positivity that gradually falls after the stimulus. The filled circles show the time at which potentials were measured for Fig. 4. There is a tonic discharge in the nerve which is stopped by the lumen-negative stimulus and augmented by the lumen-positive stimulus. B: in the isolated condition the same size current pulses cause larger potential changes. The lumen-positive stimulus causes the potential to rise up to a maintained plateau. There is little tonic discharge in the nerve. A neural response begins when the potential evoked by the lumen positive pulse begins to exhibit a concave upwards curvature indicating the beginning of calcium activation. The open circles indicate the measurements for Fig. 4. (From Obara, 1974.)

ly isolated condition, when no current flows down the canal, only a little calcium activation need be obtained for net inward current; in the shunted case the maximum calcium activation available apparently is insufficient for a sharp threshold.

Particularly clear records of PSPs have been obtained from the afferent fibers of the *Plotosus* receptors that confirm the predictions made from the tonic receptors of freshwater teleosts (Fig. 6, see also Obara and Bennett, 1972). Long lasting excitatory stimuli produce long lasting depolarizing PSPs that gradedly increase impulse frequency (unless they are large enough to inactivate the axon). Inhibitory stimuli cause hyperpolarizing PSPs and reduction in impulse frequency, and there appears to be a pacemaker potential between the impulses of the resting discharge that presumably results

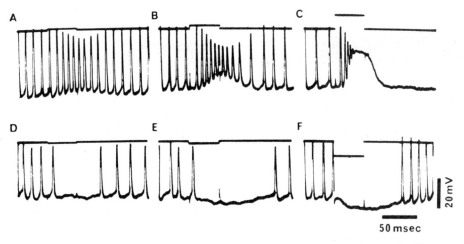

Fig. 6. Responses in an afferent fiber of *Plotosus* near the receptor terminals. The receptor was in situ and current pulses were applied at the canal opening (upper traces). A-C: lumen-positive stimuli (depolarizing the basal faces of the receptor cells) cause an acceleration of the nerve discharge. The underlying PSP is particularly clear in C where it is sufficiently large to inactivate the impulse generating mechanism. D-F: lumen-negative stimuli (hyperpolarizing the basal faces) cause hyperpolarization of the nerve and cessation of impulse activity. (From Obara and Oomura, 1973.)

from tonic release of the excitatory transmitter. The inhibitory hyperpolarization causes a slight increase in the peak height of a superimposed antidromic impulse, which suggests that this PSP is accompanied by a decrease in conductance and is due to reduction in the tonic release of transmitter rather than a separate inhibitory process. This conclusion is supported by the indication of steady calcium activation in the tonically active preparation and loss of this activation and the tonic activity when the preparation is electrically isolated or the basal face is hyperpolarized by applied current.

The effects of electrically isolating the skate ampulla are similar to those for *Plotosus* except that in this case the lumen goes 10—20 mV positive. It follows that the resting potential of the lumenal face is more inside-negative than that of the basal face. In the isolated ampulla the current-voltage relationship is linear for small voltages (Fig. 7B). When lumen-negative stimuli are given which return the potential to near the zero level, the epithelium generates an impulse of about 60 mV amplitude and 50 msec duration. The shunted epithelium is in the voltage range in which its calcium channels are turned on as can be seen by the fact that it shows a negative resistance, i.e., lumen-negative stimuli actually increase current flowing inward through the lumenal faces, and lumen-positive stimuli decrease it (Clusin and Bennett, unpublished), with corresponding effects on the basal faces and nerve discharge.

As in the shunted *Plotosus* receptor, the shunted elasmobranch receptor usually does not generate a spike; perhaps a third of the preparations show an impulse of reduced amplitude, all show graded oscillations for small stimuli (Obara and Bennett, 1972). The rising phase of the action potential is calcium-dependent and presumably results from an inward flow of calcium. The response is abolished by perfusion of the lumen with cobalt or EGTA, and is unaffected by TTX. The basis of the falling phase will be discussed later.

In the elasmobranch isolating the epithelium does not turn off transmitter release, probably because the basal faces actually are slightly depolarized. (The basal faces have a much lower resistance than the lumenal faces as evidenced by the fact that the resistance of the epithelium is greatly reduced during an action potential in the lumenal face, so that only a small depolarization of the basal faces would be expected to result from isolation.)

In the normal preparation no activity of the basal face is apparent, not even when lumen-positive stimuli are given, that should depolarize this membrane. Because transmitter release is blocked by high magnesium or low calcium solutions (Steinbach, 1974) it would be expected that calcium channels are there, although their activity is masked by parallel relatively high conductance channels. The situation is presumably the same as postulated for the innervated face of receptors of freshwater teleosts. A much more direct demonstration is possible here analogous to the experiments of Katz and Miledi (1969) with the squid giant synapse. The basal face does generate an action potential after treatment with tetraethylammonium (TEA) and excess calcium (Clusin and Bennett, 1973). Sr^{2+} and Ba^{2+} ions also lead to action potential generation but without TEA; presumably they block potassium conductance and/or are more effective in the calcium channel. These treatments have no effect on the responses of the lumenal face when applied to basal face. If transmitter release is blocked by bathing the basal face in low calcium solutions, responses of the lumenal membrane do not cause nerve responses. The calcium channels of the lumenal membrane are apparently too far from the secretory membrane to effect transmitter release.

There may be a significance to the similarity of mechanism in setting the basal membrane in *Plotosus* and the lumenal membrane in *Raja* into the non-linear regions of their voltage-current relations. There is no a priori reason why there should not be voltage-insensitive sodium and potassium conductances in these faces that set their potential at an appropriate level. Perhaps the advantage is in mediating accommodation, for the *Raja* ampullae show considerable accommodation such that the incremental sensitivity remains very high over a fairly wide range, a process of obvious utility in a very sensitive receptor likely to see significant shifts in DC background voltage (Murray, 1965 and 1967). The adjustment of an axial current through the receptor cells may for some reason be more feasible than control of an eddy current within a single face.

A CALCIUM-DEPENDENT VOLTAGE INSENSITIVE LATE OUTWARD CURRENT

The responsiveness in *Raja* turns out to have another characteristic that is of considerable interest. The delayed outward current that terminates the impulse is initiated not by a voltage sensitive conductance, but by calcium influx (Clusin et al., 1975). When receptor epithelium is voltage clamped to rectangular pulses of increasing lumen negativity, initially one sees the conventional sequence of inward then outward current that underlies most action potentials (Fig. 7). As the lumen is made still more negative, the late outward current is delayed and then supressed completely. If one extrapolates the resting or leakage resistance (dashed line) to the point where the inward current is zero, this is the potential at which the late outward current fails; this may be termed the suppression potential, for it is homologous to the suppression potential of the squid giant synapse at which inward calcium current is prevented and transmission fails (Katz and Miledi, 1967; Kusano, 1970; Llinás and Nicholson, 1975).

The leakage current extrapolation is validated by resistance measurements made immediately after the onset of a lumen-negative pulse. For potentials measured over a substantial fraction of the level required to suppress the outward current, the resistance does indeed correspond to the steady state resistance for lumen-positive pulses. Other evidence for calcium sensitivity of the late outward current is that if calcium current is blocked by perfusion of the lumen with cobalt or EGTA solution, no delayed outward current is seen. After perfusion with low calcium EGTA solution the equilibrium potential for calcium current is shifted in the lumen-positive direction (corresponding to a less inside-positive value in the lumenal face), and the suppression potential remains the equilibrium potential (Fig. 7C). A mechanism for delayed outward current is much less prominent in *Plotosus* receptors, although the small oscillations seen in the shunted preparation suggest that it is present to some extent (Fig. 5A).

There is evidence now for similar mechanisms in other tissues (cf. Meech and Standen, 1975). In a variety of excitable cells calcium entry increases potassium conductance. (There is still no good evidence for the ion mediating the late outward current in *Raja*, although comparative considerations suggest that it is K^+.) In many or all of these cells, however, there are voltage sensitive potassium channels as well, and it is difficult to be sure that the calcium is not acting on these channels in some way. The occurrence of voltage insensitive calcium channels indicates that a distinct calcium sensitive mechanism is present, one presumably mediated by distinct macromolecules.

ELECTRICAL SENSITIVITY OF THE RECEPTORS

In both kinds of marine fishes the receptors are more sensitive than are the tonic receptors of freshwater teleosts. The nerve discharge is changed to

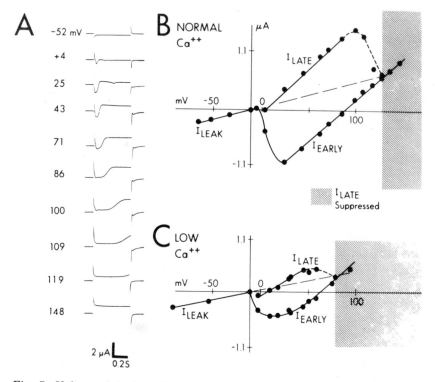

Fig. 7. Voltage clamping of the receptor epithelium of the ampulla of Lorenzini of *Raja*. On the left (A) are shown current records obtained at the indicated clamping voltages during perfusion with artificial seawater. The graph on the upper right (B) is from the same experiment. Voltages that depolarize the lumenal membranes (lumen-negative) are defined as positive and are shown to the right according to the conventions for the other excitable cells. Inward current through the lumenal membrane is shown downwards. The vertical axis is placed at the holding potential (defined as zero) which is the lumen-positive potential that the receptor assumes when electrically isolated. For voltage displacements hyperpolarizing the lumenal membranes the receptor behaves linearly. For moderate voltage displacements depolarizing the lumenal membranes there is a sequence of inward then outward current. For voltages between 25 and 100 mV both early and late currents are linearly related to voltage suggesting maximal activation. For larger displacements in this direction the early current is still linearly related to voltage but late current is suppressed. The point at which the late current is suppressed completely is that at which extrapolation from I leak indicates that no current flows through the early (calcium) channel and all the current flows through the resting resistance of the receptor. When the calcium concentration in the lumen of same preparation is reduced by perfusion with EGTA the late current is suppressed at a lower voltage (C) which is still the point at which the early current reverses. (From Clusin et al., 1975.)

an obvious extent by stimuli of a few microvolts (Akutsu and Obara, 1974; Clusin and Bennett, unpublished; Murray, 1965 and 1967; Obara, personal communication). The form of the input-output relationship is similar to that for the freshwater teleost receptor but the sensitivity is even greater. A number of factors might contribute to the sensitivity of the receptors as compared to interneuronal synapses. For one, the calcium channels might turn on over a narrower voltage range. However, in voltage clamped *Raja* the voltage range over which calcium activation occurs is comparable to that for sodium and potassium currents in ordinary tissues, and there is no extraordinary sensitivity. In the shunted *Plotosus* receptor, the deviations from the linear region seen with hyperpolarization also occur over a range of more than 5 mV, which is too wide to account for the great sensitivity.

Later stages in transmission might contribute in that the secretory process might be more sensitive to intracellular calcium, the subsynaptic chemo-sensitive membrane might be more sensitive to transmitter and the impulse generating mechanism in the postsynaptic membrane might be more sensitive to depolarization. Working backwards, the PSPs are of ordinary size (Fig. 6) and the electrical sensitivity of the terminals does not appear unusual. The transmitter is unknown, but the receptors are quite sensitive to glutamate, which is a reason to consider it a candidate transmitter (Obara, personal communication; Steinbach, 1974). Increased sensitivity to this or another transmitter may be a contributing factor. However, presynaptic vesicles are of normal appearance, and if transmitter release is quantal (for which there is physiological evidence in a vestibular receptor of the goldfish (Ishii et al., 1971)), sensitivity of the postsynaptic membrane should not be very important, particularly in view of the absence of evidence for large miniature PSPs at these synapses. Finally there is no evidence as to the amount of calcium influx required to release transmitter; this would appear to be a stage in which considerable increase in sensitivity might be obtained (and one in which the presynaptic dense body might function).

There remains the interesting coincidence of the occurrence of clearly regenerative responses in the two most sensitive tonic receptors. The relevant parameter in sensitivity is calcium activation as a function of applied voltage. Provided source impedance is sufficiently low, which it should be in the marine environment, loading of the signal source can be neglected. Then inspection of Fig. 4 suggests that the slope obtained in the shunted receptor is perhaps only twice the slope that would be obtained if the receptor were so severely shunted as to be electrically linear (Obara, personal communication), which is not enough to explain the sensitivity difference between marine and freshwater forms.

As Cole et al. (1970) pointed out the voltage gain of an impulse generating cell poised at threshold is very great. While the shunted epithelium is generally incapable of developing an impulse, it may be that some of the cells are allowed to escape from the clamping effect of the shunt by the series resistance of their otherwise electrically inactive faces. Thus, these cells could exhibit a larger response and a larger voltage gain than is represented in the transepithelial potential as a whole. The clarification of these possibilities really requires intracellular recording from the receptor cells, which unfortunately have not yet proven particularly tractable to this technique.

ELECTRICAL SENSITIVITY OF THE ORGANISM

Given receptors with a sensitivity of perhaps 2 μV, one must still account for the behavioral sensitivity of the intact animal. The longest canals in *Raja* of the size used in the behavioral experiments were probably about 20 cm. The space constant of the canals is much longer than their length and the fish is quite leaky (Waltman, 1966; Murray, 1967; Kalmijn, 1974). The result is that a voltage gradient in the direction of the axis of the canal is sensed by the receptor operating as a voltmeter measuring between the opening of the canal and just extracellular to the basal face of the receptor cells. In the examples given the actual stimulus to the receptor would be 0.2 μV or one-tenth of the established threshold. In psychophysical measurements such a discrepancy is not particularly disturbing. The physiological experiment may not have utilized the most sensitive receptors and the experimental manipulations may have reduced their sensitivity. Also, the intact animal obtains information from all its receptors and may be able to correlate the different inputs to increase sensitivity.

One may question whether it is significant that the two most sensitive receptors are in marine organisms. It is likely that electrical interference of atmospheric origin is much more severe in freshwater organisms, and streaming potentials and similar phenomena are much more prominent at low ionic strength. Thus it is reasonable that the lower sensitivity of the freshwater organisms is due to a greater background noise level (Hopkins, 1973; Kalmijn, 1974).

Another correlation is found between electroreceptors of freshwater and marine fish that can be ascribed to the difference in conductivity of the two media. The body interior of the marine fish is somewhat less conductive than the seawater in which it swims. The body interior of the freshwater fish is much more so. An electric field in the sea appears in the body of the marine fish with relatively little distortion; as noted above the canals operate as leads to measure between points that can be widely separated. The highest sensitivity to uniform fields is achieved by the longest canals; greater spatial resolution and directional sensitivity is achieved by shorter canals oriented in different directions. Many short canals radiate in the oral region and in skates and dogfish electrical sensitivity is used in prey detection (Kalmijn, 1971). In freshwater fishes the mode of operation is different. The skin resistance is very high and in the presence of an applied field most of the voltage drop occurs across the skin (Bennett, 1965 and 1967). The body interior remains nearly isopotential at a value that is some average of the potential over the entire body surface. The receptors, which have only short canals, are located in the skin and detect the potential across it at their particular location.

The values of these two distinctive arrangements for environments of different conductivity is attested to by their convergent evolution in different lines. The marine catfish *Plotosus* has developed long canals like those of the marine elasmobranchs. The freshwater ray *Potamotrygon* has developed short canals like those of the freshwater teleosts, although it retains the polarity of sensitivity typical of elasmobranch receptors (Szabo et al., 1972; Szamier and Bennett, 1971). Another marine catfish *Galeichthys* apparently has only short canals (Szamier, personal communication); it would be interesting to determine the receptor sensitivity. Perhaps adoption of the marine environment has been too recent for evolution of long canals. A number of other elasmobranchs invade fresh water, but no studies of their electroreceptors have yet been carried out.

RELEVANCE TO OTHER SYSTEMS

The properties of the presynaptic face of electroreceptors may well be quite widely spread among excitable cells. In the vestibular system many mechanoreceptors of the labyrinth are tonically active, their discharge frequency can be modulated in either direction, and (in a teleost) the sensitivity is reduced by high magnesium solutions (Highstein et al., 1974). Whether any of these receptors have regenerative responses is unknown, but one type of afferent (Fernandez et al., 1972; Goldberg and Fernandez, 1971) has a number of similarities in responsiveness to the class of phasic receptors in mormyrids in which transmission appears to be electrical and may correspond to the calyx endings in which there are gap junctions (Hamilton, 1968). In these endings the regenerative response may electrically amplify the mechanoelectrically transduced signal to a level where electrotonic transmission to the afferent fiber is possible.

An interesting question is sensitivity. The cochlear microphonic recorded at the round window is about 0.003 μV at threshold (McGill, 1959; Wever et al., 1959). If the potential across the presynaptic membrane is 300 times larger, which is not unreasonable for a ratio between amplitudes of intracellular and extracellular recordings, the signal is in the range where electroreceptors can detect it. In hair cells of two kinds of lateral line receptor, the cochlear microphonic is a fraction of a millivolt (Flock and Russell, 1973; Harris et al., 1970) which is a reasonable signal for an electroreceptor, but a very small one for the usual model neuronal synapses. These cells appear to be electrically linear like the tonic electroreceptors (Flock et al., 1973). The major difference between mechanically and electrically sensitive hair cells is likely to be the presence of a kinocilium for mechanoelectric transduction.

Synapses of the vertebrate retina, rods, cones, bipolar and horizontal cells

362

all appear to release transmitter tonically (Byzov and Trifanov, 1968; Hagins et al., 1970; Dowling and Ripps, 1973; Cervetto and Piccolino, 1974; Werblin and Dowling, 1969), and rod, cone and bipolar synapses have presynaptic ribbons as do the acousticolateralis receptors (Dowling and Boycott, 1965 and 1966). Potentials evoked by threshold light levels in rods of the toad, which are in the single quantum range, are tenths of a millivolt and well within the amplitude range of electroreceptor sensitivity (Fain, 1975). There is evidence for regenerative responses and non-linearities in the rods and horizontal cells which may provide an amplifying function (Werblin, 1975a and b). The ionic basic is not explored, but the ERG is not markedly affected by TTX and the usual sodium channels can thereby be ruled out (Murakami and Shigamatsu, 1970). A contribution of calcium channels also mediating transmitter release remains a possibility. Reciprocal and dendrodendritic synapses have been established by electron microscopy as a not infrequent component of the nervous system (Famiglietti and Peters, 1972; Pinching and Powell, 1971; Reese and Shepherd, 1972; Sloper, 1971). Here the intermediation of the action potential is not necessary to transmit signals from receptive to output portions of the neuron and tonic operation, as in the tonic receptors and in the retina, becomes possible.

The presence of voltage insensitive channels that are activated by intracellular calcium could be demonstrated particularly clearly in the ampulla of Lorenzini because of the absence of interfering conductances in parallel. The mechanism apparently occurs in very many neurons, although the experimental demonstration is more difficult. A greater richness of responsiveness over periods of seconds may well be obtained that provides a link between the rapid processes of impulse signalling, the intermediate processes of sensory accommodation, and the long term plastic changes of learning and development.

Acknowledgements

Although many of the ideas presented here have been developing for some years, the work of my friend and former associate, S. Obara, and of my Ph. D. student and colleague, W. Clusin, has made possible most of the recent progress. When the exigencies of getting a medical education have eased the new work on *Raja* that has been alluded to will be published in full with W. Clusin as senior author. Obviously this paper owes much to our discussions.

Supported in parts by grants from National Institutes of Health (NS-05512 and HD-04248).

REFERENCES

Akutsu, Y. and Obara, S. (1974) Calcium dependent receptor potential of the electroreceptor of marine catfish. Proc. Jap. Acad., 50, 247—251.

Baker, P.F., Hodgkin, A.L. and Ridgeway, E.B. (1971) Depolarization and calcium entry in squid giant axons. J. Physiol. (Lond.), 218, 709—755.

Bennett, M.V.L. (1965) Electroreceptors in Mormyrids. Cold Spr. Harb. Symp. quant. Biol., 30, 245—262.

Bennett, M.V.L. (1967) Mechanisms of electroreception. In P. Cahn (Ed.), Lateral Line Detectors. Univ. of Indiana Press, Bloomington, Ind., pp. 313—393.

Bennett, M.V.L. (1971a) Electroreception. In W.S. Hoar and D.S. Randall (Eds.), Fish Physiology. Academic Press, New York, pp. 493—574.

Bennet, M.V.L. (1971b) Electrolocation in fish. Ann. N.Y. Acad Sci., 188, 242—269.

Bennett, M.V.L., Hille, B. and Obara, S. (1970) Voltage threshold in excitable cells depends on stimulus form. J. Neurophysiol., 33, 585—594.

Byzov, A.L. and Trifonov, Y.A. (1968) The response to electric stimulation of horizontal cells in the carp retina. Vision Res., 8, 817—822.

Cervetto, L. and Piccolino, M. (1974) Synaptic transmission between photoreceptor and horizontal cells in the turtle retina. Science, 183, 417—419.

Clusin. W. and Bennett, M.V.L. (1973) Calcium electrogenesis in skate electroreceptors. Biol. Bull., 145, 429.

Clusin, W., Spray, D.C. and Bennett, M.V.L. (1975) Activation of a voltage-insensitive conductance by inward calcium current. Nature (Lond.), 256, 425—427.

Cole, K.S., Guttman, R. and Bezanilla, F. (1970) Nerve membrane excitation without threshold. Proc. nat. Acad. Sci. (Wash.), 65, 884—891.

Dowling, J.E. and Boycott, B.B. (1965) Neural connections of the retina: fine structure of the inner plexiform layer. Cold Spr. Harb. Symp. quant. Biol., 30, 393—402.

Dowling, J.E. and Boycott, B.B. (1966) Organization of the primate retina: electron microscopy. Proc. roy. Soc. B, 166, 80—111.

Dowling, J.E. and Ripps, H. (1973) Effect of magnesium on horizontal cell activity in the skate retina. Nature (Lond.), 242, 101—103.

Eyzaguirre, C., Leitner, L.M., Nishi, K. and Fidone, S. (1970) Depolarization of chemosensory nerve endings in carotid body of the cat. J. Neurophysiol., 33, 685—696.

Fain, G.L. (1975) Quantum sensitivity of rods in the turtle retina. Science, 187, 338—341.

Famiglietti, E.V., Jr. and Peters, A. (1972) The synaptic glomerulus and the intrinsic neuron in the dorsal lateral geniculate nucleus of the cat. J. comp. Neurol., 144, 285—334.

Fernandez, C., Goldberg, J.M. and Abend, W.K. (1972) Response to static tilts of peripheral neurons innervating otolith organs of the squirrel monkey. J. Neurophysiol., 35, 978—997.

Flock, A. and Russell, I.J. (1973) Efferent nerve fibres: postsynaptic action on hair cells. Nature New Biol., 243, 89—91.

Flock, A., Jørgensen, J.M. and Russell, I.J. (1973) Passive electrical properties of hair cells and supporting cells in the lateral line canal organ. Acta oto-laryng. (Stockh.), 67, 190—198.

Goldberg, J.M. and Fernandez, C. (1971) Physiology of peripheral neurons innervating semicircular canals of the squirrel monkey. III. Variations among units in their discharge properties. J. Neurophysiol., 34, 676—684.

Hagins, W.A., Penn, R.D. and Yoshikami, S. (1970) Dark current and photocurrent in retinal rods. Biophys. J., 10, 380—412.

Hamilton, D.W. (1968) The calyceal synapse of Type I vestibular hair cells. J. Ultrastruct. Res., 23, 98—114.

364

Harris, G.G., Frishkopf, L.S. and Flock, Å. (1970) Receptor potentials from hair cells of the lateral line. Science, 167, 76—79.

Highstein, S.M., Keeter, J. and Bennett, M.V.L. (1974) Some aspects of transmission at synapses in the labyrinth of the toadfish. Biol. Bull., 147, 482.

Hopkins, C.D. (1973) Lightning as background noise for communication among electric fish. Nature (Lond.), 242, 268—270.

Ishii, Y., Matsuura, S. and Furukawa, T. (1971) Quantal nature of transmission at the synapse between hair cells and eighth nerve fibers. Jap. J. Physiol., 21, 79—89.

Jørgensen, J.M., Flock, Å. and Wersäll, J. (1972) The Lorenzinian ampullae of *Polydon spathula*. Z. Zellforsch., 130, 362—377.

Kalmijn, A.J. (1971) The electric sense of sharks and rays. J. exp. Biol., 55, 371—383.

Kalmijn, A.J. (1974) The detection of electric fields from inanimate and animate sources other than electric organs. In A. Fessard (Ed.), Handbook of Sensory Physiology, Vol. III/3, Electroreceptors and Other Specialized Receptors in Lower Vertebrates. Springer, New York, pp. 147—200.

Katz, B. and Miledi, R. (1967) A study of synaptic transmission in the absence of nerve impulses. J. Physiol. (Lond.), 192, 407—436.

Katz, B. and Miledi, R. (1969) Tetrodotoxin-resistant electric activity in presynaptic terminals. J. Physiol. (Lond.), 203, 459—487.

Kusano, K. (1970) Influence of ionic environment on the relationship between pre- and postsynaptic potentials. J. Neurobiol., 1, 435—457.

Llinás, R. and Nicholson, C. (1975) Calcium role in depolarization-secretion coupling: an aequorin study. Proc. nat. Acad. Sci. (Wash.), 72, 187—190.

Lissmann, H.W. (1958) On the function and evolution of electric organs in fish. J. exp. Biol., 35, 156—191.

Lissmann, H.W. and Machin, K.E. (1958) The mechanism of object location in *Gymnarchus niloticus* and similar fish. J. exp. Biol., 35, 451—486.

McGill, T.E. (1959) Auditory sensitivity and the magnitude of the cochlear potential. Ann. Otol. Rhinol. Laryngol., 68, 193—207.

Meech, R.W. and Standen, N.B. (1975) Potassium activation in *Helix aspersa* neurones under voltage clamp: a component mediated by calcium influx. J. Physiol. (Lond.), 249, 211—239.

Murakami, M. and Shigamatsu, Y. (1970) Duality of conduction mechanism in bipolar cells of the frog retina. Vision Res., 10, 1—10.

Murray, R.W. (1965) Electroreceptor mechanisms: the relation of impulse frequency to stimulus strength and responses to pulsed stimuli in the ampullae of Lorenzini of elasmobranchs. J. Physiol. (Lond.), 180, 592—606.

Murray, R.W. (1967) The function of the ampullae of Lorenzini of elasmobranchs. In P. Cahn (Ed.), Lateral Line Detectors. Univ. of Indiana Press, Bloomington, Ind., pp. 277—293.

Obara, S. Personal communication.

Obara, S. (1974) Receptor cell activity at 'rest' with respect to the tonic operation of a specialized lateralis receptor. Proc. Jap. Acad., 50, 386—391.

Obara, S. and Bennett, M.V.L. (1972) Mode of operation of ampullae of Lorenzini of the skate, *Raja*. J. gen. Physiol., 60, 534—557.

Obara, S. and Oomura, Y. (1973) Disfacilitation as the basis for the sensory suppression in a specialized lateralis receptor of the marine catfish. Proc. Jap. Acad., 49, 213—217.

Patrizi, G. and Munger, B.L. (1966) The ultrastructure and innervation of rat vibrissae. J. comp. Neurol., 126, 423—436.

Pinching, A.J. and Powell, T.P.S. (1971) The neuropil of the glomeruli of the olfactory bulb. J. Cell Sci., 9, 347—377.

Reese, T.S. and Shepherd, G.M. (1972) Dendro-dendritic synapses in the central nervous system. In G.D. Pappas and D.P. Purpura (Eds.), Structure and Function of Synapses. Raven, New York, pp. 121—136.

Scheich, H. and Bullock, T.H. (1974) The detection of electric fields from electric organs. In A. Fessard (Ed.), Handbook of Sensory Physiology, Vol. III/3, Electroreceptors and Other Specialized Receptors in Lower Vertebrates. Springer, New York, pp. 201—256.

Sloper, J.J. (1971) Dendro-dendritic synapses in the primate motor cortex. Brain Res., 34, 186—192.

Srivastava, C.B.L. (1972) Morphological evidence for electrical synapses of 'gap' junction type in another vertebrate receptor. Experientia (Basel), 28, 1029—1030.

Steinbach, A.B. (1974) Transmission from receptor cells to afferent nerve fibers. In M.V.L. Bennett (Ed.), Synaptic Transmission and Interneuronal Communication. Raven Press, New York, pp. 105—140.

Steinbach, A.B. and Bennett, M.V.L. (1971) Effects of divalent ions and drugs on synaptic transmission in phasic electroreceptors in a mormyrid fish. J. gen. Physiol., 58, 580—598.

Szabo, J. and Fessard, A. (1974) Physiology of electroreceptors. In A. Fessard (Ed.), Handbook of Sensory Physiology, Vol. III/3, Electroreceptors and Other Specialized Receptors in Lower Vertebrates. Springer, New York, pp. 59—124.

Szabo, T., Kalmijn, A.J., Enger, P.S. and Bullock, T.H. (1972) Microampullary organs and a submandibular sense organ in the freshwater ray, *Potamotrygon*. J. comp. Physiol., 79, 15—27.

Szamier, R.B. and Bennett, M.V.L. (1971) Fine structure and physiological properties of ampullae of Lorenzini in the freshwater ray. Abstr. 11th Ann. Mtg. Amer. Soc. Cell Biol., p. 296.

Waltman, B. (1966) Electrical properties and fine structure of the ampullary canals of Lorenzini. Acta physiol. scand., Suppl. 264, 1—60.

Werblin, F.S. (1975a) Regenerative hyperpolarization in rods. J. Physiol. (Lond.), 244, 53—81.

Werblin, F.S. (1975b) Anomalous rectification in horizontal cells. J. Physiol. (Lond.), 244, 639—657.

Werblin, F.S. and Dowling, J.E. (1969) Organization of the retina of the mudpuppy, *Necturus maculosus*. II. Intracellular recording. J. Neurophysiol., 32, 339—355.

Wever, E.G., Rahm, W.E., Jr. and Strother, W.F. (1959) The lower range of cochlear potentials. Proc. nat. Acad. Sci. (Wash.), 45, 1447—1449.

Zipser, B. and Bennett, M.V.L. (1973) Tetrodotoxin resistant electrically excitable responses of receptor cells. Brain Res., 62, 253—259.

DISCUSSION

PURPURA: You see how he carefully at the end slipped in the most important problem now facing us: what to do with the dendrodendritic synapse. What you want to do about it?

BENNETT: I think one needs to know their input-output relations. They do allow a whole lot of mathematics in this continual function, of maintaining operations.

PRIBRAM: Do they have a continuous function?

BENNETT: That is true.

HORN: What is the neurotransmitter at these receptors?

BENNETT: We do not have enough data to answer that completely. There is a good deal of evidence for the vesicles containing a transmitter. The general picture is consistent about it. There is quantal release which is difficult to demonstrate at these synapses, but Ishii and Furukawa have in the other eighth nerve system. So I think there is no reason to believe that the vesicles are not containing transmitter, whether we can get sufficient recycling as Gray has got morphologically. The morphological picture without stimulation and effects of stimulation which Gray has described in retina is completely consistent with the neuromuscular junction where there is exocytosis, reclaiming of the membrane, etc.

ITO: You compared the squid giant axon and the electroreceptor. If I understand, you are assuming that the electroreceptor has an extremely high sensitivity for small changes in the membrane potential.

BENNETT: That is true. It does have an extremely high sensitivity. That is the point. There are two differences between the squid axon and the electroreceptor: one is the big increase in sensitivity and the other is spontaneous release of transmitter in the absence of applied stimuli.

ITO: But this certainly may simply be due to the high resistance of the membrane.

BENNETT: No, that it certainly could not be due to. It may be that all the calcium channels are of the same sensitivity, that is, each channel could have same sort of relation. The squid may just have a reverse population and the electroreceptor may just have a population that are all identical. That is one way that greater sensitivity could be achieved without any difference in the channels themselves, and we don't really understand what the differences are at the chemical or physical level. But yes, it is a very important point that there is this dramatic difference in slope as well as the shift in the zero point.

SUBJECT INDEX